Two Centuries
of
American Planning

edited by

DANIEL SCHAFFER

THE JOHNS HOPKINS UNIVERSITY PRESS, BALTIMORE

©The Contributors and Mansell Publishing Ltd, 1988

This book was commissioned, edited and designed by
Alexandrine Press, Oxford

Printed and bound in the United Kingdom

First published in the United States of America, 1988, by
The Johns Hopkins University Press, 701 West 40th Street, Baltimore,
Maryland 21211

Library of Congress Cataloging-in-Publication Data

Two centuries of American planning.
   (Studies in history, planning and the environment)
   "An Alexandrine Press book."
   Includes index.
   1. City planning — United States — History.   2. Regional
planning — United States — History.   I. Schaffer, Daniel,
1950 –   . II. Series.
HT167.T86   1987   361.6'0973   86 – 31293

ISBN 0 – 8018 – 3647 – 6
ISBN 0 – 8018 – 3719 – 7 (pbk)

Contents

The Contributors

HOWELL S. BAUM teaches social planning, planning theory, and organizational behaviour at the University of Maryland at Baltimore. He has studied planners' self-perceptions and attitudes towards bureaucratic power and politics. His research findings are discussed in two books: *Planners and Public Expectations* (1983) and *The Invisible Bureaucracy* (1987).

JOHN F. BAUMAN is Professor of History and Urban Affairs at California University of Pennsylvania. He has authored numerous articles and papers on the history on housing and urban planning. His book *Public Housing, Race and Renewal: Urban Planning in Philadelphia, 1920–1974* will be published in 1987.

HENRY C. BINFORD is Associate Professor of History at Northwestern University. He is the author of *The First Suburbs: Residential Communities on the Boston Periphery, 1815–1860* (1985). In addition to further work on nineteenth-century suburbs, he is currently studying the history of downtown redevelopment strategies in the twentieth century.

MICHAEL H. EBNER is Chairman of the Department of History, Lake Forest College. He has written widely for learned publications, serves on the editorial boards of the *Journal of Urban History* and *Reviews in American History*, co-chairs the Urban History Seminar of The Chicago Historical Society, and has been a Fellow of The National Endowment for the Humanities. With Eugene M. Tobin he co-edited *The Age of Urban Reform: New Perspectives on the Progressive Era* (1977). To be published in 1988 is his book *Creating Chicago's North Shore: A Suburban History*.

ROBERT FISHMAN is Associate Professor of History at Rutgers/The State University of New Jersey. He is the author of *Urban Utopias: Ebenezer Howard, Frank Lloyd Wright, Le Corbusier* (1977). He is now working on a comparative history of suburbanization from the eighteenth century to the present.

DAVID R. GOLDFIELD is the Robert Lee Bailey Professor of History at the University of North Carolina at Charlotte. His publications include numerous articles on subjects from planning in urban Sweden to city development in the American South. He has co-authored the standard American urban history text, *Urban America: From Downtown to No Town* (1979), and was the recipient of the 1983 Mayflower Award for *Cotton Fields and Skyscrapers: Southern City and Region (1982)*. His most recent book is *Promised Land: The South since 1945* (1986).

DAVID C. HAMMACK is Associate Professor of History and Director of the Social History Ph.D. Program at Case Western Reserve University. He is the author of *Power and Society: Greater New York at the Turn of the Century* (1982), and is currently working, under a Guggenhiem Fellowship, on a book about the role of national institutions in bringing about New York City's fiscal crises of 1914, 1933, and 1975.

JOHN HANCOCK is Professor of Urban Design and Planning at the University of Washington. He is currently completing a study of military and city planning in twentieth-century San Diego and a reassement of John Nolen's contributions to U.S. new town, city, and regional planning.

DAVID A. JOHNSON is a Professor of Planning at the University of Tennessee. He has lectured on the history of regional planning in the U.S.S.R. as a Senior Fulbright Exchange Scholar and has been a practicing planner on the staffs of the National Capital Planning Commission, Washington, D.C. and the Regional Plan Association of New York.

DANIEL SCHAFFER is an editor and writer for the Tennessee Valley Authority's Office of Governmental and Public Affairs and Editor of *Forum for Applied Research and Public Policy*. He is the author of *Garden Cities for America: The Radburn Experience* (1982).

EDWARD K. SPANN is Professor of History and Urban and Regional Planning at Indiana State University. His works include *Ideals and Politics: New York Intellectuals and American Liberalism, 1820–1880* (1972 – nominated for a Pulitzer Prize), and *The New Metropolis: New York City, 1840–1857* (1981 – Winner of the New York State Historical Society Manuscript Award). He recently completed a history of American utopianism and is now at work on several inter-related studies of early modernization in the United States.

DANA F. WHITE is Associate Professor of Urban Studies at Emory University. He served as the editor of *Olmsted South: Old South Critic/New South Planner* (1979) and is currently completing *The Urbanists, 1865–1915*, a monograph on the concepts of city, metropolis, and region in planning, public administration, and the applied social sciences.

WILLIAM H. WILSON is Professor of History at North Texas State University. He has written extensively on the history of urban and regional planning, including *The City Beautiful Movement in Kansas City* (1964) and *Coming of Age: Urban America, 1915–1945*. He has recently completed a manuscript on the City Beautiful Movement and is now studying Hamilton Park, a planned residential community for blacks in Dallas, Texas.

Introduction

DANIEL SCHAFFER

Metropolitan areas in the United States continue to grow – whether planned or not. That has been the American experience since the nation's beginnings. The 1970 demographic census, however, indicated that for the first time in more than one hundred years, non-metropolitan areas grew at a faster rate than metropolitan areas. The trend was hailed as historic. Demographers, social scientists and historians believed these data signalled a reordering of America's population – as significant an indicator as the 1920 census, which showed that for the first time the majority of Americans were living in urban areas. So it seemed that in less than one hundred years – or in the span of just four generations – the United States had moved from a rural to an urban to a suburban and now a post-suburban nation.

The policy implications were enormous. The problems of the cities were disappearing – not because these problems had been resolved, but rather because the cities themselves were disappearing, if not physically then as a major political force in the future of America. Small town living, twentieth-century condo-style, had helped to re-order the nation's priorities. There was a sense that we were returning to our roots of neighbourliness and co-operation, and that we were doing all this naturally, and not through the forced hand of government intervention. Benign neglect had worked. Americans had voted with their feet. In the process they had helped to reshape the contours of the American landscape, placing them more in line with traditional American values. The 1970 demographic census seemed to fit their times – on the one hand, reflecting the prevailing political mood of the 'me generation'; and on the other hand, reaffirming the wisdom of that generation's principles.

The place of professional planners in all this seemed suspect. As guardians of the physical appearance of cities and towns, their track record during the post-World War II period was not one to inspire confidence. By promoting high-rise public housing, planners unwittingly had helped to institutionalize ghetto life. Informal, but sometimes effective, poverty networks of community interaction had been supplanted by impersonal and inadequately funded social welfare agencies. In the suburbs, planners had bemoaned suburban sprawl but had been unable to halt its spread. In the yet unspoiled countryside, planners had called for farmland preservation, but laws to achieve that goal had rarely been enacted. Now the 1970 census seemed to suggest that the nation was finding its own solutions to the problems of urban decay and suburban sprawl. Planners may have disagreed (questioning both the solution and its effectiveness), but they seemed increasingly helpless to alter either its course or appeal.

Professional planners in the 1970s seemed not only to lose much of their purpose; they seemed to lose much of their constituency as well. Government bureaucracies, which provided the bulk of their employment, were either stagnant or shrinking in size. The poor, who had been a major focus of their concern, had become increasingly hostile – not only voicing doubt about the ability of planners to deliver on their promises, but also wanting a more direct role in the decision-making process. And the middle class, who at best had benignly viewed planners as experts in administration, looked more and more toward the market place and the corporate world to resolve the nation's problems.

As external pressures mounted, planners added to their own problems with internal dissension. In fact, planners themselves were finding it difficult to agree on a definition of purpose. This problem had been present since the 1930s (if not before) when the profession began to move in earnest away from its roots in landscape architecture and physical urban design to issues of economic equity and social values. But in the 1970s, the question of purpose had gained a critical edge. If planners did not rationally plan the physical shape of the city and region (or had failed in their attempts to do so), then what did they do? Were they to be welfare experts or administrators? Did they provide the site planning techniques for large-scale development and thus the conceptual base for economic growth and urban expansion? Perhaps they were to be taught the skills of arbitrators and become central figures in labour conflicts? Or maybe planning would be an ideal education for those wanting to be community organizers and political activists? In fact, was planning a process or goal; a method for rational interaction and discourse between conflicting groups, or a way to achieve certain results (where procedural mechanisms were recognized more as tactics than as ends in themselves)? And finally, if planners were not quite sure of their role in the larger society, why should the public have any appreciation for the place of this profession in their own lives and in their own communities?

There has recently been a selective resurgence of the American city. Downtown redevelopment, inspired in part by professional planners, has brought life and vitality back to some centre cities. Even the newer cities in the south and west – Pheonix, Atlanta, and prototypical Los Angeles – once noted for their sprawl and horizontal plane have developed staunch downtowns marked by the vertical bulk of skyscrapers. And some older cities in the north-east – notably New York, Boston, and Baltimore – have stabilized and expanded their once troubled economies – beneficiaries of the nation's growing service industries. Deep troubles persist – in housing, in serving the poor, in transportation, in education, in equity. But these problems are perceived as less critical than they were twenty years ago at the height of Lyndon Johnson's Great Society initiatives. Then the city was seen as a damaged national resource with ills that required political and social correctives. Now the city is seen more in terms of an accounting sheet with some significant liabilities but with some tangible assets as well. The image of pathology has been replaced by the image of accounting; the social reformer and community activist by the businessman and developer.

But if cities have recently prospered to some degree, professional planners have not. Enrolments have declined at their schools; internal disagreements persist over their appropriate role in society; and doubts continue to be expressed about their effectiveness, both from potential allies and long-time opponents. In fact the policies and popularity of the Reagan Administration in the 1980s have narrowed the planner's field of responsibilities substantially. The decade, as President Reagan so proudly proclaimed, was to be the Age of the Entrepreneur. Despite the President's fondness for Franklin D. Roosevelt, the image and reality he presented stood a great distance from FDR's sincere, although vaguely articulated, appreciation for planning and government activism. So, as the role of the federal government continued to shrink, so did the role of the planner. The two bywords of the planning profession – long-term and compre-hensive – have had no place in the political philosophy of the Reagan Administration. And apparently these words, rarely cherished in the past, have had an increasingly narrow range of use in the nation as a whole.

If we were simply discussing the troubles of a single profession, the analysis would be of limited value. But the fate of planning has in many ways been tied to the fate of the public sector. What we see happening to professional planning is a reflection of what is happening to government in the United States: a loss of public con-

3

fidence; a paralysis of purpose; an inability to forge a consensus on significant issues; and an ever-stronger belief that progress lies more in short-term, personal fulfilment than in long-term, national goals.

Thus the problems of the planning profession serve as a metaphor for the current crisis in government. And perhaps equally important, it reflects as well, the current crisis in liberal thought in America. For if twentieth-century planning is tied to any political philosophy, it appears to hold its greatest allegiance to liberalism – that middle ground of political thought based on the premises that private enterprise is good but requires public regulation to curb its worst abuses; that the quest for self-fulfilment must be matched by a concern for community; that personal satisfaction is indeed important but that it does not automatically lead to improved community welfare; and that the private sector directs the economy but that government – particularly the federal government – needs to play a vital role in our society. In short, liberals believe that greed is a significant motivating force, but that it is not enough; and that government should not promote greed as a virtue, but rather has a responsibility to ensure that the personal and corporate pursuit of wealth does not run roughshod over our more humane, national values.

These are tough times for government, planning and liberalism. During such moments of crisis, it is not unusual for the bereaved party to turn to its past for insights and answers – not as an exercise in nostalgia but rather as a means of greater understanding. This has been particularly true of professional planners: the growth of the Planning History Group; the increasing exchange of ideas between planners and historians; the intellectual movement from theoretical models to historical narratives; a rise in the number of historical sessions at the annual meetings of planning professionals; and the numerous monographs and articles devoted to planning history are all testimony to this desire to understand (but not necessarily return to) the profession's roots.

The chapters of this book, written by some of the most prominent practitioners in planning history, are another contribution to this field of inquiry. Like many previous planning history articles and monographs, they reveal as much about the traditional place of government in American society as they do about the planning profession – and in the process say a great deal about the nature of American society not only in the past but most likely in the future as well.

The collection is ordered chronologically. It begins with a discussion of the 1811 plan for New York City (the first significant city plan in the new nation outside of L'Enfant's majestic radial street pattern for Washington, D.C.). It ends with a discussion on the future course and direction of the American metropolis as we approach the twenty–first century.

In between, the reader journeys through a discussion of the development of the antebellum American suburb and its post-Civil War counterpart. We learn about the genius of Frederick Law Olmsted and his impact on his own and subsequent generations. We look at the rise of the City Beautiful Movement and preplanning professionals who were interested in ordering the growth of the city and who were able to carry out many of planning's functions before the profession was recognized as an independent one (with its own training, vocabulary and expertise). We learn about planning between the World Wars and the rising importance of professionalism during this period despite the political conservatism of the day. We see how many of the planning ideas of the 1920s were introduced at the federal and state level by the Roosevelt Adminstration during the Great Depression. We learn as well about the limits of reform in the United States, even during a period of extraordinary stress and disillusionment.

And finally, we look at post-World War II America – at its sincere, but misguided, attempts to deal with the problems of housing the urban poor; and at the economic success of its suburbs which now dominate not only the nation's domestic economy but its image and aspirations as well. Collectively displaying the nation's enormous wealth and poverty, the city and suburb – the American metropolis – perhaps most dramatically conveys the contradictions in American life. Each metropolis exists as a visible reminder of the nation's economic successes and failures. In the process each reveals the limits of planning, and more significantly of government, either to guide our prosperity or to overcome our poverty. The collection then ends very much where this introduction began. It looks at the planning profession today, not just in terms of its own internal conflicts and inadequacies, but also as a metaphor for the problems of government in American life during the 1980s.

Although chronologically cast, this collection does not lend itself to traditional methods of periodization. There are, of course, references to the romantic suburb, the city beautiful, the age of the metropolis and other standard terms which have become a common part of the planning historian's vocabulary. There are, too, assessments of the impact of important figures in the history of planning. Frederick Law Olmsted, Thomas Adams, Lewis Mumford, and Le Corbusier all receive due recognition for their accomplishments and influence. But what strikes me about this collection is not the periods or personalities which are discussed, but rather how each chapter (whether a case study of the City Beautiful Movement in Seattle or a general analysis of post-World War II suburban development) illustrates the intellectual continuity which has existed within the notion of planning since the nation's first efforts to shape the growth of its cities. Indeed the problems of planning were evident well before a group of social reformers tried to give landscape architects, housers, city administra-tors, and real estate lawyers a coherent and collective identity as professional planners during the first two decades of this century.

It is this continuity – or to state it more accurately, this conflict in purpose – which seems to typify the planning experience in the United States, whether we choose to study planning in the early nineteenth or the late twentieth centuries. So different in their approaches and subject matter, these chapters are joined by their collective portrayal of planning as a significant, yet selective, force in American development. And in the process, they also reflect the uses to which government has been put in the United States.

American planning has always possessed a bifocal quality. At one level, it is concerned with economic growth – setting the stage for private development and individual prosperity. On another level, it focuses on issues of reform and equity – concerned not so much with setting the stage as with altering the props under which the economic system operates so as to ensure a greater level of equality rather than more vigorous competition. This dual vision would not necessarily be a problem if in fact both aspects were operating equally. One can foresee pendulum shifts in policy from an emphasis on economic growth to an emphasis on social and economic equity. These shifts would generate self-corrective policy measures that would enable the nation, over a period of time, to consider both short-term and long-term goals and to establish strategies for individual satisfaction and national welfare. In fact, the dream of twentieth-century liberalism – at least in terms of its domestic agenda – has been to compress these broad concerns into the same timeframe so that policy makers could simultaneously see and react to both sides of the issue.

But planning's (or for that matter, liberalism's) bifocal quality has never been divided into equal parts. Private, economic development has always been in sharper focus than issues of equity and reform. From this aspect, planning (and more generally government) does not seek to change society as much as to embody and promote its most basic and traditional values. Thus, as you will read, the 1811 plan for New York City succeeds because it adheres to the terms of economic growth set by the larger society, and more specifically by the city's powerful business and commercial interests. The plan's gridiron pattern laid the groundwork for the enormous expansion of New York City during the nineteenth century. Later critics would lament how implementation of the plan abused the city's once attractive natural environment, but no one could deny its positive impact on the city's (and region's) economy. The 1811 plan thus had admirably fulfilled one definition of planning, but in the process seemed to have violated the tenets of another. Perhaps no greater historical image of American poverty exists than New York City's late-nineteenth-century crowded and disease-ridden tenements – built within the very framework created by the gridiron and just miles from the rising skyscrapers that signified the city's growing wealth and power.

One hundred and ten years later New York City embarked on another momentous plan, one that would also exert a significant impact on the rest of the nation. In 1921, a group of planning professionals under the leadership of Thomas Adams began research on *The Regional Plan of New York and Its Environs*. This was state-of-the-art planning, based on a meticulous survey of regional conditions and a careful analysis, by experts in the field, of potential solutions to regional problems. It cost $1 million and took ten years to complete. It produced ten volumes analysing and illustrating the physical, economic, social, and political state of affairs in the New York region.

Virtually nothing remained unnoticed by the researchers. Population trends, changing land values, governmental structures, commercial districts, recreation, buildings, neighbourhoods, and public services all came under their scrutiny. But the prime legacy of the plan resided in its impact on transportation routes in the New York metropolitan region – its proposals for a circumvential highway system and a network of bridges that, when built, melded the area together. In effect the Regional Plan, despite the sincere intentions of its researchers to do otherwise, very much served the same purpose as the 1811 plan: it provided the physical framework for future economic growth. As Lewis Mumford pointed out at the time, the plan failed to consider seriously the need for decent low-cost housing; nor did its authors fully understand the implications of allowing population growth to continue unchecked. Consequently, Mumford castigated the plan and ridiculed Thomas Adams, who had led the research effort and compiled and synthesized the findings. Mumford, in his biting style, voiced his support for planning's reformist impulse. Adams, on the other hand, had come face-to-face with the contradictions inherent in American planning. In liberal fashion, he extended his support for both economic development and social equity, but when the details of the plan unfolded, the emphasis – as it usually does with any successful American plan – lay with the forces of economic growth. Planners and government would once again serve their traditional function of providing the physical infrastructure for successful private investment.

The same story, often with a different cast of characters and a different set of specific issues, has occurred again and again in American planning history – although rarely with the drama and verve of the Adams/Mumford exchange. It is found in Depression-era politics when a combination of economic catastrophe and intellectual rigour gave planners a rare moment of influence. However, for most planners the list of New Deal programmes that ultimately failed is more impressive than those which succeeded. The National Resources Planning Board and the Resettlement Administration both had the potential to reshape our national landscape – and in the process not just to revitalize our economy but to reform it as well. Neither was ever adequately funded; neither was able to survive beyond the late 1930s and early 1940s. Conversely, the Home Owners Loan Corporation (whose functions were later folded into the Federal Housing Administration) revolutionized home mortgages in the United States. It made it possible for middle-class Americans to purchase their own homes and it protected lending institutions from possible financial losses. Thus the HOLC and later the FHA gave the federal government a direct partnership in a national programme for suburban development. Not surprisingly, the programme outlasted the economic emergency of the Depression and became the key financial element behind suburban real estate development in post World War II America. In the mix of New Deal legislation, the winning hand was held by those who wanted to revitalize and promote private investment – even if it meant the federal government would become a 'silent' partner in underwriting the risk and in insuring the players against loss.

The same competing forces of reform and growth were evident in the most important piece of urban legislation passed in the post-war period: the Housing Act of 1949. The lofty language of the Act called for 'a decent home in a decent environment for every American'. The National Association of Real Estate Boards, a conservative lobbying group for real estate developers, supported it; so did the liberal National Association of Housing Officials. In fact, here was legislation that apparently met the need to promote both profitable investment for private developers and social equity for the poor. At one level, this legislation held the potential for more and better public housing. At another level, it might also prove that the principles of planning were not flawed by inherent contradictions, but rather encompassed a large universe that – with forethought and compromise – could accommodate disparate needs and desires.

But the reality of public housing beginning in the 1950s was quite different from the hopes expressed after the Act was passed in 1949. Under this programme, the government purchased land at its 'market' value, often demolished the houses and then 'wrote down' the resale price of the land when making it available to prospective private developers. The result: the clearing of hundreds of thousands of homes without a reciprocal housing construction programme to compensate for the loss of housing stock. Moreover, the federal public housing programme, had a keen eye for shabby housing that already existed (often confusing worn paint for neighbourhood malaise), but seemed blind to the dehumanizing effects of institutionalized high-rise housing cells being built to replace razed 'slums'. And since commercial development held greater promise for profit than residential development, land that had been levelled for public housing, if it could find a market, found one for offices and retail stores, not housing.

Thus in many respects it was the fallout of the public housing programme that helped pave the way for the current selective resurgence of the city: it showed that the city still possessed a means for profit, but that attractive investment resided not with public housing but with commercial downtown redevelopment. It is indeed ironic that the rise of 'yuppy' neighbourhoods often took place at the expense of the poor – not just in terms of evictions but also in terms of programmes that were initially designed to help the least, not some of the most, fortunate Americans.

But we do not have to look to our most recent past to see this story being played out again and again – although by doing so we are able to place the issue in its sharpest relief. We will see these contradictory principles unfold in Frederick Law Olmsted's plans for Buffalo, New York in the late nineteenth century; we will find them operating in Seattle's City Beautiful Movement at the turn of the century; and they will serve a useful purpose in understanding the reform initiatives proposed by Andrew H. Green (in New York City), John H.B. Latrobe (in Baltimore), and George Cadwallader (in Philadelphia) nearly a century ago.

Thus the chapters that follow – despite their enormous disparities in time, place and subject matter – share a common theme. The evolution of the American city and suburb – and those conscious attempts to shape their growth – are not just bound by their geographical and historical setting. Rather these experiences (whether in New York City or Cambridge, Massachusetts, whether in Seattle or Chicago's Northshore, whether in Buffalo or Atlanta) all reveal a certain contradiction in American patterns of growth, as well as in the policy responses that have been developed to guide the nation's cities, suburbs and regions. Planners – and more generally public officials sponsoring liberal government initiatives – have stood at the centre of these contradictions, trying to develop principles and policies to satisfy both the need for economic growth and social equity. Their accomplishments should not be minimized; nor should they be overstated. An episodic history of urban and regional planning in the United States illustrates not just the roots and inner workings of a particular profession; it shows, as well, the outer workings of the nation's economic and political system – and with that, the fundamental values under which the nation operates. Planners – and liberals – do not possess an intellectual monopoly on the contradictions in American life. They simply choose to deal with them directly. That is why their history is so important.

Chapter One

The Greatest Grid: the New York Plan of 1811

EDWARD K. SPANN

The decades surrounding the birth of the New York Plan of 1811 constitute both an end and a beginning of urban planning in the United States. The period brought a significant shift away from earlier forms of urban design, imbued with socio-political and aesthetic concerns, to simpler and more utilitarian plans intended to facilitate the rapid urban development which occurred during the nineteenth century. In the first decades of this new century, the simple gridiron pattern of straight streets and rectangular blocks established itself as the primary basis for American city form, leaving later generations of planners to cope with its real and presumed defects. Nowhere was the triumph of the grid so decisive as in America's greatest city. In its positive and especially negative influence, the New York grid was to be a landmark in the history of American city planning.

This development eclipsed an earlier tradition of urban design which gave form to such colonial capitals as Philadelphia, Annapolis, and Savannah.[1] These capitals were designed, under the influence of European planning practices and ideals, to embody the values intended to govern them and their colonial domains. In 1681, for instance, William Penn tried to establish the simplicity and humanity of his Quakerism in the spatial openness and geometric regularity which he planned for Philadelphia (figure 1). In what was then the new gridiron form, Penn saw the opportunity to provide ample space for both people and vegetation so that his capital would become 'a green country town, which will never be burnt, and always be wholesome'. The real city fell short of these hopes, but eighteenth-century Philadelphia attained a charming and orderly character which helped popularize the grid among Americans.[2]

The greatest of these early designs was provided in 1791 by Pierre L'Enfant for Washington, D.C. Although based on European

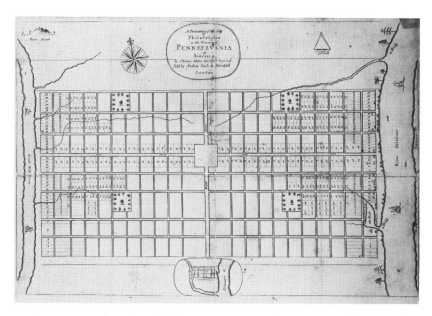

Figures 1 and 2. Two Capital Cities. The Philadelphia grid, prepared in 1683 by Thomas Holme and approved by William Penn, probably was derived from the gridiron plans proposed for London after the Great Fire of 1666. L'Enfant's plan for Washington D.C., as rendered by Andrew Ellicott in 1792, drew heavily on French baroque planning (*Source*: New York Public Library – Stokes Collection).

practice, this design for America's new capital was, as L'Enfant boasted, a new plan expressive of the special character of American government: it emphasized the constitutional separation of executive and legislative powers by placing the Presidential 'Palace' (yet to be called the White House) and the Capitol building at opposite ends of Pennsylvania Avenue; similarly, it displayed the sovereign presence of states in the American federal system by providing a square for each of the then fifteen states (figure 2). L'Enfant laid out most of Washington on the already familiar gridiron pattern, but he believed that a simple grid was 'tiresome and insipid'.[3] To provide for a more dynamic layout, he subordinated the grid to a system of diagonal avenues connecting the various squares and other principal points of the city. Such a system, he said, would not only break the tiresome repetition of right-angled streets but would 'connect each part of the city . . . by making the real distance less from place to place, by giving them reciprocity of sight and by making them thus seemingly connected, promote a rapid settlement of the whole extent'.[4] His design, then, was intended to counteract what were eventually recognized as some of the major weaknesses of the grid, notably its visual monotony, rigidity of traffic patterns, and absence of unifying focal points.

On paper, L'Enfant's plan won general acceptance, but he soon learned that planning in America involved politics and economics as well as design. Officially, he answered to a three-man commission appointed to initiate the city's development. The Commission wanted to promote rapid growth, an aim which overrode L'Enfant's resolve to protect the integrity of the design. Fearful that rapid development would distort the plan, he attempted to obstruct a major sale of Washington lots in 1792 which caused him to be fired for insubordination.[5] Even without L'Enfant his plan survived, but as early as 1803 one observer concluded that it had been mutilated, particularly by the addition of more than 130 unplanned building squares 'inserted to gratify proprietors, to whom the acquisition of an additional lot was more desirable than either the beauty or health of the city'. Other mutilations would follow, providing ample need for the replanning of the capital city in the early twentieth century.[6]

L'Enfant's plan did exert some influence on later American cities such as Detroit and Indianapolis, but the next half-century brought a rising mania among Americans for land speculation and rapid town 'development' which favoured the grid in its least restrictive form. Although the gridiron system was not as inflexible or as insipid as L'Enfant and other critics have charged,[7] the dominant concern for rapid development encouraged its application in simple and mechanical ways. Typical was the fate inflicted on Penn's plan for Philadelphia which in the first half of the century suffered serious distortions from the overcrowding of its lots, the deterioration of its squares, and the monotonous multiplication of its rectangular blocks and right-angled streets.[8]

During this period of early city growth, decisions made in the interests of towns and small cities would govern the development of a much different metropolitan world in a future as yet unknown. The New York Plan of 1811, the masterplan of the first great American metropolis, was devised to meet the needs of a moderate-sized Atlantic port not much different from the small city depicted at the tip of Manhattan Island in Bernard Ratzer's 1767 map of the area around New York Harbor (figure 3). In 1811, who could have predicted that the surrounding regions of farms and small villages would eventually merge into one complexly organized and densely populated metropolitan area?

Among several influences on the Plan was the fact that New York was emphatically not a political centre; in the 1790s, it had lost its earlier roles both as the nation's first capital under the Constitution and as the capital of New York State. Henceforth, considerations of design were subordinated to the more practical concerns of a city plainly commercial in character. Another essentially negative influence was the haphazard and inefficient layout of New York's streets. The city could boast of Broadway, its great fashionable thoroughfare, but most of its streets were narrow, crooked, crowded, and so poorly organized as a system that one visitor complained that it took at least a month to learn one's way around town. Over the next century, the increasing overload of these streets was to make one incessant headache for both business and government.[9] It was in response to this situation that New York planners developed what later critics would condemn as an excessive devotion to the grid. Even before 1811, that devotion was evident in the city's efforts to deal with its own local frontier, the yet-to-be urbanized upper four-fifths of Manhattan Island lying above Houston Street.

The municipal government had a special interest in this matter because it owned more than two square miles of 'common lands' on the Island. By the 1790s, the city wanted to sell part of this public domain to pay its debts, but haphazard patterns of both property-lines and roads north of the city made this no easy task, particularly since many parcels of city property had been left without the street frontage needed to attract private buyers.[10] This situation emphasized a related problem: the irregular character of private property boundaries, which had often been laid out in reference to the meanderings of a few main roads. To assure the orderly development of its northern territory, New York moved to replace this irregular system with one that would provide access to all lands and also establish a regular base

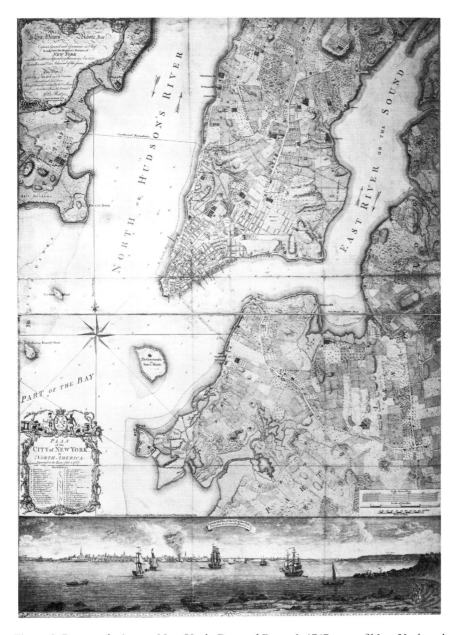

Figure 3. Pre-revolutionary New York. Bernard Ratzer's 1767 map of New York and environs, in its irregular property lines and roads, has a unique charm, but that irregularity was viewed by later developers as an obstacle to be eliminated in favour of the grid. Fifty years later, the city has grown northward only a little beyond Delancy's Square (*Source*: New York Public Library – Stokes Collection).

for property lines. In 1796, Casimer Goerck, the City Surveyor, prepared a map of the common lands divided into rectangular blocks. The Goerck map helped fix a geometric order on Manhattan, but it was only one step in the complicated process that led to the Plan of 1811.[11]

Early in the new century, two factors demanded an even more comprehensive plan to govern future development. One was the prospect for rapid urban growth resulting from the expansion of American foreign trade after 1790. The growth of commerce brought a notable increase in population, which led one newspaper to predict with apparent rashness that this city of 60,000 people in 1800 would grow to 700,000 in 1850 and to over three million by the end of the century. In anticipation of such growth, private developers hastened to lay out new streets to the north of the existing city, thereby threatening to add more confusion to street patterns and property lines unless they were guided by some comprehensive plan.[12]

Real and anticipated growth also intensified concern over public health, a problem dramatized by a series of yellow fever epidemics, which in 1803 and 1805 forced massive evacuations of the city. Although New Yorkers disagreed as to the specific causes of such diseases, they believed that their general health was threatened by the impure air and congested conditions of the old city. In 1809, a New York physician warned that the congestion associated with large cities brought 'nervous distempers, and others more rapidly fatal'.[13] Plainly, the time had come for a plan to avoid the mistakes of the past and to provide for a healthier, more orderly future. The city was ready for its first conscientious effort to shape its future environment.[14]

Early in 1804, the New York Common Council (the municipal legislature) took an important step toward comprehensive planning by instructing the Street Commissioner to prepare 'a plan on paper for new streets hereafter to be laid out and opened', a plan which would override the streets projected by private developers. The Council also added a new element by instructing the Commissioner to determine 'what grounds ought to be retained or procured by the Common Council for military parades, pleasure grounds or other public uses for ornamenting the City in its future growth and extension'. Such a plan was reported three months later, but by then city officials had concluded that comprehensive planning involved something more than the preparation of a 'plan on paper'. Aside from some doubts concerning their authority to override the rights of property-owners and developers, they were uncertain about the future willingness of the city to adhere to a comprehensive plan. In 1807, therefore, the Council requested the state legislature, its immediate sovereign, to establish a Commission to prepare a plan which would have the authority and permanence of law.[15]

In its petition to the legislature, the Council emphasized its 'highly interesting and important' duty to provide for new streets 'in such a manner as to unite regularity and order with public convenience and benefit, and in particular to promote the health of the city'. It noted, however, that 'the diversity of sentiments and opinions which has hitherto existed and probably will always exist among members of the Common Council, the incessant remonstrances of proprietors against plans however well devised or beneficial, wherein their individual interests do not concur, and the impossibility of completing these plans but by tedious and expensive course of law, are obstacles of a serious and perplexing nature'. The Council thus concluded that any plan devised by city officials without state authorization would likely be 'disregarded or annulled by their successors'.[16]

Fortunately, the petition had a powerful champion in DeWitt Clinton who at the time was both the Mayor of the city and a State Senator.[17] Even considering his support though, it is surprising that legislation intended to provide for the future of the state's largest city was passed without reported debate or recorded vote except for some controversy as to whether the Commissioners appointed under the act should be paid four or five dollars a day. By a close vote, the state assembly decided on the smaller amount.[18] Given the fact that the plan had the force of law, it is also notable that the legislature did not require review or even formal approval by either the state or the city. When the completed plan was presented to the Common Council in April 1811, it was accepted without any action other than to publish it in the public press.[19] In such a casual way were provisions made for a plan which would govern the growth of New York from a small city of some 75,000 people to a metropolis of over 800,000 a half-century later.

Under the 1807 Act, three prominent New Yorkers were appointed to the plan Commission: John Rutherford, a lawyer; Simeon Dewitt, a cousin of DeWitt Clinton and long-time State Surveyor-General; and Gouverneur Morris, a former United States Senator and ex-diplomat who had retired to his estate at Morrisania outside of Manhattan in what is now the Bronx. As Dewitt and Morris soon became involved in a prolonged effort to determine a route for the Erie Canal, most of the work probably was done by their head surveyor, John Randel Jr, a protégé of Dewitt's; later Randel laid out several upstate towns including the future city of Syracuse.[20]

The responsibilities of the Commissioners were quite explicit. In the areas to the north and east of Greenwich Village (still a suburb of the old city), they were to lay out 'the leading streets and great avenues, of a width of not less than 60 feet, and in general to lay out said streets, roads and public squares of such ample width as they may deem sufficient to secure a free and abundant circulation of air'. They were also expected to establish a definite basis for property-lines, a responsibility emphasized by requirements that they keep careful field-notes of their surveys and 'erect suitable and durable markers at the most conspicuous angles'.[21]

The Commissioners' work proved more difficult than the implication conveyed in the canard later publicized by Frederick Law Olmsted that they modelled their plan on the grid-like mesh of a mason's sieve. Although much of it entailed tedious surveys, there were moments of drama. John Randel later said that he was often arrested for trespass on the complaints of property-holders who believed that the plan threatened their rights. Survey parties were sometimes attacked by irate farmers and market-gardeners who feared, with reason, that the new streets would be run through or over their properties.[22] If these attacks did little to obstruct the work, they reminded the Commissioners that they were not engaged in the utopian task of imposing ideal forms on empty space. As creatures of their local culture, they would not repeat L'Enfant's mistake of unnecessarily antagonizing property-owners and developers.

The completed plan covered an area five times as large as old New York and extended as far north as Harlem, then a small town distant from the city. Having included all but the northern neck (Washington Heights) of the Island, the planners felt it necessary to justify the ambitious character of their work: 'It may be a subject of considerable merriment that the Commissioners have provided space for a greater population than is collected at any spot on this side of China. They have in this respect been governed by the shape of the ground. It is not improbable that considerable numbers may be collected at Haerlem [sic] before the high hills to the southward shall be built upon as a city'. The expected development of Harlem as a secondary commercial centre was not unpleasing to Morris, who was interested in promoting the development of lands near his estate on the other side of the Harlem River. It is notable, though, that no special provision was made for Harlem as its streets were planned simply as an extension of the larger grid; the effect of their work, intended or not, was to assure that Manhattan would eventually become one city.

Having overestimated Harlem's growth potential, they proceeded to underestimate that of New York itself by making the not 'unreasonable conjecture' that in half a century, the city would extend as far north as 34th Street and would 'contain 400,000 souls';[23] likely, they expected most of Middle Island to become a suburb for the well-to-do. The actual growth of the city after 1820 was greater than they anticipated, but their conjecture was a realistic projection of the

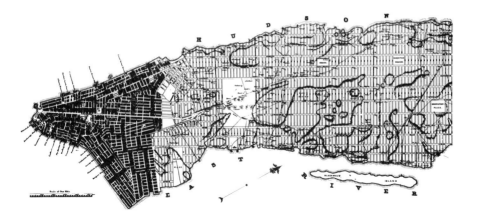

Figure 4. The Greatest Grid. The southern half of Manhattan Island as mapped for the 1811 Plan (the extreme length of the Island prevents reproduction of the whole map in any meaningful scale); the dark area is the old unplanned city (*Source*: Indiana State University Library – Special Collections).

population density of the old city into the new areas, a projection suited to the slow and costly horsedrawn transportation of their times. As responsible planners obliged to make 'realistic' projections of future development, they could not base their work on the seemingly rash prophecies made by newspapers and land speculators.

Whatever the prospects for future growth, the Commissioners did their best to facilitate the development of Manhattan in a way acceptable to the city fathers. The previous decade had indicated a clear preference for a simple geometric order to replace the chaotic and inefficient layout of the existing city. In fulfilment of that preference, the planners effaced the casual roads and property lines of the new areas in favour of a special New York variant of the grid (figure 4). To accommodate traffic up and down the Island, they mapped out twelve straight, parallel, numbered avenues, each 100 feet wide; Third through Sixth Avenues in the interior of the Island were placed 920 feet apart, while the other avenues were spaced somewhat closer together probably in anticipation of denser river front development.[24]

What gave this grid its most distinctive character were the narrow rectangular blocks created by 155 cross streets, only 200 feet apart (except for fifteen wider streets, each street was to be 60 feet wide); with considerable pride, head surveyor Randel noted that the distance between every twentieth street was a mile 'within about a yard'. This unusually high number of cross-streets may have been designed in anticipation of a heavy volume of traffic between the two river fronts, but more likely it was intended to facilitate land development. The

Plan guaranteed a vast number of uniform rectangular blocks and miles of street frontages, enough to satisfy the well–established demand for orderly property lines and for access to property which dominated the city's planning concerns.[25]

The New York Commissioners readily admitted that this simple geometry differed from the more complex plan devised for Washington, D.C.: they pondered 'whether they should adopt some of those supposed improvements by circles, ovals, and stars which certainly embellish a plan, whatever may be their effects as to convenience and utility. In considering that subject, they could not but bear in mind that a city is composed principally of the habitations of men, and that strait sided and right angled houses are the most cheap to build and the most convenient to live in'. This reasoning, the Commissioners said, was 'decisive' in shaping their decision. More broadly, however, the decision was a conceptual choice in favour of the grid as the dominant planning idea, a choice motivated also by their indifference (and, possibly, hostility as the citizens of a proud new nation) to practices associated with the European and colonial past; the United States had already repudiated that past in both its decimal coinage system (which Morris had helped devise) and the rectangular system of surveys which it had adopted for its own public lands.[26] In the interests of convenience and of the future, the Plan provided for not one circle, oval, star, or diagonal street with one exception, an unwanted anomaly at later Union Square formed by the convergence of Broadway and the Bowery (figure 5).[27]

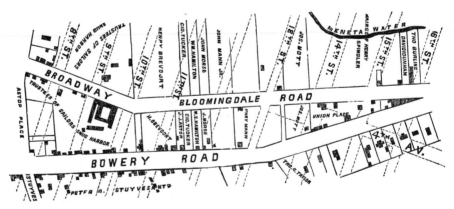

Figure 5. The Union Place Area. This map details the chief anomaly in the otherwise rectangular 1811 Plan; note the disharmony between the street plan (in broken lines) and both the existing property lines and the two main thoroughfares of the old unplanned city (*Source*: Indiana State University Library – Special Collections).

The Commissioners seemed confident that their geometry met prevailing expectations, but they were less sure that they had satisfied the newer concern over public health: 'It may, to many, be matter of surprise, that so few vacant spaces have been left, and those so small, for the benefit of fresh air, and consequent preservation of health'. Their defence was that New York required comparatively few open spaces, since it was embraced by two 'large arms of the sea' (the Hudson and East rivers) which would insure a fresh supply of air even to built-over areas, presumably through the many straight streets which would cross the narrow island; therefore, in a city where 'the price of land is so uncommonly great, it seemed proper to admit the principles of economy to greater influence'.[28]

This apologetic tone seemingly confirms later complaints that the Commissioners were miserly in their provision for open spaces, but actually they were notably more generous than those who implemented their plan over the next decades. For instance, they provided space for future neighbourhood parks in the form of Bloomingdale, Hamilton, Manhattan, and Morris Squares, each comprising eight blocks of land, to be located at 53rd, 66th, 77th, and 120th Streets respectively. Apparently, these were intended to enhance the value of nearby muncipal land; Hamilton Square had already been approved by the City Council as part of a projected sale of some of the common lands.[29]

The plan also provided for three larger open spaces, each of which was assigned some practical function. The smallest was set aside in the upper part of the island for later use as a reservoir when the city would finally construct an adequate system to supply itself with pure water, an attainment more than thirty years in the future. In the meantime, the Commissioners said, the space 'may be consecrated to the purpose of science' in the form of an astronomical observatory which they hoped the public would erect on the site; this hope was not fulfilled, although the spot was long called 'Observatory Place'.[30]

The Commissioners gave special attention to a much larger space (54 acres), on the lower east side of the planning area, designated for a wholesale market complex to be supplied by a canal dug from the East River through the marshy ground of Stuyvesant Meadow. Although they evidently designed this Market Place to make the best use of a low-lying swampy area of doubtful value for private development, they emphasized the hope that in their new city the wholesale market would become the central source of supply for a network of small private food shops to replace the existing system of public markets. The new network would bring food closer to the consumer and also avoid the need to allocate space for public markets, whose smells and organic filth made them less than 'consistent with cleanliness and health'. In their intentions to eliminate a frequently noisome and inefficient system of food supply, the Commissioners were at least half a century ahead of their time, too far ahead as soon was demonstrated by the complete failure of the city to implement this part of the plan.[31]

The largest open space, about 275 acres between 23rd and 34th Streets and Third to Seventh Avenues, was intended for a grand 'Parade', a training ground for the local militia and a place to assemble any military force required for the defence of the city, an important matter during a period of impending war with Great Britain. The Commissioners readily admitted that this site was both too small and too remote from the lower city fully to serve its function, but they argued their case in terms which New Yorkers could understand: that the remedy would incur 'a frightful expense' due to the high cost of land closer to the city.[32] To the contrary, later generations might have objected that the Parade was both too large and too far south, since it would have denied the northern areas served by Fourth, Fifth, and Sixth avenues direct access to the lower city. In mapping out this barrier, the Commissioners probably assumed that the interior of the island would develop more slowly and at a lower density than the areas closer to the river fronts, an assumption which also explains their belief that the 'two large arms of the sea' would provide adequate ventilation for the city.

By later standards, the Commissioners failed to notice several significant planning considerations: they did not determine the street grades required by the imposition of the grid on Manhattan's varied and often rugged terrain; nor did they try to resolve the problems created when their street system disrupted the Island's natural drainage systems. They did not attempt to regulate population densities, land usage, or the heights and volumes of buildings, nor did they make any effort to guide the development of New York's two waterfronts. Even more striking in the light of the importance of streets in their plan, they gave little thought to providing for the efficient movement of people and goods by diagonal thoroughfares or any other means.[33]

These failures undoubtedly resulted from the Commission's inability, understandable in these simple days of stage-coaches and small-scale enterprise, to envision the complexly-organized future city with its extensive crowding and high volume of traffic. In his boldest prophecy, for instance, Governeur Morris in 1807 could do no more than to predict that the whole of Manhattan would 'soon become a village or a town'. Essentially a country squire who believed the real strength of American society lay in its 'yeomanry', Morris was simply not able to anticipate the metropolitan future which eventually was to envelop even his own estate at Morrisania.[34] Neither he nor the other Commissioners could possibly anticipate the radically transformed world which modernization would create over the next century. Under the circumstances, it probably was better that they made no detailed plan.

That they attempted no such plan owes much to their appointed mission. Morris and his colleagues undoubtedly were influenced by the fact that their handiwork would become, in the words of the 1807 Act, 'final and conclusive' law unalterable except by state action. In order to guard the future against the inconsistencies of common councils and the caprice of land developers, New York agreed to bind itself to what one of its city-attorneys later called 'one grand permanent plan'.[35] Since their plan directly affected the property rights of many New Yorkers, the Commissioners had good reason not to stretch their legislative mandate any more than necessary. Thus they made little effort to determine land usage; any area of their grid was equally open for the construction of a mansion or a foundry. This uniformity had the distinct advantage of protecting them from complaints that their plan favoured some propertied interests over others. Unwilling to define future development in exact terms, they were content to create an open context where private development as well as public life would be 'attended with the least inconvenience', leaving it largely to individuals to fill in the empty blocks and to give details to the future city, subject to such regulation as might later seem necessary.[36]

In following this path, they succeeded in their primary mission, which was to replace the old uneven and uncertain system of property lines and roads with a regular and orderly one. The landowners of Manhattan, whatever their particular resentments against this intrusion on their property, received a general guarantee of future opportunities and restraints. The public plan thus provided a stable, assured basis for private planning.[37] As a result, the new grid was accepted as a fact of life by most New Yorkers, an inexorable future that affected their perception of land on the Island. In the 1840s, Edgar Allen Poe complained that it had doomed many 'picturesque sites for villas' in the yet-to-be developed portions of Manhattan: 'Streets are already "mapped" through them, and they are no longer suburban residences, but "town lots" '[38] (figures 6 and 7).

The implementation of the plan, however, did not always go smoothly. Initially, the Commissioners hoped to reconcile their work with the plans of private developers and landowners, but their decision to override existing property and street lines soon led to complaints, particularly over the way that the new streets cut up existing properties.[39] More resentment arose over the way that the

Figure 6 and 7. The Development of Union Square. These two views of the Union Square area in 1830 and 1848 illustrate the rapid growth that began within the lower limits of the plan some twenty years after it was prepared (Source: New York Library – Stokes and Eno Collections).

projected streets were actually built. Under state law, the city could expropriate, with compensation, the lands needed for streets and then finance street openings by levying assessments on adjoining properties, a process which antagonized many property-owners. At least a few of the resentful blamed the Plan for increasing construction costs and assessments by requiring the expensive levelling and filling of the Island's frequently rugged terrain in order to make it conform to the grid (figure 8). In 1818, some inhabitants of Greenwich Village complained that the Plan not only increased street costs but offended 'persons of taste' by destroying the natural beauty of the terrain. For decades, there were sporadic explosions of resentment over what one New Yorkers called the 'de-grading' process of street openings.[40]

The most thorough early criticism came from a Commission established by state law in 1823 to lay out streets south of 34th Street, a task complicated by the city's decision to abandon the Market Square in favour of the private development of Stuyvesant Meadows; what was perhaps the most far-sighted feature of the Plan was the first to be completely eliminated. The difficulties of preparing the often swampy ground for streets undoubtedly contributed to the petulant tone of the new Commission's complaints, some of which indicate that its members had little knowledge of the Plan. One complaint, that it involved an *entire absence of public squares*, suggests that they had not even looked at it. Their other charges were sensible enough to be echoed by some later critics: the Plan had failed to provide adequate 'direct communication between the several quarters of the city', and, moreover, the 'great uniformity in the breadth and circumstances of the streets' established by it did not afford the variety of sites 'which is necessary for the adequate habitation of classes, differing extremely in opulence, that must be found united in the population of a great city'.[41]

The chief complaint of these street planners, however, was the already familiar one: that imposition of the grid on uneven terrain entailed exorbitant costs both to prepare manageable street grades and to provide for adequate drainage;[42] no indication, however, was made even of the possibility that part of these costs were an inevitable result of the elimination of the Market Square from the Plan. Although this complaint had some merit, it probably emanated from the desire of the new Commissioners to defend their own street scheme against the protests of property-owners in the area, especially over the projected costs of the ditches and sewers required to drain Stuyvesant Meadow. The problem of planning in a highly individualistic city like New York was well illustrated by one notable protest that the scheme required that 'the proprietors of the high ground [in the planning area] contribute to the expense of regulating the low ground, without any corresponding benefit to them'. Such arguments led the Common Council not only to reject the scheme but to persuade the legislature to repeal the 1823 Act establishing the Commission.[43] Nothing was done, however, to restore the Market Place to the 1811 Plan; Stuyvesant Meadows was eventually prepared for private development along lines acceptable to the property-owners in the area.

This imbroglio highlighted the governing principles of planning during these earlier decades. The loudest voice in planning decisions was that of property-holders and businessmen: those decisions that benefited them were approved, and those that did not were dismissed. The basic grid survived the complaints against it, because it provided a predictable future for private interests. Over the decades, it promised to transform over 11,000 acres of uneven and unorganized Manhattan land into some 2,000 neatly defined blocks and uncounted lots with hundreds of miles of street frontage. In its guarantee of streets and secure boundaries, it provided an important subsidy and incentive for private land developers – a promise of profit later emphasized by one of the makers of the Plan, head surveyor John Randel, Jr. Many years after he completed his work, Randel boasted that it had enriched many New Yorkers, including some descendents of those who had once gotten him arrested for trespass:

> The Plan of New York, thus objected to *before its completion*, is now the pride and boast of the city; and the facilities afforded by it for the *buying*, and *improving* real estate, on streets, avenues, and public squares, already laid out and established on the ground by monumental stones and bolts, *at the cost of the city*, and of greater wealth and extent, safety from conflagration, beautiful uniformity, and convenience, than could otherwise have been obtained . . .; thereby avoiding the frequent error of laying *short*, *narrow*, and *crooked streets*, with *alleys* and *courts* endangering extensive conflagrations, confined air, unclean streets, etc., must have greatly enhanced the value of real estate on New York Island.[44]

For Randel and most other New Yorkers, the enhancement of real estate under the plan was linked to the progress of the city; the grid guaranteed public interest as well as private profit. In an American city, where a democratic government was to protect and not to interfere with individual rights, planning was to encourage private ambition and effort within the general limits of an ordered freedom. Essentially, the grid promised to promote the rapid development of Manhattan along lines which protected the future against the mistakes associated with the old city. Moreover, many New Yorkers found aesthetic and intellectual satisfaction in the prospect that straight streets and rectangular blocks would replace the marshes, swamps, hills, and other irregular features of the Island. For them, the grid was a plan for the conquest of both nature and the past in the interests of an advancing civilization. 'Our streets have been straightened and widened, our buildings much improved and beautified', said one observer of uptown improvements in the 1840s. 'Whoever wishes to see the process of city-creation going on – fields converted into streets and lots, ugly cliffs into stately mansions, and whole rows of buildings supplanting cow pastures, may here be gratified'.[45] In such views, the development of Manhattan was no less magnificent than the American conquest of the western wilderness. The implementation of the Plan might gash the terrain, as in the construction of Second Avenue (figure 8), but this was simply a passing phase in the process of urban improvement.

Objections to the costs of street openings, therefore, were often outweighed by complaints over the slowness with which streets were opened by a generally cautious Common Council. Even after half a century, the village of Manhattanville on the west side of the Island mapped out for streets numbered in the 80s had yet to be developed (figure 9). The laggard pace of the street openings was blamed for the crowded, unsatisfactory housing conditions of the increasingly commercialized lower city. Erastus Benedict, a prominent advocate of rapid development, charged that this had contributed to the growth of neighbouring Brooklyn, then a separate city, at New York's expense. The charge was echoed by some city fathers concerned by the flight of tax-paying citizens to suburbs outside of Manhattan. In 1856, Mayor Fernando Wood complained that, in contrast to the Commissioners in 1811, later generations had neglected 'the improvement of the unoccupied part of the island'. To counter this negligence, Wood called for a programme to facilitate the opening of streets in order to provide adequate residential space for the city's expanding population.[46]

In the ebb and flow of development, the Plan was significantly altered, an adjustment to new circumstances which the Commissioners had probably expected. The legal character of the 'one grand permanent plan' made change difficult but hardly impossible. In fact, alterations were often enacted by the state legislature, generally along lines demanded by property interests. The Plan had little protection against such pressure, since no agency had been established to maintain its integrity or even to remind the public of its existence. During its first fifty years, therefore, it was the easy victim of a process of piecemeal change that involved several distinct phases.

The first phase indicated that the Commissioners, in planning for open spaces, had not understated the prevailing expectation that most

Figures 8 and 9. An Altered Terrain. The 1860 view up Second Avenue (looking northward from 42nd Street) depicts one of the many changes in topography that took place under the 1811 Plan. The 1860 picture of Manhattanville, mapped for streets numbered in the 80s but yet to be developed, gives some idea of Manhattan's original terrain (*Source*: Indiana State University Library – Special Collections).

land be reserved for private development. Even before the Market Square disappeared, the state legislature had in 1814 approved a city scheme to reduce the size of the Parade to the area between Fourth and Sixth Avenues and 23rd and 31st Streets. This action, which halved the space assigned to military use during a major war with Great Britain, opened the way for the complete elimination in the 1820s of the Parade with the exception of a small portion that was later made into Madison Square.[47] City streets replaced what might have become a large park to serve the crowded future city.

The elimination of the Parade, though, distinctly benefited the future flow of traffic, since it removed a major obstruction to movement along the interior avenues. Even more, it served to release Broadway, which would otherwise have terminated at the Parade's southern boundary, to follow the northward wanderings of the old Bloomingdale Road, marked on the Commissioner's map with dotted lines as something to be omitted. Subsequent state legislation permitted the extension of Broadway along this route, thus giving New York its one major 'diagonal', which broke the simple geometry of the grid and created in its intersections with cross streets the triangles and other eccentric spaces which the Commissioners had attempted to rule out of their order; one of these spaces later became Times Square.

In the 1830s, a boom in Manhattan real estate brought a more positive phase that added rather than subtracted open spaces. Although the boom's primary effect was to incite a speculative rush to develop new areas for building sites, it also evoked an interest in park-like open squares, particularly for their influence in increasing the saleability and value of nearby real estate. In 1831, a committee of the Common Council urged the city to act in the interests of present and future generations by 'providing squares in various parts of the city for purposes of military and civic parades, and for parties, and what is perhaps of more importance, to serve as ventilators to a densely populated city'.[48]

The new movement failed to restore the over 300 acres lost by the elimination of the Parade and the Market Square, but it did persuade the legislator to establish Union, Tompkins, Stuyvesant, and Madison squares in the developing areas. Only one of these squares (Stuyvesant) was entirely new to the plan. Union Square was a belated realization of the provision for Union Place (figures 6 and 7), while Madison and Tompkins were remnants, respectively, of the Parade and the Market Square. The state also attempted to satisfy the city's need for thoroughfares and appetite for street frontages by adding two new avenues, Lexington and Madison, in the middle of the extra long blocks between Third and Sixth Avenues.[49]

This movement, however, came to an abrupt halt in the late 1830s, causing one of its leaders later to complain that in the following decade the whole area between 26th and 77th Streets was left 'without one single breathing space other than adjacent roads and avenues'. In fact, no new open space was added to the plan in this area except for a distributing reservoir of the new Croton Water system (figure 9)[50]. The primary cause of this failure was an economic collapse in 1837, which deflated enthusiasm for new streets and squares, particularly when the assessments levied to pay for them came due during the generally depressed years which followed.[51] In these years, urban America learned that it is much easier to provide for parks and other amenities in good times than bad.

The return of prosperity in the late 1840s renewed the enthusiasm for improvements, but in a form that was distinctly contrary to the 1811 Plan. By the 1850s, development had reached 42nd Street (figure 9) and promised to accelerate under the pressures of a rapidly expanding population. The compact city of the past was being transformed into a sprawling metropolis which threatened to cover the whole Island within decades. The magnitude of development was matched by momentus alteration of the Plan. Having for more than a decade done nothing to provide for open spaces, the new metropolis persuaded the legislature in 1854 to set aside 770 acres in the centre of the Island for a great city park. Under the design of Frederick Law Olmsted, land which had been destined for conversion into building lots within the grid was transformed into a romantic antithesis to the grid. Although framed as a giant rectangle in a sea of rectangles, the new Central Park, in its interior curves and flowing shapes, was a defiant rejection of the angular geometry favoured by the Commissioners (figure 12). It was intended, said Olmsted, to provide 'conditions remedial of urban conditions', to counter the negative influences of the city which had matured within the framework of the 1811 Plan. Most of the motives behind the Park had been known before: concern for public health and welfare closely linked to expectations that civilized open space would increase the value of surrounding lands for development. Olmsted's plan, however, also involved essential changes in scale and design suited to the desire of the new metropolis to escape from its past.[52]

The influence of Central Park on public perceptions of the grid was soon apparent. In 1865, one New Yorker complained that under the old Plan 'the city was laid out . . . on the parallel rule system' without concern for either nature or basic human needs: 'If the city had been no farther laid out than it was built upon until the advent of the Central Park Commission and had been given over to them, the whole residence portion of the island might have been a park – a

Figures 10 and 11. A Half-Century's Growth. The 1792 painting depicts the area around Corlaers Hook (the sharp angle into the East River evident in figures 3 and 4); old New York is to the right and Brooklyn is to the left. The 1855 lithograph depicts the new metropolis with 42nd Street in the foreground. (Corlaers Hook is at the top of the shaded area on the left); the diagonal street on the right is Broadway, and in the foreground the reservoir marks the site of the present New York Public Library (*Source*: New York Public Library – Stokes and Eno Collections).

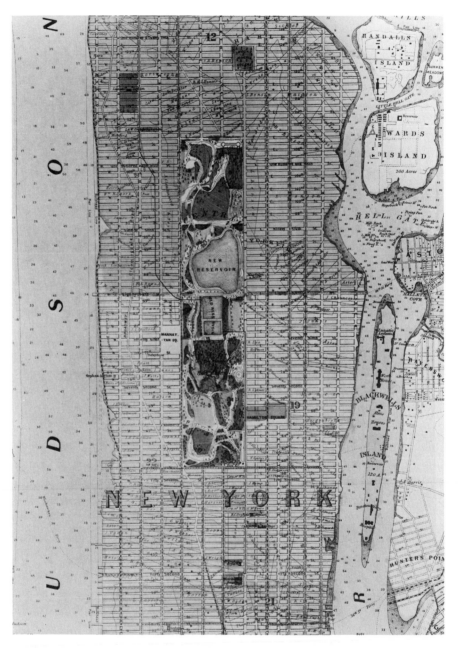

Figure 12. A New Era of Planning. This mid-Manhattan section of an 1864 map shows how the 1811 Plan was modified by the creation of Central Park; the map also gives some idea of the irregular property lines eliminated by the Plan (*Source*: Indiana State University Library – Special Collections).

perfect pleasure-garden of delight'.[53] In the general enthusiasm for their new creation, few New Yorkers noticed that its success was won, if only indirectly, at the expense of the remaining open spaces provided by the original Commissioners; between 1856 and 1870, Bloomingdale and Hamilton squares with Observatory Place were all ordered to be converted into city streets.[54]

As these changes indicated, the grid continued to dominate most of the Island, but the change in scale and taste that took place by mid-century left New Yorkers with little understanding and even less appreciation of the 1811 Plan. In the light of both the problems and opportunities of the metropolis, it became a thing of the distant past, to be ignored except as an object of criticism and as a convenient explanation for the problems of the new era. Since it could be readily associated with the well-publicized troubles of America's largest city, the Plan became a convenient target especially for those planners and developers who wanted to demonstrate that they had better ways to shape the urban future.

The first and probably the most influential of these critics was Frederick Law Olmsted who helped identify the Plan with the process which, in his eyes, had destroyed the natural beauties of Manhattan only to produce a badly flawed metropolis. For him, it had denied character and organization to New York by imposing on the city an inflexible and undifferentiated grid that had produced 'rows of monotonous straight streets and piles of erect buildings'. In the uniform 100-feet deep lots demanded by its narrow blocks, he saw building sites too small for the mansions of the rich and too large to provide inexpensive houses in a city where land was a major part of building costs. Such defects in the Plan helped make for the cramped housing which had become a major social and physical curse for New York.[55]

Later generations of critics elaborated on these themes. I.N. Phelps Stokes, the great local historian, quoted earlier praise of New York as 'an everlasting monument of the stability and wisdom' of the plan only in order to refute it: 'As a matter of fact, it destroyed the natural beauty of the island' and in other ways made for a city of little charm or variety.[56] Architectural historian, Vincent Scully, has charged that the Commissioners failed to provide adequate public space in their 'implacable gridiron', thereby evidencing in early form 'the later American tendency toward private luxury and public squalor'.[57] Others repeated the charge that the long, narrow lots associated with the grid were responsible for New York's crowded housing. Lewis Mumford, for instance, identified the Plan with 'more and more standardized boxes. Long monotonous streets that terminated nowhere, filled by rows of monotonous houses', most of which were ill-lit and poorly ventilated, a factor in the city's notoriously high rates of death and sickness.[58]

Especially in the twentieth century, critics also condemned the street system established by the Plan for complicating the crowded city's traffic and health problems. As early as 1894, a local historian, Thomas A. Janvier, said that in the interests of utility the Commissioners ('the cutting and slashing Commissioners') had planned 'in the simplest and dullest way', but even on practical grounds they had erred in not providing enough north-south avenues for traffic between a congested downtown and a growing uptown.[59] With the handicap of seemingly endless intersections created by the numerous cross-streets, the avenues became even more overloaded as a consequence of the later development of the midtown commercial district and the popular use of the automobile. This problem was noted in the 1920s by Henry James, who served as a historian for the Regional Plan of New York; James also reiterated earlier complaints that the failure of the Commissioners to consider topography in setting their grid had led to costly drainage problems that endangered the health of the city.[60]

If nothing else, these criticisms helped to develop the planning strategies and ideals that came to prevail in the half-century after 1870. This period brought the cumulating influences of Olmsted's landscape art, the development of planned suburbs, the City Beautiful movement, the revival of L'Enfant's plan for Washington D.C., and the professionalization of city planning. Criticism of the 1811 Plan helped to refine and promote the city parks, serpentine park roads, curvilinear streets, 'park-ways' and boulevards, diagonals, circles, civic centres, model housing complexes, superblocks, and other innovations that marked the advance of planning. In the light of the myriad problems which burdened the modern city, these criticisms were often valid and useful. In their failure to anticipate the character and problems of mid-century New York, the Commissioners invited Olmsted's judgement in 1877 that they viewed planning 'very nearly from the position which a small, poor, provincial village would now be expected to make'.[61] It was understandable that in 1911 New York made no effort to celebrate the centennial of its first comprehensive plan.[62]

Even the valid criticisms of the Commission's work, however, also serve to emphasize its success as an instrument for the growth and development of a city, a point conceded by Olmsted: 'Innumerable transfers and pledges of real estate have been made under it with a degree of ease and simplicity without parallel'.[63] The Plan was devised to meet the needs of the major commercial city of a new Republic interested in escaping from its European and colonial past. The planning ideals and practices of that past weighed little against the obligation to provide a simple and orderly means for the development of the land. Having made what they thought was adequate provision for public health and welfare, the Commissioners were content to establish a simple and regular basis for the organization and disposition of properties yet to be developed, leaving later developers and decision-makers to fill-in or, when necessary, to change the framework which they provided (figures 10 and 11).

Future developments within the limits of the Plan involved heavy costs in virtually every aspect of life. These, however, were the costs of later decisions often allowed but never mandated by the Commissioners. Nothing in their rectangular order required the notoriously narrow 15 to 25 feet wide lots associated with New York's congested character, and nothing invited the elimination of their provisions for open spaces. The most basic weakness was not in the Plan itself but in the failure to create some agency to guide its implementation and evolution in a future which could be barely anticipated. Without such an agency, it was inevitable that the Commissioners' work would be the object of haphazard, piecemeal alteration even though it had the character of law.

The Plan, however, was neither ineffectual nor insignificant. Rather, it effectively embodied the private expectations and public intentions of its times. If its provisions for open spaces were often eliminated, it did help establish and preserve the idea of open space. If the rigid geometry of its grid earned later scorn, it was also a significant advance away from the uncertainties and disarray produced by previous growth. If it left New Yorkers free to crowd their properties and to ravage the landscape, it above all provided them with a predictable future and a guaranteed order within which they could carry on their myriad acts of development. The collective result of this ordered freedom was a city whose aggressive character and energy was to make it one of the great metropolises of the world within half a century. 'So thrives the Paris of the American continent', said a New York weekly in 1845, 'year after year waxing greater in population, in wealth, in commerce, in civilization, in refinement, in folly, and in wickedness'.[64] It was an apt summation of the results of city growth under the Plan of 1811.

NOTES

1. Reps, John W. (1965) *The Making of Urban America*. Princeton: Princeton University Press, pp. 103–8, 157–74, and 185–202.

2. Ibid., pp. 157–74.

3. Kite, Elizabeth S. (1929) *L'Enfant and Washington, 1791–1792*. Baltimore: The Johns Hopkins Press, pp. 43–48. Tunnard, Christopher (1970) *The City of Man*. New York: Scribners, p. 91.

4. Kite, *op. cit.*, pp. 52–65.

5. Kite, *op. cit.*, pp. 144–67. Reps, *op. cit.*, pp. 253–56.

6. King, Nicholas in Glab, Charles N. (1963) *The American City: A Documentary History*. Homewood, Ill.: Dorsey, pp. 38–42. Reps, *op. cit.*, pp. 256–62.

7. See, for instance, the town plans reproduced in Reps. *op. cit.*, pp. 263–93.

8. Warner, Sam Bass, Jr (1968) *The Private City: Philadelphia in Three Periods of Its Growth*. Philadelphia: University of Pennsylvania Press, pp. 51–56.

9. Stokes, I.N. Phelps (1915–28) *The Iconography of Manhattan Island, 1498–1909*. New York: Robert H. Dodd, Volume V, p. 1449. Still, Bayrd (1956) *Mirror for Gotham*. New York: New York University Press, p. 67. Spann, Edward K. (1981) *The New Metropolis: New York City, 1840–57*. New York: Columbia University Press, pp. 284–87.

10. Rodgers, Cleveland (1943) *New York Plans for the Future*. New York: Harper, pp. 36–45. Hartog, Hendrick (1983) *Public Property and Private Power: The Corporation of the City of New York in American Law*. Chapel Hill: University of North Carolina Press, pp. 13–59, 158–59. Also Black, George A. (1891). *The History of Municipal Ownership of Land on Manhattan*. New York, pp. 10–79.

11. Stokes, *op. cit.*, Volume I, pp. 454–55; Volume III, p. 869; Volume V, pp. 1327 and 1329. Reps, *op cit.*, pp. 296–98. King, Charles (1852) *Progress of the City of New York*. New York, pp. 50 and 58.

12. Black, *op. cit.*, pp. 42, 79. Rodgers, *op. cit.*, p. 42. The population of New York City was 60,515 in 1800, 123,706 in 1820, 312,710 in 1840, and 515,547 in 1850.

13. Duffy, John A. (1968) *A History of Public Health in New York City, 1625–1886*. New York: Russell Sage Foundation, pp. 101–58. *New York Medical . . . Journal* (1809), pp. 244–45.

14. Hartog, *op. cit.*, pp. 142–57. Also see Teaford, John C. (1975) *The Municipal Revolution in America: Origins of Modern Urban Government, 1650–1825*. Chicago, pp. 102–10.

15. Stokes, *op. cit.*, Volume V, pp. 1417, 1420, 1442–43, 1454.

16. *Ibid.*, p. 1454. New York City, Common Council (1917) *Minutes*. New York, Volume IV, pp. 353–54.

17. Bobbé, Dorothie (1933) *DeWitt Clinton*. New York: Minton, Balch, pp. 110, 123,25.

18. New York State, Senate (1807) *Journal*. Albany, pp. 60, 97, 141; Assembly (1807) *Journal*. Albany, pp. 304–5, 307.

19. New York, Common Council (1917) *Minutes*, Volume IV, pp. 560–61. This was the established procedure governing the public improvement

programmes of the period, but none of the others matched the scope of the 1811 Plan.

20. Bobbé op. cit., pp. 150–65. Morris, Gouverneur (1888) Diary and Letters, edited by Anne C. Morris. New York, pp. 518–22, 532. In 1808, though, Morris did give some thought to improving the connections between the area around Morrisania and Manhattan in anticipation of New York's rapid expansion northward. Ibid., pp. 511–12. A brief sketch of Randel's life is in New York City, Common Council (1866) Manual. New York, pp. 764–65.

21. Stokes, op. cit., Volume V, p. 1457. Bridges, William (1811) Map of the City of New York and Island; with Explanatory Remarks. New York, pp. 7ff. The Act established a well-defined southern boundary for the plan area ('a line commencing at George Clinton's wharf on the Hudson River; thence through Fitzroy Road, Greenwich Lane, and Art Street; thence through North Street in its direction to the East River'), but no northern boundary.

22. For Olmsted's comment, see Sutton, S.B. (ed.) (1979) Civilizing American Cities: A Selection of Frederick Law Olmsted's Writings. Cambridge, Mass.: MIT Press, p. 45. Randel, John, Jr 'City of New York, North of Canal Street in 1808 to 1821', in New York, Common Council (1866) Manual, pp. 547–56.

23. 'Remarks of the Commissioners for Laying Out Streets and Roads in the City of New York Under the Act of April 3, 1807', in New York, Common Council (1866) Manual, pp. 756–65; also in Bridges op. cit., pp. 24–38. A somewhat misleading summary of the report and plan can be found in Reps, op. cit., pp. 297–99.

24. 'Remarks' in New York, Common Council, Manual, op. cit., p. 760; also Bridges op. cit., p. 31. The Plan was later altered to include two new avenues, Madison and Lexington.

25. Randel op. cit., p. 856. Neither Randel nor the Commissioners provided an explanation for the unusual number of cross streets. One student of early New York planning says that it resulted from the assumption that traffic on the Island 'would continue to gravitate to the water front'. Bannister, Turpin C. (1943) Early town planning in New York State, New York History, XXIV, p. 194. Perhaps this is so, but it should be noted that the long rectangular blocks formed by these streets had already been established in earlier maps of the common lands, which were often located away from the river fronts. See Reps, op. cit., 296.

26. 'Remarks', in New York, Common Council, Manual, op. cit., p. 756; also Bridges, op. cit., p. 24. Hendrick Hartog, in his able analysis of the Plan (Public Property and Private Power, pp. 158–74), argues that the decision in favour of the simple grid was influenced by two primary aims: (1) to encourage the construction of cheap, convenient houses; (2) to establish in their plan a 'public neutrality' regarding future development (circles and other distinctive points, for instance, would have made the lands surrounding them more attractive for devlopment than lands not so favoured). In a general sense, this is correct, but it should be noted that the Commissioners also made provision for several public open spaces which both reduced the land available for housing and favoured (as did their

provision for the ten wider streets) some lands over others.

27. The Commissioners themselves contributed to the Union Square situation by angling Broadway from 10th Street so as to run it as a diagonal northward to its intended terminus at the centre of the southern boundary of the Parade; otherwise, Broadway would have merged with the Bowery at 12th Street. This apparently minor decision had great future significance, since it inadvertently allows Broadway's later development as the city's only major diagonal thoroughfare.

29. New York, Common Council, *op. cit.*, *Minutes*, Volume IV, p. 388.

30. 'Remarks', in New York, Common Council, *Manual*, *op. cit.*, p. 757.

31. Ibid., pp. 758–59. For a phase in the later history of the public markets, see Spann, *New Metropolis*, *op. cit.*, pp. 124–28.

32. 'Remarks', in New York, Common Council, *Manual*, *op. cit.*, p. 758.

33. James, Henry (1929) A review of earlier planning efforts in New York and its environs, in Lewis, Harold M. (ed.) *Physical Conditions and Public Services*. New York: Russell Sage Foundation, pp. 151–61, 178.

34. *Ibid.*, p. 159. Morris, *Diary and Letters*, p. 491, 532.

35. Stokes, *op cit.*, Volume V. p. 1457. Hartog, *op. cit.*, p. 169.

36. 'Remarks', in New York, Common Council, *Manual.*, *op. cit.*, p. 757. James, *op. cit.*, p. 159–62. With perhaps more drama than truth, one critic says that 'the Grid's two-dimensional discipline also creates undreamt-of freedom for three-dimensional anarchy'. Koolhaas, Rem (1978) *Delirious New York*. New York: Oxford University Press, p. 15.

37. Hartog, *op. cit.*, pp. 162–75. Randel, *op. cit.*, p. 848. James, *op. cit.*, p. 162.

38. Poe, Edgar Allen *Doings of Gotham*, Spannuth, J. E. and Mabbott, T. O. (eds.) (1929) Pottsville, Pa.: J. E. Spannuth, pp. 25–26.

39. 'Remarks', in New York, Common Council, *Manual*, *op. cit.*, p. 757. Rodgers, *op. cit.*, p. 43. Hartog, *op. cit.*, pp. 162, 169.

40. Rosewater, Victor (1896) *Special Assessments*. New York, pp. 26–33. Hartog, *op. cit.*, pp. 167–69. Stokes, *op. cit.*, Volume III, pp. 481–82. *Knickerbocker Magazine*, No. 33 (1849), p. 185. This levelling process, however, was well underway before the Plan and would have continued even without it. Cozzens, Issacher Jr (1943) *Geological History of Manhattan*. New York, especially pp. 22–23, 27.

41. *Reports and Documents Relative to the Stuyvesant Meadows* (1832). New York, pp. 9–10.

42. *Ibid.*, pp. 9, 12–17.

43. *Ibid.*, p. 30. Stokes, *op. cit.*, Volume V, pp. 1629, 1663.

44. Randel, *op. cit.*, p. 848.

45. New York *Tribune*, April 18, 1846.

46. Benedict, Erastus C. (1851) *New York and the City Travel*. New York, pp. 3, 5, 14. Wood, Fernando (1856) *Communication . . . February 4, 1856*. New York, pp. 25–40.

47. Stokes, *op. cit.*, Volume V, pp. 1540, 1569, 1581, 1684, 1741, 1746. In 1812, the Common Council initiated the move to reduce the Parade three months before it voted a resolution thanking the Commissioners for their work. *Ibid.*, p. 1555.

48. New York, Common Council (1857) *Manual*, p. 480.

49. New York State Assembly (1832) *Documents*, No. 115, p. 1; No. 239, pp. 1–2. Stokes, *op. cit.*, Volume V, pp. 1701, 1705, 1711, 1740, 1741, 1746.

50. Ruggles, Samuel B. (1878) *Memorial . . . on the Social and Fiscal Importance of Open Squares*. New York, pp. 8–11. In the 1830s, Ruggles demonstrated one of the possibilities of the grid by turning a block between 19th and 20th Streets into a park-like residential square, Gramercy Park. Pine, John B. (1921) *The Story of Gramercy Park*. New York: Gramercy Park Associates, pp. 5–11.

51. Rosewater, *op. cit.*, pp. 19–31. *New York Evening Post*, Jan. 15, 1846.

52. Olmsted, Frederick Law, Jr and Kimball, Theodore (1929) *Frederick Law Olmsted, Landscape Architect, 1822–1903*. New York: Putnam, Volume II, pp. 46, 173. Among many studies of Central Park, see Spann, *op. cit.*, pp. 157–73. For a critical view of Olmsted's design and a defence of the 1811 Plan as 'the most orderly plan of its size in the world', see Peets, Elbert (1968) *On the Art of Designing Cities*, edited by Paul D. Spreiregen. Cambridge, Mass,: MIT Press, pp. 184–85.

53. Kendall, Isaac C. (1865) *The Growth of New York*. New York, pp. 34–39.

54. Stokes, *op. cit.*, Volume III, pp. 970–971.

55. Olmsted and Kimball, *op. cit.*, Volume, I, p. 46. Olmsted, Frederick Law and Croes, James R. (1877) Preliminary report, in Sutton, S. B. (ed.) *Civilizing American Cities: A Selection of Frederick Law Olmsted's Writings*. Cambridge, Mass.: MIT Press, pp. 43–49.

56. Stokes, *op. cit.*, Volume I, p. 407; Volume V, p. 1532.

57. Scully, Vincent (1969) *American Architecture and Urbanism*. New York: Praeger, p. 78.

58. Mumford, Lewis (1924) *Sticks and Stones*. New York: Boni and Liveright, p. 68. Also see Ford, James *et al.* (1936) *Slums and Housing*. Cambridge, Mass.: Harvard University Press, Volume I, p. 259.

59. Janvier, Thomas A. (1894) *In Old New York*. New York, pp. 62, 207–217.

60. James, *op. cit.*, pp. 158–60.

61. Olmsted and Croes, *op. cit.*, p. 44.

62. In 1911, the only apparent attention to the Plan came from an architect who, in the interests of rounding off the street-corners of buildings, condemned it for doing what the Commissioners had intended it to do: A whole city of straight-sided and right-angled houses must necessarily be a depressing spectacle'. Winkler, Franz K. (1911) Mitigating the 'gridiron' street plan. *The Architectural Record*, p. 380.

63. Olmsted and Croes, *op. cit.*, p. 43.

64. *Working Man's Advocate*, March 4, 1845.

Chapter Two

The Early Nineteenth-Century Suburb: Creating a Suburban Ethos in Somerville and Cambridge, Massachusetts, 1820–1860

HENRY C. BINFORD[1]

The American residential suburb, which first appeared between 1820 and 1860, was a new kind of community that encouraged new thinking about the arrangement and functioning of the city. So important was this new form of settlement that it permanently changed the meaning of the word 'suburbs'. For centuries the term denoted an undifferen-tiated zone outside the city limits, containing various city-related (and often undesirable) facilities: dumps, noxious manufactures, the homes of the poor. By the 1850s suburbs meant a collection of separate communities housing many city-employed (and often affluent) workers, linked to the city through commuting, but frequently independent in government.

The evolution of these communities was in part a response to new technological capabilities, not only in transportation but in food distribution, water supply, sewerage, and home construction. But it was also a response to long-term changes in the structure of the city economy, as commerce and manufacturing took over huge sections of the central city. Finally the creation of independent suburban municipalities was a reflection of the powerful emphasis on local autonomy that prevaded much of nineteenth-century U.S. political history.

Thus the suburbs were not merely locations where prosperous people could build state-of-the-art homes, commuting to the city whose dirt and immigrants they had left behind. They were also cooperative ventures in community-building according to a new view of domestic life, efforts that drew in non-commuters as well as those who rode to work. This essay draws on the experience of two nineteenth-century Boston suburbs, Cambridge and Somerville, Massachusetts, to illustrate a process that occurred, with variations, outside all the largest American cities before the Civil War.[2]

Looking back from a twentieth-century vantage, it is easy to think of all suburbs as communities created by city-based developers for out-migrants from the city. In a common conception of suburban history, technological innovation (railroad, streetcar, automobile, superhighway) encouraged land speculators and builders, who attracted city workers to ever more distant locales, where promoters and commuters joined to lay out and incorporate residentially-oriented suburban municipalities. From Olmsted's Riverside to the postwar Levittowns, the making of suburbs seems to have been a repetition of this process.

But early nineteenth century suburb-building frequently did not involve such a clearcut sequence of events or so clearly defined a goal. As Sam Warner has shown, post-Civil War streetcar suburbs were not generally laid out by developers. Rather, thousands of small builders created communities ordered by the routeing of streetcar lines, the gradients of land values, and the informal regulation of shared desires and tastes.[3]

If we press back further in the century, we find even fewer grand designs and even more 'planning' through collective activity – a planning drawn not through the conscious design of experts but rather through a vaguely stated core of shared values. Those who created the first suburbs were small entrepreneurs, hustlers, local politicians, and a few venturesome city workers, who shared loosely parallel aims in promoting residential property. Over the course of four decades, in a trial-and-error process, they created not only the first residential suburbs but also the vision of a residential community that would guide suburban growth in future generations.

Thus the history of the first American suburbs is in large part a history of evolving community self-consciousness. Suburban leaders came to think of their communities as distinctive places, different from country towns or city districts, and to form policy accordingly. Early debates about what a suburb should be, debates that took place primarily among suburbanites, played a key role in making the suburbs what they became: primarily residential, stubbornly independent.

Antebellum suburbs were different in important ways from the rail-based varieties that came later. It is appropriate to begin by spelling out what these communities were and were not, before discussing how their leaders developed policy.

First, how did antebellum suburbs differ from those of the late nineteenth and twentieth centuries? Perhaps the biggest difference lay in the assumptions their inhabitants made about transportation. For late-nineteenth-century suburbanites, rail transportation was a given. Although the rail system grew and electricity made it faster in the 1880s, the daily movement of thousands into and out of the city by rail did not emerge as a new phenomenon after the Civil War. Residents of earlier suburbs had to learn about and experiment with rail transportation, and indeed with public transportation in general, first in coping with railroads and omnibuses in the late 1830s and early 1840s, then in promoting streetcars, which appeared in the mid-1850s.[4]

Inhabitants of late-nineteenth-century suburbs were also accustomed to living in a metropolis that was politically and governmentally complex. After the Civil War, residents of all the biggest American cities took it for granted that the metropolitan area included a central city and a number of peripheral communities, each with its own charter, its own leaders and agenda. Relations between particular communities might vary, boundaries might change, but it was a fundamental fact that the metropolis would be a mosaic of governmental units, and that municipal autonomy and annexation were always at least potential issues for discussion. Residents of many suburbs, on the other hand, were in the process of defining the place of their communities in a metropolitan setting – learning how to be suburbs. Between the 1820s and the Civil War, their leaders came to attach new meaning to boundaries, to place a new importance on a competitive or defensive posture *vis à vis* other municipalities, and to cope with the issues and the rhetoric of annexation.[5]

Many of the features and problems of later suburbs thus had surfaced earlier but only appeared in their full dimension at the end of the period here considered. And yet if antebellum communities were not just antecedents of the streetcar suburb, then what were they? To begin with, they shared many traits with other small communities of the early nineteenth century. They were, for example, growing very rapidly. The two communities here studied – Cambridge and Somerville – doubled their population between 1820 and 1840, and then tripled it between 1840 and 1860 (see table 1). Rapid growth was characteristic of the whole semicircle of communities adjacent to Boston. By 1860 these suburbs contained a population equivalent to two-thirds of that of the city itself.[6]

Suburban growth in this period was marked by a proliferation of distinct villages, often separated by empty land, rather than the

Table 1. Village population growth, 1820–1860
(Non-institutional population)[1]

	Mainland Charlestown (Somerville)	Old Cambridge	Cambridge-port	East Cambridge	Total
1820 Total	– [2]	1,296	1,360	384	3,040+
Increase, 1820–30		414	728	1,533	
% gain		32%	54%	399%	
1830 Total	1,154	1,710	2,088	1,917	6,869
Increase, 1830–40	319	270	1,395	620	
% gain	28	14	67	34	
1840 Total	1,473	1,980	3,483	2,537	9,473
Increase, 1840–50	2,067	1,920	3,817	1,463	
% gain	140	97	110	58	
1850 Total	3,540	3,900[3]	7,300[3]	4,000[3]	18,740
Increase, 1850–60	4,485	2,487	5,272	3,101	
% gain	127	64	72	78	
1860 Total	8,025	6,387	12,572	7,101	34,085

1. *Source*: recompilation of MS Census data. Omits McLean Asylum, Cambridge Jail, Cambridge Almshouse, Harvard College.
2. 1820 Charlestown data are recorded in a peculiar way. Discrimination of Mainland and Peninsula proved impossible.
3. Estimates based on sample data.

outward sprawl from a city centre that would characterize later periods. Figure 1 shows the main villages emerging in the two municipalities here studied. Of those identified, only the Old Cambridge Centre and the Charlestown seaport were there at the beginning of the nineteenth century. All the others were new. This pattern of growth, through the addition of new centres, resembled that of Michael Frisch's Springfield, Massachusetts or Stuart Blumin's Kingston, New York more than it did the pattern of the late-nineteenth-century suburbs. Because of this differentiation of villages, and because of the strains of growth in general, the suburbs faced problems of internal cohesion and self-definition not unlike those Blumin has associated with crossing 'the urban threshold'.[7]

Yet early-nineteenth-century suburbs had some peculiar problems of their own. Unlike any other version of urban growth in this period, suburban development involved an immediate, intimate, and

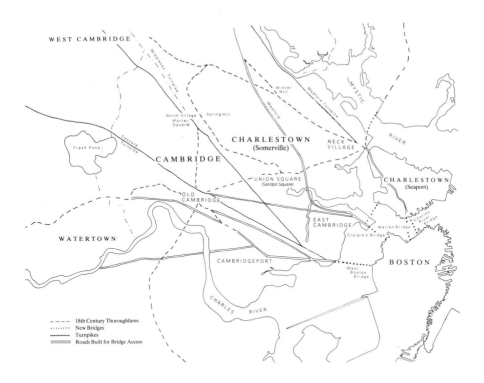

Figure 1.

multifaceted relationship with a much larger neighbour. As individuals, and on behalf of their communities, suburbanites had to deal with a far more diverse mixture of opportunities, intrusions, and threats than did the residents of any free-standing urban centre. Antebellum suburbs were, finally, charged with a heavy burden of expectation in the minds of some reformers. They were the kinds of communities Andrew Jackson Downing had in mind when he advocated cottage residence, the ones favoured by devotees of Catherine Beecher in promoting a new vision of domesticity, and the ones frequently mentioned in city guidebooks, which took their readers on tours of the 'picturesque environs' of all the major cities.[8] In Cambridge and Somerville the vision of suburbs as places specially suited to new domestic and moral reforms was evident in newspaper editorials and in residents' discussion of political issues from the 1840s onward.[9]

These distinctive suburbs also had a distinctive political history. In the two communities here studied, a process of interplay between economic and social development on the one hand and the evolution of local government on the other brought suburban leaders to a sharp recognition of their communities' role in the metropolis, and to a determination to defend it. The process of suburban identity-formation had two stages – one from the 1820s until the early 1840s, the other from the late 1840s to the Civil War.

The first stage involved a revolution in the physical mobility of suburbanities and dramatic changes in suburban forms of government. In the 1820s and 1830s residential development became an important goal for influential suburban residents – as part of a general promotion of the peripheral economy, in which agricultural marketing, industry, and lot sales were all seen as complementary parts of a healthy suburb.

The second stage, which began in the late 1840s and accelerated in the ensuing prosperity, saw a sifting and refinement of suburban objectives. The railroad, the streetcar, heavy industry, and mass commuting forced suburbanites to deal with conflicting land uses and incompatible lines of growth. In a series of political confrontations in the late 1840s and early 1850s, the promoters of commuter residential growth made that form of enterprise dominant in the suburban economy, and began to corral and purge some industrial and commercial pursuits. They also rejected annexation to Boston, and thus bequeathed to post-Civil War suburban residents a completed model for suburban growth: residentially-oriented, commuter-dominated, and politically independent.

THE MOBILITY REVOLUTION AND THE RESIDENTIAL VISION

Among fundamental changes in nineteenth-century urban life, the shift from walking to public transportation was at least as important as the spread of work in factories. Indeed, the two kinds of change were in many ways similar. Like industrialization, the revolution in mobility did not begin with complex technology, did not occur all at once, and affected some places and some people far more quickly than others. Like industrialization, it accelerated and changed character in the late 1840s and 1850s, when urban mobility came to involve corporate organization, sophisticated equipment, and large numbers. Although relatively few people worked in factories before 1860, and relatively few rode omnibuses, trains, or horsecars, the organized activity of these few gradually changed the habits and expectations of the whole society.

Between the 1820s and the 1840s, the revolution in mobility changed the pattern of community building in the suburbs from one based on small, road-centred villages and irregular contact with the city, to one based on continuous, predominantly residential settlement and routine daily movement through the metropolis. The overall change took in every mode of travel from walking to commuter trains. It involved new possibilities as much as new devices: a lowering of barriers and costs to moving about; an increase in the variety and reliability of carriers; a new set of expectations about possible journeys; and ultimately a new vision of how the metropolis would grow, how its parts would fit together.

The walking city of the early nineteenth century was actually several cities – with different boundaries for different purposes. Long before mass transportation appeared, many individuals were accustomed to occasional long trips, and a few were involved in routine travel. The shift from walking to riding was revolutionary because it *combined* distance and regularity. The exceptional trip became ordinary; the realm of ordinary trips expanded. The initial pressure for expanding these various limits of walking mobility arose from the suburbs, and arose naturally from their economic and social interests.

Even before the introduction of any significant new technology, many people in the Boston metropolitan area expanded the walking city considerably for special purposes and on special occasions. Truck farmers and suburban artisans made regular if infrequent trips to the city to sell their goods. A few energetic members of the mercantile elite, who had flexible schedules and private carriages, made daily trips from suburban estates to the city exchanges.

The first steps toward a change in the role of suburban communities came from suburban entrepreneurs who sought to cater for the needs of these occasional walkers and uncommon riders. Beginning in 1823 peripheral residents launched campaigns to shake off the burden of tolls on bridges to the city. One such effort, the Warren Free Bridge Corporation in 1828, won fame in U.S. history when it built a toll-free span next to the old bridge between Charlestown and Boston. The lawsuit brought by proprietors of the old bridge led to Supreme Court Chief Justice Taney's decision in favour of the new bridge. Yet in its origins the Charles River Bridge Case was but one of several suburban efforts to gain 'free avenues to the city', affecting several bridges and also some turnpikes.[10]

Freeing the bridges was a long-term project, but the efforts to do so changed the climate for other kinds of enterprise. By the early 1830s it seemed likely that all routes to the city would one day be free, and other suburbanites had already begun to reduce the time and energy required for city-suburban mobility through the introduction of scheduled public vehicles. In the mid-1820s citizens of Roxbury, Cambridge, and Charlestown took the radical step of instituting coaches to Boston every hour. The young and obscure proprietors of these lines quickly found a pool of demand, bought more vehicles, hired extra drivers and attracted rivals. The 1830s saw the introduction of omnibuses, the first vehicles designed specifically for local service. The first true omnibus in the United States was built from French plans and began service in New York in 1831. The first omnibus in New England appeared on the Cambridge-Boston run, making its maiden trip on Harvard's Commencement Day in 1834.[11]

From the mid-1830s until the coming of the streetcar in 1856, through good times and bad, coach and omnibus proprietors continuously expanded their operations. Competition also reduced the cost of the ride. During the late 1830s and early 1840s all the omnibus proprietors offered fare reductions through the sale of tickets in package lots. In this 'commutation' of fares they borrowed a device from the turnpikes and steamboats. Within a few years more, railroads and streetcar companies carried the procedure to higher levels of refinement, and introduced the word 'commuter' to the language.

The coach-omnibus network was a booming business, but it was inefficient, a patchwork of 'lines' rather than a transportation system. Some of its flaws were obvious from the start, some became more serious with the growth of demand. Its management was unstable; it was expensive; it served only the most populous villages in the suburbs; and it encountered the same impediments as walking or private carriages: tolls, bad roads, inclement weather, and traffic.

Given all these limitations, the omnibus could not replace walking or driving. In a sense it was an improved version of the private vehicle, a better mode of conveyance for well-to-do people on flexible schedules. Yet it did provide a regular means of mass access to Boston, and it demonstrated a substantial demand for the service.

Suburban residents persuaded even the wealthy Bostonians who built the first railroads that suburban demand counted. Although several early railroads traversed the suburbs between 1835 and 1845, the promoters had no initial interest in local travellers. When their companies languished in the depression of 1837–43, however, and when they were confronted with constant and vociferous demands from the suburbs for suburban service, the railroad men experienced a wholesale change in their thinking, rebuilding their facilities to encourage commuters, introducing specially designed and scheduled suburban trains, and plunging heavily into advertising and selling suburban house lots.[12]

Though they were expensive, the omnibus and the railroad stretched the realm of occasional riders and spread the riding habit to shoppers and businessmen who would not previously have ventured as far. This first round of changes in mobility set the stage for a sequence of policy responses. In the 1830s and early 1840s the suburbs experienced massive changes in political geography. The central events were struggles over modifying the town form of government to meet suburban needs. But what seemed to be straightforward arguments over corporate forms also reflected much deeper currents of thinking about the suburban role.

In the beginning of the nineteenth century every community in Massachusetts was incorporated as a town, ruled by a town meeting in which all eligible votes disposed of policy issues and chose a board of selectmen and other officers to execute policy. Boston itself was a town until 1822, when it received a charter from the state legislature authorizing a shift to representative government. The area north-west of Boston was mostly included in two large towns: Cambridge, centred in the very old village near Harvard College, and Charlestown, which contained a seaport village on a peninsula at the eastern end, and a large amount of less settled land to the west. The proliferation of new villages in the early nineteenth century created a variety of strains and conflicts within these towns. Beginning in the 1820s, there were efforts to separate the western part of Charlestown from the peninsula. In 1842, these efforts culminated in the creation of a new town called Somerville. In Cambridge the 1820s and 1830s saw the growth of two new villages in the eastern areas. Here too there were efforts to separate the western part of the town, but these efforts failed in the early 1840s. In the aftermath of that failure a coalition of leaders from all three Cambridge villages petitioned the state legislature for a city charter, in the belief that ward-based city government would better serve all interests within the town. The new charter made Cambridge the fourth city in Massachusetts, after Boston, Lowell, and Salem.[13]

These changes in government represented more than a simple adjustment of boundaries to accommodate population shifts. The incorporation of Somerville and the creation of Cambridge as a city reflected an alliance between two kinds of entrepreneurs, and a reshaping of government instruments for the promotion of a new vision of the future for peripheral communities.

Both of the main kinds of enterprise were based on efforts to exploit the suburbs' unique position on the city's edge. In one category were those pursuits characteristic of an urban fringe economy: light manufacturing for the city and brokerage or processing of farm goods. New villages in Cambridge and western Charlestown became centres for brickmaking, soapmaking, the production of rope and other maritime goods, cattle marketing, slaughtering, and the trans-shipment of farm products. The centres of such activity attracted artisans in related fields – coopers, smiths, wheelwrights – as well as teamsters and stable operators. The people who entered these pursuits were frequently young migrants from rural New England or

Figure 2. Fringe Industry. The Middlesex Bleachery in Somerville. (*Source*: Somerville Historical Society)

Figure 3. Porter's Hotel, Cambridge Market. A successful urban fringe enterprise of the 1830s. (*Source*: The Boston Athenaeum)

sons of old farm families in the vicinity. The most successful of these fringe entrepreneurs came to exert considerable influence in town meetings.

The other kind of enterprise involved speculative dealing in and development of land for residential purposes. This kind of activity went back to the beginning of the nineteenth century, and expanded along with the urban fringe. In the 1820s there was a surge in lot sales as Cambridgeport attracted artisans and small factories. In the 1830s residential lots in both Cambridgeport and mainland Charlestown became popular with a small number of well-heeled men who worked in Boston. These early Boston-employed suburbanites were not what we think of as commuters. Some had lived in the suburbs and took up a daily journey to and from the city in connection with fringe-related work – selling the products of suburban factories or acting as agents of suburban brokerage firms. A few were young specialized merchants with flexible schedules who found suburban lots preferable to Boston's high-priced crowding and who did not mind long walks or expensive carriage or omnibus rides to the city.[14]

Beginning in the 1830s, first in Cambridgeport and then in the other suburban villages, entrepreneurs representing both of these two kinds of development articulated and implemented a new vision of the suburban role. In Cambridge the pioneers included a soap manufacturer, a surveyor, a local lawyer, and a minister turned railroad investor. In Somerville the leaders were brickmakers and grain dealers. These promoters sought institutions and services that were appropriate to much larger places – a fire department, paved streets and sidewalks, graded schools. It was desirable to make such improvements in advance of need, they argued, to make a suburb

> more eligible as a place of residence. This will not only add to the value of property in and about our villages, but will tend to the healthy increase of population among us, by giving us constant accessions of citizens from a class of people who will not only add to our respectability, but give us accessions of wealth, and thus diminish our public burdens.[15]

But their vision was not that of a dormitory annex to Boston. When they spoke of attracting desirable residents they clearly meant not only residents who would work in Boston but residents who would find work in the rapidly growing local economies of the suburbs. Their reports and petitions refer constantly to the peculiar mixture of external linkages and local self-sufficiency that characterized suburban growth. The justification for sidewalks, in the Cambridge of 1838, was that the town was 'constantly thronged, not only with strangers passing through its principal streets from the country to the city . . . but with a busy population of its own of nearly 8,000 persons'. Promoters on mainland Charlestown were proud that 'the enterprise and energy of our own people is exciting the industrial population of the neighbouring towns and cities', who would soon come to live and work in the new suburb.[16]

It was this conception of the suburb as an independent residential community attractive to both a locally employed and a Boston employed population that inspired the reincorporation of local government in the 1840s. An analysis of petitions in the Massachusetts state archives indicates that the two kinds of suburban entrepreneurs worked together to create the town of Somerville and to secure a city charter for Cambridge. Early petitions to split off mainland Charlestown, backed by farmers in the 1820s, and full of agrarian, anti-city rhetoric, failed because they were opposed by tavernkeepers and artisans who valued their connection to the seaport peninsula. In the late 1830s young members of the same artisan families became convinced that their land would be more valuable and their taxes lower if they created a separate town. They joined with land speculators and a few early commuters in the successful effort of 1842. In Cambridge a similar alliance failed to split off the western sector, but when residential promoters from Cambridgeport and East Cambridge mounted a city incorporation drive, tradesmen and speculators in the west abandoned separatism to join the new movement.

Commuting and Residential Dominance

Although the new town of Somerville and the new city of Cambridge were promoted by men who had a vision of growth and who sought urban services, neither of the new communities was meant to be a big city, and neither of the new governments was truly a big city government. The founders of Somerville tried hard to behave as town leaders had in the past, giving oral reports to infrequent town meetings, avoiding debts, and running the town largely through consultation among leading landowners. Cambridge residents spoke of their charter as a way to preserve the best features of town government: cheapness, accountability, and centralization of decisions in a body of respected citizens (now the aldermen instead of the selectmen). In promoting these small-town suburbs of the 1830s and 1840s, the founders made assumptions that would be violated in the 1850s, and this violation of assumptions would lead to another round of suburban identity formation, which involved a narrowing of goals.[17]

The reformers of the 1830s assumed, first, that the interests of the artisan-industrial fringe and the interests of residential promotion could coexist, both feeding the growth of prosperous suburbs. They further assumed that if there were conflicts between areas or interests, gentlemen like themselves could reach agreement in the caucuses and small-scale meetings of the town and city, and that politics would be sustained by voluntarism – by the stewardly efforts of 'the best men'.

In the late 1840s and early 1850s all of these assumptions were undermined. Suburban growth followed new and unforeseen paths, which destroyed the harmony of fringe and residential interests. On the one hand the railroads encouraged heavier industry – big factories, foundries, meat-packing plants. These establishments attracted large numbers of immigrant workers, who had been a negligible part of the suburban population in 1840. By 1850 the population of the two suburbs was 25 per cent foreign born, and by 1860 that proportion rose to two–fifths. In some areas large tracts of land were covered with the shanties and cottages of the Irish. On the other hand, railroads and omnibuses opened the way for commuters – true commuters who depended on public transportation and had no roots in the suburbs. Linkage of names from a series of Boston and suburban directories with the census demonstrates that, between 1845 and 1860, the number of Boston-employed in the two suburbs rose from about 100 to at least 1500, and that the practice of commuting spread to new occupational groups, especially lawyers and bank employees. In this period before the streetcar, and before the end of bridge tolls in 1858, the new commuters were still well-heeled. But they did not possess quite the same flexibility of schedule as the pioneers of the 1830s. In the suburbs of the 1850s, commuters were less likely to be loyal stewards of the community, more likely to be demanding consumers of services and transportation.[18]

Not only did these changes increase the scale of activity in the suburbs and strengthen city-suburban links, they also brought the two parts of the suburban economy into sharp juxtaposition and conflict. New residential developments in Cambridgeport and northern Cambridge were very close to the factory-and-immigrant districts. Residential promoters and commuter residents of the late 1840s and early 1850s increasingly saw the industrial areas and their unwashed inhabitants as a threat. They sponsored churchs and schools as explicit weapons against the 'ungodliness and moral destitution' of such districts.[19]

Meanwhile, as economic and demographic change eroded some parts of the vision of the 1830s, political changes eroded others. The temperance movement, especially the crusades to enforce prohibition under the so-called Maine Law of 1852, gained strong support in the

Figure 4. Streetcars in the centre of Old Cambridge in the late 1850s. (*Source*: Harvard University Archives)

Figure 5. Middle-class housing development in Somerville in the 1850s. (*Source*: Somerville Historical Society)

elite residential clusters, and alienated those who worked in fringe industries. Temperance crusades not only widened the gap between residential and fringe interests, but also destroyed the idea that gentlemen in small groups would agree. In 1852 prohibition advocates began a campaign of systematically informing on illegal drinking spots, in which teetotallers would enter a targeted establishment, buy a drink, and then file a complaint in court. But there were temperance men who renounced this informer crusade, preferring to rely on moral suasion, and who were in turn denounced for their timidity.[20]

Matters got worse between 1852 and 1854, when the collapse of the Whig party statewide had local repercussions. Suburban politics depended on the idea that parties did not matter, which in turn depended on the reality that most suburban leaders were of one party. Now in the mid-1850s the Whig local caucuses distintegrated. Every local election saw the appearance of candidates narrowly identified with one or another factional interest – temperance, nativism, anti-slavery, as well as Democrats and a few die-hard Whigs.[21]

At its peak the political turmoil of the 1850s seemed to threaten the very integrity of the suburbs. Between 1852 and 1854 Boston and the suburbs debated annexing Roxbury, Cambridge, and Charlestown. The rhetoric of these debates involved all the issues common in annexation struggles: the city's desire for an expanded tax base and an attractive boost in its population; the suburbs' division between those who wanted to share Boston's resources and those who preferred local autonomy. In this argument, however, there was also a hidden agenda. Die-hard Whigs in Boston and Charlestown sought to join forces through annexation, creating a voting base they hoped would bolster their strength in the state legislature. Their scheme failed narrowly because of a massive opposition campaign organized by Democrats and Free Soilers all over the state.[22]

From our vantage it would be easy to see these developments of the 1850s as an array of external challenges to the suburbs. After all, big factories, immigrants, demanding commuters, the temperance crusade, and the political crisis of the 1850s were all phenomena that came, to some extent, from 'outside' the suburbs. Thus it might seem that the story of suburban government and politics in this period was primarily one of the spillover effects from Boston's growth, or one in which the former suburban villages became units in a metropolitan economy or society.

Suburbanites certainly recognized and talked about the regional and national transformations that affected them. They expressed anxiety about intrusions from Boston, and as individuals they participated enthusiastically in debates about larger political issues.

Yet suburbanites of this era were also engaged in a separate redefinition of local politics and government, and the most important issues, events, and changes at that level were different from those which occupied the state and national stages. In suburban politics of the 1850s we may see not only increasing sensitivity to relationships between the suburbs, Boston, and the larger world, but also a desire to strengthen local institutions in the face of local problems, and an argument between suburbanites about priorities internal to the suburbs.

The strains of increased commuting, for example, never led to a conflict that pitted commuters against 'locals'. Rather, the key issue for suburbanites was the growing tension between the two major parts of the suburban economy – the industrial-commercial sector and the residential sector. In the 1850s this tension resolved itself into a struggle over the allocation of local resources. Those oriented to residence and domesticity – including not only commuters, but land speculators, investors in omnibuses and streetcars, and most of the local clergy – turned against their former allies in the suburban promotions of the 1830s, allies who included not only factory owners and employees but artisans, innkeepers, stablemen, teamsters, and other representatives of the old fringe.

A symptom of this shift was the conversion of John Ford, the editor of the Cambridge newspaper. Since the 1840s he had been a generalized booster with a special interest in the manufacturing and commerical centre of Cambridgeport. But in the mid-1850s he swung his support to residence, acknowledging that 'Cambridge will not be likely to have very great facilities for business'. Beginning in the early 1850s and continuing into the 1860s, those with residential interests steadily and openly gained the upper hand in local politics. They secured ordinances confining if not banning noxious trades, they pressed for municipal support for streetcars and residential water supplies, while at the same time denying aid to manufacturers who sought dock and canal improvements and water for their factories.[23]

In a similar fashion, the spillover of temperance and partisan politics into the suburban arena did not, in the long run, make suburban politics like the politics of the city or the state. In the crises of the early 1850s, suburban leaders expressed at least as much concern about the fragmenting of local leadership – the loss of trust in and agreement among the town stewards – as they did about drinking or party preferences. The key question for suburbanites concerned the simple, cheap, voluntaristic local governments they had set up in the 1840s. How could they preserve their virtues while coping with the demands of a population growing more rapidly than anyone expected? This question dominated the 1850s, long after the larger political crises ended with the rise of the Republican party to dominance in Massachusetts in 1857.

The long-term answer required that suburbanites give up voluntarism and strengthen local government as a provider of services. In 1856–57, for example, the Somerville selectmen found themselves repeatedly stymied by petty conflicts in town meetings. They placed the blame squarely on a breakdown in voluntarism, scolding residents who, 'migrating from cities, accustomed to a different administration of affairs . . . forget that on them personally rests the responsibility and the consequences of the acceptance or defeat of the various measures proposed for their consideration'. Yet such exhortations did not work. Instead, the selectmen worked harder, and delegated more of their responsibilities to salaried employees. By the late 1850s, Somerville had the rudiments of a service bureaucracy, employing dozens of paid workers to maintain roads, schools, and sidewalks, to fight fires, keep a lid on crime, and keep records of their activities.[24]

Cambridge residents reacted against political confusion by electing a new kind of mayor. John Sargent, an attorney and former commuter, explicitly rejected both partisan politics at the local level and the old pattern of stewardship. He united representatives of Republican, Democratic, and Nativist parties to redraw the ward boundaries and to set up a Municipal Nominating Convention. He also greatly enlarged the city apparatus for providing residential services. On both fronts he aimed to improve the representation of areas and groups, and to ensure that the 'best men' continued to play a prominent if more formal role in meetings to nominate slates of local officers.[25]

The result by the 1860s was a dramatic expansion of services and a strengthening of local leadership in both Cambridge and Somerville. In 1845 the two towns had five volunteer fire companies, eighteen small and mostly frame schoolhouses, thirty-nine teachers, and a few road workers. By 1860 they had hundreds of paid firemen, organized into companies, had thirty large brick school buildings, 133 teachers, and well over 100 maintenance personnel.

It was no wonder then, that in both the 1850s and the 1860s Cambridge and Somerville leaders treated annexation with contempt. In both the communities there were a few who argued for 'one grand New England metropolis'. But there were also powerful coalitions of commuters and local workers, who controlled local government, and who agreed with the editor of the *Cambridge Chronicle* when he said that the public affairs of the suburbs 'can be better administered in their present form of separate independencies than by union with the scheming city of notions'.[26]

Cambridge and Somerville had both become 'separate independencies' through a two-stage process of local evolution. The first stage was largely experimental, and based on assumptions appropriate to small peripheral villages. The second stage narrowed and clarified the suburban leaders' conception of their role, and committed resources and local government apparatus to fulfilling it. In both stages, the unifying theme was neither the clearcut and overwhelming expansion of Boston nor a consistent effort by suburbanites to create dormitory adjuncts of the city. Rather the political history of these early suburbs reveals a recurrent process of coping with the unique and changing circumstances of growth on the city's edge, and a continuous redefinition of community in those circumstances.

By the Civil War the suburban definition of community, here and in many other similar settings, gave primacy to the interests of commuters, making the municipality a provider of services and amenities as props of middle-class domesticity. But the same definition involved selective urbanization, and a vigorous defence of the suburban community against what were deemed undesirable aspects of city growth. These suburbanites had also clarified for future generations what suburbs should strive to be, and in the process created a landscape design and a pattern of response to problems of growth that would stand as a formidable challenge to those who had sought more comprehensive and systematic approaches.

NOTES

1. This essay draws on material from Binford, Henry C. (1985) *The First Suburbs: Residential Communities on the Boston Periphery, 1815–1860*. Chicago: University of Chicago Press. I am indebted to the Press for permission to reprint parts of the text and some of the illustrations. The essay also draws on my paper entitled 'The Political History of Romantic Suburbs', read at the annual meeting of the American Historical Association on December 18, 1984. I thank my commentators and audience for their valuable criticisms and suggestions on that occasion.

2. On the suburban growth process elsewhere, see Schwartz, Joel (1976) The evolution of the suburbs, in Dolce, Philip C. (ed.) *Suburbia: The American Dream and Dilemma*. Garden City, New York: Anchor Books; and Teaford, John (1979) *City and Suburb: The Political Fragmentation of Metropolitan America, 1850–1970*. Baltimore: Johns Hopkins University Press, chapter 1.

3. Warner, Sam Bass, Jr (1978) *Streetcar Suburbs: The Process of Growth in Boston, 1870–1900*, 2nd ed. Cambridge: Harvard University Press.

4. *Ibid.* Led by Kenneth Jackson, a few historians have done pioneering research on antebellum suburbanization. These studies, though too few, have clearly shown that the roots of the modern suburb lie well before the Civil War. See Jackson, Kenneth (1975) Urban deconcentration in the nine-

teenth century: a statistical inquiry, in Schnore, Leo F. *The New Urban History: Quantitative Explorations by American Historians*. Princeton: Princeton University Press, pp. 110–42; Taylor, George Rogers (1966–67) The beginning of mass transportation in urban America (2 parts) *Smithsonian Journal of History* 1, pp. 35–50, and 2, pp. 31–54; Goldfield, David R. and Brownell, Blaine A. (1979) *Urban America: From Downtown to No Town*. Boston: Houghton Mifflin, pp. 142–46.

5. On the distinctive traits of American residential suburbs, see Teaford, *op. cit.*, chapter 1–5; Warner, *op. cit.*, Introduction to 2nd edition; and Schwartz, Barry (1976) Images of suburbia: some Revisionist commentary and conclusions, in Schwartz, Barry, (ed.) *The Changing Face of the Suburbs*. Chicago: University of Chicago Press, p. 330.

6. Boston in 1860 contained 133,563 people. The contiguous communities housed 120,248. *Eighth Census* of the United States (1864). Washington: United States Government Printing Office.

7. Frisch, Michael (1972) *Town into City: Springfield, Massachusetts and the Meaning of Community, 1840–1880*. Cambridge: Harvard University Press. Blumin, Stuart (1976) *The Urban Threshold: Growth and Change in a Nineteenth Century American Community*. Chicago: University of Chicago Press.

8. Sklar, Kathryn Kish (1973) *Catherine Beecher: A Study in American Domesticity*. New Haven: Yale University Press, esp. chapter 11; Clark, Clifford (1976) Domestic architecture as an index to social history: the romantic revival and the cult of domesticity in America 1840–1870. *Journal of Interdisciplinary History*, 7, pp. 33–56: Handlin, David (1979) *The American Home: Architecture and Society, 1815–1915*. Boston: Little Brown, chapter 1; Wright, Gwendolyn (1980) *Moralism and the Model Home: Domestic Architecture and Cultural Conflict in Chicago, 1873–1913*. Chicago: University of Chicago Press, chapter 1.

9. See Binford, Henry C. (1985) *The First Suburbs: Residential Communities on the Boston Periphery, 1815–1860*. Chicago: University of Chicago Press, pp. 171–78.

10. Handlin, Oscar and Handlin, Mary F. (1969) *Commonwealth: A Study of the Role of Government in the American Economy – Massachusetts, 1774–1861*. Cambridge, Massachusetts: Harvard University Press, p. 238. *Review of the Case of the Free Bridge, between Boston and Charlestown, 1827*. Boston: n.p., p. 93.

11. Raylor, George Rogers (1966) The beginnings of mass transportation in urban America: Part 1. *Smithsonian Journal of History*, 1, pp. 40–43.

12. The details may be found in Binford (1985) *op. cit.*, pp. 91–95.

13. Paige, Lucius (1877) *History of Cambridge, Massachusetts, 1630–1877*. Boston: H.O. Houghton.

14. Information on the early commuters is based on linkage of Boston and Suburban directories with the census schedules.

15. *Report of a Committee, appointed August 4, 1834, to consider the Subject of a Reorganization of the Public Schools in the Town of Cambridge*. Cambridge: 1834, pp. 8–9.

16. Hayward, James (1838) *Report of the Survey of the Roads of Cambridge*, p. 13; Paige, Lucius (1877) *History of Cambridge*. Boston: H.O. Houghton, pp. 244–46. Remonstrances of Samuel P.P. Fay and others, Massachusetts Archives, original documents relating to Acts of 1846, chapter 109.

17. Tyler, Columbus, Report of a Committee on a Fire Engine, April 28, 1845, Somerville Town and City Papers (MS, Somerville City Vault; hereafter cited as STCP); *Cambridge Chronicle*, May 7, 1846; March 1, 1848.

18. The pattern of growth in the suburbs is evident in the maps in Cambridge Historical Commission (1965–77), *Survey of Architectural History in Cambridge*, 5 vols. Cambridge: Cambridge Historical Commission, Volume 3; pp. 113–14; Volume 5; pp. 28–29.

19. Pope, Augustus R. (1851) *An Address at the Laying of the Corner Stone of a House of Worship for the Allen Street Congregational Society, 1851*. pp. 5, 6, 9, 22; *A Brief History of the Perkins Street Baptist Church, Somerville*. Somerville, 1887, pp. 6–7.

20. *Cambridge Chronicle*, 31 July 1852. On the Maine law enthusiasm, see Griffin, Clifford S. (1960) *Their Brothers' Keepers: Moral Stewardship in the United States, 1800–1865*. New Brunswick: Rutgers University Press, pp. 147–51; *Cambridge Chronicle*, 18 September 1852, 31 July 1853, 24 December 1853.

21. *Cambridge Chronicle*, 4 March, 2, 9 December 1854. Here and elsewhere, statements about the composition of local slates are based on comparison of tickets published in the *Chronicle* with information in the biographical file based on record linkage.

22. Derby, E.H. (1850) Commercial cities and towns of the U.S. – No. XII – Boston. *Hunt's Merchant's Magazine and Commercial Review*, **XIII**, November, pp. 483–97; *Report of the Committee in Favor of the Union of Boston and Roxbury*, Boston, 1851, pp. 20–22. *Cambridge Chronicle*, 9 September 1854; Butler, Benjamin F. (1892) *Autobiographical and Personal Reminiscences*. Boston: A.M. Thayer & Co., 1000–1002.

23. Drafts of Somerville By-laws, Somerville Town Papers, 1855 (Somerville City Vault). Requests for nuisance abatement: letter from A. Houghton to the Somerville Selectmen, November 3, 1858; record of Board of Health notices dated June 4, July 16, 1859, STCP, 1858, 1859; *Cambridge Chronicle*, 12 December, 1853, 14 October, 11 November 1854, 4 August 1855, 12, 26 September, 24 October, 14, 21 November, 5, 12 December, 1857, 30 April, 22 October, 1859.

24. Reassertions of the importance of meetings, nonpartisanship, and voluntarism: *Cambridge Chronicle* 8, 15 March, 1851; 17 January, 21 February, 6 March, 1852; G.W. Warren, *Address* (as first Mayor of Charlestown), April 26, 1847. Charlestown, 1847, 19–21.

25. *Cambridge Chronicle*, 8 December 1855, 6 December 1856, 12 December 1857; Cambridge Mayor's Address . . . 1857.

26. *Cambridge Chronicle*, 20 March 1852, 26 March 1853, 29 April 7, 21 October 1854.

Chapter Three

The Late Nineteenth-Century Suburb: Creating a Suburban Ethos for Chicago's North Shore, 1855–1900

MICHAEL H. EBNER

This chapter examines the origins, evolution, and applications of the place name *North Shore* as it denotes eight contiguous suburbs of Chicago situated on the western shoreline of Lake Michigan. The label achieved currency by 1890 and now urban historians regard it as an early effort to affect a regional self consciousness.[1] Central to what follows is an assumption that by the time residents adopted this label each community possessed a well-formed sense of self, or what Asa Briggs regards as *the sense of place*.[2] 'What begins as undifferentiated space', writes a geographer, 'becomes place as we get to know it better and endow it with value'.[3] An astute local observer recognized this in writing,

> To an unitiated eye these attractive villages stretching along the lake from the city limits . . . look very much alike. But oh, the differences, really![4]

This observation brings to mind the notion of 'local frames of awareness' envisaged by Clifford Geertz in his wide-ranging anthropological studies.[5] While it would not comfort residents past or present, obsessive devotion to locale amounted to the suburban variety of a deeply-rooted cultural attachment within cities to neighbourhood or ward. Nonetheless, it is the purpose of this chapter to demonstrate that such identification limited but did *not* completely negate efforts which fostered loyalty to a more inclusive North Shore ethos.

THE NORTH SHORE AND SUBURBAN AFFLUENCE

What transpired on the North Shore between 1855 and 1900 reflects an essential dimension of the North American suburban experience. It is best characterized as metropolitan fragmentation: each community simultaneously viewed itself as separated physically and culturally from the central city as well as distinctive from its neighbouring suburbs.[6] Henry C. Binford, an urban historian, has astutely written of the nineteenth-century milieu: ' . . . residential suburbs stand as monuments to their enterprise and reflections of their outlook on the world: innovative, competitive, localized, stubborn, at once parochial and urbane'.[7] Or as the late Kevin Lynch, the distinguished planner, once observed of the contemporary metropolis, 'Our senses are local, while our experiences are regional'.[8]

'Enduring affluent suburbs' is a geographer's definition of the type of locales we shall consider.[9] A foremost student of the metropolis of Chicago writes of its North Shore: 'This long-settled lakeshore area, with its attractive physical features, good rail transportation, and freedom from obnoxious industry, contains the greatest number of high income suburbs in the Chicago area'.[10] Their historical development resulted from the advent of railroad service in 1855.[11] The North Shore includes – in increasing distance away from The Loop – Evanston (13 miles), Wilmette (16 miles), Kenilworth (17 miles), Winnetka (18 miles), Glencoe (22 miles), Highland Park (28 miles), Lake Forest (31 miles), and Lake Bluff (35 miles). Each community was incorporated prior to the twentieth century: two in the late 1850s (Evanston and Lake Forest), three before the Great Fire of 1871 (Highland Park, Glencoe, and Winnetka), one in the immediate aftermath of the conflagration (Wilmette), and two in the mid-1890s (Lake Bluff and Kenilworth).

But before getting down to particulars, we turn to the use of the word *ethos* for studying suburban history. It is my objective not only to explore the history of one notable aggregation of communities but also to suggest how ethos may be applied to this and other networks.[12] Not unlike most conceptual labels, this one has the pitfall of being overly inclusive and indiscriminately invoked. It must be used discreetly, with keen attention devoted to the particular community or network of communities. In some instances, ethos is readily portrayed in bold and active terms, 'a set of ideas and assumptions . . . which apparently guided the community leaders in their individual and collective actions'.[13] In other settings, ethos constitutes something more than 'a compendium of booster nonsense' but less than a 'coherent policy' or a 'structured ideology'. Acknowledging these limitations, Blaine A. Brownell concludes, and rightfully so, that the ethos of a community be accorded 'serious' attention.[14]

To appreciate the nineteenth-century origins of the North Shore, a brief review of its modern-day condition will prove instructive. A 1980 survey of median family income in the 262 communities surrounding Chicago revealed four among the top ten in this network: Kenilworth ranked first ($90,751), Winnetka was fourth ($76,119), Glencoe was fifth ($75,947), and Lake Forest was seventh ($70,964). All the more telling is an analysis that includes residents who were listed in the 1980 editions of *Who's Who in America* and *The Social Register*: in the former only 12 per cent did *not* live along the North Shore, in the latter only 3 per cent.[15] Little wonder that the North Shore was recently described, half in jest and half seriously, as a 'posh, luxurious, and exclusive . . . baronial strip of lakefront . . . not related to the rest of Illinois any better than it is to the middle or lower classes'.[16]

A history of enduring affluent suburbs is incomplete, however, without discussion of places that are *not* counted among the communities constituting the North Shore, be the reason social, cultural, or economic. A few examples illustrate this circumstance. Waukegan, on the shoreline 40 miles from The Loop, is part of the network of Chicago's satellite cities.[17] Also very much out of place among the neighbouring communities, despite proximity to Lake Michigan, are Highwood and North Chicago, each serving an adjacent federal defence installation, Fort Sheridan and Great Lakes Naval Training Centre respectively. Indeed, anyone undertaking to study suburban history must be guided by the advice offered by Harold M. Mayer and Richard C. Wade at the outset of *Chicago: the Growth of a Metropolis* (1969): 'The modern metropolis, with its central city, suburbs, and "satellite cities", is a single historic and geographic entity'.[18]

A SENSE OF PLACE

But we turn to the nineteenth century to understand the North Shore as a suburban system. Convergence of three factors stood critical to the process of forming a distinctive suburban ethos: transportation, nature, and population.

The advent of rail passenger service in 1855 – the line known today as the Chicago & North Western Railroad's North Division – made the lakeshore accessible for daily commuting, at least in a rudimentary fashion. This link results directly from the ascent of Chicago between 1848 and 1856 as the railroad hub of the nation; in the former year only ten miles of track entered the city, while in the latter the figure exceeded 3,600 as eleven new lines were constructed.[19] During the third quarter of the century – as Carl Abbott has detailed for us – 'railroad suburbs' would radiate north, west, and south of the city.[20] What evolved was the Chicago version of a cultural phenomenon that John R. Stilgoe calls the 'metropolitan corridor', whereby railroading 'reshaped the American built environment and reoriented American thinking.[21] But railroading itself did *not* make the North Shore distinctive; it merely provided ready access to a stretch of terrain blessed with certain natural endowments.

Lake Michigan distinguished the North Shore from other suburbs. In 1873, landscape architect Horace W.S. Cleveland, although talking about Chicago's Lincoln Park, fastened on the lake's 'intrinsic sublimity and unceasing interest'. Proximity to the lake stimulated suburban growth in three ways: it offered something especially conducive to the germination of villages, namely the prospect of seemingly ample supplies of pure water as population increased and artesian wells became inadequate; its breezes proved something of a buffer against climatic extremes; and its shoreline areas were, in a word, beautiful. The rolling topography, with its deep ravines, bluffs, and sylvan shade, afforded visual relief from the flat, open, prairie to the immediate west. Little wonder that the influence of landscape architects working in the romantic idiom was evident in the design of several of these suburbs.[22] The ridges parallel to Lake Michigan constituted the Chicago version of what urban historians – most notably Zane L. Miller – term 'The Hill Tops', although lacking the actual rises associated with such places as Cincinnati or San Francisco.[23] One observer, writing in 1873, termed Chicago's 'Northern Suburbs' the 'Highlands' of the metropolis.[24]

Finally, the momentous expansion of Chicago – human, economic, and physical – affected the metropolis, including the North Shore. After 1860 it was the fastest growing city not only in the United States but in the world. A population of 109,260 would grow by 1900 to almost 1.7 million. But even prior to the Great Fire of 1871 these embryonic villages attracted those anxious – and possessed with the means – to relocate away from the less desirable aspects of urban life. After the Fire, the nexus of technology and nature spawned the visage of idyllic suburban havens differentiated from all else in the burgeoning metropolis.[25]

Quickly the North Shore solidified its budding reputation. An Evanston resident observed many more 'strangers' after the Fire: 'They are learning, now, how much cleaner and more quiet and pleasant is our village than the city, and how much better it is for their children'.[26] Residents of Highland Park were advised to think of their community, as well as other nearby locales, in the same way Bostonians regarded Brookline, and Roxbury or New Yorkers the 'inviting and justly appreciated' charms of suburbs on Long Island or in New Jersey.[27] Every major city, wrote the author of a booklet promoting real estate, had its 'suburban windows at which nature may be seen in her many expressions' but the distinctiveness of 'natural advantages' along Chicago's 'northern lake shore' was unsurpassed.[28]

Evanston was the most important of the North Shore suburbs not only because it stood first chronologically but also because it set the cultural tone for the nearby communities.[29] When Perry R. Duis writes of 'the triumph of moral geography', there is no better example than Evanston. Its founders in the 1850s prided themselves on establishing a sanctified village that was free of spirited beverages and a seat of higher education, namely Northwestern University. This setting was to become the venue of the Women's Christian Temperance Union. Correspondingly, it was the adopted hometown of Frances E. Willard, regarded by Clyde D. Foster, a local historian, as 'incontestably Evanston's greatest citizen'; Ruth Bordin acclaims her as 'unquestionably America's leading heroine to her contemporaries and the most famous woman of her day'. All seven suburban communites along the lakeshore would readily follow the example of banning liquor, wine, and beer upon achieving corporate status. Residents of Evanston scrupulously watched over the entire metropolis as self-annointed moral custodians. Each new local ordinance − at Woodstock in McHenry County, Oak Park or Hyde Park at some distance, or adjacent places such as Niles Township and Wilmette − was dutifully called to the attention of the people of Evanston for the purpose of edification and reiteration. A handbook for travellers published on the eve of the World's Columbian Exposition of 1893 portrayed Evanston as 'quiet, grave, and in part distinguished'.[30]

Lake Forest epitomized the cultivated landscape and social whirl associated with the North Shore. As early as 1869 one astute observer had labelled Lake Forest *romantic* in contrast to *orthodox* Evanston. Wrote Everett Chamberlin, author of a guide to Chicago's suburbs published in 1874: ' . . . Lake Forest boasts of more elegant private residences than almost any other suburb'. By 1878 this haven for Chicago's society set had come to be regarded as the 'Newport of the West'. Herbert Warren Wind, the foremost historian of golf, tells of its Onwentsia Club, established in 1895, as 'a very posh preserve' among the country clubs founded in and around Chicago at the end of the nineteenth century. To an admiring resident of Evanston the club was 'exclusive and aristocratic'. F. Scott Fitzgerald later affirmed this impression in *The Beautiful and Damned* as he set Lake Forest into the same league as Newport, Southampton, and Palm Beach.[31]

'Tediously full of good works' is the characterization of Winnetka by one local historian. To be sure this place also was dry and valued its well-tended landscape, but from its start was devoted to civic-mindedness with particular attention lavished on supporting its schools. The arrival of the Lloyd family in 1878, Henry Demarest Lloyd and Jesse Bross Lloyd (well known to students of late-nineteenth century reform), added to its reputation. Their activities culminated in experiments with direct democracy within Winnetka akin to the New England town meeting tradition. One result was the establish-ment of a municipally-owned lighting plant in 1896. Equally notable was the decision reached in 1899 by the citizens of New Trier Township – which included Winnetka – to establish a high school that would almost immediately achieve acclaim for its standard of excellence.[32]

Highland Park's founders had dreams of replicating the beauty and social milieu of Lake Forest, only to find their aspirations dashed by undercapitalization. This helps to explain why its leaders encouraged all comers, resulting in a suburb that became socially inclusive. Instructive is the fact that by the mid-1870s four distinct Protestant denominations plus Roman Catholics had established local congregations. (In Lake Forest, boosters in 1872 told of only a single congregation, the First Presbyterian Church, unrivalled until 1899 when an Episcopal congregation was founded; ignored was the presence of the Roman Catholic and African Methodist congregations.) 'Refinement without exclusiveness, cultivation without arrogance . . .', was the estimation of Highland Park by a local journalist in 1874. Then again, its public treasury perpetually suffered from the threat of imminent depletion, be it imagined or real. Although citizens valued such institutions as a library and high school, each started in the 1880s, they lived with uncertainty as to the fiscal stability of their community.[33]

To be sure, the remaining communities that constitute the North Shore deserve individual attention. 'There is an expectation of a special quality of human relationship in a community', writes Thomas Bender, 'and it is this experiential dimension that is crucial . . .'.[34] Each possessed a distinctive tone and tenor. But for purposes of this chapter the preceding sketches of four suburbs represent the variety of experiences contained within a network.

THE GROWTH OF REGIONAL IDENTITY

Early signs of an emerging regional suburban consciousness date to the 1850s. Walter S. Gurnee, a real estate speculator, deserves credit for first envisaging a string of railroad suburbs along the western

Figure 1. Lake Forest Station, c. 1930. (*Source*: Lake Forest Foundation for Historic Preservation)

shoreline of Lake Michigan. Gurnee was a former Democratic mayor of Chicago (1851–52) and subsequently the president of the Chicago & Milwaukee Railroad (corporate predecessor to the Chicago & Northwestern). Before Gurnee went bankrupt and departed for New York City, he had a major hand during the 1850s in the formation of locales we now know as Lake Bluff, Highland Park, Glencoe, and Winnetka.[35]

Further evidence exists to corroborate Gurnee's vision. By 1857, two years after the railroad commenced service, a Chicago newspaper reported on the 'beautiful and flourishing towns along the Lake Shore . . .'.[36] In April, 1869 commuters from several of these suburban communities joined successfully to protest a rise in ticket prices.[37] Baseball teams hailing from particular locales, such as the 'Pioneers' and 'Lake Shores' of Waukegan, the 'Nine' of Lake Forest Academy, and the 'University 9' of Evanston, regularly competed beginning in the spring of 1871.[38] When the Chicago, Milwaukee & St. Paul Railroad began to construct its route along a right-of-way some five miles west of Lake Michigan in early 1871 (ultimately creating a new string of railroad suburbs, among them Morton Grove, Glenview, Northfield, Northbrook, and Deerfield), at least some along the lakeshore expressed concern about the ramifications of a rival line.[39] Finally, intramural rivalries – for the most part petty, frivolous and shortlived – existed between the various communities along the shoreline. One illustration suffices. When a handsome railroad station was constructed in Wilmette in 1873, a citizen of Evanston deplored the depot in that community as 'a wretched inconvenience'.[40]

Specific use of the label *North Shore* to describe these communities dates to the winter months of 1889. In a formal sense the founding of an organization called the North Shore Improvement Association (N.S.I.A.) in February, 1889 provided the impetus. No community eschewed sending a representative to its initial meeting, and probably for good reason as we shall soon discover. Moreover, the newly-coined descriptive label achieved instantaneous acceptance.[41] Wherever one resided, be it *dry* Evanston or *fashionable* Lake Forest, this common denominator called to mind enough similarities to win approval. Notably, the organization's first president was Potter Palmer, thus lending this cause the imprimatur of one of Chicago's most socially prominent citizens. An editorial in the *Evanston Index* added:

> The interests of all the north shore suburbs are practically identical, and there is no reason why they should not unite their forces and pull together for the common good.[42]

Not that the foregoing transpired by chance. Rather the founding of the N.S.I.A. coincided with a momentous turn in the history of Chicago. In the late 1880s a movement was in process that culminated on June 29, 1889 with the city's annexation of 125 square miles to its existing 43, including the townships of Lake, Hyde Park, Jefferson, and Lake View. This accession was symptomatic of what Kenneth T. Jackson aptly discerns as a wave of urban imperialism during the second half of the nineteenth century. Jackson refers, of course, to the actions of other world-class cities such as Philadelphia, London, Paris, and New York that consolidated political or administrative control over major portions of their peripheries. Not lost upon the citizens still beyond the newly-expanded corporate limits of Chicago was the fact that one *very* desirable suburban locale – Hyde Park on the Southside – no longer possessed its political autonomy and communal identities.[43]

As a result, and understandably, a wary relationship existed between Chicago and the suburbs along the North Shore. Because of Evanston's proximity it was the city's primary object of desire. When Chicago proposed consolidation with Evanston in 1894, 78 per cent of the voters in that suburb cast negative ballots. 'True Evanstonians', proclaimed Mayor Oscar Mann, valued their community for its 'individuality'. And when the Civic Federation of Chicago proposed enabling legislation in 1899 to unite Chicago and Cook County into a single unit of metropolitan government, residents organized themselves as if anticipating an 'earthquake'. A delegation of prominent citizens of Evanston stood at the fore among those who journeyed to Springfield and killed the bill.[44] It is not unreasonable to surmise that these experiences over the course of ten years heightened the value placed upon political autonomy in the minds of citizens residing along the North Shore.

SHERIDAN ROAD: A PATH TO REGIONAL IDENTITY

Add to the foregoing situation the course of action pursued by the N.S.I.A. in the 1890s. We know that its leaders devoted substantial attention to formulating a uniform design for a suburban extension of Chicago's Lake Shore drive. It was designated *Sheridan Road* in memory of General Philip Sheridan, the Civil War hero who had won the hearts of Chicagoans as a keeper of the peace in the aftermath of the Fire of 1871 and again during the momentous railroad strike of 1877. The plan was to construct a pleasure thoroughfare, 100 feet in width, running immediately along the shoreline not unlike the project launched in 1886 at Brookline, Massachusetts to transform Beacon Street into 'a grand boulevard'. Its promoters, writes Bessie Louise Pierce, were 'ambitious and farseeing citizens'. Surely the leaders of the N.S.I.A. envisaged the completed roadway project as their instrument for creating a regional self-consciousness. Possibly its leadership saw virtue in fostering cooperation as a check against future manifestations of the annexation mania.[45]

The initial idea for Sheridan Road, proposed in 1873, was to extend Lake Shore Drive northward, offering access to Chicago's Lincoln Park from Evanston via the intermediate locales of South Evanston, Rogers Park, and Lake View. Although some progress would be achieved by 1880, concern existed in the aftermath of the prolonged economic downswing of the mid-1870s about cost and utility. Midway through 1884, as another 1.5 miles of roadway was improved, pleas were issued to private citizens and the trustees of Northwestern University to offer assistance in the defrayal of expenses. But almost five years later financial problems persisted. Early in January of 1889, a public meeting of Evanston's 'property holders and well-known progressive men' again considered how to underwrite completion within their community.[46]

Lack of progress in constructing the northerly extension of Lake Shore Drive within Evanston stood in stark contrast to the headway achieved at the Chicago terminus. Two factors contributed to this situation. First, prospects for Chicago's North Side had been enhanced by an act of the state legislature in April, 1879 granting sole authority for the development of Lake Shore Drive to a single agency, the Lincoln Park Commission. Second, the desirable nature of the North Side as a place for residential habitation – it had previously been inhabited by grazing cows – received impetus in 1882 when Bertha and Potter Palmer erected their lakefront 'castle' at a cost of $150,000. As others constructed mansions, the value of real estate advanced from $160 a front foot in 1882 to $800 by 1892; what was taking place was the evolution of the North Side into Chicago's Gold Coast, supplanting Prairie Avenue.[47]

From its inception the leadership of the N.S.I.A. was single-mindedly devoted to the northerly extension of Lake Shore Drive. But from the moment that Sheridan Road was proposed its design was plagued by the confusion resulting from the multiplicity of governmental jurisdictions bordering on its right-of-way. Ideal would have been expansion of the authority of the Lincoln Park Commissioners into the suburbs, but such a resolution was politically and legally unrealistic in the 1890s. What took place was very different, indicative of the tradition of municipal autonomy which confounded ventures aimed at achieving cooperation within the late-nineteenth-century metropolis. Each agency of government – namely townships and assorted municipal entities – struggled to preserve its own imperatives. All of them feared responsibility for imposition of any new burden on taxpayers.[48]

Perhaps the suburban promoters of Sheridan Road sensed potential legal and political obstructions. Clearly they proceeded with notice-able care from the time the N.S.I.A. had been organized in 1889. Volney W. Foster, a resident of Evanston destined to be the plan's single-most important advocate, left no stone unturned. Favourable press reports had been appearing since 1888, setting the stage for the effort about to be launched. On February 12, 1889 a circular letter was distributed by 'A Committee of the citizens of Evanston', among them the soon-to-be famous architect Daniel H. Burnham. Addressed to influential citizens in Chicago and along the North Shore, it solicited membership in an organization composed of 'all public spirited citizens' to promote extension of the road. Marshall Field sent $10. John V. Farwell, Jr of Lake Forest claimed no interest but sent the letter to his uncle, Senator Charles B. Farwell in Washington, D.C. Robert W. Patterson, managing editor of the *Chicago Tribune* answered: 'Mr Medill desires me to say in reply to your letter to him that you can count upon the co-operation of the THE TRIBUNE in the work you are carrying forward to the fullest extent'. Buoyed by this outward enthusiasm, leaders of the new association spoke of having the project nine-tenths finished within two years.[49]

SHERIDAN ROAD: OBSTACLES TO SUCCESS

But the project confronted obstacles. Two replies to the circular letter of February 12, 1889, each in the form of private correspondence rather than public declarations, are instructive. Elisha Gray, the Highland Park inventor, tempered enthusiasm with a general qualification: 'Of course a great deal will depend upon how the details are marked up . . .'. Henry Demarest Lloyd, closely identified with village affairs in his beloved Winnetka, responded in similar fashion:

> I trust the promoters of the plan will give it sufficient elasticity to adjust it to local pecularities. A *widening* of the drive where it passes through Winnetka would destroy hundreds of beautiful trees, and where it touches my place would completely wreck a little hill, which I consider the chief beauty of the place. What is needed is a good drive and a beautiful one, and that can best be got by preserving the beauties that already exist.

The *Evanston Index* editorially embellished this concern: 'This drive is a magnificent conception, and it can be carried to a successful end *only* by the cooperation of all the towns'.[50]

Evanston was the focal point. Beginning in early March of 1889, steps were taken to obtain from the government of the village an ordinance for a lakefront right-of-way. Surely Volney Foster and his associates understood that if misgivings about Sheridan Road were to be allayed, progress was imperative in the community where the design originated. By early March, 1889, however, dissenters were making themselves heard. Eldon Lee Brown, a founder of the preservation-minded Village Improvement Society of Evanston, was concerned about damage being done to the cherished vista of the lakeshore. 'Mudsill', the *nom de plume* employed in a letter written to the *Evanston Index*, expressed more interest in paying taxes for 'a nice clean street in front of my own residence'. The trustees of Northwestern University disputed the precise cost of a special assessment for improving Sheridan Road adjacent to their campus. Finally, Daniel P. O'Leary entered into protracted litigation in pursuit of just compensation for property that he held legal rights to, thereby preventing construction along 196 feet of prime property. Before this case was settled in 1902, the original plaintiff had been joined by Daniel Burnham and his neighbours, who expanded the issues in litigation. Their concern was for the shoreline of Lake Michigan, their fear that undue harm might be inflicted on it by construction of Sheridan Road.[51]

In the face of disappointments, Volney Foster attacked on other fronts. His objective, no doubt, was to demonstrate to those who lacked his enthusiasm that the concept was worthy. Five issues deserve

Figure 2. University Hall of Northwestern University was completed in September 1869 and remains standing today. It was the first modern structure on the campus. (*Source*: The Archives of Northwestern University)

Figure 3. Sheridan Road, looking at the south end of the Northwestern University Campus where Sheridan Road turns west, c. 1900 or earlier (*Source*: The Archives of Northwestern University)

attention: negotiations between the N.S.I.A. and Archbishop Patrick A. Feehan of Chicago seeking a lakefront right-of-way for Sheridan Road through Calvary Cemetery at the point where Chicago and Evanston meet; advocacy of state legislation expanding the authority of the Lincoln Park Commission northward to the city line; prolonged deliberations with the United States Department of War about the possibility of designating Sheridan Road a military highway; support of a state law known as the Sheridan Road Bill allowing municipalities to create special park districts to facilitate construction; and a campaign in the legislature of Wisconsin to pass a bill extending Sheridan Road from the Illinois-Wisconsin border to Milwaukee via the cities of Kenosha and Racine.

Discussions with Archbishop Feeham proceeded with alacrity, to the joy of those favourably disposed to the Sheridan Road project. The *Chicago Inter-Ocean* unknowingly claimed that the agreement reached in March of 1889 constituted 'the last obstacle of any importance to the constructions of "Sheridan's Road" '. By late May a subscription campaign within Evanston had raised donations totalling $2,500 toward completing this stretch.[52] Surely when Volney Foster, an Episcopalian, reflected on this successful episode he must have appreciated the hierarchical authority bestowed upon a sole religious leader.

As for the northerly extension of authority for the Lincoln Park Commissioners in 1892, developments on this issue must have been reassuring to the N.S.I.A. Evanston's representative in the Illinois Assembly had proposed enabling legislation during April of 1889. Thereafter Foster and his allies had lobbied strenuously among politicians in Chicago and Springfield. The Baker Bill empowered commissioners to engage in the necesary condemnation proceedings and ensuing construction from Fullerton Avenue (the original limit of their authority) north to Chicago's limits. In one instance a portion of an existing street, Sheffield Avenue, was renamed Sheridan Road by the Lincoln Park authorities and who then ordered its improvement to conform with the overall design. On the whole, progress proved swift, certainly by comparison to what the N.S.I.A. was able to achieve in the suburbs.[53]

Foster's extended campaign to link the destiny of Sheridan Road to Fort Sheridan had commenced with the circular letter of February 12, 1889. Among those who replied was an Assistant Quartermaster General of the United States Army. General J.D. Bingham, not unlike others who had received this solicitation, mixed enthusiasm with local concern: 'It would not be practicable to construct the drive through the Fort Sheridan Reservation, the drill ground, rifle range, etc., would interfere with its use'. Within two months, seeking to reverse this attitude, Foster was in Washington, D.C. meeting with the Secretary of War. It was at this point, despite failings to win the right-of-way through the grounds, that Foster described Sheridan Road as a military *highway* and proposed that upon its completion between Chicago and Fort Sheridan responsibility should be assumed by the federal government. But until late 1898 the issue stood dormant, at which stage exploratory discussions were renewed with officials at the War Department, thanks to prodding by Congressman George E. Foss who represented the North Shore district. An editorial in the *Sheridan Road Newsletter* – a weekly whose purpose was embedded in its name – forcefully made the case: 'In a word, there must be not only a Fort but quick and ample means of transit between it and the city'.[54]

Amplification on the proposal to convert Sheridan Road into a military highway helps us to appreciate what was involved. The founding of Fort Sheridan in 1887 stemmed from the turmoil associated with the Haymarket Riot of May, 1886. It had been established at the behest of wealthy residents of Chicago who now claimed a federal military presence was required within the metropolis. It is commonly assumed that the N.S.I.A. had the military reservation in mind from the start of its promotional activities in February of 1889; the decision to adopt the name 'Sheridan Road' as well as Foster's visit to the War Department in April affirm this. Designation as a national defence corridor would have reinforced the utility of the fort. And having achieved this, Foster would have been endowed with authority to sweep aside local civil barriers.[55]

The unfavourable decision announced in December 1900 surely proved disheartening to Volney Foster, although he termed it satisfactory. The army would allow the right-of-way *through* Fort Sheridan and accept responsibility for the cost of construction within the grounds, but judged as unnecessary the road's designation as a military highway. The rationale for the decision is not clear. By this point Foster obviously was frustrated and even desperate over an unfulfilled goal he now regarded as a beloved 'hobby'. Possibly he had abused his substantial political leverage (he was president of Chicago's Union Club and influential in Republican party affairs nationally) when he gained an audience to make his plea before Secretary of War Elihu Root in 1900. It is also plausible that residents along the North Shore now recognized that Sheridan Road as a military route promised more harm than good, containing the possibility of inflicting damage on well-tended landscape. By the late 1890s the presence of a military installation amid the cultivated suburbs had come to be viewed as a mixed blessing; its existence already had changed the adjacent village of Highwood from an aspiring suburb not unlike its neighbouring communities into a post town where soldiers spent idle hours pursuing undesirable leisure activities. But the best explanation is that Secretary Root remained unconvinced. (That General Nelson A. Miles, a former Evanston resident currently serving as army commander, was seemingly aligned with Foster's campaign served no constructive end. Miles and Root were locked in bitter dispute over the latter's plan to reorganize the United States Army, a scheme opposed by the general.) Entering into Root's reasoning may have been the fact that the railroad connection between Fort Sheridan and Chicago was strategically more important. Perhaps the War Department drew a fundamental conclusion that the coveted designation as a military corridor constituted not an imperative so much as an inventive ploy.[56]

The Sheridan Road Bill was enacted by the Illinois General Assembly in June of 1895, again the result of a sustained lobbying effort extending back to the earliest days of N.S.I.A. The legislation proved sensitive to concerns about usurpation of municipal authority, its proponents denying any attempt to approximate the broad powers held by the Lincoln Park Commissioners. Claiming the intent 'local in character', the secretary of the N.S.I.A. explained that 'pleasure drive districts' – linking the desired roadway to a network of accompanying parkways – would be constituted *only where welcomed* in Cook and Lake counties. A clarification also was issued outlining the circumscribed fiscal powers granted such districts, an ongoing concern reinforced by the long downswing in the national economy following the Panic of 1893. Still another key provision of the legislation essential to the original design of Sheridan Road was the restriction imposed upon commercial traffic.[57]

SHERIDAN ROAD: THE END OF THE ROAD

Despite attentiveness to local concern, the promise of the Sheridan Road Bill went unfulfilled. Evanston voters conducted an election on July 30, 1895 for the purpose of creating a park district. But hope that this would spark dramatic progress was dashed when 61 per cent of the participating voters opposed the proposition. Although little opposition had manifested itself prior to election day, proponents recognized the principal reason for defeat involved misgivings about taxation authority. And when citizens in Highland Park voted in January 1901, the merits and liabilities of the highway were debated passionately before 58 per cent of the ballots were marked negative.[58]

The campaign to extend Sheridan Road to Milwaukee took hold in August of 1894, with Volney Foster once more at the helm. Working with a committee based in Milwaukee, he proposed a 100 foot wide improved roadway on the path of an existing lakeshore road. 'The Chicago road is already a splendid pleasure drive', claimed one of the Milwaukee representatives, 'and the widening of the road and the connection with Sheridan drive, will make it one of the finest roads in the country'. No doubt Foster was gratified by this turn of events, which stimulated a flurry of construction activity within Illinois. In Wisconsin, promotional committees were formed by interested residents of Kenosha and Racine, culminating in the submission of a bill to the legislature during 1897 seeking aid from the three countries it would traverse. Some enthusiasts expanded their horizons, one proposing that the road be extended beyond Milwaukee to Green Bay, another that the sought-after military highway designation be applied to the entire length between Milwaukee and Chicago.[59]

This effort failed for familiar reasons. Farmers in southeastern Racine County lobbied in opposition, fearing that the cost of a coastal survey requisite to constructing Sheridan Road imposed too great a burden. As a second initiative commenced early in 1899, an editorial in the *Milwaukee Sentinel* admonished readers to cooperate with a plan 'so useful and desirable'. Although the perfected bill freed individual property owners from assessments for the survey, the prospect of a publically-financed roadway still did not inspire support. Three years later, obviously recognizing the futility of his mission, Foster went after representatives of the Chicago & North Western Railroad about the Wisconsin extension.[60]

Sheridan Road's fate appeared sealed when, in the summer of 1904, came the unexpected death of Volney Foster at the age of fifty-six. Fittingly, Evanston authorities waived the ordinance prohibiting funeral processions along Sheridan Road in recognition of his contribution. But without his singular force, most activity lapsed. Another referendum for a lakefront park district in Evanston was defeated in July 1905 with nearly 54 per cent of the voters opposed. Interest in the project revived, briefly, in 1910, 1915, and again in 1918. In retrospect, the decision of the federal government in December, 1900 not to grant Foster's longstanding petition designating Sheridan Road a military highway had been decisive. What is clear is that for a goodly number of years – as early as 1895 and for long thereafter – the N.S.I.A. had ceased to function, its sole objective single-handedly perpetuated by Foster. Some months after he died, the remaining officer of the N.S.I.A. inquired of J. Seymour Currey, secretary of the Evanston Historical Society, as to whether its archives might yield records that could illuminate past deliberations.[61]

Foster's inability to realize his goal ultimately proved a blessing. Had his design been implemented with the enthusiasm he believed Sheridan Road deserved the North Shore might have been changed in unintended ways. In the looming age of the automobile a modern artery – be it a pleasure drive or military highway – might have transformed adjoining suburban communities. What could have transpired is reminiscent of the unanticipated havoc wrought on Long Island by the road-construction projects launched in the 1920s by Robert Moses. Instead the character of Sheridan Road has been perpetuated and even enhanced for future generations.[62] Pursuing its meandering route, it adheres to the physical contours of the landscape rather than imposing a uniform roadway upon the North Shore.

THE NORTH SHORE SUBURBAN ETHOS

That the ethos of the North Shore was highly circumscribed should by now be readily apparent. Anyone familiar with the political economy of the American metropolis – be it the 1890s or 1980s – recognizes the constraints that inhibit efforts to achieve coordinated action even among relatively homogeneous but autonomous communities. Whatever preconceptions the outsider might conjure up, the place name *North Shore* certainly was *not* a magic wand waved to achieve a uniform response to knotty problems. Those who expected more, as Volney Foster had learned, would readily encounter disappointment, and sometimes frustration. What they discovered was that this rubric was *not* a political instrument to be used for collectively implementing tangible, programmatic goals.[63] It may be that the lessons of Chicago's momentous consolidation of June 29, 1889 as well as the thwarted designs for absorbing Evanston in 1894 and 1899 had cured these suburbanites of immediate thoughts about cooperating on a metropolitan scale. Even when issues arose of greater immediacy than Sheridan Road, proponents of quick action found themselves thwarted.

Take the concern manifested by the outbreaks of typhoid in 1898 and scarlet fever in 1899. The prospect of epidemics prompted officials representing municipalities along the shoreline to consider the problem of controlling sewage discharge so as not to perpetuate contamination of the supply of drinking water drawn from Lake Michigan. Despite calls for a concerted, unified response, including the proposed formation of a suburban federation to address the issue, no formal action was undertaken. Mayor Edward F. Gorton of Lake Forest lamented in 1899, 'I am afraid more years will pass . . . before the people will be brought to realize the dangers they are harboring and the North Shore towns are sure in time to acquire [a] . . . bad reputation . . . '. Not until 1909 would this concern be heeded with the formation of the North Shore Sanitary Association. And this achievement was itself burdened by additional legel problems rooted in the fact that the eight suburbs are spread over two countries, thus prolonging a resolution for another five years.[64]

Yet despite these difficulties, I still draw the conclusion that a suburban ethos, albeit limited, had been created. It took form as a cultural expression rooted in the common historical experience of the eight locales and the imagery they evoked. *North Shore* by the 1890s amounted to a definition of what was socially proper and politically desirable. This rubric separated this network from Chicago, the singular symbol of urbanism and imperialistic designs. It constituted a *boundary* (to borrow the words employed by John Brinckerhoff Jackson) that stabilized and clarified social relationships between the North Shore and the metropolis.[65] But more ambitious efforts to apply this suburban ethos, at least initially, impinged upon another set of boundaries created by strong feelings of autonomy so cherished by residents of the individual communities.

Peter O. Muller, the historical geographer, places the preceding setting into context when he writes of 'closed social cells' being formed during the nineteenth century.[66] Underscoring this was the firm opposition within well-established suburbs to various designs for metropolitan cooperation. Instead of suburbs becoming harbingers of democracy, something else took place: *each* locale prized its independence over nearby suburbs as well as the central city. Hence the reluctance to join into collective efforts such as the uniform design of Sheridan Road. Indeed the laboured quest to create an ethos along Chicago's North Shore is instructive to those viewing such circumstances from the vantage point of the late twentieth century. Even among like-minded suburban neighbours nearly one-hundred years ago, suspicions existed that were grounded in local frames of awareness.

NOTES

Support from Lake Forest College, the National Endowment for the Humanities, the Albert Beveridge Memorial Fund for Research in American History, and the American Association for State & Local History has been instrumental to this research.

1. Schwartz, Joel (1976) The evolution of the suburbs, in Dolce, Philip C. (ed.) *Suburbia, the American Dream and Dilemma*. Garden City: Anchor Press/Doubleday, p. 18. Currey, J. Seymour (1908) Chicago's North Shore. Illinois State Historical Library, No. 13, *Transactions of the Illinois State Historical Society for the Year*, p. 103, dates the common application of the place name to 1890.

2. Briggs, Asa (1985) *The Collected Essays of Asa Briggs*, Volume 1, *Words,*

Numbers, Places, People. Urbana: University of Illinois Press, p. 6.

3. Tuan, Yi-Fu (1977) *Space and Place, the Perspective of Experience.* Minneapolis: University of Minnesota Press, p. 6.

4. Meeker, Arthur (1955) *Chicago, with Love, a Polite and Personal History.* New York: Alfred Knopf, p. 82.

5. Geertz, Clifford (1983) *Local Knowledge, Further Essays in Interpretive Anthropology.* New York: Basic Books, p. 6.

6. Teaford, John C. (1979) *City and Suburb, the Political Fragmentation of Metropolitan America,* 1850–1970. Baltimore: Johns Hopkins University Press, pp. 5–31.

7. Binford, Henry C. (1985) *The First Suburbs, Residential Communities on the Boston Periphery, 1815–1860.* Chicago: University of Chicago Press, p. 229.

8. Lynch, Kevin (1976) *Managing a Sense of Region.* Cambridge: MIT Press, p. 10.

9. Burns, Elizabeth K. (1980) The enduring affluent suburb. *Landscape,* 24(1), pp. 33–41.

10. Cutler, Irving (1972) *Chicago: Metropolis of the Mid-continent.* Chicago: The Geographic Society of Chicago, p. 100.

11. Ebner, Michael H. (1982) 'In the suburbes of Toun': Chicago's North Shore to 1871. *Chicago History,* 11(2), pp. 66–77. These circumstances are qualita-tively and chronologically different from those discussed in Warner, Sam Bass, Jr. (1962) *Streetcar Suburbs, the Process of Growth in Boston,* 1870–1900. Cambridge: Harvard University Press, pp. 158ff.

12. Connell, John (1974) The metropolitan village: spatial and social processes in discontinuous suburbs, in Johnson, James H. (ed.) *Suburban Growth, Geographical Processes at the Edge of the Western City.* London: John Wiley & Sons, pp. 77f. writes about the 'illusive' nature of the suburban ethos and the lack of attention devoted to it by scholars. Since Connell wrote some important additions to the literature on suburbanization have been made by geographers and historians. Refer to Ebner, Michael H. (1985) Re-reading suburban America: urban population deconcentration, 1810–1980. *American Quarterly,* 37(3), pp. 368–81.

13. Bloomfield, Elizabeth (1983) Community, ethos and the local initiative in urban economic growth: review of a theme in Canadian urban history. *Urban History Yearbook,* p. 56.

14. Brownell, Blaine A. (1975) *The Urban Ethos in the South, 1920–1930.* Baton Rouge: Lousiana State University Press, p. 40.

15. *Chicago Sun-Times,* September 16, 1982 provides a ranking of communities. I conducted the tabulations of listing in *Who's Who* and *Social Register.*

16. *Chicago Tribune,* June 14, 1981.

17. Monchow, Helen Corbin (1939) *Seventy Years of Real Estate Subdividing in the Region of Chicago.* Evanston: Northwestern University, p. 21; Cutler, Irving (1965) *The Chicago-Milwaukee Corridor: A Geographic Study of*

Intermetropolitan Coalesence. Evanston: Department of Geography, Northwestern University, pp. 26–28.

18. Mayer, Harold M. and Wade, Richard C. (1969) *Chicago: The Growth of a Metropolis*. Chicago: University of Chicago Press, p. ix.

19. Cronon, William J. (1981) 'To be the central city': Chicago, 1848–1857. *Chicago History*, **10**(3), pp. 130–40; Pierce, Bessie Louise (1940) *A History of Chicago*, Vol. 2 *From Town to City, 1848–1871*. New York: Alfred Knopf, pp. 35–76.

20. Abbott, Carl (1980) 'Necessary adjuncts to its growth': the railroad suburbs of Chicago. *Journal of the Illinois State Historical Society*, **73**(2), pp. 117–31. Also consult Posadas, Barbara (1978) A home in the country: suburbanization in Jefferson Township, 1870–1880. *Chicago History*, **7**, pp. 134–49.

21. Stilgoe, John R. (1983) *Metropolitan Corridor, Railroads and the American Scene*. New Haven: Yale University Press, pp. ix.

22. Cleveland, Horace William Shaler (1873) *Landscape Architecture as applied to the Needs of the West*. Chicago: Jansen, McClurg & Co., pp. 40; Archer, John (1983) Country and city in the American romantic suburb. *Journal of the Society of Architectural Historians*, **42**(2), pp. 139–56.

23. Miller, Zane L. (1968) *Boss Cox's Cincinnati, Urban Politics in the Progressive Era*. New York: Oxford University Press, pp. 41–55; Burns, Elizabeth K. (1974) The process of residential suburban development: The San Fransisco Peninsula. *Great Plains–Rocky Mountain Geographical Journal*, **3**, p. 14. McCarthy, Michael P. (1977) On bosses, reformers, and urban growth: Some suggestions for a political typology of American Cities. *Journal of Urban History*, **4**(1), pp. 29–38 raises important question about how topography affects patterns of metropolitan growth.

24. n.a. (1873) *North Chicago: Its Advantages, Resources, and Probable Future including a Sketch of its Outlying Suburbs*. Chicago: Henry C. Johnson, p. 8 (available at Chicago Historical Society).

25. Published too late to be consulted was the much awaited study by Rosen, Christine (1986) *The Limits of Power, Great Fires and the Process of City Growth in America*. New York: Cambridge University Press.

26. *Evanston Index*, July 6, 1872 (available at Northwestern University Library).

27. *Highland Park News*, August, 1874 (available at Highland Park Public Library).

28. *North Chicago: Advantages, Resources, and Probable Future, op. cit.*, p. 8.

29. Blumin, Stuart M. (1983) When villages become towns, the historical contexts of town formation, in Fraser, Derek and Sutcliffe, Anthony (eds.) *The Pursuit of Urban History*. London: Edward Arnold, Ltd., p. 56 writes: '. . . town formation, even in long settled-regions, must not be understood as a purely random process in which all the region's villages have an equal chance for inclusion'. Although Blumin's focus is different from my own, his observation provides much insight for considering the chronological

progression of suburban development.

30. Perkins, Margery Blair (1985) (compiled and edited by Buchbinder-Green, Barbara J.) *Evanstoniana, an Informal History of Evanston and its Architecture.* Evanston & Chicago: Evanston Historical Society & Chicago Review Press, pp. 3–27; Ebner, Michael H. (1984) The result of honest hard work: creating a suburban ethos for Evanston. *Chicago History,* 13(2) pp. 48–65; Foster, Clyde D. (1956) *Evanston's Yesterdays, Stories of Early Evanston and Sketches of some of its Pioneers.* Evanston: n.p., p. 56; Bordin, Ruth (1981) *Women and Temperance, the Quest for Power and Liberty, 1873–1900.* Philadelphia: Temple University Press, p. 166; Ruegamer, Lana (1982) 'The Paradise of Exceptional Women': Chicago Women Reformers, 1863–1893. Unpublished doctoral dissertation, Indiana University, pp. 116–45; and Duis, Perry R. (1983) *The Saloon, Public Drinking in Chicago and Boston.* 1880–1920. Urbana: University of Illinois Press, pp. 204–229, esp. 211ff.

31. (Runnion, James B.) (1869) *Out of Town, Being a Descriptive, Historical and Statistical Account of the Suburban Towns and Residences of Chicago.* Chicago: Western News Company, p. 32 (available at Chicago Historical Society); Chamberlin, Everett (1874) *Chicago and its Suburbs.* Chicago: T.A. Hungerford & Co., p. 397; (Farwell, Grace) Mrs. Robert Greaves McGann (1919), Early Lake Forest, in Kirkland, Caroline (ed.) *Chicago Yesterdays, a Sheaf of Reminiscences.* Chicago: Daughaday and Company, p. 253f.; (Farwell, Anna) Mrs. Reginald DeKoven (1926) *A Musician and his Wife.* New York: Harper & Brothers; Arpee, Edward (1964) *Lake Forest, Illinois, History and Reminiscences.* Lake Forest: Rotary Club, p. 151; Wind, Herbert Warren (1975–76) Golfing in and around Chicago. *Chicago History,* 4(4), pp. 246–9; Fitzgerald, F. Scott (1922) *The Beautiful and Damned.* New York: Charles Scribners, p. 191; and Jaher, Frederic Cople (1982), *The Urban Establishment, Upper Strata in Boston, New York, Charleston, Chicago, and Los Angeles.* Urbana: University of Illinois Press, pp. 531f.

32. Meeker, *op. cit.,* p. 83. On the history of this community refer to Hood, Hester Marie (1924) The Study of a Suburban Community, Winnetka, Illinois, M.A. thesis, Northwestern University; Glick, Clarence Elmer (1928) Winnetka: A Study of a Residential Suburban Community. M.A. thesis, University of Chicago; Dickinson, Lora Townsend (1956) *The Story of Winnetka.* Winnetka: Winnetka Historical Society; and Harnsberger, Caroline Thomas (1977) *Winnetka: The Biography of a Village.* Evanston: Schori Press. On the Lloyds and their influence see Ginger, Ray (1958) *Altgeld's America, the Lincoln Ideal versus changing Realities.* New York: Funk & Wagnalls; Destler, Chester MacArthur (1963) *Henry Demarest Lloyd and the Empire of Reform.* Philadelphia: University of Pennsylvania Press; Frederick, Peter J. (1976) *Knights of the Golden Rule, the Intellectual as Christian Social Reformer in the 1890s.* Lexington: University Press of Kentucky, pp. 56–77, and Thomas, John L. (1983) *Alternative America, Henry George, Edward Bellamy, Henry Demarest Lloyd and the Adversary Tradition.* Cambridge: Harvard University Press.

33. *Highland Park News,* June 1874; Beckmire, Reginia Marie (1932) The Study of Highland Park as a Residential Suburb, M.A. thesis, University of

Chicago; Wittelle, Marvyn (1958) *Pioneer to Commuter, the Story of Highland Park*. Highland Park: Rotary Club; and Frooman, Mary E. (1972) The History of the Highland Park Public Library. M.A. qualifying paper, Northern Illinois University (available at Highland Park Public Library).

34. Bender, Thomas (1978) *Community and Social Change in America*. New Brunswick: Rutgers University Press, p. 6.

35. Parkerson, D.H. (1981) Walter S. Gurnee, in Holli, Melvin G. and Jones, Peter d'A (eds.) *Biographical Dictionary of American Mayors, 1820–1980, Big City Mayors*. Westport: Greenwood Press, pp. 143f.

36. *Chicago Tribune*, January 13, 1855.

37. *Waukegan Gazette*, March 27, April 17, May 1 and 22 and June 12, 1869 (available at Waukegan Public Library).

38. *Waukegan Gazette*, April 22, May 27, June 10 and 17, August 5 and 19, and September 30, 1871.

39. Halsey, John J. (ed.) (1912) *History of Lake County, Illinois*. Chicago: Roy S. Bates, pp. 384–89; Andreas, A.T. (1884) *History of Cook County, Illinois, from the Earliest Period to the Present Time*. Chicago: A.T. Andreas, pp. 471–77; and Cutler, *op. cit.*, pp. 135–41.

40. Bushnell, George (1976) *Wilmette: A History*. Wilmette: Wilmette Bicentennial Commission, p. 46; Mayer and Wade, *op. cit.*, p. 70; Stilgoe, *op. cit.*, pp. 189–243; and *Evanston Index*, December 5, 1874.

41. *Evanston Index*, December 29, 1888 and January 5 and February 2, 1889; *Chicago News*, February 21 and March 4, 1889; *Chicago Tribune*, March 3, 1889; *Chicago Herald*, March 4, 1889; and *Chicago Inter-Ocean*, March 9 and 20, 1889.

42. Smith, Henry Justin (1931) *Chicago, a Portrait*. New York: The Century Co. pp. 46–57 and *Evanston Index*, March 2, 1889.

43. Jackson, Kenneth T. (1985) *Crabgrass Frontier, the Suburbanization of the United States*. New York: Oxford University Press, pp. 138–56. Three case studies, each set in Chicago, illustrate the ramifications of urban imperialism: Block, Jean F. (1978) *Hyde Park Houses, an Informal History, 1856–1910*. Chicago: University of Chicago Press, pp. 25–28; Jebsen, Harry Jr. (1981) Preserving suburban identity in an expanding metropolis: the case of Blue Island, Illinois. *Old Northwest*, 7, pp. 127–43; and Posadas, Barbara M. (1983) Suburb into neighbourhood: the transformation of urban identity on Chicago's periphery – Irving Park as a case study, 1870–1910. *Journal of the Illinois State Historical Society*, **76**(3), pp. 162–76. Also consult Hoyt, Homer (1933) *One Hundred Years of Land Values in Chicago, the Relationship of the Growth of Chicago to the rise in its Land Values, 1830–1933*. Chicago: University of Chicago Press, pp. 153–55.

44. McCarthy, Michael P. (1977) Chicago, the annexation movement and progressive reform, in Ebner, Michael H. and Tobin, Eugene M. (eds.) *The Age of Urban Reform: New Perspectives on the Progressive Era*. Port Washington: Kennikat Press, pp. 43–52; Cain, Louis P. (1983) To annex or not to annex? A tale of two towns: Evanston and Hyde Park. *Exploration in Economic History*, **20**, pp. 58–72; Ebner (1984) *op. cit.*, p. 49; and *Evanston Index*, April 1, 8 and 15, 1899.

45. Duis, Perry R. (1984) The scenic route to the suburbs. *Chicago*, **33**(3), pp. 120–23; Pierce, Bessie Louise (1957) *A History of Chicago*, Vol. 3, *The Rise of the Modern City, 1871–1893*. New York: Alfred Knopf, p. 318; and Karr, Ronald D. (1984) Brookline and the making of an elite suburb. *Chicago History*, **13**(2), p. 44.

46. Duis *op. cit.*, pp. 120–23 is especially helpful, but does not recognize the importance of the Lake Shore Drive project dating to the 1870s; for an appreciation of this relationship see Mayer and Wade, *op. cit.*, p. 74. For local detail: *Evanston Index*, February 22, 1873, May 23 and June 6, 1874, May 22, 1880, August 19, 1882, July 10 and October 13, 1883, August 23 and September 13, 1884, March 7, 1885, January 23, February 27, March 27, and November 13, 1886, August 18 and December 29, 1888, and January 5 and February 2, 1889; *Chicago Tribune*, January 17, 1886 and February 6, 1889; *Chicago News*, May 9 and September 15, 1888; and *Chicago Herald*, August 22, 1888.

47. Smith, *op. cit.*, pp. 246–57 is superb on the 'Gold Coast' and the influence of Bertha Honore Palmer. Also consult: Pierce, *op. cit.*, pp. 60 and 318; Hoyt, *op. cit.*, p. 189; Meeker, *op. cit.*, pp. 142–45; and Mayer and Wade, *op. cit.*, p. 150.

48. Teaford, *op. cit.*, pp. 5f.; Pierce, *op. cit.*, p. 318.

49. On Volney W. Foster consult *Memorial Service in Honor of Volney William Foster* (Evanston, August 28, 1904), *passim*, Sheppard and Hurd *op. cit.*, pp. 503–5 and the obituaries (he died on August 28, 1904) in file marked 'Volney W. Foster' at Evanston Historical Society. Also refer to : Duis, *op. cit.*, p. 121; *Evanston Index*, December 29, 1888 and January 5 and February 2, 1889, *Chicago News*, February 21 and March 4, 1889, *Chicago Tribune*, March 3, 1889, *Chicago Herald*, March 4, 1889, and *Chicago Inter-Ocean*, March 9 and 20, 1889. The following letters in the *Sheridan Road* folder at Evanston Historical Society offer evidence of Foster's behind-the-scene efforts: Letter of 'A Committee of the citizens of Evanston' February 12, 1889; R.W. Patterson to A.W. Foster February 12, 1889; John V. Farwell, Jr. to V.W. Foster, Esq. February 16, 1889, and Arthur Jones on behalf of Marshall Field to Alexander Clark, Esq. March 15, 1889.

50. Elisha Gray to Charles F. Grey, Arthur Orr and Others February 15, 1889 and H.D. Lloyd to V.W. Foster February 18, 1889 (both letters are in the *Sheridan Road* file, Evanston Historical Society). I have added italics to the editorial opinion of the *Evanston Index*, March 2, 1889. Also consult *Chicago Herald*, May 11, 1889.

51. *Evanston Index*, March 9 and 16, August 3, September 28, October 12 and 26, November 16, and December 21, 1889, March 29, 1890, and January 3 and 24, 1891.

52. *Chicago Inter-Ocean*, March 17, 1889; *Evanston Index*, May 25, 1889; and *Chicago Globe*, January 24, 1890.

53. Pierce *op. cit.*, p. 318; Duis, *op. cit.*, p. 121; and *Evanston Index*, May 4, 1889 and January 3 and 24, 1891.

54. J.D. Bingham and V.S. Foster February 15, 1889 *(Sheridan Road* file,

Evanston Historical Society); *Evanston Index*, April 13, 1889, May 4, 1890, October 1, 1898, and December 22, 1900; *Chicago Times*, April 28, 1889; *Highland Park News*, February 4, 1899; *Sheridan Road Newsletter*, December 11, 1899; *Chicago Times-Herald*, December 10, 1900; and *Lake Forester*, March 2, 1901.

55. Schall, Robert 2nd Lt., AUS (1944) The History of Fort Sheridan. Unpublished report prepared for the Clerical School & the Visual Training Aids Section, 1672 Service Unit, p. 12 (available at Highland Park Public Library); Haberkamp, Douglas B. (1980) The History of Fort Sheridan, From Its Beginnings to World War I. Unpublished seminar paper, Trinity College, Deerfield, Illinois, pp. 11f. (I am indebted to the author for allowing me to make use of his work); Duis, *op. cit.*, p. 120; and Ginger, *Altgeld's America, The Lincoln Ideal Versus Changing Realities*, p. 159.

56. *Evanston Index*, January 3, 1903. In Memorial Service in Honor of Volney William Foster, p. 38 is a letter of condolence from General Miles. For a recounting of the Miles-Root dispute over the army's reorganization consult Dawson, Joseph G. III (1984) Miles, Nelson Appleton, in Roger J. Spiller (ed.) *Dictionary of American Military Biography*, 3 vols. Westport: Greenwood Press, 2:pp. 769f. and Jessup, Philip C. (1938) *Elihu Root*, Vol. 1, *1845–1909*. New York: Dodd, Mead and Company, pp. 240–64.

57. Barrett, Paul (1983) *The Automobile and Urban Transit, the Formation of Public Policy in Chicago, 1900–1930*. Philadelphia: Temple University Press, p. 51 is instructive on roadways with restricted usage; Duis, *op. cit.*, p. 122; *Evanston Index*, May 4, 1889, August 20, 1892, August 20 and December 9, 1893, March 30, June 22, 1895.

58. *Evanston Index*, July 6, 13, and 27 and August 3 and 10 1895; and *Sheridan Road Newsletter*, October 5, November 23, December 7, 14, and 21, 1900, and January 4, 11, and 18, 1901.

59. Cutler, *op. cit.*, *passim* is essential for an appreciation of the geographic ties between the two cities. For local detail: *Evanston Index*, August 11, 1894, December 14, 1895, April 18 and August 22, 1896; Duis *op. cit.*, p. 122.

60. *The Sheridan Road and the Beautiful North Shore* (Chicago 1902) n.p.; *Evanston Index*, March 13 and 27 and July 10, 1897, October 1 and 15, 1898, April 22, June 10, and December 16, 1899; *Milwaukee Sentinel* quoted in *Highland Park News*, January 28, 1899; *Sheridan Road Newsletter*, February 11 and December 30, 1899; and *Lake Forester*, November 8 and 29, 1902.

61. George H. Miller to J. Seymour Currey January 4, 1905 in Volney W. Foster File, Evanston Historical Society; *Evanston Index*, July 7 and 14, 1905 and November 6, 1909.

62. Duis, *op. cit.*, p. 123. Caro, Robert A. (1974) *The Power Broker, Robert Moses and the Fall of New York*. New York: Alfred Knopf, *passim* is instructive as to possible ramifications of highway improvement projects in the metropolis; for an excellent case study of a singular planned undertaking consult Weigold, Marilyn E. (1980) Pioneering in parks and parkways: Westchester County, New York, 1895–1945. *Essays in Public Works History*, No. 9, especially pp. 1–10.

63. Another key illustration of the strength of local autonomy during the 1890s involved the advent of the electrified street railway along the North Shore. Despite popularity elsewhere, this innovation met with firm opposition. Although the first tracks for a projected Waukegan-to-Evanston line were built in the former city in 1891, not until August 1899 was the connection completed. The circumstances contributing to the protracted delay resembled the concurrent opposition to Sheridan Road and also reflected the opposition to electrified tract in long-established suburbs elsewhere: concern over preserving local autonomy, fear of encroachment by people and corporations deemed *foreign* because of their *urban* addresses as well as corporate ties, and uncertainty as to how this latest advance in transport technology would affect the landscape. Schwartz, Joel (1977) Suburban progressivism in the 1890s: the policy of containment in Orange, East Orange, and Montclair, in Schwartz, Joel and Prosser, Daniel (eds.) *Cities of the Garden State: Essays in the Urban and Suburban History of New Jersey.* Dubuque: Kendall-Hunt, pp. 53–70 reports on similar opposition; contrast with the effects of electric traction companies in metropolitan Boston as discussed in Warner, *op. cit.*, p. 160.

64. *Evanston Index*, December 18, 1897 and October 21 and 28, 1899; *Highland Park News*, May 27, July 8, September 2, 1898; *Sheridan Road Newsletter*, February 25, March 4, April 8 and 22, October 14, 21 and 28, November 4 and December 23, 1899; *Lake Forester*, October 28, 1899; and *North Shore Sanitary Association Bulletin*, October 31, 1910, pp. 1–35 (available at Chicago Historical Society).

65. Jackson, John Brinckerhoff (1984) *Toward a Vernacular Landscape.* New Haven: Yale University Press, p. 15. My thinking about how residents of the North Shore thought about their own environs has been influenced by Darnton, Robert (1984) *The Great Cat Massacre and other Episodes in French Cultural History.* New York: Basic Books, pp. 3–7 and Warner, Sam Bass Jr. (1983) The management of multiple urban images, in Fraser and Sutcliffe, *op. cit.*, pp. 383–94, *must* reading for historians engaged in studying cultural phenomenon.

66. Muller, Peter O. (1981) *Contemporary Suburban America.* Englewood Cliffs: Prentice-Hall, p. 30.

Chapter Four

Frederick Law Olmsted, the Placemaker

DANA F. WHITE

With the nationwide celebration in 1972 of the 150th anniversary of his birth, Frederick Law Olmsted joined the pantheon of American heroes. Since these sesquicentennial festivities, there has been a remarkable outpouring of Olmstediana: the publication of the initial three (of a projected twelve) volumes of *The Papers of Frederick Law Olmsted*;[1] one major, as well as several specialized biographies;[2] regionalized studies of his work in Atlanta, Boston, Buffalo, Chicago, New York City, and the Commonwealth of Massachusetts;[3] the acquisition by the National Park Service of his home and offices at Brookline, Massachusetts;[4] a National Endowment for the Arts 'Greening of Cities' project to document the landscape resources of central city parks and to develop appropriate plans for their revitalization;[5] the passage by the U.S. House of Representatives of the 'Olmsted Heritage Landscapes Act';[6] and the establishment of a National Association for Olmsted Parks (N.A.O.P.).[7]

At the fourth (but first 'international') convocation of N.A.O.P., Grady Clay, long-time editor of *Landscape Architecture*, put all these achievements and events in context when, in his keynote address, he offered the 'New Olmsted Movement' that requisite of 'all great religions . . . a Code of Conduct, a catechism, a set of commandments about how one must act . . . not only among one's fellow creatures, but also how one must act in Holy Places'. Clay's scriptural mandate reads, in part:

> Go ye among the multitudes and preach this,
> the Way of the Great Designer, so that all may
> come and share his handiwork forevermore.
>
> Impose not thy foreign will upon this place.

Figure 1. Frederick Law Olmsted, circa 1890s. (*Source*: National Park Service, Frederick Law Olmsted National Historic Site)

Seek ye its Spirit and all else will follow . . . .
　Make no undue noises unto the high heavens.
Nor shall ye push and shove thy neighbor between
a rock and a hard place. Carry thyself gently
and there shall be space for all . . . .
　Do this in remembrance of the great place-maker,
whose firm hand can make us free to enjoy his places
forever.[8]

To many of the assembled Olmstedians, Clay's gentle satire smacked of the sacrilegious. In their eyes, Olmsted stood as the nonpareil among designers of the built environment – eclipsing even a Roebling, Richardson, Burnham, or Wright. Surely, to his devotees, FLO seemed above criticism.

OLMSTED IN THE 1920s: PRAISE AND CRITICISM

So, too, it must have seemed to Theodora Kimball when, in 1922, she proclaimed: 'This year marks the centennial of the birth of Frederick Law Olmsted, the great landscape architect, one of the first exponents of our modern city planning in America'.[9] To celebrate the occasion, Kimball and Frederick Law Olmsted, Jr. announced *Forty Years of Landscape Architecture: Being the Professional Papers of Frederick Law Olmsted, Sr.*, and they projected a lengthy series covering his writings and design efforts in 'public parks and park systems, town plans, land subdivisions, grounds for public and semi-public buildings, private estates, and so on'.[10] 'So on', it turned out, meant but two volumes – a slim anthology of his early writings for 1922 and a sizable collection about Central Park in 1928. Indeed, while the sesquicentennial celebration of 1972 would boast a flood of Olmstediana in its wake, the morbid (rather than the aquatic) connotation of wake better described the afterflow of the centenary. Two modest works of note appeared soon after 1922, only one of them concerned with Olmsted the place-maker.[11]

Under the banner 'Landscape Design' for the fledgling *American Mercury* in 1925, Elbert Peets asked 'why must Central Park be an amalgam of a Herefordshire sheepwalk and the location for a movie version of "Hiawatha"? We know the answer: Central Park is Nature and Nature is man's Great Solace, the only sure antidote to hurdy-gurdies, pool-rooms, factories, tenements, and all the other vicious influences of a great city'. According to whom, Peets asked rhetorically? 'Such Eighteenth Century scientists as Thomson and Cowper discovered this quality', he answered, 'and the sociologically enlightened Americans of the '50s confirmed their researches'.

Prominent among the latter, Peets noted, was 'F.L. Olmsted, co-designer, with Calvert Vaux, of Central Park'.[12] From this point on in Peets's assault, Vaux's name disappears, while FLO stands as solitary target.

> Olmsted's claim that only his true counterfeit of nature's bosom could compensate the city dweller for the nervous irritations that harrass him is only another proof that love will find a reason. He knew and loved the style he worked in. He identified it with nature, the holy word of his time, and so made of it a religion.[13]

Thus, in his foray against 'the fog of inherited sentiment through which we now look at the prettiness of Central Park'[14] did Elbert Peets anticipate Grady Clay's elevation of the Olmsted Movement from mere matters of design to the higher concerns of theology.

In a second contribution to the *Mercury*, Peets renewed his attack. His approach remained the same: heavy frontal assault, extravagant wording, an iconoclastic tone – all typical of editor H.L. Mencken's 'compound of prejudices, hyperbole, and a kind of free-wheeling diction just this side of rant' that marked 'Menckenism' and 'Menckenese'.[15] (In Mencken's editorial universe, then, the bark might well supersede the bite.) At the same time, Peets was provided space to expand upon his initial criticisms: whereas his first piece had been sandwiched in 'The Arts and Sciences' department between notes about Latin American culture and history and race, his second was a full-fledged article. Its heightened visibility was significant on two counts, one contemporary, the other historical. First, because of its iconoclastic departure from the polite norms of contemporary magazine editing, the *American Mercury* was one of the most discussed journals of opinion during the 1920s: publication in its pages guaranteeed attention in intellectual circles. Then, too, since it was the only extended treatment of Olmsted and his legacy between Mariana Griswold van Rensselaer's 1893 panegyric in the *Century* and Lewis Mumford's 1931 laudatory portrait in *The Brown Decades*,[16] this article maintains a singular place historiographically: it marked a clear break between two generations of like-minded Olmsted scholarship and stood as a landmark in design criticism.[17] Thematically, it continued the frontal assault; stylistically, it retained the divine metaphor as signalled in its title 'The Landscape Priesthood'.[18]

When Olmsted relocated his practice from New York City to Brookline during the 1880s 'chance', according to Peets, presented 'the priests of the inner temple a firm hold on the training of the novices'. Since one of these tyros was Charles Eliot, the son of the incumbent president of Harvard University, it was only 'natural' when 'Harvard began instruction in landscape architecture, . . . that the new department should become practically a branch of the Olmsted office'. What is more, because most of its students were graduates not of Ivy League schools but 'of State universities where under-graduate instruction in horticulture and ornamental gardening is given' and were returned 'to their old schools, or to others, as instructors, on the recommendation of the Harvard faculty', the reach of 'old Olmsted men' extended nationwide:

> This interchange of personnel produces a strong spiritual connection between the Olmsted-Harvard tradition and hundreds of men and women who go from the State universities with a smattering of garden design, enough to get them jobs as draftsmen, or with a general impression to guide them in forming the settings of their own homes or as members of city-beautiful committees.[19]

Beyond the academy stood the professional organization, the American Society of Landscape Architects. Membership in this body, Peets continued, 'is essential to respectable standing – and helps get jobs . . . Every royal academy has its chorus of ancients. In the A.S.L.A. it is the Boston crowd. Olmsted men are preponderant in the society, if not numerically in the majority'.[20] Their mission, all in concert – professional colleagues, teachers, students – was to propagate 'the Logos incarnated in Olmsted'.[21]

With his own heretical preachments, Elbert Peets sought to challenge this Word Incarnate, based as it was upon what fellow *Mercury* contributor Harry Elmer Barnes ridiculed as 'The Drool Method in History'. 'With all its admitted defects', Barnes offered in its place a Menckenian 'Sneer Method', which Peets applied avidly to FLO.[22] By the very overstatement of his case, he posed essential questions about style, vision, and influence in the Olmsted tradition – questions which remain central to comprehending the Olmsted spirit and its legacy.

THE ROMANTIC TRADITION IN LANDSCAPE DESIGN

That Frederick Law Olmsted was committed to what Elbert Peets identified as 'the English landscape style of gardening' cannot be challenged.[23] This commitment took root during FLO's early childhood on family trips through New England and Upstate New York – 'tours', Olmsted later described them, 'in search of the picturesque'.[24] It blossomed during his first visit to England.

When he set sail for Liverpool on April 30, 1850 the 28-year-old Olmsted was also setting out on a career search that would extend into the mid-1860s. Before 1850, his record was unremarkable: spotty formal schooling, a brief clerkship in the dry-goods business, a venture before the mast to the Orient, and three years of scientific (or gentlemanly) farming – first in Connecticut, then in New York. After 1850, his achievements as author, editor, administrator, designer, manager, and planner were exceptional and wide-ranging. Olmsted's public life, which began with this English trip, found first expression in his 1852 *Walks and Talks of an American Farmer in England*.[25]

As he relates in *Walks and Talks*, Olmsted's first visit to the new public park in the Liverpool suburb of Birkenhead convinced him of the immense value of this civic amenity. 'Five minutes of admiration, and a few more spent in studying the manner in which art had been employed to obtain from nature so much beauty, and I was ready to admit', the patriotic Olmsted confessed grudgingly, 'that in democratic America there was nothing to be thought of as comparable with this People's Garden'.[26] Soon after, venturing beyond the city limits, Olmsted enthused over his initial encounter with rural England: 'There we were right in the midst of it! The country – and such a country! – green, dripping, glistening, gorgeous! We stood dumbstricken by its loveliness . . . '[27] (figure 2). Farther along, inspired by a visit to the Marquis of Westminster's Estate at Eaton Hall, Olmsted penned his most memorable prose on landscape design and the designer:

> What artist so noble, has often been my thought, as he, who with far-reaching conception of beauty and designing power, sketches the outline, writes the colours, and directs the shadows of a picture so great that Nature shall be employed upon it for generations, before the work he has arranged for her shall realize his intentions.[28]

Certainly, his aesthetic encounters with the English landscape, so engagingly recounted in *Walks and Talks*, both supported Olmsted's already-established tastes and influenced his later choice of design styles. Two stylistic elements, which lie squarely within the English tradition of landscape gardening, became central to his work: the Pastoral or Beautiful, 'the basic mode of his park designs'; and the Picturesque, the style he employed for emphasizing the 'mystery and Bounteousness' of nature.[29] These design elements describe his preferred style, much as would the terms Romanesque, Neoclassical, International, or Postmodern characterize the stylistic approach of an architect. The preferred style, nonetheless, was more manner than method: rather than being wedded irrevocably to either Pastoral or Picturesque, FLO was ever ready to cut himself free from their bounds whenever site or situation required him to do so.

When he judged the Pastoral mode inappropriate for a site, Olmsted not only refused to recommend it, but urged strongly against its consideration. Thus, as early as 1866, in a proposal for a San Francisco park, his design not only disavowed Eastern and English models, but also demonstrated a marked sensitivity for the singular

Figure 2. Frontispiece to Volume I of *Walks and Talks of an American Farmer in England* (New York, 1852). (Untitled sketch by Olmsted, redrawn by Marryat Field)

topography of that city and the potential for indigenous trees, shrubs, and grasses. Similarly, as late as 1886, upon being commissioned by California Senator Leland Stanford to set out a new campus in the San Jose Valley, Olmsted's plan not only argued against the suitability of his client's conception of a tree-lined quad in the arid West, but also worked to 'educate' Stanford about the challenge of creating a truly regional university setting.[30] Finally, from his initial proposal for Chicago's South Park in 1870 through his plans for the World's Columbian Exposition of 1893, Olmsted demonstrated a like sensitivity for that city's lake site and prairie environment.[31] Again, Olmsted selected the style to suit the situation.

Even when his preferred style seemed to dominate the scene, appearance was not necessarily an end in itself. Thus, while exquisitely blending the Picturesque with the Pastoral, along shaded curvilinear side roads winding gracefully into a sweeping central parkway bordered by a sequence of small parks, Olmsted's Druid Hills (figure 3) in Atlanta was an exercise in practicality. Situated along the verdant southern Piedmont, where lush forests provided both amenity and natural screening, and laid out astride an established transportation corridor that promised easy access for commuters,

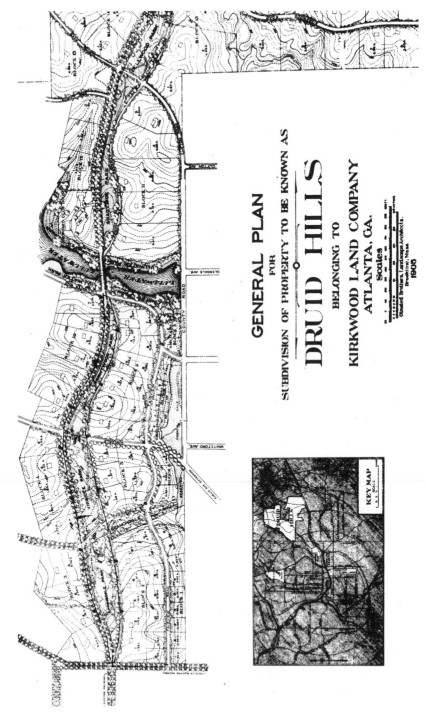

Figure 3. Olmsted Brothers Plan for Druid Hills, Atlanta, Georgia; based upon preliminary concepts for a plan by Frederick Law Olmsted, Sr., c. 1895. (*Source:* National Park Service, Frederick Law Olmsted National Historic Site)

Druid Hills is an innovative, brilliantly-conceived linear suburb.[32] As such, it illustrates neatly the potential for variation within Olmsted's use of the Romantic tradition in landscape design.

FROM PARK SITES TO CITYWIDE SYSTEMS

John Higham's concept of 'boundlessness' as applied to early nineteenth century America could just as readily have been coined to describe the Olmsted vision.[33] Linking FLO with such contemporary innovators as Paxton, Roebling and Eiffel, architectural historian James Marston Fitch has suggested that their era produced 'a special type of personality'.

> [It included] a kind of synoptic intuition, a capacity to perceive and absorb new needs almost osmotically, even before they had been coherently formulated by society at large. And the times demanded the courage, if not that of ignorance then at least that of innocence, to tackle assignments of unprecedented size and complexity.[34]

To Olmsted, even 'assignments of unprecedented size and complexity' could prove limiting. Consistently, he would extend the boundaries of an already ambitious project to an extent inconceivable to his contemporaries by redefining its scope.

As with his preferred style, Olmsted's approach to planning may be traced to his first English trip. With the critical success of *Walks and Talks*, FLO gained admission to what he called the 'literary republic', where he would reside from the end of 1852 through mid-1857. His major effort during these years was the notably-ambitious trilogy, 'Our Slave States', later condensed into *The Cotton Kingdom*, which Lawrence N. Powell has described recently as being 'without equal among the five hundred or so books and pamphlets written by visitors to the South in the three and a half decades preceding the Civil War . . .'

> Where other travelers spent only one or two months in the region, Olmsted spent fourteen months, spread over two separate trips. Where previous visitors hewed closely to established seaboard routes, traveling by boat, train, or coach, Olmsted often departed from the major thoroughfares, roughing it on horseback into the back country and venturing westward as far as Texas . . . He claimed to have talked with five hundred southern white men, and he probably did. He seems to have missed nothing.[35]

Nevertheless, all this was still not enough for Olmsted; in fact, only the Panic of 1857, which ended his career in publishing, turned him from considering trips to – for books about – Kansas, Utah, and Jamaica.[36] His youthful ambition, energy, and vision seemed limitless.

From the literary republic, Olmsted carried these same qualities into his next career – that of management. When he was appointed

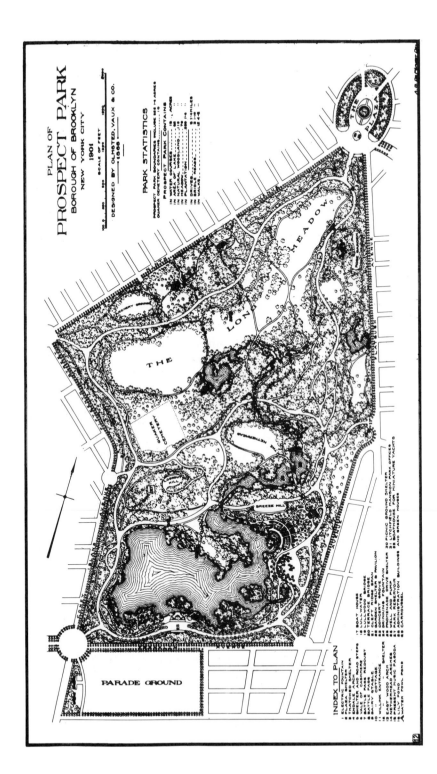

Figure 4. Plan of Prospect Park. (*Source:* National Park Service, Frederick Law Olmsted National Historic Site)

'Superintendent of the Central Park' in 1857, prior to his design efforts there, FLO undertook the day-to-day supervision of as many as 3,800 labourers.[37] Then, with the outbreak of the Civil War in 1861, as Secretary General of the newly-organized United States Sanitary Commission (forerunner to the American Red Cross), Olmsted directed the relief effort for Union forces. Finally, from 1863 to 1865, in his last career shift before settling into the profession of landscape architecture in 1866, FLO managed for an Eastern syndicate the Mariposa Estate, some 70 square miles of mining land in California. His career pattern between 1857 and 1865 enabled him to supplement the boundless vision of a social critic/author with the nuts-and-bolts perspective of a manager. It represented a singular range of experience; in the process, FLO advanced from writing about what should be, to recognizing what could be, to getting it done.

As landscape architect, Olmsted's first commission, in partnership with Calvert Vaux, was the 1858 Greensward Plan for Central Park. Their second major project, an 1866 design for Prospect Park in Brooklyn (figure 4), represented a quantum leap in planning. Whereas their effort in Manhattan had been a relatively straightforward park design, their Brooklyn venture extended beyond circumscribed property limits to include (by 1868) not only park entrances, which they had provided for Central Park, but also roadway approaches. To assure a parklike ambiance for their roads, Olmsted and Vaux conceived of the 'park-way': their boulevard-picturesque. At its finest, the parkway transcended convenience to achieve amenity. The planning of the Chicago suburb of Riverside (figure 5), a concurrent commission during 1868–69, advanced them still another step beyond the park – and city – into the metropolitan hinterland. With the separate pieces set out, it remained only to fit them together – a planning puzzle readily solved by theorist-manager Frederick Law Olmsted.

As early as 1870, Lewis Mumford has pointed out, 'less than twenty years after the notion of a public landscape park had been introduced in this country, Olmsted had imaginatively grasped and defined all the related elements in a full park programme [for] . . . comprehensive city development'.[38] FLO linked together these related elements – the central park, parkway, satellite suburb – in a notable address on 'Public Parks and the Enlargement of Towns' before the American Social Science Association, meeting in Boston on February 25, 1870.[39] According to his scheme of things, a major park – such as Prospect Park – could provide a focus for development: one 'fairly well managed', Olmsted promised, '. . . will surely become a new centre of that town'. Emanating from the park, 'new trunk lines of communication between it and the distant parts of the town existing and

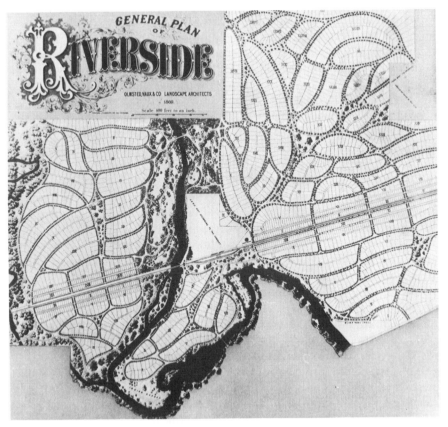

Figure 5. General plan of Riverside. (*Source*: National Park Service, Frederick Law Olmsted National Historic Site)

forecasted' would provide corridors for controlled growth. These action paths, whether 'narrow informal elongations of the park' or, as in Brooklyn, 'formal Park-ways', would lead ultimately to a planned community such as Riverside or, as Olmsted called it, the 'open town suburb'.[40] His 'full park programme' for 'comprehensive city development' anticipated by a generation the Anglo-American Garden City/ New Towns movement;[41] indeed, the sketch maps from Ebenezer Howards's *Garden Cities for To-Morrow*, with a few parkways pencilled in, could well have illustrated 'Public Parks and the Enlargement of Towns'.

Although he never had the opportunity to carry out his ambitiously-conceived park/parkway/suburb scheme, Olmsted did manage to complete comprehensive plans based on the first two of the three related elements. Between 1868 and 1876, FLO provided Buffalo

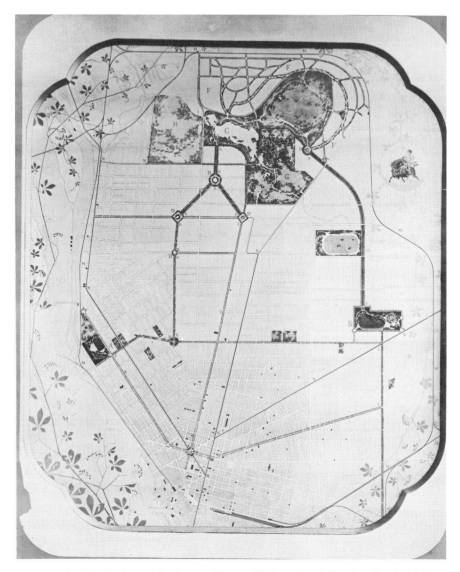

Figure 6. Buffalo Parks and Parkways. (*Source*: National Park Service, Frederick Law Olmsted National Historic Site)

with the 350-acre Delaware Park ('C' in figure 6); the grounds for the Buffalo State Hospital ('H'), in collaboration with H.H. Richardson, on the park's western border; the 32-acre Front ('A'), to the city's lower west side; and the 56-acre Parade ('B'), on the east side. And although it had been laid out years before his arrival in the city, Olmsted included the rural cemetry of Forest Lawn (*c.* 1850: 'G') in his

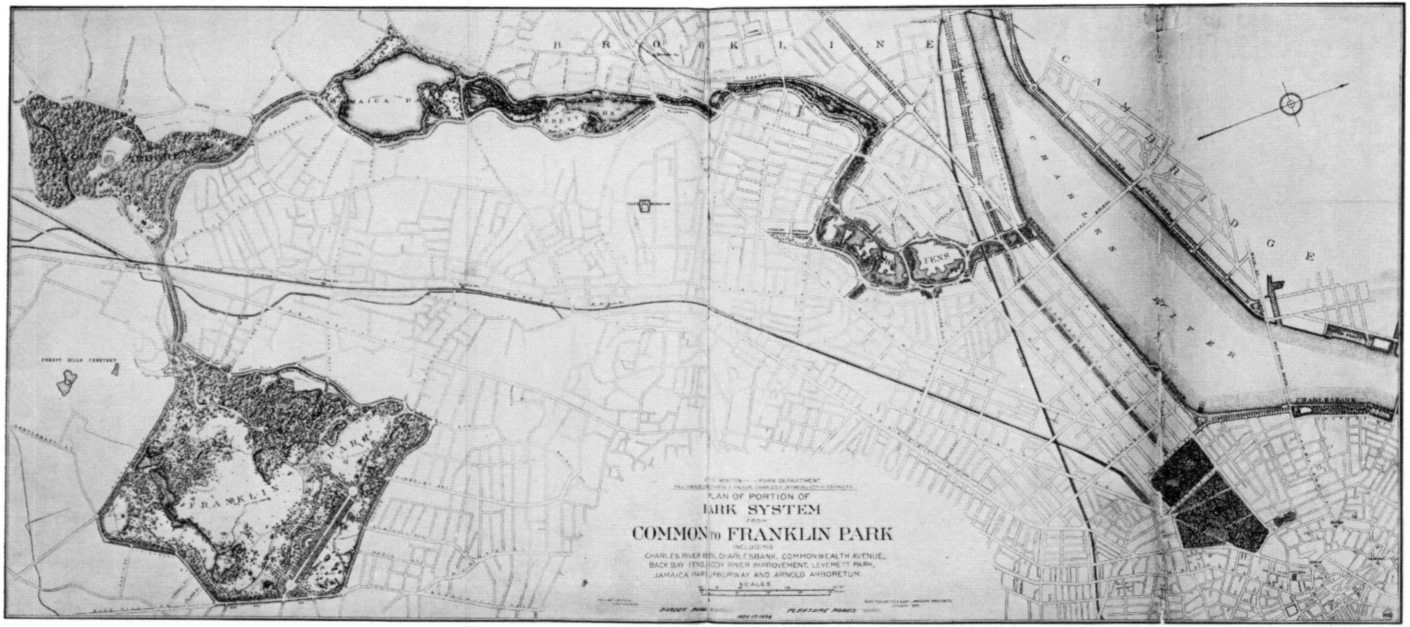

Figure 7. Boston Park System. (*Source*: National Park Service, Frederick Law Olmsted National Historic Site)

comprehensive scheme. All of these he linked together, as a recent analysis demonstrates, with an interrelated 'series of wide, shaded parkways and streets that connected the Park, Front, and Parade with each other and with the rest of the city', thereby serving 'the need for open space of the neighborhoods through which they passed'.[42] For Olmsted, the desired end was experiential:

> Thus, at no great distance from any point of the town, a pleasure ground will have been provided for, suitable for a short stroll, for a playground for children and an airing ground for invalids, and a route of access to the large common park of the whole city, of such a character that most of the steps on the way to it would be taken in the midst of a scene of sylvan beauty, and with the sounds and sights of the ordinary town business, if not wholly shut out, removed to some distance and placed in obscurity. the way itself would thus be more park-like than town-like.[43]

'By making nature urbane' through such devices, Mumford sums up, Olmsted 'naturalized the city'.[44]

Between 1878 and 1895, FLO created for Boston (figure 7) a still more extensive system of related open spaces encompassing over 2,000 acres. Five separate parks (Back Bay Fens, Muddy River Improvement, Jamaica Park, Arnold Arboretum, and Franklin Park) and their connecting parkways (Fenway, Riverway, Jamaicaway, and Arborway) graced the city with its famed 'emerald necklace'.[45] Between 1869 and 1878, numerous proposals had been put forth for such a system, not a one of them accomplished.[46] That Olmsted not only conceived a coherent plan for a unified Boston park system, but that he also translated his conception into reality attests to his development from writing about what should be, to recognizing what could be, to getting it done. Given the scale at which he operated, it is little wonder, as landscape architect Bruce Kelly has observed, that 'Olmsted has become a generic term, symbolizing those teams of men whom he supervised and the work which he so ably administered'.[47]

A Representative Man for his Times

In reporting his death during 1903, *The Nation* remarked that Olmsted 'had outlived not only his powers, but the friends of his early manhood'. That influential weekly, which he helped to create and sustain, described its co-founder as a man whose 'name has been actively perpetuated in the profession of landscape gardening and architecture, which . . . he brought to an unsurpassed pitch of achievement and propaganda'.[48] For *The Nation* in 1903, 'propaganda' held none of the negative connotations later attached to it; instead, the term derived from that Papal body instituted during the seventeenth century, which held jurisdiction over missionary territories: the *Congregatio de propaganda fide*. Once again, with his 'propagation of the faith', the theological metaphor attaches itself to Frederick Law Olmsted.

Propagating the Faith well describes FLO's several careers. 'The aesthetically suggestible traveller' like the Olmsted of *Walks and Talks*, literary historian Christopher Mulvey has suggested recently, was among 'the active creators of a new mode of perception' based on 'picturesque principles'.[49] The investigative reporter (in modern parlance) like the Olmsted of *The Cotton Kingdom* both laid bare a pernicious system and helped demarcate more sharply the lines between South and North. The modern manager like the Olmsted of the Sanitary Commission and of Mariposa Mining practised advanced administrative techniques, lobbied for a planned reconstruction of the Union, and promoted the sanitary ideal. The innovative editor like the Olmsted of *Putnam's Monthly Magazine* (1855–56) and *The Nation* (1865–66) took part in the transformation of the literary republic into a communications empire. Thus, even before entering his chosen profession of landscape architecture in 1866, Olmsted had established precedence in the major movements of his day: the creation of a new aesthetic, the abolition of slavery, the preservation of the Union, the advancement of public administration, the metamorphosis of periodical publishing, and the introduction of sanitary science into American life.[50] Then, too, there was the New York park – the Central Park, as contemporaries called it: the initial and premier example of its kind; a demonstration project for design and administration of national, even international significance; a public enterprise of unprecedented proportions; a model for all urban America.[51] Informed contemporaries who might not have known the Olmsted of *The Cotton Kingdom* or the Olmsted of the Sanitary Commission would certainly have heard of the Olmsted of *the* Central Park.

Through his vigorous involvement in the major movements of the age, Olmsted developed remarkable networks of association. Such famous and quasi-familiar names as Charles Francis Adams, Charles Loring Brace, William Cullen Bryant, George William Curtis, Edward Everett Hale, Richard Morris Hunt, William Le Baron Jenney, Charles Eliot Norton, Robert Treat Paine, Augustus Saint Gaudens, and numerous others – reformers, authors, designers, scholars – crowd the index of his biography to the point that the reader often feels that he is sampling the *Dictionary of American Biography* or *Who was Who in America*.[52] How Olmsted exploited his relationships with this influential gentry – these triple-tagged friends, associates, clients – in his efforts to shape American cities may be seen, once again, both early and late in his career.

In Buffalo, where he completed his first comprehensive park-parkway system between 1868 and 1876 and where his firm consulted during the 1880s and 1890s, FLO worked closely with that municipality's civic elite through a semi-autonomous Park Board. An analysis of the late nineteenth-century composition of that body by Leonard H. Gerson, who has made the most detailed study of the agency, revealed 'that more than two-thirds of the identifiable commissioners were from the city's elite and 46 per cent of the total number of commissioners were members of the exclusive, upper class Buffalo Club'.[53] As opposition to park expenditures mounted, particularly within the eastside German community where five out of seven wards often voted against Park Board measures, petitioners to the Common Council urged on October 11, 1869 that the park-parkway system was 'all out of proportion to the size, wealth, and needs of this city, either present and [sic] prospective', and suggested that municipal funds might better be spent on buildings, bridges, and public utilities rather than on such 'a questionable luxury'. Similarly, toward the close of 1872, another group of petitioners from the same side of town, requesting street-paving monies, addressed the Council: '. . . whereas the city has been induced to purchase a large tract of land for park purposes, *mostly at the instigation and seemingly for this special benefit, gratification and pleasure of the wealthy of our community*', its own needs demanded equal attention.[54] The validity of the specific claims of each set of petitioners is not at issue here, but their perception that a highly-visible elite seemed to exercise disproportionate power is. That elite group had introduced Olmsted to Buffalo, afforded him the support of the Park Board that it dominated, and retained his firm to plan for its own extensive land holdings – some of them in close proximity to the main park. Thus, as the city approached financial crisis in 1877, at which point the municipal debt had risen from $882,500 in 1870 to $7,139,291 in 1876, the open space system and its champions became losers in the austerity programme that followed, and the official Olmsted influence in Buffalo diminished.[55]

In Boston, where he crafted that city's 'emerald necklace' between 1878 and 1895 and where he relocated his firm in 1883, FLO found his ideal planning milieu. There, under the leadership of 'a gentlemanly cosmopolitan elite', historian Geoffrey Blodgett has argued, Olmsted 'discovered a ninteenth-century political community which had not yet been torn apart by factional strife, class resentment, or ethnic rancor' – a municipality totally unlike the Tammany-dominated New York from which he had been all-but evicted by boss Honest John Kelly. In Boston, his park system 'developed in a pattern of fruitful interaction among wealthy Back Bay and suburban landowners, museums, colleges, and other cultural institutions which migrated to the edges of his park chain'.[56] There, Olmsted transformed what for a decade had been 'an essentially one-man office' into 'a full-scale professional firm, operating from . . . his new home in Brookline'. In his office at Fairsted, Cynthia Zaitzevsky explains in the fullest account yet of Olmsted's professional procedures, 'he developed a system of education and apprenticeship that was unique among practitioners of landscape design'.[57] From Fairsted would emerge such founding members of the 'landscape priesthood' as FLO's own son and namesake; the son and namesake of Charles Eliot, then president of Harvard; and Henry Sargent Codman, heir on both sides of his family to a position in Boston's gentlemanly elite. Eventually, 'graduates' of the Brookline firm would exert what Peets charged was disproportionate influence upon Landscape Architecture at Harvard and, more widely, the American Society of Landscape Architects; ultimately, some of them would enter planning at Harvard and exercise considerable influence in the nascent American Institute of Planners; unquestionably, their role in shaping urban America was substantial.[58] For the Fairsted alumni, as for their fathers and uncles before them, their students and associates after, Frederick Law Olmsted was indeed a force, one of Emerson's 'Representative Men': '. . . persons who, in their character and actions, answer questions which I have not skill to put'.[59]

THE RECENT OLMSTED REVIVAL

At the height of the Olmsted Sesquicentennial celebrations, late in 1972 *Landscape Architecture* published a sweeping but penetrating 'Report on the Profession of Landscape Architecture'. Written by Olmsted scholar Albert Fein, it condensed the conclusions of a larger three-year 'Study of the Profession', funded by the Ford Foundation and the ASLA, under Fein's direction. Its portrait of the profession was not a pretty one. Among its findings: since 'the profession was more craft oriented then theoretical in its outlook', its practitioners tended to isolate themselves from potential colleagues in planning and the applied social sciences. 'When one looks at the relative incomes among the design professions – architecture, city planning, and engineering – it becomes clear . . . that landscape architects average lower salaries' and, consequently, their 'job status . . . is low'. Since 'this profession continues to draw its membership and students from the rural areas and small towns of America' and because 'of the location of the overwhelming majority of schools of landscape architecture' in such areas, the profession suffered from 'the absence of a more representative [i.e., urban] membership'. What is more the 'Report' noted that despite its celebrated heritage which could be traced back to Olmsted, his colleagues, their successors, and 'such contemporaries as Lawrence Halprin, Ian McHarg, Garrett Eckbo, Hideo Sasaki, John O. Simonds, Thomas Church and others', it was 'not accepted by this profession' that it was 'part of a historical stream'. 'Without an adequate appreciation of history', the Report laments, 'it is difficult to understand how members of any profession can view themselves as part of a humane and scientific discipline'.[60] The bottom line: 'It is clear, therefore, that landscape architecture is probably confronted with the most formidable of challenges it has ever encountered during its 73-year history as a formal profession'.[61] Thus in 1972, as Frederick Law Olmsted's reputation was taking off, his profession's seemed to be hitting bottom.[62]

That his profession would some day approach so parlous a state as that spelled out in the 1972 Report would not entirely have surprised the senior Olmsted as he approached retirement in 1895. Throughout the 1890s, he had fretted over the prospects of his firm and the future of his profession. Thus FLO advised his stepson: 'You should above all things aim to keep up and advance the reputation of the House. Better make little money and live low for a while than fail in that'. Yet, at other times, he could boast of the 'grand professional post-graduate school' operating within the firm and confess that: 'My office is much better equipped and has more momentum than ever before'.[63] The Olmsted Brothers (figure 8), recent research indicates, maintained and even accelerated that momentum.[64] In 1903 and 1904, for example, the firm was active on both coasts, producing comprehensive park plans for Baltimore, Portland, and Seattle, which were comparable in scope to the earlier Buffalo and Boston efforts.[65] 'The reputation of the House', which had so concerned FLO, soared: the firm readily survived its founder; so, too, did the profession, but not without problems. Albeit that the sons identified the Olmsted name with the professionalization of landscape architecture by assuming leadership roles in both the new ASLA and the degree programme at Harvard, they did so reluctantly.[66] Perhaps they were sceptical that the individualized 'grand professional postgraduate school' ambience at Brookline could be institutionalized in the academy, nevermind carried forward in a national association. Perhaps they anticipated increasing competition from other rising professionals who also sought to shape the environment – architects, engineers, housers, managers, planners, recreation directors, specialists of one kind or another. Whatever their expectations, landscape architects faced mounting challenges: their City Picturesque would be transformed

Figure 8. Upper Drafting Room, Olmsted Brothers, Brookline, Mass., April 1930. (*Source*: National Park Service, Frederick Law Olmsted National Historic Site)

radically over succeeding generations into a City Beautiful, a City Efficient, an Exploding Metropolis, a Megalopolis. With such change, over so long a period, the questions remain: Why, given the recent problems of the profession, the revival of interest in its founder? Why, with the failure of the Centennial, the success of the Sesquicentennial? What, granted the totally-different conditions now confronting the profession, can today's planners draw from the Olmsted legacy?

Since what Grady Clay christened the 'New Olmsted Movement' is alive, rather than a fact of history, any answers to these questions must be speculative and thus tentative. Still, it is clear that the Olmsted revival is no mere resurgence of interest in landscape architecture or, for that matter, comprehensive planning. Each profession may lay claim to him, but he transcends both. While it is true that he provided landscape architects and their clients a national style with his coherent, yet reasonably-flexible adaptations of the Pastoral and Picturesque design modes and offered planners a method for advancing from site to system FLO provides his new constituency with something else – himself.

The 1972 Sesquicentennial celebrations promoted Frederick Law Olmsted as a potential standard-bearer for a variety of mutually-supportive, if not always interrelated, popular causes – historic preservation, the back to the city movement, neighbourhood revitalization, and environmentalism. In New York, for example, five to ten thousand civic activists staged a 'happening' in Central Park to mark both FLO's 150th birthday (April 26) and the third Earth Day (April 22). Singing 'Happy Birthday . . . happy Earth-Day . . . to Olmsted' as they shared a 24 by 8 foot cake (made of green cheese) in the shape of Central Park, the assembled enthusiasts were celebrating the park, its adjacent neighbourhoods, a rejuvenated downtown, and what Olmsted's generation hailed as Nature.[67]

For all their good spirits that day – there were similar happenings in other places, then and since – the Central Park celebrants of the Olmsted ideal were also protesting a century-long succession of conflicting urban visions: the neoclassical City Beautiful, the stream-lined City Efficient, the sanitized City Renewed, the automotive Spread City. Theirs were voices echoing such disparate protests against the modern metropolitan region as those of Lewis Mumford, Clarence Stein, and others in the Regional Planning Association of America during the 1920s and 1930s; William Whyte, Jane Jacobs, and other *Fortune* contributors during the 1950s; and numerous commentators on the 'urban crisis' during the 1960s.[68] In the fifty years between the 100th and 150th anniversary of FLO's birth then, both a built reality based upon conflicting urban visions and a vast body of critical literature – professional and popular – were in place. All that remained was identifying a central figure, one of Emerson's represen-tative men, to rally around. Thus did the man and the moment meet; whereas in 1922 Olmsted seemed only of antiquarian interest, in 1972 he achieved near-mythic stature.

For the planning professional today, the Olmsted legacy is likely to prove more inspirational than practical. A gifted amateur who was instrumental in creating his own profession, FLO functioned in an urban America seemingly without bounds, certainly with minimal constraints – procedural, bureaucratic, legal. That world and the interlocking networks of association that he exploited so effectively are no more, nor will they return; thus, the historical Olmsted, while a figure of interest, can be no role model. But what of the mythic Olmsted? What does he say to a new constituency? What can planning professionals learn from his message?

To begin with, while the man himself seems larger than life, his works are markedly human scale. Then, too, although he manipulated his landscapes tirelessly, his creations appear to be natural, pristine, eternal. Next, despite an occasional fussiness in his designs, overall they seem expressions of a no-nonsense, back-to-basics Yankee commonsense. And finally, when his works and words are joined, FLO's essential comprehension of the land and those who inhabit it, work it, and are influenced by it are made manifest. It is this wisdom, rather than any mere knowledge, that is essential to the

Olmsted spirit: a wisdom earned by a man daring, seeking, experiencing, feeling, and living – one of Emerson's representative men, a man for his time and ours.

NOTES

1. The first three volumes of *The Papers*, all published by the Johns Hopkins University Press, are: McLaughlin, Charles C. and Beveridge, Charles E. (eds.) (1977) *The Formative Years, 1822–1852*, Volume I; Beveridge and McLaughlin (eds.) (1981) *Slavery and the South, 1852–1857*, Volume II; Beveridge and Schuyler, David (eds.) (1983) *Creating Central Park, 1857–1861*, Volume III.

2. Although a half-dozen biographies have been published over the past decade, Roper, Laura Wood (1973) *FLO: A Biography of Frederick Law Olmsted*. Baltimore: Johns Hopkins University Press, is – and is likely to remain – the standard source on his life.

3. References to the Atlanta, Boston, Buffalo, and Chicago studies will be found in the notes below. For New York City, see Barlow, Elizabeth and Alex, William (1972) *Frederick Law Olmsted's New York*. New York: Praeger Publishers; and Simpson, Jeffrey and Hern, Mary Ellen H. (ed.) (1981) *Art of the Olmsted Landscape: His Works in New York City*. New York: NYC Landmarks Preservation Commission and The Arts Publisher, Inc. – both volumes emanating from exhibitions, the first at the Whitney Museum of American Art, the second at the Metropolitan Museum of Art; and for the Commonwealth, see McPeck, Eleanor M., Morgan, Keith and Zaitzevsky, Cynthia, (eds.) (1983) *Olmsted in Massachusetts: The Public Legacy; A Report of the Inventory Committee of the Massachusetts Association for Olmsted Parks*. Brookline: MAOP, which offers itself as 'A Pilot Project for a National Inventory'.

4. The Frederick Law Olmsted National Historic Site, acquired by the Park Service in October 1979, maintains the records and drawings of the Olmsted, Sr. and successor firms.

5. Under the direction of Frederick Gutheim of Sugarloaf Regional Trails, Inc. (Dickerson, Maryland), this project has published Morris, Eleanor Kenner Smith (1984) *An Anglo-American Comparative Glossary of Open Space and Related Terms*. Dickerson: SRT, Inc.; and Morgan, Keith N. and McPeck, Eleanor M. '(1984) *Adaptation of Urban Landscape Parks: A Bibliography*. Dickerson, SRT, Inc.

6. The so-called Seiberling Bill, 'to identify, commemorate, and preserve the legacy of historic landscapes of Frederick Law Olmsted' was passed by voice vote in the Second Session of the 98th Congress during August 1984. At this writing, a revised Seiberling Bill (H.R. 37) has been reintroduced in the House to the First Session of the 99th Congress, in conjunction with a compatible bill in the Senate by Daniel Patrick Moynihan.

7. Founded in 1980 upon Moynihan's recommendation, NAOP is a not-for-

profit public advocacy organization of design professionals, planners, preservationists, park administrators, scholars, elected officials, and business and community leaders from thirty-two states, Puerto Rico, Mexico, Canada, and Great Britain.

8. Clay, Grady (1984) Exploring the next landscape. *National Association for Olmsted Parks Newsletter.* 3(2), p. 19.

9. Kimball, Theodora (1922) Centenary of Frederick Law Olmsted, Senior. *The American City,* 27, p. 500.

10. Olmsted, Frederick Law, Jr. and Kimball, Theodora (eds.) (1970) *Frederick Law Olmsted: Landscape Architect, 1822–1903,* Two Volumes in One. New York: Benjamin Blom, Inc., Preface, n.p.

11. Writing under the influence of the Regionalists at Chapel Hill, Broadus, Mitchell (1924) produced *Frederick Law Olmsted: A Critic of the Old South.* Baltimore: Johns Hopkins University Studies in Historical and Political Science Series, No. 42; (1968) New York: Russell & Russell.

12. Peets, Elbert (1925) Central Park. *American Mercury,* 4, p. 339. Facetiously identified here as 'scientists', James Thomson (1700–48) and William Cowper (1731–1800) were early English nature poets.

13. *Ibid.,* p. 340.

14. *Ibid.,* p. 341.

15. Mott, Frank Luther (1968) *A History of American Magazines,* Volume 5: *Sketches of 21 Magazines.* Cambridge: Harvard University Press, p. 11. Stylistically, Peets's *American Mercury* contributions bear little resemblance to his many other articles in print. See Spreiregen, Paul D. (1968) *On the Art of Designing Cities: Selected Essays of Elbert Peets.* Cambridge, Mass.: MIT Press.

16. van Rensselaer, Mariana G. (1893) Frederick Law Olmsted. *The Century Illustrated Monthly Magazine* 46, pp. 860–67; Mumford, Lewis (1931 and 1955) *The Brown Decades: A Study of the Arts in America, 1865–1895.* New York: Dover, pp. 79–96.

17. See White, Dana F. (1979) A Connecticut Yankee in Cotton's Kingdom, in White and Kramer, Victor A. (eds.) *Olmsted South: Old South Critic/New South Planner.* Westport, Conn.: Greenwood Press, pp. 28–37, for a bibliographical overview.

18. Peets, Elbert (1927) The Landscape Priesthood. *American Mercury,* 10, pp. 94–100.

19. *Ibid.,* p. 96.

20. *Ibid.,* p. 97.

21. *Ibid.,* p. 96.

22. Barnes, Harry E. (1924) The drool method in history. *American Mercury,* 1, p. 37.

23. Peets, (1927) *op. cit.,* p. 94.

24. Quoted in Beveridge, Charles E. (1977) Frederick Law Olmsted's theory of landscape design. *Nineteenth Century,* 3, p. 38.

25. Olmsted, Frederick Law (1852) *Walks and Talks of an American Farmer in*

England, 2 vols. New York: G.P. Putnam and Company.

26. *Ibid.*, Volume 1, p. 79.

27. *Ibid.*, pp. 86–87.

28. *Ibid.*, p. 133.

29. Beveridge, Charles E. (1977) Frederick Law Olmsted's theory of landscape design. *Nineteenth Century*, 3, pp. 41–42.

30. Roper, Laura Wood (1973) *FLO: A Biography of Frederick Law Olmsted*. Baltimore: Johns Hopkins University Press, pp. 303–07 and 406–14. The San Francisco design was never executed.

31. Ranney, Victoria Post (1972) *Olmsted in Chicago*. Chicago: The Open Lands Project, pp. 25–39.

32. See Lyon, Elizabeth A. (1979) Frederick Law Olmsted and Joel Hurt: Planning for Atlanta, in White, Dana F. and Kramer, Victor A. (eds.) *Olmsted South: Old South/Critic New South Planner*. Westport, Conn.: Greenwood Press, pp. 165–93.

33. Higham, John (1962) The American Experience. Lecture given at George Washington University, 9 July 1962.

34. Fitch, James Marston (1981) Design and the designer: 19th century innovation, in Kelly, Bruce *et al. Art of the Olmsted Landscape*. New York: NYC Landmarks Preservation Commission and The Arts Publisher, Inc., pp. 73–74.

35. Powell, Lawrence N. (1984) Introduction to *The Cotton Kingdom: A Traveller's Observations on Cotton and Slavery in the American Slave States*, edited by Arthur M. Schlesinger, Sr. New York: Modern Library, pp. ix–x.

36. White, *op. cit.*, pp. 17–18.

37. Beveridge, Charles E. and Schuyler, David (eds.) (1983) *Creating Central Park 1857–1861*, volume 3 in *The Papers of FLO*. Baltimore: Johns Hopkins University Press, p. 2.

38. Mumford, *op. cit.*, pp. 91–92.

39. Olmsted, Frederick Law (1871) Public parks and the enlargement of towns. *Journal of Social Science*, 3, pp. 1–36.

40. *Ibid.*, pp. 24–25 and 8–9.

41. See Creese, Walter L. (1966) *The Search for Environment; The Garden City: Before and After*. New Haven: Yale University Press, chap. 6: 'Morris and Howard – Boston and Chicago', for the initial suggestion concerning the links between Olmsted and Howard.

42. Beveridge, Charles (1981) Buffalo's park and parkway system, in *Buffalo Architecture: A Guide*. Cambridge, Mass.: MIT Press, pp. 15–18. 'Parkside', encircling Delaware Park ('F' in figure 7), was developed only in part and over many years. It more closely approximates the ring development of English models such as Birkenhead and Sefton Park than Olmsted's ideal for the 'open town suburb'.

43. *Ibid.*, p. 18.

44. Mumford, *op. cit.*, p. 88.

45. Zaitzevsky, Cynthia (1982) *Frederick Law Olmsted and the Boston Park System*. Cambridge, Mass.: The Belknap Press of Harvard University, pp. 3–4.

46. *Ibid.*, pp. 34–47. FLO's execution – really transformation – of the Boston Park Commission's preliminary plan of 1876 will be treated in the next section.

47. Kelly, Bruce (1981) Art of the Olmsted landscape, in Kelly, Bruce, *et al.*, *Art of the Olmsted Landscape*. New York: NYC Landmarks Preservation Commission and The Arts Publisher, Inc., p. 69.

48. Notes (1903) *The Nation*, 76, p. 191 (Sept. 3). For FLO's role in its founding, see Roper, Laura Wood (1973) *FLO: A Biography of Frederick Law Olmsted*. Baltimore: Johns Hopkins University Press, pp. 294–98.

49. Mulvey, Christopher (1983) *Anglo-American Landscapes: A Study of Nineteenth-Century Anglo-American Travel Literature*. Cambridge: Cambridge University Press, pp. 130, 159, 254, and 263; for *Walks and Talks*, which is treated here as a major example of the genre, see pp. 43–59.

50. Bibliographical references to all of these topic areas would prove too lengthy; for the last-named, see Peterson, Jon A. (1983) The impact of sanitary reform upon American urban planning, 1840–1890, in Krueckeberg, Donald A. (ed.) *Introduction to Planning History in the United States*. New Brunswick, N.J.: Center for Urban Policy Research/Rutgers University, esp. pp. 27–29.

51. See Beveridge and Schuyler (eds.), *op. cit.*

52. FLO's networking is best traced in the writings of Fein, Albert (1964) Parks in a democratic society. *Landscape Architecture*, 55, pp. 24–31; (1970) The American city: the ideal and the real, in Kaufmann, Edgar Jr. (ed.) *The Rise of an American Architecture*. New York: Praeger Publishers, pp. 51–112; and (1972) *Frederick Law Olmsted and the American Environmental Tradition*. New York: George Braziller.

53. Gerson, Leonard H. (1973) Nineteenth Century Parks: Building Blocks of the Pre-Automobile City, unpublished paper in the possession of the author, p. 4.

54. Gerson, Leonard H. (1971) The Buffalo Park Movement in the 1870s, unpublished paper in the possession of the author, pp. 12 and 14, italics added.

55. *Ibid.*, pp. 8–9. In his later essay (1973), Gerson traces FLO's continuing influence in Buffalo's private sector by detailing the suburban development schemes of the Rumseys, *pere* (an early client) and *fils* (an admirer), on into the 1920s (pp. 4–8).

56. Blodgett, Geoffrey (1976) Frederick Law Olmsted: landscape architecture as conservative reform. *Journal of American History*, 66, pp. 871, 884, and 885.

57. Zaitzevsky (1982) *op. cit.*, Part 3: The Design Process, quote from p. 127.

58. The early and long-term role of Frederick Law Olmsted, Jr. in the

relationships between the two fields is a case in point. See, for example, Hancock, John L. (1967) Planners in the changing American city, 1900–1940. *Journal of the American Institute of Planners*, **33**, pp. 290–304.

59. Emerson, Ralph Waldo (1850 and 1876) *Representative Men: Seven Lectures.* Boston and New York: Houghton Mifflin Company, pp. 6–7.

60. Fein, Albert (1972) Report on the profession of landscape architecture. *Landscape Architecture*, **63**, pp. 36 and 40.

61. *Ibid.*, p. 37.

62. The Fein Report was challenged, but never answered. See Newton, Norman T. (1974) Critique. Landscape architecture: profession in confusion? *Landscape Architecture*, **65**, pp. 256–63.

63. Zaitzevsky (1982) *op. cit.*, pp. 133, 130, and 132. His statements are dated 1893, 1895, and 1890, respectively.

64. See Peterson, Jon A. (1983) FLO and FLO, Jr.: practical visionary and statesmanlike professional, in National Association for Olmsted Parks, *Summary of Workshop Proceedings: September 23–24 1983*. New York: NAOP, SL6; and Levee, Arleyn A. (1983) The Olmsted legacy: John Charles Olmsted, *ibid.*

65. See Olmsted Brothers (1904) *Report on the Baltimore Parks*. Balt.: The Lord Baltimore Press; *Report of the Park Board, Portland, Oregon* (1903), reprinted during the late 1970s by the 40 Mile Loop supporters; and the *First Annual Report of the Board of Park Commissioners, Seattle, Washington, 1884–1904* (1905) Seattle: Lowman & Hanford, reprinted by the Friends of Seattle's Olmsted Parks in 1984.

66. Kesler, Gary (1982) The role of the Olmsted office in the development of professional organizations in landscape architecture, in National Association for Olmsted Parks, *Abstracts of Conference Proceedings: June 3–6, 1982*. Chicago: NAOP, No. 9.

67. Johnston, Laurie (1972) Central Park buffs mark designer's birthday, *New York Times*, May 1, Pt. 2, pp. 1 and 39.

68. For the first, see Sussmann, Carl, ed. (1976) *Planning the Fourth Migration: The Neglected Vision of the Regional Planning Association of America*. Cambridge, Mass.: MIT Press; for the second, see *Fortune*, Editors of (1956, 1957) *The Exploding Metropolis*. Garden City, N.Y.: Doubleday Anchor Books; and concerning the third, its history has yet to be written.

Chapter Five

The Seattle Park System and the Ideal of the City Beautiful

WILLIAM H. WILSON[1]

When John C. Olmsted arrived in Seattle during March 1903 to create a park system, he went about his work guided by a complex theory of urban design. Its components were associated with the City Beautiful movement, but they derived from three distinct sources. The convictions inherited from Olmsted's famous stepfather, Frederick Law Olmsted, were the most influential. Second were the ideals and justifications of comprehensive city planning, some of which the senior Olmsted had enunciated, but which were more closely identified with the maturing City Beautiful movement. Third, the burgeoning playground movement impinged upon the younger Olmsted's design decisions, though he was ambivalent about its demands for open space.

FLO AND THE CITY BEAUTIFUL MOVEMENT

The senior Olmsted grounded his park and planning ideology upon a qualified rejection of the city. He accepted the dominant thought of the mid-nineteenth century about cities, that they were unnatural, unappealing places filled with din and tumult, producing anxiety and exhaustion in their residents. But he kept an open mind. From his 1858 *Greensward* plan for Central Park to his 1870 major theoretical statement about cities, Olmsted's experiences in New York, Europe, the rural South, roughhewn California, and other places softened his anti-urban attitude.[2]

Olmsted conceded much to cities when he delivered 'Public Parks and the Enlargement of Towns' in 1870. He discovered a close relationship between urbanization and 'civilized progress', which he identified with the rise of schooling, the arts, organized and commercial recreation, the division of labour, rapid advances in transportation, communication, utilities and public health, and the mechanization of agriculture. All these positive developments were associated with urbanization, and with 'the emancipation of both men and women from petty, confining, and narrowing cares'. He predicted that the exodus from country to city would accelerate, that cities 'are likely to be still more attractive to population in the future' . . .[3]

Against the aesthetic norms of his day, Olmsted proclaimed the potential beauty of cities. He declared: 'Let your buildings be as picturesque as your artists can make them. This is the beauty of a town'. As much as he welcomed urbanism however, Olmsted never abandoned his prejudice against cities. Suburbanization and deconcentration would ease the lot of a majority of their residents, their public health could be increased, their streets widened and better lighted, and their institutions improved, but cities they remained. They still would be crowded, dirty, inhospitable, and unyielding.[4]

Olmsted found the anodyne to the city's destructive qualities in the large landscape park, the psychic alternative to urban pressures. Romanticism shaped but did not control Olmsted's outlook and designs. His secular vision was of a perfect democracy, with the poor and deprived raised to a cultural level of genteel refinement. While he hoped for the political and cultural triumph of genteel thinkers with views similar to his own, those hopes should not be overemphasized at the expense of his ideals of democracy and design. His ideals directed him, not the possibilities of a simple, mechanistic social control through city planning. As a park planner, Olmsted most desired to create a work of art, just as evidently a work of art as a landscape painting. The romantic influence showed in his belief that landscape artistry was most expressive when it followed nature, which was God's creation.[5]

A landscape park, however, was no more God's creation, at least not directly, than it was solely romantic. The best term for Olmsted's realization of his rich, complex heritage is naturalistic constructivism. His parks resulted from artistic inspiration springing from nature, but they were realized through elaborate construction. Olmsted's parks featured traffic separation, open and closed vistas, looping and winding drives, formal areas such as Central Park's Mall, and focal points such as fountains. The existing topography sometimes offered no more than hints for the location and arrangement of these features, and sometimes not even that. Olmsted's later practice of locating athletic fields, playgrounds, zoos, and other features on the periphery of his large parks demanded further compromises with topography.

His naturalistic constructivism was most pronounced in two later lakefront designs, for Buffalo's proposed South Park along Lake Erie, and for the World's Columbian Exposition on the shore of Lake Michigan. The physical purpose behind all these alterations was the creation of the middle landscape, an artistic delight shorn of the gross, ugly, or fetid elements sometimes found in nature.[6]

The resulting landscape would help realize Olmsted's democratic vision. That vision encompassed a peaceful society, with masses and classes coexisting harmoniously. The display of riding horses and luxurious carriages amid throngs of ordinary citizens in a holiday mood, moving against a naturalistic scene, would be the visual affirmation of an interdependent, organic society. The park offered an escape from the city, an environment designed to soothe the anxieties and diminish the nervousness of 'tired workers', 'poor mothers', and businessmen. Psychically restored, they would carry on the world's work in a reasonably contented fashion. It was a socially conservative goal, to be sure.[7]

There were other values for Olmsted, however. He valued the individual human being, a creature of God's who shared some of His divine attributes. He valued, too, the warm, friendly mingling of park patrons, each rejoicing in the regeneration of the other. If the heterogeneous, cosmopolitan population of New York could find a common ground in the park, there was hope for cheerful, democratic, interclass gregariousness in urbanizing America. 'The poor and the rich come together in [Central Park] in larger numbers than anywhere else', he declared, 'and enjoy what they find in it in more complete sympathy than they enjoy anything else together'.[8]

The City Beautiful movement took over great expanses of Olmstedian social and psychological argument and converted them to its own uses. The arguments were altered in the conversion, but Olmsted's less exalted, more material justifications for beauty survived practically unimpaired. That was because American society, intellectual permutations aside, was consistently materialistic and conscious of public costs. Olmsted advanced these arguments because he well knew that paeans to the restored human spirit would carry him only so far. Parks might make potentially disruptive people benign, promote interclass concord, and contribute to familial harmony; or they might not. The assertion was problematic, but the expenses of park acquisition, construction, and maintenance very real. Therefore Olmsted developed a 'pocketbook' rationale for beauty only partly dependent on his assumptions about behaviour modification and the psychic restoration of the workforce.

Urban beauty paid off, Olmsted argued, because it attracted people of substance and leisure, people 'who are not deeply absorbed in the mere *pursuit* of wealth . . .'. As early as 1866 he contended that the wealthy came to New York, Paris and London because of those cities' institutional culture and inducements to leisure, including parks. When monied people departed they took along their culture, income, and expenditures. Lesser cities should respond with public improvements designed to retain the rich. For similar reasons, parks paid by attracting visitors and permanent residents who considered cultural conditions when making their travel and living arrangements. Landscape beauty also paid enterprising cities directly by raising property values and swelling tax revenues. Olmsted's and Calvert Vaux's 1868 Brooklyn report noted how Prospect Park had increased nearby property values more than four times. In his 1870 address Olmsted spoke of the opponents of Central Park who assumed that the park would attract undesirable uses on its periphery. They were confounded when the property 'immediately about the Park, . . . advanced in value at the rate of two hundred per cent. per annum'. Finally, park beauty paid because it encouraged activities that required recreational equipment. In the course of using Central Park, he maintained, 'the number of private carriages kept in the city was increased tenfold, the number of saddle horses a hundredfold, the business of livery stables more than doubled, the investment of many millions of private capital in public conveyances made profitable'. Surely these economic arguments would convince observers that parks could pay.[9]

Olmsted made other proto-City Beautiful assertions. His reports expressed a conviction about the inevitability of urban growth. Environmental planning, therefore, should begin at once, with improvements projected for much larger cities than those existing. Land purchases should be made before urbanization drove up prices. From his concern for immediate beginnings came Olmsted's insistence on the value of expert planning by a specialist capable of designing for large civic purposes. Only a disinterested expert could conceive of a city-wide plan of improvements. Moreover, he continually referred to the value of studying European precedents. Finally, he understood his work to be comprehensive beyond the conventional framework of city plans. Planning, to be fully effective, had to advance in relation to political and administrative improvements, the growth of public education, and the development of public appreciation for the arts.[10]

THE CITY BEAUTIFUL

The City Beautiful movement that coalesced after 1900 owed much to Olmsted, but its origins and growth were more complex than the

Figure 1. John Charles Olmsted, the designer of Seattle's park, boulevard, and playground system, at work in the drafting room at Olmsted Brothers, Brookline, Massachusetts. (*Source*: National Park Service, Frederick Law Olmsted National Historic Site)

continued development of parks and boulevards. The City Beautiful retained and elaborated several of Olmsted's ideas while sometimes twisting them loose from their intellectual moorings. These changes affected John C. Olmsted, whose active career continued well beyond the progressive era. The City Beautiful's striking departure from Olmsted was its optimism about the city. No longer was it a stark, inhuman place. In the Darwinian, progressive age the city became organic, thus malleable and infinitely improveable. Urban conditions could be transformed, not merely meliorated. There would be no merely temporary, psychic return to a rural or arcadian past, no beauty which was in the city but not of it.[11]

In other ways, the City Beautiful represented continuity with Olmstedian planning. Its solution to urban ills – a beautiful, rationalized city – would occur within the existing social, political, and economic arrangements. City Beautiful advocates were committed to a liberal-capitalist, commercial-industrial society, and to the concept of private property. They recognized society's abuses, but they assumed a smooth transition to a better urban world. Thus the reformist and optimistic City Beautiful was the civic improvement and city planning aspect of the progressive movement.[12]

Despite their hopefulness, City Beautiful advocates recognized and indeed emphasized the aesthetic and functional shortcomings of

American cities. Few cities could, by the early twentieth century, boast well-distributed or well-improved parks. Factory smoke, inefficient street cleaning, poor trash collection, indifferent or non-existent street tree planting and care, all contributed to a dirty, ugly environment. These conditions persisted despite advanced technologies in sanitary engineering, street paving, utilities systems, and smoke abatement which could foster a healthful urban life.[13]

The City Beautiful justified itself by joining beauty and utility. City Beautiful partisans did so explicitly. They were unwilling to rest on the implications of Olmsted's arguments about the positive social effects of natural beauty. To them the beautiful was useful, and the useful could be beautiful at no greater cost than the ugly or the plain. It was necessary for the champions of the City Beautiful to reiterate this venerable argument. They realized that their vocal opponents – solid middle and upper-middle citizens like themselves – were content with a smoky, noisy, unkempt city so long as it got the job done: distributed goods, provided housing, and brought together employer and employee. The trick was to combine the beautiful, on which no value could be placed, with the functional, which paid in discernable ways. That is why Daniel H. Burnham, when speaking at the Chicago Merchants' Club in 1897, announced that 'Beauty has always paid better than any other commodity and always will'.[14]

The City Beautiful strove for efficiency. It would be too much to say that the search for efficiency was the progressive era's quest for the grail, but efficiency was an important goal, one closely related to utility. City Beautiful planners depreciated the chaos around them in part because it was inefficient. Palls of factory smoke were not simply ugly or distasteful. They represented the 'waste' of fuel, wrote a City Beautiful spokesman, a waste compounded when fly ash 'spread upon houses, clothes, goods and food'. The idea of the civic centre often associated with the City Beautiful was promoted in part because clustered civic buildings would ensure the efficient and economical conduct of the city's business.[15]

Those who endorsed the City Beautiful believed less in the senior Olmsted's view of beauty's restorative power, and more in the shaping influence of beauty. To put it another way, they believed less in man as a natural, God-like creature who required a beautiful reprieve from his imprisonment in the artificial city; and more in man as remote from his Creator, a malleable being who was little more than the sum of his experiences. Therefore, an urban dweller's whole environment and experience was extremely important to them. Their belief in a controllable, flexible city led them to advocate a comprehensive plan that addressed a significant number of a city's problems, and that offered multiple solutions to those problems. This environmentalism certainly involved social or moral control, but the control was essentially benevolent. Generally speaking, City Beautiful advocates desired to create environmental conditions evoking a spontaneous and unified appreciation for civic values that would lift the working class to the cultural level of the middle and upper middle classes.[16]

City Beautiful ideologues were class-conscious in a non–Marxian sense. They believed in individual mobility and in limited class fluidity, but they accepted a functional distinction between an upper, or professional-managerial class, and a lower, or working class. The working class required parks for Olmstedian reasons: workers and their families lacked the means to vacation away from the city; and both workers and professionals could mingle in a friendly, non-threatening way in parks. The civic centre, however, not the landscape park, became the idealized site for interclass mingling and reconciliation. This transfer occurred because of several geographical and social realities. Most landscape parks were too remote to serve as gathering places for a cross-section of society. And, as Galen Cranz and Roy Rosenzweig have demonstrated, the design of some parks altered over the years, reflecting in part the wishes of nearby users. The alterations were potentially discouraging to more distant users who belonged to other socio-economic groups.[17]

The civic centre, on the other hand, combined the Olmstedian ideal with the City Beautiful's quest for efficiency. A civic centre on the rim of the urban retail-commercial core would draw all population groups because virtually everyone went downtown to work or shop, to transact government business, or to visit a cultural institution. Grouped buildings would speed a citizen's business while monumental architecture quickened civic pride and an awareness of a common bond, through government, with fellow urban dwellers. The centre's plaza would accommodate concerts, civic celebrations, and national festivals. The architecture and spatial arrangements were practically immune from popular control, unlike those in the more plastic landscape park. Parks and civic centres were essential to urban life, not so much because working-class people would revolt if they did not exist, but because without them the working class would eventually become demoralized and debased.[18]

Finally, City Beautiful advocates revered expertise. Reverence for the expert was related to the progressive creeds of efficiency and non-partisanship, and diffused among the middle class. In contrast to the senior Olmsted's era, expertise was no longer solely an elite, class-based preoccupation tainted with partisan overtones. The progressives revered the expert partly because his civic work stood in welcome relief against the inept, piecemeal, 'political' patchwork efforts to stay abreast of urban needs. Then, too, from Olmsted's day forward, experts had prepared plans based on assumptions that appeared proven in hindsight. They had predicted headlong urban expansion, asserted that their improvements would increase property values, called for buying public property while land was yet relatively cheap, laid out functional designs of broad scope, subordinated and integrated details, and allowed for gradual improvement within the context of a grand scheme. Whatever their commitment to a set of ideals, it was important for the experts to get along with the members of the local boards and commissions who oversaw the preparation and execution of their plans. Usually they did so because of shared values of ideology and class, and because of some politic compromises on both sides.[19]

THE PLAYGROUND MOVEMENT

The playground movement was the third influence on John C. Olmsted. When he first visited Seattle in 1903 the movement had not jelled organizationally. That would come in 1906 with the founding of the Playground Association of America, but the outlines of the movement's principles were clear. The playground movement was a feature of the child-saving impulse of the progressive years but its thrust was universal.[20]

Playground advocates believed in reaching out to all children, irrespective of age and ethnicity. Team sports for older children and adolescents taught them that their differences were less important than their similiarities. Team play required the sacrifice of individuality or at least the tempering of it, to attain a common goal. This training socialized children, making them receptive to the discipline of the work environment, to an efficiently-organized polity, to national partiotism and to civic idealism. A Darwinian ontogeny lay behind the inculcation of moral values, from the sandpile to team sports. Morality, in this view, was not independent and divine, but environ-mentally conditioned. The playground movement saw itself as providing an alternative to the depraved, socially centrifugal city. The playground supplied the corrective for bad forms of recreation, including illicit drinking establishments, vaudville theatres and burlesque halls. The street gang's primitive civicism could be nurtured and its destructive appetites discouraged if only an innovative play director would inveigle its members to the playground and redirect its leadership to more productive pursuits.

Two of the playground movement's goals, its quest for social efficiency and its drive to re-establish community, have been held to be incompatible. But this was less apparent in 1903, when the movement was still forming. Nor were the philosophical or practical conflicts among the devotees of Olmstedism, the City Beautiful, and the playground movement so obvious as they have become to historians. As with the young Jews and Italians on the idealized playing field, what united them was more significant than their divisions.[21]

THE MERGING OF MOVEMENTS

Olmstedism, the City Beautiful, and the playground movement intersected at several points. All were environmentalist, although the post-Darwinian beautifiers and playgrounders were in agreement that man's nature was less teleological than conditioned. All subscribed to the concept of recreation. The Olmstedian tradition emphasized the restorative value of observing or strolling through naturalistic scenery, although Olmsted allowed for active recreation on the margins of his later parks. City Beautiful thought embraced the values of organized play. Further, Olmstedism and the City Beautiful desired to re-establish community, a goal that the playground movement pursued from the young citizen's cradle. Olmstedians, beautifiers, and playgrounders believed in the expert, while the City Beautiful and the playground movement upheld efficiency. Because of these common concerns there was not much conflict among the movements in the early twentieth century. The City Beautiful movement faced both ways, advocating parks, boulevards, and neighbourhood playing fields located close to their potential users. Devotees of landscape parks were willing to concede a few acres to playgrounds provided the surrender did not involve the destruction of landscape values.[22]

BEAUTIFYING SEATTLE

John C. Olmsted's task was to translate this loose system of ideas into a park and boulevard plan for Seattle. The small, unkempt, but booming Pacific Northwest city presented Olmsted with unique opportunities and problems. In 1903 Seattle had boomed for six years on the strength of Alaska-Yukon gold strikes, and of other developments. In that year it held some 90,000 souls, and was growing toward a population of 237,194 in 1910. On a map, Seattle resembled a giant hourglass, pinched at its waist by Puget Sound on the west and Lake Washington on the east. A series of bays and inlets, plus Lake Union just north of the city's waist, made for a richly varied pattern of land and water. Steep hills, plateaus, and ridges offered spectacular views of deep ravines, of lakes and the sound, and of the Olympic Mountains on the west and the Cascade range on the east. Mount Rainier's near-perfect cone, visible on a clear day to the south-east, was the centrepiece of this visual delight.[23]

Puget Sound, the nearby Pacific, and other bodies of water moderated the temperature. A well-distributed rainfall supported a luxuriant coniferous and deciduous vegetation. Cloudy and cool days, or mottled days varying from light rain and clouds to mostly clear conditions, combined with more typically mid-continental days of sun or rain. The meterological mixture varied still more the optical experience of water and land. The weather, Olmsted wrote, was 'like England or Ireland'. Olmsted's problems were in part the reverse of this spectacularly scenic coin. The hills and steep slopes enforced heavy construction penalties. The expense of bridging waterways virtually assured that some boulevard traffic would enter major commercial streets, then mingle on bridges with commercial traffic before returning to a boulevard route. Other limitations included earlier plans which had enlivened the public expectations of certain beautification improvements, notably a boulevard running south from Union Bay on Lake Washington. Olmsted had to bring the few existing public parks into a system, and he had to allow for the eventual absorption of private amusement parks.[24]

From March through June Olmsted and his assistant studied Seattle, 'an extensive city', and wrote up his recommendations. The city council accepted the report in October. In 1904 the board of park

Figure 2. (opposite) A Board of Park Commissioners map of 1908 showing Seattle's prominent features. The northernmost lake is Green Lake, while the lake directly south of it is Lake Union. Lake Washington's Union Bay is to the east of Lake Union, with Lake Washington proper beyond. Queen Anne Hill, showing a boulevard loop on its west, north, and east summits, is directly west of Lake Union. Magnolia Hill, with Fort Lawton at its northwest corner, is west of Queen Anne Hill. Salmon Bay of Puget Sound is north of Magnolia Hill while Eliott Bay is south and east. West Seattle is south across Elliott Bay from Magnolia Hill. Woodland Park is at the southwestern corner of Green Lake, while Ravenna Park is east of the lake at the end of the eastward boulevard. The university grounds are south of Ravenna Park and are marked 'A.-Y.-P. Exposition 1909'. Washington Park is directly south of Union Bay. Volunteer Park is the large square to the west of Washington Park. City or Beacon Hill (now Jefferson) Park is the large oblong a few miles south of Volunteer Park. Except for the boulevards west of Woodland Park and most of the complex west and south of City Park, the system was eventually built, with significant additions not shown. (*Source:* Historical Photography Collection, University of Washington Libraries)

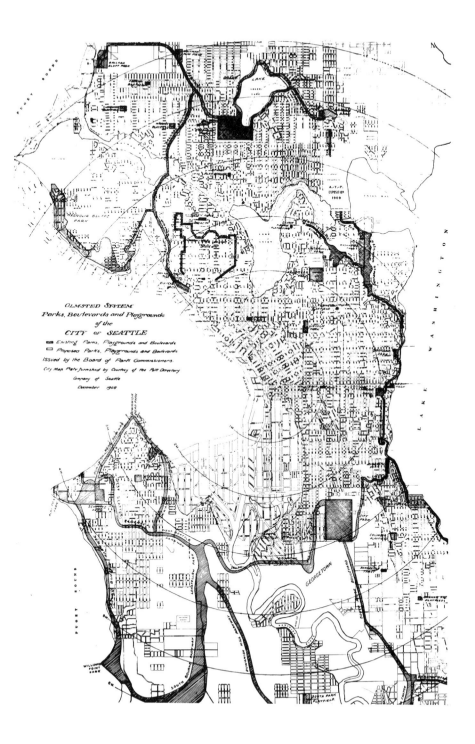

commissioners secured a charter amendment granting it greater independence and income. It built a park, boulevard, parkway, and playground system until an economic panic forced a sharp curtailment after a decade's work.[25]

Olmsted proposed, as an untimate goal, an ambitiously conceived 'comprehensive and satisfactory system of parks and parkways', with supplemental drives and playgrounds. He began at the undeveloped Bailey Peninsula, almost 200 acres jutting like a cocked thumb into southern Lake Washington. He proposed taking and preserving the peninsula, then laying out a parkway that, for the most part, hugged the lake's western shore until it reached Washington Park, across Union Bay and south-east from the new University of Washington grounds. Olmsted drew a proposed boulevard from a suggested expansion of Washington Park west to a crossing of the Lake Washington ship canal, then north through the university grounds along the bluff overlooking Union Bay. The boulevard continued to the east end of the privately-owned Ravenna Park, a park he advocated bringing into the system.[26]

At Ravenna Park the proposed boulevard swung north-west along the edge of the ravine, and, continuing in the same direction, followed the creek then running between Green Lake and Ravenna Park. At Green Lake Olmsted suggested an extension around the western shore of the lake, to Woodland Park. From there it would continue south-westerly to the western ship canal, where a bridge would carry it to the north-western flank of majestic Queen Anne Hill. From Queen Anne Hill Olmsted would have had a boulevard run southerly to a cove between Queen Anne and Magnolia Hills, thence west and north along the upper shore of Elliott Bay and the rim of Magnolia Bluff to the Fort Lawton military reservation. Branch parkways on Queen Anne Hill, one to link with the existing Kinnear Park; from Washington Park to the existing Volunteer Park, and along high ground west of Lake Washington, rounded out the proposed driveways. Other smaller proposed takings included six playgrounds, mostly in the east central or southern part of the city. The main parkway system, including its major intrapark drives, would have reached almost 24 miles. Unfortunately it could not be made continuous. Olmsted, to achieve a true loop, would have had to draw a boulevard through expensive property at the city's waist, north of the commercial-retail core and south of Lake Union, to say nothing of additional miles to the east and south.[27]

Unfortunately, too, the costs of the proposed system were estimated to be $1,198,000 while only about $280,000 was available for purchases. Under the press of circumstances Olmsted met in May with a group of park commissioners and landowners along the

Figure 3. A bird's-eye view of Seattle in 1900, three years before John C. Olmsted's arrival, looking south southwest from a point approximately above the present NE 55th Street and Roosevelt Way NE. The body of water directly in front of the viewer is Portage Bay of Lake Union. The prominent white building left (east) of Portage Bay is the new University of Washington, while east and south of it is Union Bay of Lake Washington. Queen Anne Hill is the prominent rise beyond Lake Union proper, while beyond Queen Anne Hill, at the extreme upper right, is Magnolia Hill. (*Source*: Historical Photography Collection, University of Washington Libraries)

proposed Lake Washington Boulevard. It was a private meeting at the home of Park Commission Chairman Elbert F. Blaine, called to discuss a 'reduced system for the near future'. This truncated system dropped the Bailey Peninsula and the southern portion of the Lake Washington Boulevard (both outside the city limits at the time), the Washington Park expansion, and the boulevard through the University grounds from the University to Ravenna Park, to and around Green Lake. It excised Ravenna Park itself. Olmsted dropped the boulevard from Woodland Park to Queen Anne Hill. He modified the Queen Anne boulevard, and eliminated the drives through Fort Lawton. The recommended playgrounds he reduced to three. He retained a few spur or substitute boulevards of no great consequence.[28]

The reduced system symbolized the juncture of the Olmstedian and City Beautiful approaches to the practical problems of city planning. First, neither Olmsted nor the park commissioners ever abandoned the Olmstedian vision, as the detailed narrative made clear. The comprehensive system remained the ultimate goal. Second, the reduced system represented an empirical solution, a tough-minded application of the senior Olmsted's injunction to make a beginning on an elaborate plan. This time there would be no dazzling vision of a resplendent parkway system such as Frederick Law Olmsted and Calvert Vaux offered the Prospect Park commissioners in 1868, but without any concrete suggestions for its realization. Instead, the beginnings in Seattle were definite and explicit. Finally, though the

Mt Baker Park Boulevard, Seattle, Washington

Figure 4. Mt. Baker Park Boulevard along Lake Washington. Although the juxtaposition of curvilinear driveways and light concrete work was evidently admired in Seattle, John C. Olmsted deplored stiff, straight stairs such as those at the left. He believed them to be out of keeping with naturalistic scenery. (*Source*: Historical Photography Collection, University of Washington Libraries)

playsteads separate from in-park recreation areas were reduced in number, they were not eliminated.[29]

With Olmsted's report in hand, the financially strengthened board plunged into construction, and kept Olmsted busy responding to requests for designs and advice. In 1906, 1908, and 1910, Olmsted wrote supplementary reports on parks, parkways, and playgrounds, which revealed a distinct difference between the commissioners and their advisor. Bond issues fuelled the board's land purchases partly because of rapid park improvements, but partly, as Mansell Blackford has observed, because the commissioners catered for the rising public demand for neighbourhood playgrounds. Contrarily, Olmsted pressed to resolve any conflict between traditional parks and playgrounds in favour of perpetuating the Olmstedian ideal. In his 1906 park and playground report he conceded that 'the time is now near when some of the expenditure for improvements can advisedly be made in the play grounds', but cautioned against capitulation to the popular desire for small parks and playgrounds in each neighbourhood. Delays in providing larger, close-in landscape parks and parkways would deprive the masses of their benefits and would hold the commission hostage to the demands of urban sectionalism. Besides, he wrote, 'I do not think the city is yet so large and the working population so crowded as to make it so vitally essential to provide play grounds in the midst of the dense population as it is in cities of two or three times the population of Seattle'. Therefore, 'I do not believe that even such play grounds as have already been acquired, or will be secured in the immediate future, should be improved in any very comprehensive or expensive manner'. Not surprisingly, the bulk of his report concerned park and parkway improvements.[30]

Olmsted's 1908 report followed an extensive annexation programme incorporating large suburban areas, including Ballard to the north-west, Ravenna to the north-east, West Seattle, and districts to the south. Accepting the board's charge to examine these areas, plus Magnolia Hill, Olmsted devised a formula for each based on pre-annexing Seattle's park areas, playgrounds larger than an acre, and parkways. Then he suggested smaller parks, parkways, and playfields of various sizes and uses.[31] Olmsted recommended thirteen play spaces, but his commitment to landscapes and to City Beautiful practicality dominated the report. The board followed neither Olmsted's recommendation for elaborate parkways around and through the southern portion of the city, nor his suggestion for funding most of the parks and playgrounds from special assessments on the newly annexed areas. Ultimately it purchased land at or near eighteen of the twenty-five locations designated in the report. With the exception of the present Lincoln Park in West Seattle, the commissioners did not buy large scenic and recreational grounds, unless Olmsted's suggestions made in the 1903 report and repeated in the 1908 report are counted. The principal lesson from the 1908 report and the board's response is the divergence between Olmsted's continuing emphasis on naturalistic constructivism and the commissioners' concern with meeting the popular demand for active recreation.[32]

The contrast was more pronounced in 1910, when Olmsted presented the last of his formal reports. With unconscious irony the commissioners had instructed their advisory landscape architect to prepare recommendations on playground sites throughout the city. Olmsted chided the board for 'yielding to public pressure' by maintaining playgrounds in school yards. 'The primary duty of the Park Board is to provide parks – not school playgrounds', Olmsted reminded his readers. Then he coupled a concession to play ideology

Figure 5. Looking south along Lake Washington in the Mt. Baker Park area, 1914. The towering cone of Mount Rainier is a sublime counterpoint to the romantic-naturalistic foreground (*Source*: Historical Photography Collection, University of Washington Libraries, photo by Asahel Curtis)

with a call for administrative and functional clarity. He conceded that

> the City needs and must have playgrounds', because 'they surely are necessary as a matter of public health and good morals. But . . . most of them ought to be provided and all of them should be managed, . . . by the School Board as a matter of right education of the physical, mental and moral natures of children . . . If the Park Board diverts its income from park work to teaching children in playgrounds, it is not accomplishing what it should in its proper line and is doing . . . what could probably be better done by the School Board.[33]

Olmsted advised the board 'to go on providing playgrounds', but 'only incidentally and subordinately to parks' . . . He urged the park commission to surrender its small playgrounds 'bodily to the School Board whenever that Board is prepared to take them' . . . And he recommended combined landscape treatment and play space development for each subsequent acquisition. He insisted 'that the local parks should be larger and more park-like than several which have been

Figure 6. The Lincoln Park (Broadway) Playfield, about 1911. The 1909 park board report took particular pride in this playground, pointing to the recent installation of a shelter house, shrubs, trees, and other improvements. The city's low service reservoir, with its fountain plume, is north of the play area. The cylindrical object on the horizon is the water and observation tower in Volunteer Park. (*Source:* Historical Photography Collection, University of Washington Libraries, photo by W & S)

acquired and improved by your Board under the name of playgrounds'. Olmsted advised the board, where possible, to locate the parks 'on steep hillsides or on the shores of lake, harbour, or river where they will afford the pleasure and refreshment due to their command of views, even at some sacrifice of advantage of shortest distance from the greatest number of homes or of uniformity of distribution'.

Olmsted made fifteen recommendations for playgrounds or other active recreational spaces, including his call for a water-front park repeated from the 1903 report. Of these, the city eventually provided eleven, counting partial and nearby purchases, or provisions within the same general area. A few, such as the Hiawatha Playfield in West Seattle, were elaborately landscaped, fulfilling Olmsted's vision. Walks, shelter, field, and toilet houses, surviving trees, planted shrubs, and grass relieved the stark outlines of a few others, but most were play areas, not small neighbourhood parks with play apparatus integrated into landscape design.[34]

During 1914 the park commissioners virtually exhausted their remaining bond funds and were forced to live within a strict budget. An era of active acquisition and construction, of the partial realization of the Olmstedian, City Beautiful, and playground movement ideals, was closing. Two years before, Seattle's voters had approved a park bond issue but had overwhelmingly defeated the Bogue plan, an extensive traffic, street improvement, harbour, park and parkway development having as its focus a civic centre in the City Beautiful mode.[35]

In 1916, forty-four parks of all sizes and stages of improvement were scattered through the city. They comprised 1,439 acres. The twenty-four playgrounds totalled 139 acres and were reasonably well distributed. Parkways and boulevards wound through the city for 31 miles while contributing 231 additional acres of roadway and open space. Forty-three small squares and places added another 6 acres. Between 1906 and 1912 Seattle's citizens voted $4,000,000 in park bonds, underwriting the major part of the cost of land and improvements totaling more than $5,100,000.[36]

SEATTLE AND THE LEGACY OF THE CITY BEAUTIFUL MOVEMENT

How well the Seattle system compared with the prevailing goals of urban design is not an issue open to an absolute answer. In a fundamental way it failed to realize the Olmstedian dream of a large landscape park where, as John Olmsted phrased it, 'the markedly artificial conditions of city life' are 'kept out of sight . . .'. Such a park, he thought, required 'an area in one compact body of 500 acres or more'. Seattle's largest park was just under 194 acres. Many parks offered spectacular views of water, land and sublime mountain scenery, interspersed with urban scenes. But it was hardly the senior Olmsted's vision of quiet, contemplative restoration amid family, friends, and well-disposed strangers. Moreover, John Olmsted disliked modifying boulevard designs to the dictates of rapacious landowners. He criticized the unimaginative planting, the obvious rectilinearity of walks, drain inlets, and stairs in Seattle's parks. He also 'regretted to see that the lines of the drives were in many cases conspicuously stiff and formal, consisting of a succession of simple radial curves and straight lines, as is customary in railroads, instead of gracefully varying curves as is customary in the best parks'.[37]

On the other hand, Olmstedism, by the last decade of the nineteenth century, embraced much more than a simple pastoralism;

it included active recreation areas, elaborate formal elements, and diverse uses. John Olmsted doubted 'whether, considering the tremendous natural advantages of the Sound and the lakes, it will be necessary that the city should have anywhere within its present boundaries' a large landscape park. As it was, Seattle enjoyed a people-to-parks ratio of slightly less than 208 persons per acre, close to the park enthusiasts' minimum of 200 persons per acre. Further, the parks were pleasant and restful though they never met the senior Olmsted's social claims. It is improbable that a series of large and varied landscape parks would have dampened Seattle's reputation for labour radicalism or prevented the city's general strike of 1919. As for the 'pocketbook' arguments, parks and parkways may have helped to draw visitors and population, retain the well-to-do, and meliorate the economic stagnation that continued for several years after 1915, but these claims are unproveable. Parks and related improvements probably contributed to the rise in Seattle real estate though it is difficult if not impossible to control for other variables when attempting to assess the contributions of parks to rising land values and tax revenues. The parks were the product of expertise, though modified by local contingencies. They were, generally, traditional in layout and design, and they did reflect, if very imperfectly, comprehensive planning.[38]

The boulevard and parkway system diverged most radically from the Olmstedian–City Beautiful ideals of comprehensiveness. The city was neither defined nor shaped by its parkways. John Olmsted found it impossible to plan a circumferential system, given Seattle's topography. The park board claimed sixteen boulevards, but one of those was unconstructed, one was a speedway track for horse fanciers, and three were, by other names, the Lake Washington Boulevard planned to run south from Union Bay to the Bailey Peninsula (by then Seward Park). The boulevard began about a mile and a half north of Seward Park, and ran north to Washington Park and Union Bay, where the construction of the Lake Washington ship canal severed connections with the University of Washington. University Boulevard ran north through the western edge of the campus, far from its eastern rim and the fine views of Lake Washington that Olmsted had wished to incorporate into the system. University Boulevard continued over 17th Avenue NE until it joined Ravenna Boulevard just south of Ravenna Park. Ravenna Boulevard slanted north-west to Green Lake, although along a route about a block south of the line which Olmsted first suggested. After skirting Green Lake, this boulevard segment ended some six blocks west of Woodland Park. A boulevard looped around the ridge of Queen Anne Hill, and Magnolia Boulevard ran from the south-eastern corner of the

Magnolia district to Fort Lawton. The boulevards were not connected, nor was either linked with the Lake Washington-Green Lake segment. The park board gamely suggested that a southbound traveller could, by leaving Lake Washington Boulevard and taking Mt. Baker and Cheasty Boulevards to Jefferson Park, make something of a loop by returning northbound to the downtown area over paved streets. None of these parkways, however desirable in themselves, defined or organized the city.[39]

Other City Beautiful ideas were realized in part. The parks combined utility and beauty, while the playgrounds were utilitarian and sometimes attractive. The parks were efficiently built and maintained under the leadership of Park Superintendent John W. Thompson, hired on the Olmsted Brothers' recommendation. Thompson served the park commission for almost a generation as an economical and capable leader. Unfortunately for City Beautiful ideals, there were too many other environmental, not to mention genetic, influences on Seattle's population for its parks and boulevards to work a fundamental change. This is not to argue, however, that parks and playgrounds did not meliorate conditions. They did, unless one believes that the crowds who went to the parks and playgrounds came away repeatedly deluded and unfulfilled. What parks and playgrounds could not do was transform human behaviour.[40]

The ideas of the playground movement came the closest to realization, except, again, regarding any measurable modification of human behaviour over the long term. The Seattle Playgrounds Association, the daily press, and the Park Board consistently promoted playgrounds. In 1910 the board promised the voters four additional playgrounds if they would approve a $2,000,000 bond issue. By 1916 the board was operating an active recreation programme with paid playground supervisors and team sports. If playgrounds were not always within a half-mile of one another, as a few enthusiasts advocated, they were generally no more than a mile apart. Where in-park playgrounds existed, as at Kinnear Park, they met with public approval without seriously compromising landscape values.[41]

The work of John Olmsted and the park board realized fairly well a set of complex, overlapping, and occasionally contradictory planning ideals. In this they illustrated how City Beautiful success came most often in the growing, yet plastic, commercial cities of the middle and far west, rather than in the largest cities or industrial towns. Their failures to attain the City Beautiful ideal suggested, as well, some limitations on City Beautiful planning. They did not bring forth the grander progressive vision of a new age of community marked by a strifeless society. But then neither Frederick Law Olmsted, nor the dreamers of the City Beautiful, nor the playground advocates assumed that their unaided efforts would perfect humanity. They believed their planning work to be only one part of a broad continuous movement. Unfortunately for them, they were less the leaders of an evolving effort than they were keepers of the flame, and the urban public did not always travel by the light of their reform lamp.

NOTES

1. Released-time grants from the Organized Research Fund of North Texas State University have assisted in a study of the City Beautiful movement, of which this chapter is a segment. Some of the structure and conclusions presented here were first developed in Wilson, W.H. (1980) The ideology, aesthetics and politics of the city beautiful movement, in Sutcliffe, A. (ed.) *The Rise of Modern Urban Planning 1800–1914*. London: Mansell, pp. 165–98, while other portions draw upon an unpublished paper, Wilson, W.H. (1984) John C. Olmsted in Seattle: the successes and other experiences of a planner-consultant in the early twentieth century, prepared for the National Association for Olmsted Parks conference, Seattle. The author is grateful for permission to quote from the John Charles Olmsted – Sophia White Olmsted Correspondence, Frances Loeb Library, Graduate School of Design, Harvard University.

2. Major studies and interpretations of Olmsted include Stevenson, E. (1977) *Park Maker: a Life of Frederick Law Olmsted*. New York: Macmillan; Roper, L.W. (1973) *FLO: A Biography of Frederick Law Olmsted*. Baltimore: Johns Hopkins University Press; Fein, A. (1973) *Frederick Law Olmsted and the American Environmental Tradition*. New York: Braziller; Bender, T. (1975) *Toward an Urban Vision: Ideas and Institutions in Nineteenth-Century America*. Lexington: University Press of Kentucky, pp. 161–87; Blodgett, G. (1976) Frederick Law Olmsted: landscape architecture as conservative reform. *Journal of American History*, **62** (March), pp. 869–89, and Simutis, L.J. (1972) Frederick Law Olmsted, Sr.: a reassessment. *American Institute of Planners Journal*, **38** (September), pp. 276–84.

3. Olmsted, F. (1970) *Public Parks and the Enlargement of Towns*. New York: Arno Press & the New York Times, pp. 5, 10.

4. *Ibid.*, p. 23.

5. For Olmsted, parks, and the social control issue, see Bender, *op. cit.*, pp. 164–72; Boyer, P. (1978) *Urban Masses and Moral Order in America, 1820–1920*. Cambridge: Harvard University Press, pp. 236–42, and Blodgett, G. (1976) Frederick Law Olmsted: landscape architecture as conservative reform. *Journal of American History*, **62** (March), pp. 869–89. For English design, see the text and illustrations in Newton, N.T. (1971) *Design on the Land: The Development of Landscape Architecture*. Cambridge: Belknap Press of Harvard University Press, pp. 182–232. For Italian design, see *Ibid.*, pp. 55–152. For Olmsted's philosophy of landscape design see Fisher, I.D. (1978) *Frederick*

Law Olmsted and the Philosophic Background to the City Planning Movement in the United States. Ann Arbor: University Microfilms.

6. Simutis, *op. cit.*

7. Olmsted, F. (1970) *Public Parks and the Enlargement of Towns* New York: Arno Press & the New York Times, pp. 22, 23, 32–4, and Olmsted, F.L., Jr., and Kimball, T. (eds.) (1970) *Frederick Law Olmsted: Landscape Architect, 1822–1903*, vol. 2. New York: Blom, p. 46.

8. Olmsted (1970) *op. cit.*, p. 18, and for quotation see Sutton, S.B. (ed.) (1971) *Civilizing American Cities: A Selection of Frederick Law Olmsted's Writings on City Landscapes*. Cambridge: MIT Press, p. 255.

9. Sutton, *op. cit.*, pp. 111–12, 115, 171, 255; Fein, A. (ed.) (1967) *Landscape Into Cityscape: Frederick Law Olmsted's Plans for a Greater New York City*. Ithaca: Cornell University Press, pp. 156–7, 163; Olmsted and Kimball (eds.) *op. cit.*, Vol. 2, p. 46; Olmsted (1970) *op. cit.*, pp. 19–22, 34–5; and Peterson, J.A. (1967) The Origins of the Comprehensive City Planning Ideal in the United States, 1840–1911. Unpublished PhD. thesis, Harvard University, Cambridge, p. 104.

10. Olmsted (1970) *op. cit.*, pp. 10, 17, 26–8; Fein, *op. cit.*, pp. 135–56, 157–8; and Sutton, *op. cit.*, pp. 110–7. 130–1.

11. For analyses of the movement see Peterson, J.A. (1976) The city beautiful movement: forgotten origins and lost meanings. *Journal of Urban History*, 2 (August), pp. 415–34, and Wilson (1980) *op. cit.*, pp. 165–98.

12. A study of one optimistic reformer is Wilson, W.H. (1981) J. Horace McFarland and the city beautiful movement. *Journal of Urban History*, 7 (May), pp. 315–34.

13. J. Horace McFarland to Charles H. Kilborn, 28 May 1908, J. Horace McFarland Papers, box 15, manuscript group 85, Pennsylvania State Archives, and speech, The crusade against ugliness, box 14. Melosi, M.V. (1981) *Garbage in the Cities: Refuse, Reform, and the Environment, 1880–1980*. College Station: Texas A & M University Press, especially pp. 105–33; Grinder, R.D. (1973) The Anti-Smoke Crusades. Unpublished PhD. thesis, University of Missouri, Columbia; Wilson, W.H. (1975) More almost than the men: Mira Lloyd Dock and the beautification of Harrisburg. *Pennsylvania Magazine of History and Biography*, 99 (October), pp. 490–9, and U.S. Department of the Interior, Census Office (1895) *Report on the Social Statistics of Cities in the United States at the Eleventh Census: 1890*. Washington: Government Printing Office, p. 35.

14. Peterson (1967) *op. cit.*, pp. 102–6; Wilson, W.H. (1964) *The City Beautiful Movement in Kansas City*. Columbia: University of Missouri Press pp. 2–6; McFarland, J.H., Abstract of an illustrated address on the crusade against ugliness. J. Horace McFarland papers, box 14, manuscript group 85, Pennsylvania State Archives, and (1904) Beautiful America. *Ladies Home Journal*, 21 (January), p. 15. For quotation see Moore, C. (1921) *Daniel H. Burnham*, vol. 2. Boston: Houghton Mifflin, p. 102.

15. McFarland, J.H., Abstract of an illustrated address on the crusade against ugliness. J. Horace McFarland papers, box 14, manuscript group 85, Pennsylvania State Archives, and Wilson, W.H. (1983) A diadem for the city

beautiful: the development of Denver's civic center. *Journal of the West*, **22** (April), p. 75.

16. For environmentalism, see Shuey, E.L. (1901) Commercial bodies and civic improvement. *Home Florist*, 4 (January). p. 35; and McFarland, J.H. (1904) Beautiful America. *Ladies Home Journal*, 21 (January), p. 15; Robinson, C.M. (1903) *Modern Civic Art, Or The City Made Beautiful*. New York: G.P. Putnam's Sons, p. 346, and Wilson (1981) *op. cit.*, pp. 316–7.

17. *Harrisburg Telegraph*, 6 June 1901; Moore *op. cit.*, vol. 2, p. 101; Wilson (1983) *op. cit.*, p. 75; Cranz, G. (1982) *The Politics of Park Design: A History of Urban Parks in America*. Cambridge: MIT Press, pp. 61–99, and Rosenzweig, R. (1979) Middle-class parks and working-class play: the struggle over recreational space in Worcester, Massachusettss, 1870–1910. *Radical History Review*, 21 (Fall), pp. 31–46.

18. Burnham, D.H. and Bennett, E.H. (1909) *Plan of Chicago*. Chicago: Commercial Club, p. 116; Aitken, R.I. *et al.* (1926) *Arnold W. Brunner and His Work*. New York: American Institute of Architects, pp. 29–30; Lubove, R. (1959) The twentieth century city: the progressive as municipal reformer. *Mid-America*, 41 (October), p. 198; Robinson, C.M. (1903) *Modern Civic Art, Or The City Made Beautiful*. New York: G.P. Putnam's Sons, p. 246, and Jeffreys-Jones, R. (1974) Violence in American history: plug uglies in the progressive era, *Perspectives in American History*, Volume 8. Cambridge: Charles Warren Centre, Harvard University, pp. 486–9.

19. Weinstein, J. (1968) *The Corporate Ideal in the Liberal State: 1900–1918*. Boston: Beacon, pp. ix–x, 94–5; Wiebe, R.H. (1967) *The Search for Order: 1877–1920*. New York: Hill and Wang, pp. 149–55, 160–1, 169–76; Olmsted and Kimball (eds.) (1970) *op. cit.*, vol. 2. pp. 45–7, 214–32; Wilson (1964) *op. cit.*, p. 48; Harrisburg League for Municipal Improvements (1901) *The Plain Truth About the Improvements*, 2nd ed. Harrisburg, p. 10; Robinson, *op. cit.*, pp. 280–1; Hines, T.S. (1974) *Burnham of Chicago: Architect and Planner*. New York: Oxford University Press, pp. 317–9, 321, 324, 352, and Peterson (1967) *op. cit.*, pp. 342–7.

20. This discussion of the playground movement is based on Cavallo, D. (1981) *Muscles and Morals: Organized Playgrounds and Urban Reform, 1880–1920*. Philadelphia: University of Pennsylvania Press, and Boyer, *op. cit.*, pp. 242–51.

21. For conflicts between the organized play movement and park advocates see Finfer, L.A. (1974) Leisure as Social Work in the Urban Community: The Progressive Recreation Movement, 1890–1920. Unpublished PhD. thesis, Michigan State University, East Lansing, pp. 121–6, 132; Burnap, G. (1916) *Parks: Their Design, Equipment and Use*. Philadelphia: J.B. Lippincott, p. 168, and Curtis, H.S. (1917) *The Play Movement and Its Significance*, reprint ed. Washington: McGrath, pp. 126–7, 129–30, 315. For Olmstedian attacks on the City Beautiful see Peterson (1967) *op. cit.*, pp. 182–3; Simutis, L.J. (1971) *Frederick Law Olmsted's Later Years: Landscape Architecture and the Spirit of Place*. Unpublished PhD. thesis, University of Minnesota, Minneapolis, pp. 196–200, 206–7, and John C. Olmsted to Sophia Olmsted, 10 April 1907, box 15A, folder 103, John Charles Olmsted – Sophia White Olmsted Corres-

pondence, Frances Loeb Library, Graduate School of Design, Harvard University.

22. For a later Olmsted plan see Ziatzevsky, C. (1982) *Frederick Law Olmsted and the Boston Park System*. Cambridge: Belknap Press of Harvard University Press, pp. 96–9.

23. Relevant studies of Seattle include Sale, R. (1976) *Seattle, Past to Present*. Seattle: University of Washington Press, and Blackford, M.G. (1980) Civic groups, political action, and city planning in Seattle. *Pacific Historical Review*, **49** (November), pp. 557–80.

24. For quotation see John C. Olmsted to Sophia Olmsted, 27 May 1903, box 5A, folder 37, John Charles Olmsted – Sophia White Olmsted Correspondence, Frances Loeb Library, Graduate School of Design, Harvard University. For early park planning in Seattle and another view of the Olmsted plan, see Burke, P. (1973) The City Beautiful Movement in Seattle. Unpublished master's thesis, University of Washington, Seattle, pp. 28–44.

25. For quotation see John C. Olmsted to Sophia Olmsted, 30 April 1903, box 5A, folder 35, John Charles Olmsted – Sophia White Olmsted Correspondence, Frances Loeb Library, Graduate School of Design, Harvard University. For a brief historical review of the park system see Seattle Board of Park Commissioners (1916) *Thirteenth Annual Report*. Seattle, pp. 12–5. For the depression's effects see Blackford, M.G. (1980) Civic groups, political action, and city planning in Seattle. *Pacific Historical Review*, **49** (November), p. 578.

26. The Seattle Board of Park Commissioners of 1904 renumbered board reports beginning with its (1905) *First Annual Report, 1884–1904*. Seattle: Lowman & Hanford. It reprinted the Report of Olmsted Brothers, pp. 44–85. For quotation see p. 44, and for description see pp. 44–5.

27. *Ibid.*, pp. 45–8.

28. *Ibid.*, pp. 48–51, and for the meeting see J.C. Olmsted memorandum, 29 May 1903, in Records of the Olmsted Associates, box 130, folder 2690, Manuscript Division, Library of Congress.

29. Fein (ed.) (1967) *op. cit.*, pp. 158–64, and Seattle Board of Park Commissioners (1905) *First Annual Report, 1884–1904*. Seattle: Lowman & Hanford, p. 50.

30. John C. Olmsted to J.E. Shrewsbury, 28 November 1906, in Records of the Olmsted Associates, box 130, folder 2690, Manuscript Division, Library of Congress, and Blackford, *op. cit.*, p. 561.

31. Olmsted Brothers to J.M. Frink, 25 January 1908, in Records of the Olmsted Associates, box 130, folder 2690, Manuscript Division, Library of Congress.

32. Seattle Board of Park Commissioners (1916) *Thirteenth Annual Report*. Seattle, pp. 17–43.

33. John C. Olmsted to J.T. Heffernan, 4 October 1910, in Records of the Olmsted Associates, box 130, folder 2690–1, Manuscript Division, Library of Congress.

34. Seattle Board of Park Commissioners (1916) *Thirteenth Annual Report*. Seattle, pp. 17–43.

35. *Ibid.*, p. 11. For the defeat of the Bogue Plan see Blackford, *op. cit.*, pp. 562–76.

36. Seattle Board of Park Commissioners (1915) *Eleventh and Twelfth Annual Report*. Seattle, p. 11.

37. Olmsted Brothers to J.M. Frink, 25 January 1908, and John C. Olmsted to Edward C. Cheasty, 14 June 1909, in Records of the Olmsted Associates, box 130, folder 2690, Manuscript Division, Library of Congress.

38. Olmsted Brothers to J.M. Frink, 25 January 1908, in Records of the Olmsted Associates, box 130, folder 2690, Manuscript Division, Library of Congress, and Robinson, *op. cit.*, pp. 323–5. The calculation is based on 1,445 acres in parks and squares and an assumed population of 300,000.

39. Seattle Board of Park Commissioners (1916) *Thirteenth Annual Report*. Seattle, pp. 39–43.

40. For Thompson see Olmsted Brothers to Board of Park Commissioners, 24 March 1904, and James F. Dawson to Charles W. Saunders, 29 November 1920, in Records of the Olmsted Associates, box 130, folder 2690, Manuscript Division, Library of Congress.

41. Seattle Playgrounds Association (1909) *The Playground Movement in Seattle*. Seattle, pp. 3–4, 11–14. For the press see *Seattle Post-Intelligencer*, 4 April 1911, p. 6. For the bond issue promises see John C. Olmsted to J.T. Heffernan, 4 October 1910, in Records of the Olmsted Associates, box 130, folder 2690–1, Manuscript Division, Library of Congress. For park board activities see Seattle Board of Park Commissioners (1916) *Thirteenth Annual Report*. Seattle, 49–53. For recreation enthusiasts see *Seattle Post-Intelligencer*, 25 April 1909, p. 8, and Cavallo, D. (1981) *Muscles and Morals: Organized Playgrounds and Urban Reform, 1880–1920*. Philadelphia: University of Pennsylvania Press, p. 105. For Kinnear Park see Seattle Board of Park Commissioners (1916) *Thirteenth Annual Report*. Seattle, p. 23.

Chapter Six

Comprehensive Planning before the Comprehensive Plan: A New Look at the Nineteenth-Century American City

DAVID C. HAMMACK[1]

When Lewis Mumford denounced the nineteenth century's 'insensate industrial towns' in *The Culture of Cities*, he renewed a venerable tradition of complaint. Like many humane critics of that century, Mumford found the ugliness and unhealthiness of its astonishing mushroom cities deeply disturbing. The problem, he insisted, was unrestrained, short-sighted industrial growth. Industry had 'laid its diseased fingers on the new cities and stultified the further development of the old ones'. In America as in England the cities of the industrial age were 'man-heaps, machine-warrens, not organs of human association'. These cities, Mumford insisted, were the products of mechanical growth, or blind individualism: not of anything that might be called intelligent forethought.[2]

In the twenty-five years since Mumford restated his views in *The City In History* we have learned a great deal about the people, the policies, and the politics that shaped nineteenth-century American cities. These cities grew with a rapidity that was almost incomprehensible to their residents, and they offered living conditions that were often appallingly unhealthy. But nineteenth-century cities did not 'just grow' without the intervention of human intelligence and forethought. To a very large extent, men (and, often indirectly, women), made conscious decisions that shaped their cities. Sometimes their decisions reflected thinking that was so comprehensive, and so concerned about long-term developments, that it can only be called planning.

Many scholars have contributed to our new knowledge about the decision-makers and the planning process of the nineteenth-century American city. Because these scholars' preoccupations diverge widely, the elements of nineteenth-century city planning have never been described as a whole, and some elements remain elusive. Yet if we pull together our knowledge of nineteenth-century city-building, we can see that a form of comprehensive planning was in process long before the age of the formal comprehensive plan. And if we look carefully, we can identify some of the early comprehensive planners, and learn a good deal about their work and its effects.

HISTORIANS ON NINETEENTH-CENTURY AMERICAN CITY-BUILDING

Historians of landscape architecture and of formal urban design, often stimulated by Mumford, have made especially large additions to our knowledge of comprehensive planning. In their effort to define a canon of exemplary plans and designs, they have written impressively about Pierre L'Enfant, Alexander Jackson Davis, and Andrew Jackson Downing, Frederick Law Olmsted and Horace W.S. Cleveland, Charles Eliot and Daniel Burnham, as well as lesser figures and their works. In the words of Christopher Tunnard, one of the leading historians of design, their emphasis is on the creation of 'beauty in American cities'. Tunnard and others have splendidly demonstrated that nineteenth-century Americans produced many impressive plans for their cities. Their work identifies an American planning tradition whose great triumphs run from Central Park and its successors, to park systems like that of Boston's Metropolitan District Commission, to the grand civic centre and park system plans for the Chicago World's Columbian Exposition and the McMillan Plan for Washington D.C.

Unfortunately this planning tradition had only a limited influence on the general design of America's cities. Time after time, historians of this design tradition are forced to lament that so many of the best plans were never built. Despite their many successes as designers, city planners and landscape architects found it very difficult to gain acceptance for their plans, or to secure recognition and deference. In his text for aspiring professionals, Norman T. Newton traces the proud title 'Landscape Architect' to the letter that Frederick Law Olmsted and Calvert Vaux wrote when they *resigned* out of frustration at the Central Park Commission's 1863 rejection of their recommendations.[3]

Progressive historians inclined to denounce the failure of nineteenth-century cities to meet acceptable standards of public health and housing have also tended to agree with Mumford that those cities just grew. Much of their work complements that of the historians of planning and design by documenting the chaotic, unplanned fashion in which housing and public facilities were built, and by showing that private developers proceeded with a single-minded emphasis on short-run profits.[4] In *The Urban Wilderness*, his powerful indictment of the quality of urban life in America, Sam Bass Warner, Jr., concludes that although 'the multiplication of public and private utilities was a major accomplishment of the nineteenth-century city', the 'entire century' saw urban living conditions decline in the face of 'timid regulations against the behaviour of landlords and the excessive individualism of the land law'.[5]

Neither the urban designers nor the progressives – with the partial exception of Warner – take very seriously the activities of the landowners, builders, merchants, engineers, lawyers, and municipal officials who actually built American cities between 1820 and 1900. Other historians, however, have gradually been recovering their stories. These new historians of city-building and of city-builders suggest that three distinct forces – the demand for improved public health, the response of small investors to the market, and the strategies of large land developers – all encouraged the creation of a sort of order, and of planning.

As scientific and technological knowledge increased, especially after about 1850, urban residents insisted that water and sewer facilities be improved. Civil and sanitary engineers eagerly took up the challenge. Indeed, historians Raymond Merritt, Jon Peterson, Joel Tarr, Stanley Schultz, and Clay McShane have argued that the unsung civil and sanitary engineers made a more pervasive contribution to the building of American cities than the most widely celebrated landscape architects.[6] Often, it is true, economic pressures forced delays in sanitary improvements – but only until it made sense to provide them in a comprehensive fashion. A careful analysis of the economic history of Baltimore's sewers, for example, persuaded Alan D. Anderson that the timing of improvements reflected eminently rational thought about costs and benefits – thought that tolerated unhealthy conditions in neglected neighbourhoods for all too many years, but then produced order and a comprehensive system without advance planning.[7]

Market forces of course played an even more pervasive part in the development of American cities, but contrary to common impression market forces did not always foster disorder. As they went about the business of buying and selling houses and shops, large numbers of people who possessed only very modest resources established routines and fashions that gave distinct patterns to certain new urban districts. Warner himself has shown that Boston's subdividers, utility companies, and housebuilders created 'a weave of small patterns' that gave their city's streetcar suburbs a characteristic, if not entirely satisfactory, shape.[8] Roger Simon has similarly shown that developers and builders in early-twentieth-century Milwaukee provided generous lots, wide, paved, curvilinear streets, and complete utilities to prosperous buyers who could afford them, even as landowners in other sections of the city offered very small lots on narrow, unpaved, unsewered streets to poor immigrant labourers who wanted to build their own houses but could not afford even the most minimal sanitation.[9] At the other end of the scale, as I will argue in this essay, the few people who controlled large tracts of urban land sometimes planned their developments on a large – and in effect on a *comprehensive* – scale in order to reap the largest return from their capital.

NINETEENTH-CENTURY CITY-BUILDING: AN ALTERNATIVE VIEW

None of the historians discussed above claims that his protagonists engaged in comprehensive planning. Merritt, Tarr, Schultz, and McShane are more concerned with the evolution of the engineering profession than with the planning of cities. Warner and Simon dis-covered their small patterns and systematic variations through the careful analysis of behavioural evidence: they do not argue that the patterns were products of forethought. Taken together, however, these and other studies reveal such regularity in the development of nineteenth-century cities that they force us to ask whether some sort of comprehensive planning did not go on? How, if not through carefully considered intentional action, did public officials and private individuals create distinctive street patterns, transportation, water supply and drainage systems, and park networks? How did they create middle- and even lower-middle- as well as upper-income neighbour-hoods of consistent housing quality and style?

Jon Peterson has offered the most thoughtful answer to this question. He argues that the nineteenth-century American city produced many antecedents to the comprehensive urban planning ideal of the second quarter of the twentieth century. He finds these antecedents in water supply and drainage systems that date to the 1830s or earlier; in the park movements that began in the 1850s and the playground movement that began in the 1880s. And he finds them in the passion for monumental civic architecture and patriotic display that reached an apotheosis in the White City of the 1894 Chicago World's Fair and in the patriotic arches and monuments of the late 1890s.[10]

Peterson insists, however, that because such activities were pursued separately they did not add up to comprehensive planning in the twentieth-century sense. Surely this was often the case. And yet, as Peterson himself has shown – and as is apparent from the works of Warner, Simon, Merritt, Tarr, McShane, and others – nineteenth-century American cities did exhibit a considerable degree of order and regularity. Much of this order was surely the result not only of 'blind' market forces, but of forethought and intent. Even if the all-embracing comprehensive planning celebrated in the twentieth century was rarely seen in the nineteenth, some sort of coordination must have gone on. At the same time, it is important to remember that twentieth-century planning has rarely met the exacting standards of the ideal that Peterson has described so well. The planning that actually occurs, in fact, closely resembles that of the nineteenth century.

As the comprehensive planners of the nineteenth century sought to satisfy the market and respond to the public demand for sanitary and aesthetic improvements, their actions were shaped by their economic and political environment. It is always necessary to decide where buildings and public works should be located, and when to build them. As urban facilities grew in scale and in cost during the nineteenth century, and as the capital markets became more sophisticated and institutionalized, profit-maximizing and municipal governments found it more and more important to make real estate and utility investments on a large scale, and to plan them well in advance. In doing so, real estate investors only followed the innovative practices of investors in railroads and manufacturing.[11] Often, and it would be interesting to know *how* often, investors in these distinct fields were the same people.

The political environment of the American city also encouraged large-scale planning. As the cities grew they became politically more diverse and more competitive. Investors were forced to argue that proposed projects offered benefits to a wide variety of special interests, as well as to the public at large.[12] Thus Seymour J. Mandelbaum has suggested that much of the corrupt activity of the notorious New York City political boss, William Marcy Tweed, was designed to persuade local and small-business interests to accept large-scale public works projects. Later in the century, New York's rapid transit and suburban development policies were shaped by the conflicting pressures of disparate economic elites, aided and abetted by competing social and political elites.[13] These economic and political pressures encouraged a commercially-motivated planning that was remarkably wide-ranging – although definitely not ideally comprehensive – in its scope.

If historians have neglected the comprehensive planning of the nineteenth century, they have done so for a variety of reasons. Neither professional urban designers nor progressive advocates of public control and social justice find much to admire in the period's practical, profit-oriented, deal-making plans. Advocates of planning as a *public* service can hardly be expected to devote much attention to the attorneys and engineers who planned for *private* clients. Indeed, to an advocate of public planning these private activities do not qualify as 'planning' at all. And insofar as recent historians have thought that planning must necessarily be carried out by qualified, specialized planners, they have found it very difficult to find such figures in the much less specialized public and private decision-making environment of the nineteenth-century city.

In important ways, however, nineteenth-century planners closely resembled their twentieth-century counterparts. When planners make a significant contribution today, they almost always do so as generalists and political managers whose role is to coordinate the efforts of others. The most effective planners – New York's Robert Moses and John Zucotti, Philadelphia's Edmund Bacon, Edward Logue in New Haven and Boston – have taken a very broad view of their city or region and have urged public officials and private parties to consider the likely long-run consequences of their actions. These planners succeed when they persuade developers, landowners, bankers, public officials, and others that they can serve their own self-interest even as they advance the long-term interests of the community as a whole.[14] Although they worked within very different intellectual and institutional constraints, their nineteenth-century predecessors made much the same sort of contribution.

ANDREW H. GREEN:
THE CAREER OF A NINETEENTH-CENTURY PLANNER

The role of comprehensive planners in the nineteenth-century city can best be demonstrated through an account of the extraordinary career of Andrew H. Green of New York.[15] Although he has long been all but forgotten, Green rivalled Robert Moses in the longevity and breadth of his influence – and also in the intensity of the criticism he received. For more than fifty years he insisted, with considerable success, that major developments in the city ought to be planned carefully, and on a comprehensive scale, for the long-run advantage of the metropolitan region as a whole. Like Moses, he played a major role in planning public facilities of all kinds. Following a characteristic nineteenth-century pattern, however, Green did not draw a sharp line between public service and private interest. As an attorney and

144

consultant, he had considerable influence on the location and shape of a wide variety of private undertakings, ranging from transportation and industrial facilities, to commercial and residential developments, to the buildings and grounds of charitable and cultural institutions.

Far from hampering his career, Green's private activities were essential to his success with public as well as private projects. Characteristically, he promoted voluntary agreements, worked out in private discussion, and designed to appeal to as many interests as possible. He won acceptance of his plans by arguing that they would promote long-term economic growth. Green was able to operate in this way because he was one of the chief lawyers to New York's mercantile elite. And because he lived to a very old age, his planning career paralleled the last fifty years of that elite's long dominance, until its ultimate decline at the turn of the twentieth century.[16]

We can appreciate Green's work as a nineteenth-century planner if we consider the outlines of his career, and then turn to a more detailed look at the substance of his plans. Born to a pious, prosperous, professional family in Worcester, Massachusetts in 1820, Andrew H. Green was destined to take his place among the mercantile and legal elite of New York City. At the age of fifteen he entered one of the city's leading dry goods establishments, where he received 'a thorough commercial education'. Nine years later, at twenty-four, he began to study law in the firm of Samuel J. Tilden, who had become, as his biographer says, the nation's 'first master mind in consolidating independent railroads and other business concerns on a profitable basis'.[17]

By 1852 Green was promoting railroad consolidations and handling land and mining deals throughout New York, Massachusetts, Vermont, New Jersey, and Pennsylvania.[18] By this time his brother, Martin Green, had similarly become a close associate of William B. Ogden, the great railroad and real estate promoter who had been the first mayor of Chicago. In 1857 Green would write, during a visit to Chicago, that 'the activity, the stir, the upturning' of that city were almost great enough to tempt him to leave New York.[19]

Despite Chicago's attractions, Green was already bound to New York by an extraordinary set of political and economic connections that would keep him near the centre of affairs for half a century. As early as 1845 he was working to keep Tilden's name on the Assembly ticket despite Tammany opposition. Three years later he was appointed, no doubt with the help of Tilden, William Cullen Bryant, and other anti-Tammany or 'Swallowtail' Democrats, as a Ward School Trustee. From 1855 to 1860 he served on the city's Board of Education, winning fame 'for his punctilious regard for economy' and for his devotion to the interests of property. As a two-term president of the Board of Education he sought to reduce the share of state school tax levied on city property and, as he put it, to manage the schools so as to 'ensure order, and economy'.[20]

Thus Andrew Green had become one of the city's leading defenders of the rights of property when in 1857 he gained the most important appointment of his career as one of the original members of the Central Park Commission. Created at Bryant's urging by a state legislature dominated by Republicans and by 'Swallowtail' Democrats, the Central Park Commission possessed extraordinary power. Like the simultaneously created Metropolitan Police Commission (and like the Metropolitan Fire, Excise, and Health Commissions set up in 1865 and 1866), the Central Park Commission was designed to seize patronage from Tammany – and to assure taxpayers of services that were economical yet responsive to their desires.[21]

In effect, these commissions placed the daily management of New York City's affairs in the hands of appointed officials chosen by the state legislature. As the leading Swallowtail Democrat on the Central Park Commission Green not only held its most important formal offices: he was its guiding spirit. His subordinates often chafed under his direction, but even Frederick Law Olmsted, who bitterly resented his emphasis on economy, wrote that Green 'did a hundred times more work than all the rest [of the commissioners] together'.[22]

The Tammany 'Home Rule' charter of 1870 abolished the Central Park Commission, returning its power to the city's departments of parks and public works. Tilden's counter-attack against the 'Tweed Ring', however, almost immediately brought Green back to prominence. When the city's chief creditors refused to renew their loans while Tweed's men remained in office, Tilden and former mayor William F. Havemeyer arranged for Green to become the city's Comptroller.[23]

During the next six years Green provided records for the prosecutions of Tweed Ring members, sorted out the city's tangled finances, resisted wage and other claims issued by the Ring, and secured a market for the city's notes by signing them himself.[24] His tenacious defence of the city's taxpayers and creditors – its 'substantial people', as he called them – made him so unpopular that in 1876 he felt obliged to quash a movement to nominate him for mayor out of fear that his candidacy might hurt Tilden's bid for the presidency.[25] After 1876 Green's reputation for grim, tight-fisted loyalty to the interests of property made it impossible to consider him for elective office.[26]

Green's reputation, however, did secure him an influential and well-paid later careeer as the manager of large landed estates and as a private comprehensive planner of transportation, public works, and real estate investments throughout the metropolitan region. On retiring in 1877 as Comptroller of the City of New York, Green became the chief trustee of the estate of William B. Ogden, who had owned extensive real estate in New York and Chicago. He helped Tilden draft his famous will creating a trust for the New York Public Library, and on Tilden's death became one of the three executors and trustees of Tilden's estate. By 1894 the Tilden trustees were considering proposals to join forces with the Ogden trustees and a few other major landowners who together controlled, according to Tilden trustee John Bigelow, 'all the real estate of any value over which New York must march in its necessary growth' toward the north.[27] Green continued to expand his real estate practice until his death in 1903.[28]

Green's planning expertise and experience as a commissioner also won him seats on the boards of trustees of most of the city's leading cultural institutions. As Comptroller of Central Park he had helped the Metropolitan Museum of Art and the American Museum of Natural History secure their sites on the park's land. In the 1870s and 1880s he took a seat on the board of each of these institutions, as well as on those of the New York Academy of Science, the New York Geographical Society, the New York Zoological Society (which he helped to locate in what became Bronx Park), and the New York Historical Society.

In all these institutions, Green urged that public funds be used to support institutions that remained under private control. He 'very early' concluded, he wrote Governor David B. Hill in 1887, 'that the public might aid by financial means to erect the buildings' but that the city's museums, arboretums, and zoos should be privately owned and controlled. 'The collections', he wrote, should be 'made by private contribution'. Even more importantly, 'the management of these institutions' should be 'intrusted to intelligent citizens men of leisure & scientific men'.[29] As a member of the boards of at least three private charities, he advocated similar policies – and also arranged for new buildings to be located in accordance with the general plans he favoured.[30]

Even as Green's private estate-managing practice flourished, he continued to hold important appointive offices relating to public works, transportation, and land-use planning in the New York region. He served as Park Commissioner of the City of New York in 1870 and again in 1880 and 1881. Named as one of the original trustees of Brooklyn Bridge in the 1870s, he served until the end of the century on commissions to promote or build bridges over the East, Harlem, and Hudson Rivers that surround Manhattan. He had a hand in the planning of the Toombs prison, in the preservation of the old City Hall building and in retaining it on its site, and in the location of the

New York Public Library. In 1880 he sat on a state commission to revise state tax and assessment laws, a matter he was still pursuing as an elected delegate to the state's 1894 constitutional convention. In 1888 he launched a movement to expand New York City's water supply reserve.

In these as in his private activities Green worked largely behind the scenes, but in 1890 he returned to the metropolitan region's central, public, planning-policy position as President of the Greater New York Inquiry Commission. From this post he dominated the discussion of planning issues for five years. Despite declining health he remained at the centre of planning affairs, serving on the 1896 Greater New York Charter Commission and then, at the very end of his life, on the New York Commerce Commission of 1898.[31]

The parallels between Green's career and that of Robert Moses are extraordinary. Moses, the twentieth-century park, highway, bridge, and housing commissioner and public works 'czar', was also highly influential for a very long span of years, serving under New York governors from Al Smith to Nelson Rockefeller and under mayors from Fiorello LaGuardia to John V. Lindsay. Green and Moses both developed plans for a very wide variety of public facilities. To justify the scale of their proposals, both evinced a fanatical commitment to economy and emphasized the contributions long-term planning could make to economic growth. Both carried out plans that were desired by popular political leaders, and eagerly accepted full credit for schemes that were not entirely their own. Like Moses, Green became the object of attack by people who did not like the schemes he promoted; and like Moses, he found it impossible to realize his ambition to win election to a major office.

But Green's career also differed from Moses's and the differences are as significant as the similarities because they reflect the changes that took place in the urban decision-making environment between the nineteenth century and the twentieth. Green was trained in private mercantile and law firms; Moses held degrees in public administration from Yale, Oxford, and Columbia Universities. Green's primary career was as a railroad and real estate lawyer; Moses continuously held governmental appointments. Moses derived his power from private pressure groups, from the press, and above all from elected officials; Green enjoyed the direct support of the city's private property-owners and creditors as well as of a close-knit group of political-and-commercial associates.[32]

The largely private nature of Green's career should not mislead us into concluding that he did not play a significant public role, or that his clients and supporters did not make use of planning and forethought. Instead, his career shows that in the nineteenth century, city planning was largely a private matter in the United States. For fifty years Green sought to guide and control the development of public works, charitable facilities, and private real estate investments to promote the long-term interests of landowners and bondholders. He insisted that the plans he advocated would benefit not only his clients, but the public at large. Nevertheless, Green performed his planning functions as a real estate lawyer and estate manager at least as much as a public official. And he owed much of his success to the fact that his clients believed he was acting in their interest. Although he sometimes proposed actions that they resisted, he never lost their confidence.[33]

GREEN'S RATIONALES:
LONG-TERM PROFIT AND THE PUBLIC INTEREST

Throughout his fifty-year career, Green justified his plans with a consistent body of planning principles. He stated these principles first and in greatest detail in reports for the Central Park Commission, but he restated them again and again, and with particular emphasis during the debate over Greater New York. In essence, Green urged that comprehensive planning was the best way to reconcile the conflicting interests of competing property-owners with one another – and with the interest of the public at large. In every case, Green stressed the long-term economic advantages of planning.[34]

The first of Green's arguments for comprehensive planning, printed in 1865, was in many ways the most remarkable of all. By that time plans for Central Park itself were complete, and construction was well under way. Green then persuaded the owners of several large estates in upper Manhattan that his Commission ought to have a significantly wider scope. In 1865, the state legislature empowered the Commission to revise New York City's street plan between 59th and 155th Streets, to draft an entirely new plan for the northern end of Manhattan, and to manage the construction of public works throughout the entire area. In a lengthy report published at the end of 1865, Green discussed the principles that ought to control the new plans.[35]

For its date, Green's report was extraordinarily comprehensive: in its geographic scope, in the range of public works facilities it sought to coordinate, in its attention to aesthetic matters, and in its advocacy of what amounted to zoning. Green's report also gave extraordinary attention to the long-run implications of initial locational, design, and street-pattern decisions.

Green began by urging the commission to expand the already very large territory over which it had just been given jurisdiction. The appropriate unit for planning, he argued, was the entire metropolitan region. A good plan for upper Manhattan must therefore necessarily be part of a plan for Westchester County, or at least that portion of it that later became the Borough of the Bronx. In effect, Green would have his commission prepare a single comprehensive plan for the entire area between the Hudson River and the East River–Harlem River–Long Island Sound waterways, for a distance of at least 10 miles above 59th Street.

Within this vast area, the plan Green envisaged would coordinate the location and sequence of construction for public works and utilities of all kinds. It would provide routes for rail, rapid transit, streetcar, industrial and commercial trucking, local shopping, and pleasure travel. It would provide for parks and squares, parkways and boulevards, riding trails, and a fairground. It would locate underground water and gas lines, and storm and sanitary sewers, as well as above-ground reservoirs, sewage treatment plants, and dumps. Casting aside the relentless gridiron plan imposed on Manhattan between Houston and 155th Streets in 1811, Green urged that the dead hand of inadequate earlier plans not be allowed to control construction in the new area. Instead, each element of the plan for the territory above 59th Street should be designed to fit the local topography, to meet the practical requirements of existing and probable future bridges and traffic routes, and to make the new portion of the city as attractive as practical.

Even more remarkably, Green urged that his commission's plan should anticipate and facilitate, if not dictate by zoning, the location of separate districts for specific purposes, including upper-income residences, public buildings, retail shops, wholesale markets, and warehouses, as well as the slaughterhouses, dumps, and other activities traditionally segregated as nuisances under the common law. Three years later he emphasized the need to plan carefully for distinct residential districts for both 'artizans and merchants'.[36]

The significance of Green's proposal that specific land uses be segregated in accordance with a plan becomes clear when we recall that the standard history of city planning places the earliest effort to legislate for such a purpose in 1885, and that the first comprehensive zoning scheme in the United States was not adopted until 1916, when New York City finally acted on the implications of Green's 1865 report.[37] Sam Bass Warner, Jr., has demonstrated that in large cities like Philadelphia and St. Louis some economic activities and several ethnic and occupational groups had already begun to be segregated into distinct districts by 1860.[38] Green's 1865 advocacy of zoning suggests that mid-nineteenth-century landowners and land managers knew that such segregation was occurring and that they welcomed and encouraged it. If this is so, then zoning was in part simply a technique to ratify, systematize, and enforce patterns of land use that had long been established through less public means by owners of large pieces of property.

Green intended to reach such owners through the reports he addressed to the Central Park Commission. Such owners' support was essential to the success of his proposal to expand the Commission's jurisdiction, since these owners would have to agree to the Commission's recommendations. In effect, Green expected that his *public* agency would arbitrate among competing *private* landowners – and then carry out the plan they agreed to follow.

Green put the point clearly, if a bit hopefully, in his 1865 report. In great European capitals like Paris or Berlin, he wrote, it might be possible to employ the coercive power of the state to control urban development. But in the United States it was necessary to assume that 'a common interest of landed ownership and a common perception of the most profitable use of the land will generally assure symmetry in the plan of the city'.[39] The plan he advocated would assure 'salubrious and agreeable habitations' for future residents. But first, it would reconcile conflicting interests and promote long-term profitability.

Green admitted that no plan could be equally satisfactory to all property-owners, that 'the views of private owners will to some extent be subordinated to requirements of the public interests'.[40] Thus it would be advisable to change the location of Broadway Boulevard, Manhattan's ancient main road, to a shorter route with fewer steep grades. This would damage the interests of some current owners of property. But, Green wrote, 'if a different location is deemed detrimental to their property, it will be because the new drive will take the travel . . . [and] if it takes the travel, it will be because it is the better route'.[41]

Similarly, careful advance planning could reduce the long-run cost of public works, although again at a potential inconvenience and expense to some property-owners. Green argued that such costs could be minimized if only the city and the landowners would, at the outset, construct wide, carefully located, well-paved streets furnished with adequate sewers, water mains, and gas lines. If streets and boulevards could be made wide enough, they could serve both the 'dwellings of a costly character' that would first appear, and then could serve the crowded commercial districts that would develop in the future. Green anticipated change. 'After having served their day and generation', he argued, the expensive dwellings of a new, fashionable residential district would 'give way . . . to the pressures of business'. Thus he justified the high initial cost of a wide boulevard complete with a tree-lined median strip not only by its initial attractiveness, but also by the ease with which it might later be converted to other uses.[42]

Green's emphasis on change was very different from the approach of the landscape architects whose work has been emphasized by the historians of planning. Even as he wrote, Frederick Law Olmsted and Calvert Vaux were themselves breaking new ground by urging the development of boulevards and pleasant residential neighbourhoods for harried business and professional men. But Olmsted and Vaux hoped to create *permanent* boulevards and neighbourhoods, pathways and oases of tranquility set apart from the disturbing, contentious, changing city.[43] Green sought instead to enable landowners – and the city as a whole – to plan for changes and conflicts that he believed were inevitable. In this respect, as in his advocacy of functional segregation, Green the advocate was probably closer to the purposive practice of his time than were Olmsted and Vaux, the visionary founders of a new and not-very-well accepted profession.

GREEN'S GREATER NEW YORK: THE PUBLIC INTEREST ON A GRAND SCALE

By 1868 Green's enthusiasm for comprehensive long-range planning led him to conclude that the municipal boundaries of New York City should be enlarged. Intelligent planning required a geographic unit that included the lower half of Westchester County to the north, much of Queens County and all of Kings County to the east, and at least part of Richmond County to the south. Under 'one common municipal government', he insisted, it would be possible 'to endeavour to guide . . . the progress of improvements in Westchester' and in the other countries 'in conjunction with those of this city, for the ultimate best interests of both'.[44] The vision of unified metropolitan development was not Green's alone; the park and boulevard proposals of Frederick Law Olmsted and Calvert Vaux collected in Albert Fein's *Landscape Into Cityscape* were commissioned not only by Green's Central Park Commission but also by similar agencies in Brooklyn and Staten Island. In effect, these proposals were designed to solve the problems that Green had defined for the property-owners who were his clients.[45]

But discussion of New York's metropolitan problems was delayed for nearly twenty years. Aided by citizens who believed that too many separate agencies governed New York, Boss Tweed persuaded the state legislature in 1870 to abolish the metropolitan police, fire, public health, excise, and Central Park commissions. Green had expected that these agencies would implement his plans. Just a year later, the campaign against Tweed and his 'Ring' threw New York City's politics into a turmoil that lasted well into the 1880s. The depression that followed the Panic of 1873 intensified the political turmoil and discouraged all thought of large public works expenditures.

After devoting six years to Tilden's effort to restore the city's financial reputation, Green returned to his real estate law and estate management practice. Working privately and behind the scenes, he continued to push the complex plans he had helped develop as Commissioner of Central Park. He was not entirely successful. But through his influence on landowners, estates, charities, and public agencies, he had a considerable impact on the city's growth. Again and again, he advised agencies and individuals seeking to develop parks, bridges, shipping facilities, the water supply, and cultural and charitable facilities of all sorts.[46]

During the 1870s and 1880s Green continued to play the role of a comprehensive planner while he followed the career of a highly specialized, and successful, real estate lawyer. But he continued to favour a more public and official form of comprehensive planning. When the Chamber of Commerce of the State of New York and the New York *Times* revived the idea of enlarging New York City's boundaries in 1888, Green was ready with a fully developed rationale for what became known as the Greater New York movement.[47]

A consolidated city, Green argued, could develop the Port of New York more intelligently and aggressively than could New York, Brooklyn, and the numerous small municipalities of Westchester, Queens, Kings, and Richmond Counties acting separately. It could protect the general interest against owners of waterfront property 'who by encroachment, appropriation and misuse, deplete the general system' and concern themselves only with 'niggard schemes of individual profit'. To encourage trade and manufacturing, Green argued, a Greater New York might even apply the logic of zoning to the entire port region, including Staten Island, creating zones for 'factories, docks, bridges, terminals and markets', so as to 'economize space, promote convenience, and insure dispatch'.[48]

Andrew Green always sought to identify a public interest that was compatible with the interests of his clients.[49] Property-owners, investors in real estate or in municipal bonds, and New York-based merchants all stood to gain from the orderly, economical development of public works, just as they stood to gain from equitable laws of taxation and assessment, or from practices that reduced the cost of their transactions. Steady, predictable development also benefited contractors and their workers, all users of New York's public facilities, and taxpayers. Green's plans suited all these interests; they never went beyond.[50]

Nineteenth-Century Planners:
Patterns Outside New York

Although neglected by historians, city planning of the sort that Green engaged in was by no means confined to New York City alone. In large part it was simply a response to the pressures generated by urban growth and technological change. Anthony Sutcliffe has pointed out that in Baron Haussmann's Paris, which Green visited in 1868, 'the construction of new sewers and water ducts' under the grand boulevards 'was an integral part of the Second Empire's improvement policy'.[51] On the examination of a small provincial town much nearer to New York, Michael Frisch found that street, water, and sewer system improvements were all being planned together, in accordance with a systematic plan for the city as a whole, after 1870.[52] Indeed, Blake McKelvey's evidence suggests that a need for more systematic planning of public improvements accounts for the decline of special-purpose water and sewer commissions and for the rise of the 'strong mayor' form of city government after 1870.[53]

Operating in private as well as public capacities, Andrew Green played a central role in bringing comprehensive planning to nineteenth-century New York City. Green was able to do this while working out of a small law office because he was able to devote himself both to the narrowest and most technical legal questions in the fields of real estate and estate law, and to the broadest questions of urban development policy. New York's large size and highly evolved pattern of specialization (a pattern that was particularly marked in the field of investment advice) may well have made it easier for his career to take this form.[54] But similar careers in other large American cities suggest that Green was by no means the only comprehensive planner of his era.

Several of these planners were lawyers who like Green specialized in real estate and trusts. John H.B. Latrobe of Baltimore fits this mould very well. The son of Benjamin H. Latrobe, the noted architect, he was trained as an engineer at West Point and then as a lawyer in a prominent Baltimore office. He established himself in the latter profession by helping to draft the original charter for the Baltimore and Ohio Railroad and by successfully negotiating the purchase of much of the road's right of way. His successful legal career, together with what the contemporary historian of Baltimore, J. Thomas Scharf, called his 'long inculcation in society of the best sort', eventually led to a subsidiary career as a specialist in the location and development of parks, museums, and libraries in Baltimore. Like Green, Latrobe did very well financially although he started out with no great capital of his own. But even more than Green he exercised his planning role as an inside member of his city's mercantile elite.[55]

George Cadwallader of Philadelphia, an attorney who followed in his father's footsteps as agent for the Penn family's estates, appears, through the somewhat enigmatic pages of Scharf, and Westcott's *History of Philadelphia*, to have played a role somewhat similar to John H.B. Latrobe's.[56] Green, Latrobe, and Cadwallader were lawyers who were closely affiliated with their cities' merchants, bankers, and railroads. At the other end of the country, and at the end of the nineteenth century, another lawyer, Thomas Burke, played such an active role in the layout and development of his city that it was said 'he built Seattle'. Like his eastern counterparts, Burke played his coordinating role simultaneously as a private attorney and investment advisor, and as a public official.[57]

In other cities, however, the available secondary literature suggests that the comprehensive planner was himself a leading merchant, manufacturer, or investor. Neither Scharf's *History of St. Louis City and County* nor Justin Winsor's *Memorial History of Boston* identifies a lawyer who played Green's role. But both of those mercantile cities seem to have produced individuals who concerned themselves with comprehensive planning, not because they were lawyers who specialized in giving real estate advice but because they were directly involved in civic improvement and often in real estate investments themselves. Charles H. Dalton, the author of the influential report that called for a comprehensive park system for Boston in 1875, learned business in an old-fashioned mercantile house, became the chief financial officer for several textile manufacturing and coal companies, and went on to the vice presidency of two important banks. For thirty years after 1875 he played leading roles on Boston park and subway commissions.[58] John O'Fallon, one of the earliest and most successful merchants and real estate developers of St. Louis, played an even more direct and prominent role in the planning of his city.[59]

Railroad men and manufacturers, rather than merchants, built Cleveland, Ohio, and they also supplied that city with its nineteenth-century planners. To judge from Samuel P. Orth's *History of Cleveland, Ohio* (1910), screw and bridge manufacturer Amasa Stone and iron manufacturer Samuel Mather participated directly in decisions about the location of the fairgrounds, hospital, home for the aged, manual training school, settlement house, and colleges they built for their city. Mather also served on a very important Public Improve-ments Commission that launched major improvements in the city's water works, sewer, and garbage disposal facilities in the mid-1890s. Jeptha H. Wade, Jr., whose investments in mining and in the Western Union company brought him a fortune, devoted much of his time during the

1880s and 1890s to the problem of locating colleges and schools and laying out a large-scale park system.[60]

Within their particular nineteenth-century contexts, each of these men played the role of a comprehensive city planner. They were not, of course, social reform or civic centre planners, or professional specialists, in the twentieth-century mould.[61] But each took a broad, long-term view of the public interest, and of the implications – particularly the long-term economic and financial implications – of urban development.

All these men promoted comprehensive planning, even though none was trained as a professional planner or claimed the title of landscape architect. In their professional and civic activities, however, each came to specialize in the problems of urban development. Andrew H. Green and, to a somewhat lesser extent John H.B. Latrobe and George Cadwallader, all of whom worked in relatively large and highly specialized communities, devoted all their energies to the field. Because they worked in the institutional and business context of the nineteenth century, these comprehensive planners worked most effectively as advisors to, if not as members of, their cities' mercantile and real estate elites – and not as the holders of public office. Sometimes they advised those elites directly, sometimes they advised the executors and trustees of estates and charities, sometimes they advised semi-public, special-purpose commissions. Coordinating generalists and not technical specialists themselves, the nineteenth-century comprehensive planners served in effect as patrons and supervisors to the landscape designers and civil engineers who produced detailed physical plans.

Comprehensive planning of this sort flourished during the era when the American economy, and American cities, were effectively dominated by well-defined mercantile elites – an era that lasted, according to business historians Glen Porter and Harold Livesay, into the 1870s.[62] By the end of the nineteenth century such planning was becoming increasingly difficult. In the largest cities, at least, private economic interests had become more diverse, professionally-trained planners were asserting themselves, and groups formerly excluded from participation in policy-making were successfully demanding a share of influence. The stage was set for the twentieth-century form of comprehensive planning.

For most of the nineteenth century, however, Green and his counterparts were effective comprehensive planners. Nineteenth-century American cities were the intended product of their work. Whatever we think of the results, these men played a large role in the creation, the location, and the design of the central business and warehouse districts, the clusters of museums and concert halls, the isolated and consistently designed upper- and upper-middle-income residential districts, the parks systems and boulevards, the railroad and trolley networks, the thoroughfares and bridges of those cities. They not only made a market in land, they gave shape to some market forces and left an identifiable imprint on many parts of their cities.

NOTES

1. I presented earlier versions of this essay at the Princeton University School of Architecture and Urban Planning, at the 1980 Annual Meeting of the Organization of American Historians, and at the 1984 meeting of the Law and Society Association; it benefited greatly from comments offered by Chester Rapkin and Julian Wolpert at Princeton, by Helen Lefkowitz Horowitz, Eugene Wise, Jon Peterson, Marlene Wortman, and Stanley Buder at the OAH, and by Robert Gordon and Stephen Diamond at the Law and Society meeting. I did not accept all the good advice offered, however, and so I retain responsibility for the paper in its current form.

2. Mumford, Lewis (1938) *The Culture of Cities*. New York: Harcourt, Brace & Co., p. 148.

3. Tunnard, Christopher (1970) *The City of Man: A New Approach to the Recovery of Beauty in American Cities*. New York: Charles Scribner's Sons; and Tunnard and Reed, Henry Hope (1953) *American Skyline*. Boston: Houghton Mifflin Co., emphasize the list of great fore-planners who intentionally set out to create physical beauty, although both works deal with a broader range of subjects. Reps, John W. (1965) *The Making of Urban America: A History of City Planning in the United States*. Princeton: Princeton University Press, presents the plans of eminent, as well as not-so-eminent, planners of the nineteenth century. Newton, Norman T. (1971) emphasizes the nineteenth-century background in *Design on the Land: The Development of Landscape Architecture*. Cambridge, Mass, Harvard University Press; for Olmsted and Vaux's use of the title 'Landscape Architect' see p. 273. Among the important recent biographies are Roper, Laura Wood (1973) *FLO: A Biography of Frederick Law Olmsted*. Baltimore: The Johns Hopkins University Press; and Hines, Thomas S. (1974) *Burnham of Chicago: Architect and Planner*. Chicago: University of Chicago Press. Kreukeberg, Donald A. (1980) The story of the planner's journal, 1815–1980, and Birch, Eugenie Ladner (1980) Advancing the art and science of planning: planners and their organizations, 1909–1980. *Journal of the American Planning Association* **46**, pp. 5–21 and 22–49, characterize the American Institute of Planners.

4. The progressive tradition dates at least to Jacob A. Riis's classic exposé, *How The Other Half Lives*. New York: Charles Scribner's Sons, 1890. More recent exemplars include Bremner, Robert (1956) *From The Depths: The Discovery of Poverty in the United States*. New York: New York University Press; Lubove, Roy (1962) *The Progressives and the Slums*. Pittsburg: The University of Pittsburg Press; and Jackson, Anthony (1976) *A Place Called Home: A History of Low-Cost Housing in Manhattan*. Cambridge, Mass: MIT

Press. Scott, Mel (1969) *American City Planning Since 1890*. Berkeley: University of California Press, accepts the progressive perspective even as he looks at a wider range of topics, including street platting traditions, the park and playground movements, metropolitan water and sewer commissions, and the City Beautiful. Tunnard and Reed (1953), *op. cit.*, who also accept the progressive tradition, recognizes the contribution to the planning of American cities made by some of the nineteenth century's landfill, park, subdivision, and bridge development schemes. For a more analytic view of the housing, park, playground, and City Beautiful movements, see also Boyer, Paul (1978) *Urban Masses and Moral Order in America, 1820–1920*. Cambridge: Harvard University Press.

5. Warner, Sam Bass, Jr. (1972) *The Urban Wilderness: A History of the American City*. New York: Harper & Row, p. 26.

6. Merritt, Raymond H. (1969) *Engineering in American Society, 1850–1875*. Lexington: The University of Kentucky Press; Peterson, Jon A. (1979) The impact of sanitary reform upon American urban planning, 1840–1890. *Journal of Social History*, 13, pp. 82–103; Tarr, Joel A. (1979) The separate vs. combined sewer problem: a case study in urban technology design choice. *Journal of Urban History*, 5, pp. 308–39; Schultz, Stanley K. and McShane, Clay (1978) To engineer the metropolis: sewers, sanitation, and city planning in late nineteenth-century America. *Journal of American History*, 65, pp. 389–411.

7. Anderson, Alan D. (1977) *The Origin and Resolution of An Urban Crisis: Baltimore, 1890–1930*. Baltimore: The Johns Hopkins University Press.

8. Warner, Sam Bass, Jr. (1962) *Streetcar Suburbs: The Process of Growth in Boston, 1870–1900*. Cambridge, Mass: Harvard University Press.

9. Simon, Roger S. (1978) *The City-Building Process: Housing and Services in New Milwaukee Neighborhoods, 1880–1910*. Philadelphia: *Transactions* of the American Philosophical Society, Volume 68.

10. Peterson, Jon A. (1967) The Origins of the Comprehensive City Plan Ideal in the United States, 1840–1911. Unpublished Harvard University PhD. dissertation.

11. On the increasing scale of business and the increasing need for specialized management capable of advance planning in the nineteenth century, see Porter, Glenn, and Livesay, Harold C. (1971) *Merchants and Manufacturers: Studies in the Changing Structure of Nineteenth-Century Marketing*. Baltimore: The Johns Hopkins University Press; and Chandler, Alfred D., Jr., (1977) *The Visible Hand: The Managerial Revolution in American Business*. Cambridge, Mass: Harvard University Press.

12. For an analysis of the public decision-making environment in one nineteenth-century American city, see Hammack, David C. (1982) *Power and Society: Greater New York at the Turn of the Century*. New York: Russell Sage Foundation; for a more general account of the institutional forces and assumptions that shaped nineteenth-century decision-making, see Keller, Morton (1977) *Affairs of State: Public Life in Late Nineteenth-Century America*. Cambridge, Mass: Harvard University Press.

13. For the argument that power became more widely dispersed in

American cities during the nineteenth century, see Hammack, David C. (1978) Problems in the historical study of power in the cities and towns of the United States, 1800–1960. *American Historical Review*, **83**, pp. 323–349. Mandelbaum, Seymour (1965) *Boss Tweed's New York*. New York: John Wiley & Sons, chapters 6 and 7. On the rapid transit and suburbanization policies of the 1890s, see Hammack (1982), *op. cit.*, chapters 7 and 8.

14. The most famous twentieth-century comprehensive planner is surely Robert Moses, whose career is described in exhaustive, if not always very careful, terms in Caro, Robert A. (1974) *The Power Broker: Robert Moses and the Fall of New York*. New York: Alfred A. Knopf. Edward Logue's work in New Haven is more persuasively documented in Polsby, Nelson (1963) *Community Power and Political Theory*. New Haven: Yale University Press, pp. 70–76, and Wolfinger, Raymond E. (1974) *The Politics of Progress*. Berkeley: University of California Press. Edmund N. Bacon's impact on Philadelphia, is noted in Weigley, Russell F. (ed.) (1982) *Philadelphia: A 300-Year History*. New York: W.W. Norton & Co., pp. 694–97. John Zucotti served as city planner and deputy mayor under New York City mayors John V. Lindsay and Abraham D. Beame.

15. Three dissertations discuss Green's career in detail: Mazaraki, George (1966) Andrew H. Green. New York University; Hammack, David C. (1973) Participation in Major Decisions in New York City, 1890–1900: The Creation of Greater New York and the Centralization of the Public School System. Columbia University; and Kaplan, Barry J. (1975) A Study in the Politics of Metropolitanization: The Greater New York City Charter of 1897. State University of New York at Buffalo. Kaplan (1979) is an account of Green that generally follows my own interpretation: Andrew H. Green and the creation of a planning rationale: the formation of Greater New York City, 1865–1890. *Urbanism Past and Present*, **8**, pp. 32–41; I discuss aspects of Green's career in Hammack (1982) *op. cit.*, chapter 7.

16. Because Green accomplished much of his impact by working behind the scenes, a full analysis of his role would require an examination of his papers; unfortunately the bulk of these has been lost. Yet it is still possible to reconstruct the outlines of his career, to identify his political and commercial allies, and to work out the content of his planning principles and objectives by examining his numerous printed reports and the fragments of his correspondence that still exist.

17. The details of Green's biography appear in the dissertations cited in note 15, above, and also in Foord, John (1913) *The Life and Public Services of Andrew H. Green*. New York: Doubleday, Page & Co., pp. 10 and *passim*; Green, Richard Henry (1904) A biographical sketch of Andrew H. Green. *New York Genealogical and Biographical Record*, **35**, pp. 77–83; Greene, Samuel Swett (1904) Andrew Haswell Green: a sketch of his ancestry, life, and work. *Proceedings of the American Antiquarian Society*, **16**, pp. 200–20; Hall, Edward Hagaman (1904) A Short Biography of Andrew Haswell Green. *Ninth Report of the American Scenic and Historic Preservation Society*, pp. 11–122; Henry Mann, typescript account of the official aspects of Green's career, Green Papers, New York Historical Society; unsigned, undated memorandum on Green's

life in a folder entitled 'Municipal Government # 2', Albert Shaw Papers, New York Public Library; New York *Times*, November 14 and 15, 1903. On Tilden, see Flick, Alexander C. (1939), *Samuel Jones Tilden: A Study in Political Sagacity*. New York: Dodd, Mead and Company, Inc., p. 74, and *passim*.

18. Green's pocket diaries for 1852 through 1855, in private hands.

19. Letter, Andrew H. Green to Lydia Green, August 14, 1857, Andrew H. Green Papers, New-York Historical Society.

20. Green, Andrew H. (1857) *Address . . . on his Re-Election as President of the Board of Education*. New York: William Cullen Bryant & Co., pp. 11, 35.

21. For the political purposes behind these metropolitan commissions, see Mohr, James C. (1973) *The Radical Republicans and Reform in New York During Reconstruction*. Ithaca: Cornell University Press, chapters 2, 3 and 4; Syrett, Harold C. (1944) *The City of Brooklyn, 1865–1898*. New York: Columbia University Press, pp. 41–43; and Pleasants, Samuel A. (1948) *Fernando Wood*. New York: Columbia University Press, pp. 73–83.

22. Letter, Olmsted to John Bigelow, reprinted without date in Bigelow (1909) *Retrospections of an Active Life*. New York: The Baker and Taylor Co., vol. 1, p. 342. On other occasions Olmsted railed against Green's 'constitutional reluctance to pay' the most legitimate bills, and against his 'politico-legal alliances' in general; Bigelow, *Retrospections*, pp. 342–3; letter, Olmsted to H.R. Towne, Oct. 2, 1889, Olmsted Papers, Library of Congress. Bigelow also disagreed sharply with Green over the management of the Tilden estate in the 1890s; see Bigelow's manuscript 'Journal', vol. IX, part XXX, pp. 9, 21, Bigelow Papers, New York Public Library; and letter, Andrew H. Green to Richard Watson Gilder, May 2, 1894, Gilder Papers, New York Public Library. In evaluating Olmsted and Bigelow's frequently cited critical comments, it is important to take account of George Templeton Strong's 1871 remark, 'I believe A.H. Green an honest man. People generally think well of him. I have known him since 1844, more or less. The only person I ever heard speak ill of him was F.L. Olmsted, who . . . has a rather *mauvaise langue*;' Nevins, Allan and Thomas, Milton Halsey (eds.) (1952) *The Diary of George Templeton Strong*. New York: Macmillan Co., vol. IV, p. 385.

23. Callow, Alexander B., Jr. (1965) *The Tweed Ring*. New York: Oxford University Press, pp. 271–73.

24. Foord (1913) *op. cit.*, pp. 98–165.

25. Mandelbaum *op. cit.*, pp. 84, 90–91, 100, 118, Foord, *op. cit.*, pp. 158–160.

26. Green was mentioned as a possible candidate for Comptroller of the State of New York in the early 1880s (New York *Times*, December 6, 1880; October 11, 1881; November 7, 1882). He was considered as a candidate for mayor or city controller several times in the years after his wing of the Democratic Party had given up its effort to work with Tammany Hall (letter, Abram S. Hewitt to William Hogg, September 28, 1888, Hewitt letterpress copybooks, New-York Historical Society; Foord *op. cit.*, p. 242; New York *Sun*, June 18, 1897; letter, J. Field to James B. Reynolds, September 14, 1897, Reynolds Papers in the University Settlement Society of New York Papers, State Historical Society of Wisconsin). Green recognized that after 1887 his

faction of Democrats lacked the standing to help him to high office; letters to Thomas B. Carroll, January 8 and April 1, 1887, Green Papers, New-York Historical Society.

27. Foord *op. cit.*, p. 216; Hall, E. Hagaman (1898) *The Second City of the World.* New York: The Republic Press, p. 26; Flick *op. cit.*, p. 115; Bigelow, 'Journal', vol. IX, part XXXII, pp. 17–18. Green also provided estate advice to Oswald Ottendorfer, publisher of the *New Yorker Staats-Zeitung*, and served on the board of the Isabella Heimath, a home for German-American widows that was one of Ottendorfer's favourite charities.

28. Bigelow, *op. cit.* In 1902, Green signed a *Report on an Investigation of the Rapid Transit Railroad in Park Avenue, New York* (New York, 1901), concerning the impact of subway construction on property values; as early as 1852, at least half the legal matters recorded in his pocket diaries concerned real estate. Scattered references to Green's real estate practice appear in the Green Papers, New-York Historical Society, the *Real Estate Record and Builder's Guide*, February 1, 1890, July 28 and August 24, 1894, and November 30, 1895; in the Crane Family Papers, New York Public Library; and in the New York *Times*, April 5, 1904, which noted that of his estate of $1,625,034, over $1,000,000 consisted of small mortgages issued by Green himself. On Green's work for the Ogden estate, see the Worcester *Evening Post*, January 23, 1905.

29. Letter, Green to Hill, June 21, 1887, Hill Papers, Syracuse University. Green supported an effort to organize a meterological society as early as 1845; letters, Green to Luther Bradish, May 23 and 29 and July 4, 1845; Green Papers, New-York Historical Society. Other references to Green's relation to scientific and cultural organizations occur in Henry Mann, "Andrew H. Green and Central Park," written under contract to Green and now with his papers at the New-York Historical Society; Foord *op. cit.*, p. 205; a letter, Green to Richard Watson Gilder, May 2, 1894, Gilder Papers, New York Public Library; and Lydenberg, Harry Miller (1923) *History of the New York Public Library, Astor, Lenox, and Tilden Foundations.* New York: New York Public Library, pp. 301–11.

30. Hall (1898) *Second City, op. cit.*, p. 27; *Fourteenth Annual Report of the Isabella Heimath Home* (1903), pp. 25, 29; New York Juvenile Asylum (1903) *Fifty-Second Annual Report.*

31. Foord *op. cit.*, Hall *op. cit.*, p. 27; A.H. Green memorandum in the Albert Shaw Papers; New York *Tribune*, January 30, 1886, and March 11, 1891; New York *Times*, March 31 and December 3, 1880; April 11, 1888; April 14, 1892; New York Commerce Commission (1900) *Report.* One case illustrates Green's persistence. As Comptroller of the Central Park Commission in 1868, he recommended the construction of a span to carry traffic over the Harlem River at High Bridge. He secured the necessary legislation in 1869, continued to insist that the city's Department of Public Parks take and then build on the necessary land, and finally secured legislation transferring power to build the bridge to a special Commission in 1885. This Commission completed the bridge in early 1889. Hutton, William R. (1889) *The Washington Bridge.* New York.

32. Caro *op. cit.*

33. For Green's role in the creation of Greater New York, see Hammack (1982) *op. cit.*, chapter 5.

34. On this tendency in the courts, see Horwitz, Morton (1977) *The Transformation of American Law*. Cambridge, Mass: Harvard University Press.

35. Green, Andrew H. (1866) *Communication to the Commissioners of Central Park, Relative to the Improvement of the Sixth and Seventh Avenues . . . And Other Subjects*. New York: William Cullen Bryant. Green dated this report December, 1865.

36. Green, Andrew H. (1868) *Communication to the Commissioners of Central Park*. New York, privately printed, p. 6.

37. Scott, *op. cit.*, pp. 75, 152–63.

38. Warner, Sam Bass Jr. (1968) *The Private City: Philadelphia in Six Periods of its Growth*. Philadelphia, University of Pennsylvania Press, p. 13; Scott, *op. cit.*, pp. 154–60.

39. Green (1866) *op. cit.*, pp. 44–45.

40. *Ibid.*, p. 52.

41. *Ibid.*, p. 54.

42. *Ibid.*, pp. 38, 48–49, 52–54, 62–65, 67–69.

43. Olmsted, Frederick Law, and Vaux, Calvert (1866) *Preliminary Report to the Commissioners for Laying Out a Park in Brooklyn, New York: Being a Consideration of Circumstances of Site and Other Conditions Affecting the Design of Public Pleasure Grounds*. Brooklyn, New York, reprinted in Fein, Albert (1967) *Landscape Into Cityscape: Frederick Law Olmsted's Plans for a Greater New York City*. Ithaca: Cornell University Press.

44. Green, Andrew H. (1868) *Communication to the Board of Commissioners of Central Park*. pp. 17–18.

45. Fein (1967) *op. cit.*

46. Green's efforts to realize during the 1870s, 1880s, and 1890s the planning goals he had set in the 1860s are documented in sources previously cited, and also in his letter to Governor Levi P. Morton's secretary, Ashley W. Cole, June 12, 1895, now in the Syracuse University Public Library, urging Morton to sign a bill authorizing the acquisition of parkland in upper Manhattan, and in a letter to ex-Governor David B. Hill, March 18, 1896, now in the Hill Papers, New York State Library, commending Hill for his support of Green's just-realized plan to 'connect the Harlem River with Long Island Sound'. Green's 1866 *Communication* recommended the construction of virtually all of the parks that were subsequently built in upper Manhattan; his 1868 *Communication* called for a comprehensive park system for Manhattan and what would become the Borough of the Bronx. He spearheaded the drive for federal construction of the ship channel that connects the Hudson and the Harlem river, and secured the construction of Washington Bridge between upper Manhattan and the Bronx, and of the park surrounding the bridge. Albert Shaw's *American Monthly Review of Reviews*, **13** (June, 1896), p. 648, gave him credit for 'the reservation of the great new parks north of the

Harlem River, the utilization of the Hudson Bank for the magnificent River-side Drive and Park', and related projects. According to the *Real Estate Record and Builder's Guide*, December 7, 1895, Green took up, *pro bono publico*, an effort to clean up Newtown Creek and eliminate the notorious 'Long Island nuisance'.

47. For an account of the movement to create Greater New York, see Hammack (1982), *op. cit.*, chapter 7.

48. Green, Andrew H. (1890) *Communication on the Subject of a Consolidation of Areas About the City of New York Under One Government*. Assembly Document 71: Albany, New York, pp. 7–10, 17, 24–25.

49. Opponents of Green's plans, most notably of his plan for Greater New York, often tried to dismiss him as an eccentric enthusiast. Yet although the Chamber of Commerce of the State of New York publically critized the Greater New York scheme that was finally approved by the legislature – and that Green endorsed – it accepted him as a member of a New York Commerce Commission appointed by the state in 1898 to consider the future of the Port of New York. Two members of this commission, including its chairman, belonged to the Chamber of Commerce, but they joined the other members in a 1900 *Report* that endorsed Greater New York for 'creating the basis for one systematic plan of development . . . a material advantage that few appreciate at the present day'. (p. 92).

50. A somewhat narrower consideration of the evidence led Mandelbaum to conclude that although Green 'always argued for orderly advance', he was most closely allied 'with "reform" groups whose principal concern was the expansion of minority power in city politics in order to cut the public budget'; *Boss Tweed's New York*, p. 89. Yet in 1874 Green re-affirmed all the planning objectives he had identified in 1866 and 1868 and stated that for eight years he had favoured the consolidation of New York City and Brooklyn, even as he restated his view that 'for the future the money paid by our tax-payers and raised to the credit of the city, instead of going into the pockets of conspirators, must be honestly and intelligently expended on needed works, based on thoroughly matured plans, and so carried out that for each dollar expended there shall be a fair equivalent in materials or labor'. Honest administration and systematic advance planning, Green was arguing, were necessary not to *prevent* the expenditure of funds on public works, but to *persuade* 'this community . . . [to] cheerfully sustain and justify liberal expenditures for the development of the city'. Green, Andrew H. (1874) *Public Improvements in the City of New York*, p. 27 and *passim*.

51. Sutcliffe, Anthony (1970) *The Autumn of Central Paris: The Defeat of Town Planning, 1850–1970*. London: Edward Arnold, p. 30.

52. Frisch, Michael H. (1972) *Town into City: Springfield, Massachusetts, and the Meaning of Community, 1840–1880*. Cambridge, Mass: Harvard University Press, pp. 139–40, 170–75.

53. McKelvey, Blake (1963) *The Urbanization of America, 1860–1915*. New Brunswick, New Jersey: Rutgers University Press, chapters 5, 6, 7.

54. For the increasing specialization of occupations in New York City

during the second half of the nineteenth century, and for evidence that New York supported a much larger proportion of specialists in relation to its population than any other large American city, see Hammack (1982) *op. cit.*, chapter 2.

55. Scharf, J. Thomas (1881) *History of Baltimore City and County*. Baltimore, pp. 272–79, 715–16; Semmes, John E. (1917) *John H.B. Latrobe and His Times*. Baltimore, The Norman, Remington Co.

56. Scharf, J. Thomas and Westcott, Thompson (1884) *History of Philadelphia, 1609–1884*. Philadelphia: L.H. Everts & Co., p. 819. *Ibid.*, p. 842, and the *Dictionary of American Biography* both suggest that Philadelphia merchant John Welsh may also have specialized in the management of planning decisions in his city between his election to its Sinking Fund Commission in 1857 and his service as Finance Chairman for the Centennial Exposition of 1876. As a Fairmont Park Commissioner between 1867 and 1886, according to the *D.A.B.*, Welsh advocated the development of a comprehensive park system for Philadelphia.

57. Nesbit, Robert C. (1961) *'He Built Seattle'. A Biography of Judge Thomas Burke*. Seattle: University of Washington Press.

58. Eliot, Charles W. 2nd, The Boston Park System, in Herlihy, Elisabeth M. *et al.* (1932) *Fifty Years of Boston: A Memorial Volume*. Boston: Tercentenary Committee, pp. 640–66; Coolidge, T. Jefferson (1923) *Autobiography*. Boston and New York: Houghton Mifflin Company, pp. 81–82; Boston *Evening Transcript*, February 24, 1908, p. 9. Significantly, by the 1890s a merchant, manufacturer, and active Republican like Dalton was being replaced by full-time planning specialists like Sylvester Baxter of the Boston Metropolitan Park Commission, and landscape architect Charles W. Eliot 2nd.

59. Scharf, J. Thomas (1883) *History of St. Louis City and County*. Philadelphia: Louis H. Everts Co., Inc., volume I, pp. 344–54. Darby, John F. (1880) *Personal Recollections . . . Relating to the History of St. Louis*. St. Louis: G.I. Jones and Company, (reprinted in New York by Arno Press, 1975), suggests that he was another attorney who played a role comparable to the one that Andrew H. Green played in New York.

60. Orth, Samuel P. (1910) *History of Cleveland, Ohio*.

61. After about 1890 critics began to apply twentieth-century criteria to Green's achievements, and to assert that his accomplishments fell short. Thus 'J.D.' author of 'A Plan to Improve and Beautify New York City', *The Social Economist* (December, 1891), pp. 65–70, asserted that 'there are few, if any, cities which possess so many natural advantages as the city and harbor of New York, and there is hardly any city for whose beautifying and improvement its inhabitants and government have done so little', p. 65. The *Real Estate Record and Builder's Guide* (which represented the interests of the industry it served) insisted, on March 5, 1898, that 'there never has been, and there is not today, any plan, tentative or well thought out, local or comprehensive, for the improvement and development of this city. As a consequence we have some magnificent works to show, Central Park, the Riverside Drive, the Brooklyn Bridge, and at the same time forty-seven miles of streets, twelve or fifteen below 59th street including five miles below

Grand Street without sewers; paving that would disgrace a fifth-rate town, and docks that are out-of-date, unspeakably inadequate to known requirements . . . This state of affairs is the result of the policy of expedience, which seems to have characterized our whole past, and the absence of deliberate plan and provision'. Yet at the same time, Green's efforts to promote planning in the Greater New York region impressed Albert Shaw, the widely experienced author of *Municipal Government in Great Britain* and *Municipal Government in Continental Europe*, so much that he urged Boston officials to consult Green as they grappled with the problem of the Metropolitan District Commission (letter, Shaw to Charles P. Curtis, Jr., October 16, 1894, Shaw papers, New York Public Library). Similarly, Lyman S. Andrews praised Green's comprehensive plans for *transportation* development in the New York region in a letter to Mayor William L. Strong printed in the New York *Sun* April 9, 1896, and Julius F. Harder cited Green's Greater New York plan as a valuable contribution to comprehensive planning in 'The City's Plan', *Municipal Affairs*, 2 (1898), pp. 25–45.

62. Porter and Livesay (1971) *op. cit.*

Chapter Seven

Regional Planning for the Great American Metropolis: New York between the World Wars

DAVID A. JOHNSON

American metropolitan planning took its modern shape in the two decades between the end of World War I and the beginning of World War II. During the 1920s nascent ideas about planning generated in the 1880s and 1890s came to be accepted and institutionalized. And in the Depression of the 1930s, many of the plans and projects based on those ideas were actually carried out.

The most striking example of this process occurred in the New York Metropolitan Region. Here, it is possible to trace the movement for metropolitan planning back to the mid-nineteenth century vision of Frederick Law Olmsted for a Greater City and forward to President Franklin Delano Roosevelt's pump-priming public works and regional planning programmes. This continuity is clearly visible in the origins and implementation of the 1929 Regional Plan of New York and Its Environs, certainly one of the most important and well-funded efforts in the history of American planning. This remarkable plan brought together many of the planning and reform ideas, person-alities, and forces at work in American society in the early twentieth century. The contradictions and conflicts it generated reflected the internal division within that society and the tension between progressive reformers – those who wished to remake the basic structure of society – and meliorist reformers – those who sought only to remedy its negative consequences. This chapter examines the Regional Plan of New York and Its Environs – its origins, its critics, and its impact – as a metaphor for American planning as a whole, with its unexpected successes and predictable failures in a highly privatized business-oriented milieu.

THE PATH TO THE REGIONAL PLAN

The metropolitan regional planning tradition began in New York in 1868 with Frederick Law Olmsted's extraordinary vision of a Greater City linked together by a web of open spaces and parkways. Olmsted, with a small band of fellow reformers, offered New York City a comprehensive and humane vision of what it could become. His greatest achievements were his parks, but his regional concept extended far beyond the simple provision of open space.

Central Park had been acquired in 1856, Prospect Park between 1864 and 1869, and Riverside Park in 1872. Subsequently, the Central Park Commission and its successor, the Department of Public Parks, was designated to plan the northern part of Manhattan and the western part of the Bronx[1]. Olmsted, who became chief landscape architect of the Department of Parks in 1869, designed a street pattern adjusted to the uneven terrain of the area and proposed low-density neighbourhoods with shops, schools, public gardens and transit facilities. But Olmsted's vision was unfortunately incompatible with the municipal government's desire to develop the area quickly at conventional densities and patterns. Olmsted was fired in 1877, his concept discarded.[2]

Olmsted had somewhat more success with his grand plan to link the major parks and shore areas of Manhattan and Brooklyn by means of a system of parkways. First proposed in 1868, the plan contained a variety of proposals, many of which would be repeated in subsequent plans and ultimately carried to completion. The plan's key idea was that large parks should be established throughout the city and should be interconnected by parkways to form a natural framework for future growth. To carry out this design principle, Olmsted proposed a great loop parkway extending from the Brooklyn side of the Narrows to Riverside Park. The parkways were to serve as green spines softening the city's otherwise undifferentiated, interminable gridiron development. While only fragments were completed, Olmsted's 1868 scheme was the first definitive step toward regional environmental planning in the New York area.[3] Another forty years would pass before the consolidation of Greater New York in 1897 stimulated renewed interest in Olmsted's visionary conception.

THE NEW YORK CITY IMPROVEMENT COMMISSION PLAN, 1907

In 1897, after decades of discussion and debate, New York and Brooklyn joined with three other counties to form the Greater City of New York. In December 1903 the reform administration of Mayor

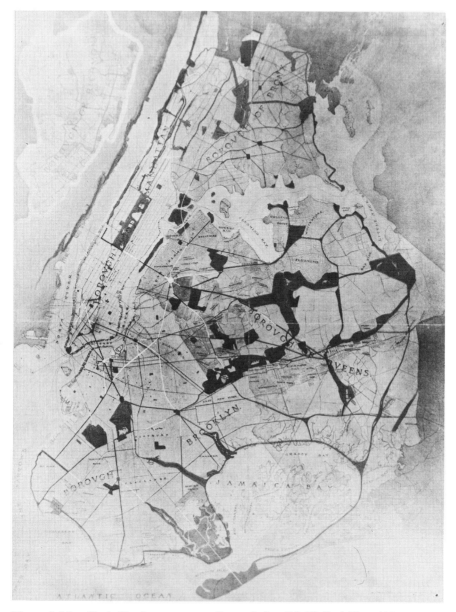

Figure 1. New York City Improvement Commission (McClellan) Plan, 1907. (*Source*: New York City Improvement Commission, *Report to the Mayor*, 1907)

Seth Low approved the creation of a New York City Improvement Commission with a mandate to prepare a comprehensive plan for the development of the newly consolidated city. The Commission was comprised of prominent businessmen, architects, and artists,

169

including sculptor Daniel Chester French and architect Whitney Warren.

The Commission, given an impossible task to complete a comprehensive plan within a year, presented instead a preliminary report in 1905 emphasizing urban aesthetics and city beautification.[4] A final report, submitted in 1907 as a general plan for the City, addressed more fundamental planning questions of parks, highways, and the location of city buildings (figure 1). The basic feature of the plan was an elaboration of Olmsted's parkway system linking the City's largest parks. The Commission looked on the integrated parkway system as an expression of unity for the consolidated city:

> The salient feature of the general plan as it affects the City as a whole is to afford adequate, proper and suitable avenues of connection between the different parts of each borough, as well as between the different boroughs themselves and the outlying disticts . . . [and to] connect as far as possible the parks of the different boroughs with each other by suitable parkways so as to make them all parts of one harmonious whole.[5]

The Commissioners' Plan of 1907 was an extraordinarily influential document in the development of the City. A felicitous blend of Olmsted's regional vision and City Beautiful formalism, it was both sufficiently broad in scope and precise in detail to provide a foundation for planning and development through two subsequent decades. Indeed, it served as the blueprint from which Robert Moses would later draw many of his proposals for park and parkway projects in New York City.

THE PLAN OF THE BROOKLYN COMMITTEE ON CITY PLAN, 1914

Seven years after the New York City Improvement Commission report was published, a private group of businessmen commissioned a new plan for the Borough of Brooklyn. The plan was prepared by Chicago architect Edward H. Bennett for the Brooklyn Committee on the City Plan and published in a special supplement of the Brooklyn *Daily Eagle* on January 18, 1914.[6] The Plan had its origins in a series of sermons on 'Great Cities' delivered in October 1911 by the Reverend N.D. Hillis at historic Plymouth Church in Brooklyn Heights, where Henry Ward Beecher had preached the abolition of slavery a generation earlier.

At the suggestion of Hillis, Daniel Burnham, the principal architect of the influential 1909 Plan of Chicago, was invited to come to Brooklyn to inspire and advise the Brooklyn City Plan movement. A citizens' committee was commissioned by the Brooklyn borough

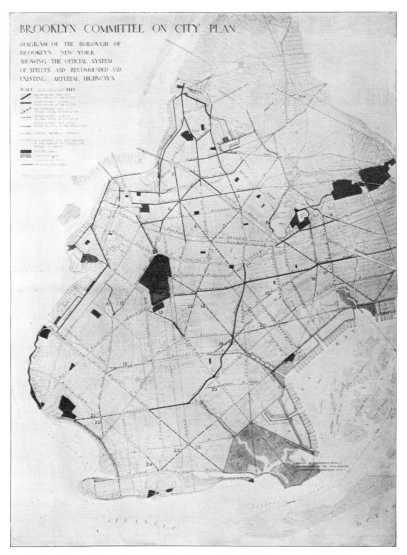

Figure 2. Brooklyn Committee on City Plan: Plan for Streets and Highways, Edward
H. Bennett, 1914. (*Source*: 'City Plan Number', *Brooklyn Daily Eagle*, 18 January, 1914)

president to meet Burnham on his arrival in the city on December 16,
1911. The aged Burnham toured Brooklyn by automobile and then
stirred the Committee with visions of a Brooklyn embracing all of
Long Island:

> The City Planning Movement means that men have arrived at a certain
> level of intelligence, and having arrived there they inevitably desire to
> have good air. The first sign in that direction is the feeling that they

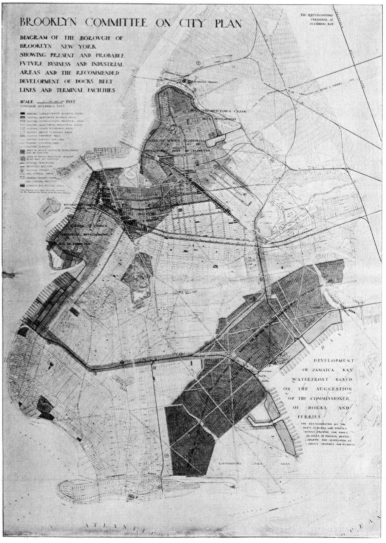

Figure 3. Brooklyn Committee on City Plan: Plan for Business and Industrial Areas, Edward H. Bennett, 1914. (*Source*: as figure 2)

must have their town in good order. Their streets, their transportation, their sewer and water facilities must be in good order.

Now shall all these elements be allowed to go on and develop in their own way? No, they are to work together and be welded into a logical whole. That's what town planning means.

In the matter of your plan here you cannot go too far. My own opinion is that when you get down to it you are likely to take in the entire Long Island . . . If there is any feasible way of uniting it to the city, a way that is beneficial to both, that ought to be recorded in your diagram.[7]

The Brooklyn Committee on City Plan was formed soon after Burnham's visit. Burnham declined the position of architect and advisor but the Committee accepted his suggestion that his Chicago associate Edward H. Bennett be selected. Bennett's plan was completed in 1914 (figures 2 and 3).

Bennett projected an ultimate population for Brooklyn of 5 million people, three times its 1910 population of 1.6 million. He followed Burnham's general prescriptions but added important new ideas of his own. King's highway was proposed to be widened into a major circumferential. Several dozen new diagonal arteries were to be cut Chicago-plan style through the existing gridiron of streets. New parks, ports, and industrial sites were proposed for the marshy lands surrounding Jamaica Bay. Of great interest in the Bennett Plan was his proposal for three great boulevards 'running the entire length of Long Island along each shore and through the center'. This, along with several other Bennett proposals, would continue to appear in planning documents, eventually to be carried out by Robert Moses in modified form as the Long Island parkway system.[8]

THE PORT OF NEW YORK AUTHORITY PLAN, 1921

One of the most significant events in the development of planning activities in the New York Region was the creation of the Port of New York Authority in 1921. The Port Authority was established after years of promotional effort by prominent business groups, mostly on the New York side of the harbour. Port development had become an obsession in cities on both the east and west coasts following the opening of the Panama Canal in 1914. The Canal symbolized the emerging industrial supremacy of the United States and demonstrated in a dramatic way the practical results produced through the combination of public capital, engineering skills and military discipline, brought together under a government attuned to the needs of business.[9]

The port's importance was recognized by successive New York City administrations, which between 1870 and 1914 had spent over $100 million to improve pier and dock facilities. In 1914, New Jersey, hoping to attract a larger share of total port trade, established a permanent New Jersey Harbor Commission with power to approve all plans for the development of its waterfront. The Commission initiated litigation to obtain a reduced rate for shipments terminating on the west side of the Hudson, hoping that the cost differential would attract industries that might otherwise dock on the New York side. The Interstate Commerce Commission denied New Jersey's brief for rate differentials and urged instead that the two states work jointly in solving their mutual problems of port development and trade. With Republicans sympathetic to business interests in control in both states, the New York, New Jersey Port and Harbor Development Commission was established by the two state legislatures in 1917. General George W. Goethals, the builder of the Panama Canal, was retained as consulting engineer to the Commission.[10]

The Commission reported back a year later with a recommendation that an autonomous port authority be established for New York Harbor similar to the Port of London Authority. To substantiate the need for such an authority, the Commission devoted the next three years to an exhaustive study of the geography, history and condition of the port. The 500-page report issued in 1920 concluded that rail freight movement was the basic problem. A comprehensive plan was presented to rationalize freight handling around the harbour. Circumferential belt lines were proposed, one along the waterfont, and one at the exurban fringe of development in the New Jersey countryside. A tunnel linking New Jersey and Brooklyn also was proposed to minimize the need for water-borne freight transport across the harbour. And an underground-automated electric goods delivery system was suggested as a way to solve truck congestion on Manhattan streets. While the plan was concerned solely with freight systems, its potential for shaping regional land development patterns was enormous.[11]

The legislatures of the two states strongly supported the proposal for a new Port of New York Authority. Despite strong opposition of New York City's Democratically-controlled Board of Estimate and a veto by Governor Edwards of New Jersey, also a Democrat, the Port Authority bill was successfully passed in both states in 1920. The legislation specifically required the Port Authority to adopt a physical plan for port development. A board appointed to propose a plan, chaired by General Goethals, recommended in 1921 one almost identical with the 1916 Comprehensive Plan of the New York, New Jersey Harbor Commission (figure 4).

Successful implementation of the plan was dependent on two factors: the cooperation of the region's eleven private railroads, and the economic feasibility of individual projects in the plan, since the Authority was legally required to pay its bonds out of revenues and could not levy or receive tax monies. As early as 1922 it was evident that the railroads would not support any Port Authority proposals for belt line connections. Each railroad was reluctant to give up the local monopoly it enjoyed along its right-of-way for the benefit of partici-

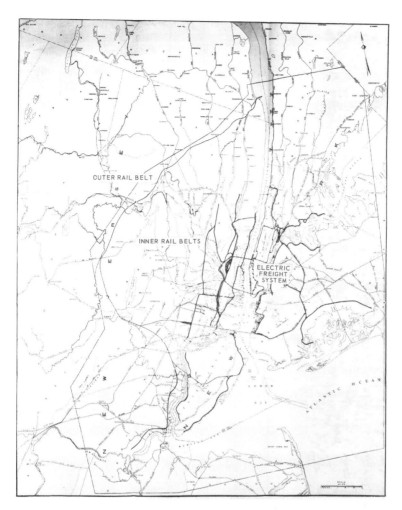

Figure 4. Comprehensive Plan for Port Development, New York, New Jersey Port and Harbor Development Commission, 1916. (*Source*: N.Y., N.J. Port and Harbor Development Commission, Comprehensive Plan for Port Development)

pating in a more efficient overall system. An impasse resulted which prevented the Port Authority from carrying out its original mission (the consequences of which would later prove regrettable for the long-term development of the region). What seemed to be required was a 'Plan of New York Authority' which could look at the region as a whole, an agency whose scope could go beyond the narrow legislative mandate of the Port Authority and yet work closely with it. This was exactly what Morgan banker, Charles Dyer Norton, had in mind when he proposed a new regional plan for New York and its environs.

THE MAKING OF THE REGIONAL PLAN OF NEW YORK
AND ITS ENVIRONS

The most important regional plan for the New York Metropolitan
Area, and certainly the best funded, was the monumental Regional
Plan of New York and Its Environs, begun in 1921 and published in
1929. Two remarkable men with roots in Chicago were the driving
forces behind the New York plan: Charles Dyer Norton, a banker
with the House of Morgan and former secretary and counsellor to
President William Howard Taft, and Norton's close friend, Frederic
A. Delano, an engineer and uncle of an aspiring New York politician,
Franklin Delano Roosevelt. Norton and Delano, who had worked
closely with Daniel Burnham on the 1909 Plan of Chicago, hoped to
generate a similar plan for New York, but on a much broader scale.[12]

Funded for a decade by generous grants from the Russell Sage
Foundation totalling $1.2 million, the plan broke new ground but also
synthesized many earlier ideas and proposals put forward by the
Olmsteds and by the Port Authority. Following the dictum of Patrick
Geddes, an elaborate regional survey was undertaken to provide a
basis for the regional plan. Economic forces, social trends, and
physical conditions were mapped and analysed for their future
regional importance. The planning staff, directed by Thomas Adams,

Figure 5. Regional Plan of New York and Its Environs: Advisory Group of Planners
1923. Thomas Adams is second from the left in the front. (*Source*: Olin Library,
Cornell University)

a Scotsman who had helped plan Letchworth and Welwyn Garden Cities near London, was assisted by the nation's leading planners: John Nolen, Edward Bennett, Harlan Bartholomew, George B. Ford, and Frederick Law Olmsted, Jr. (figure 5). In preliminary studies for the regional plan each consultant was assigned a geographic sector and asked to prepare sketch plans and policies.

From these studies Adams was able to fashion a preliminary set of bold and imaginative policy statements to guide the design of the regional plan:

1. Regional zoning should be established on the basis of a regional plan to serve as a guide to local zoning plans.

2. Special wedge-shaped agricultural zones should be established to provide more open space than could be provided through park or forest preserves alone.

3. To ease congestion, new transportation facilities should emphasize circumferential rather than radial movements.

4. Activities that did not require central locations should be decentralized; conversely, functions that could not be decentralized without loss to the region as a whole should be kept centralized.

5. High buildings were generally not desirable as they did not pay the public costs they generated in congestion and transportation requirements.

6. More public open space should be acquired, particularly at river and harbour edges.

7. Large sites should be acquired in advance for future airport needs.

8. Subdivision design and location practice should be improved, particularly to avoid gridiron plots on hilly terrain and premature development.

9. A system should be established to reduce the inequitable distribution of property taxes among industry-rich and industry-poor towns and cities.

10. Development corporations should be established to help industries relocate and to build satellite towns.[13]

Written in 1923, this was an early and comprehensive statement of the concerns which would preoccupy planners and officials in the region for decades thereafter. It neglected two critical issues, however: how were housing needs to be met, and what steps were to be taken to rebuild and revitalize the old decaying parts of the region? When the Regional Plan and Its Environs was published in 1929 it, too, failed to address these critical issues. And it timidly dropped several of the

177

more controversial original draft policies such as John Nolen's interesting proposal for satellite industrial towns.[14]

The final version of the Regional Plan assumed that population in the twenty-two county region would grow from 8.9 million people in 1920 to 21 million in 1965, an increase of more than twelve million. (This forecast turned out to be about 4 million above the actual 1965 population of 17.3 million.) Despite the absence of much vacant land, the plan envisaged a growth in population of 3.9 million more people in New York City and other older cities surrounding the Port. Large population increases were also projected for the inner suburban ring – 3.1 million people – just beyond the old core cities.

The plan called for a 'recentralization' of industry and business. Carefully selected new areas for industry were proposed while other areas, locally zoned for industry, were recommended for non-industrial uses. Economic studies had shown that the region was greatly over-zoned for industry. Regional survey studies also concluded that while some industries needed to remain in central locations such as Manhattan, others would do better to relocate in industrial tracts outside the core. Recentralization was intended to solve these problems.

THE PLAN AND ITS CRITICS

Although generally well received, the plan was severely criticized by Lewis Mumford, Benton MacKaye, and others largely for its unexamined assumption that population growth was a given and that the problem was simply one of finding the best ways to accommodate it. Mumford also criticized the plan for lacking any underlying principle of growth and development; recentralization was interpreted by Mumford as 'drift', though Adams saw it as redirection. Mumford, a disciple of both Ebenezer Howard and Patrick Geddes, had expressed scepticism about the premises of the Regional Plan as early as April of 1925 when the International Town, City and Regional Planning, and Garden Cities Congress convened in New York. After the Regional Plan staff presented their preliminary maps and plans, Garden City proponents, including Mumford, were disappointed at the absence of proposals for new communities. Raymond Unwin, C.B. Purdom, and the venerable Ebenezer Howard each expressed their concern over the regressive, over-dense growth of the metropolis and reiterated the desirability of decanting excess population into self-sufficient garden cities beyond the fringe of urban development. The Garden City was, they emphasized, not simply a planned suburb. It was an entirely new form of settlement and implied new patterns of life and work. As Mumford wrote shortly after the conference, 'anyone who went away still believing that [Howard, Purdom, and Unwin] meant a fancy kind of suburban land subdivision or a particular variety of landscape gardening must have been both deaf and blind'.[15]

The Regional Plan premise of accepting and coping with growth was clearly at odds with the Garden City ideal of stringent control and channelization. Much closer to this ideal was Henry Wright's 1926 sketch scheme of a future pattern for New York State, developed for the State Housing and Regional Planning Commission. Wright's scheme envisaged a far wider distribution of activities and transportation across New York State in the hope of reducing the economic denudation of the rural areas and the over-concentration of population in New York City.[16]

'These plans', Mumford wrote,

> stand symbolically at opposite poles: one assumes that technical ability can improve living conditions while our existing economic and social habits continue; the other holds that technical ability can achieve little that is fundamentally worth the effort until we reshape our institutions in such a way as to subordinate financial and property values to those of human welfare.[17]

By the time the first volume of the plan was issued in 1929, Mumford's scepticism had grown. He was convinced that the Regional Plan promised a continuation of the worst trends toward over-centralization and concentration. In an article for *The New Republic*, he awarded a 'prize in "Applied Logic" ', one of a number of 'Booby Prizes for 1929', to the Committee on Regional Plan –

> for its admirable demonstration that by providing for a population of 20,000,000 in the New York area, the problems of transportation which are now insoluble would become less so, and park areas and playgrounds, which are now non-existent or impossible to reach, would then be more numerous and easier to reach.[18]

Adams was deeply hurt by the attack and responded to Mumford by letter the day after publication of the article:

> The writing of that article in the *New Republic* must have given you great fun, but why direct a shaft at the Regional Plan, when you couldn't have time enough to study it to enable you to understand it?
>
> I am certain that anyone who takes the trouble to study our report on the Plan will be satisfied that we have both logic and good sense behind our proposals . . . Unfortunately we cannot prevent the growth of New York to 20,000,000 but we may do something to give that growth the right direction with more spaciousness.
>
> I am sorry we cannot count on support from your able pen because, with all deference, your duty to the public is more important than your intellectual enjoyment as a critic.[19]

Mumford remained unconvinced that his public duty was to support a plan which seemed to him to guarantee an extension to the congested, inhuman urban fabric he deplored. Writing to Adams a few weeks later, he expressed admiration for the technical work of the survey but demurred about the basic assumptions underlying the Plan:

> The chief difficulty is not with the Plan's conclusions but with its premises: namely, that continued growth at the present rate in the metropolitan area is inevitable, and that the first duty of the Plan is to facilitate such growth . . . On the basis of past experience, I see no reason whatever for hoping that this growth and vast expenditure will be compatible with a sufficient and timely provision of parks, playgrounds, and housing facilities: so long as growth and the maintenance of land values are the ends in view, it is rather safe to say that these vital facilities will remain in 'embellishments' – scamped and squeezed in order to accomodate the budget . . .
>
> [Our] points of difference . . . are not disagreements over mere matters of detail, but fundamental differences of principle and method, that cut at the very root of the whole matter. Since the chief function of the Regional Plan is educational, I cannot accept with any pleasure or equanimity a series of recommendations that seem to me wholly unsound in their general tendency, however appropriate or necessary any particular one may be. Remembering the disastrous work of the City Plan Commissioners of 1811, I had rather see a continuance of the present muddle and shortsightedness, than the general acceptance of an able and comprehensive plan which works in the wrong direction.[20]

Adams asked Shelby Harrison, the staff sociologist in charge of social surveys and perhaps most sensitive to a social welfare viewpoint, for his interpretation of the Mumford critique. Harrison thought Mumford quite wrong in his reading of the plan:

> As I see it, either the metropolitan area will grow at something like its present rate, or it will not. If its population does not grow any more at all, a better distribution is desirable; and if it does grow, a better distribution is still more desirable. And, as I understand it, such better distribution is one of major purposes of city and regional planning, and particularly the purpose of the New York Regional Plan. The only thing left in [Mumford's] implied criticism . . . seems to be . . . his thinking the Regional Plan should somehow limit the number of persons who shall stay in the New York Region, or come to it in the future. I wonder how he would do that through the agency of City and Regional planning without making just about exactly the same recommendations for future development which the plan is making![21]

Adams made one last attempt to convince Mumford by letter that their views were not irreconcilable. Adams argued that to plan for unavoidable growth was not to be construed as supporting or encouraging such growth:

> I can imagine that if you do not believe in the continued growth of the metropolitan area at some rate approximate to that which has been occurring in recent years, you will not be able to look upon the Regional Plan with favor. We have been forced as a result of our studies to face this growth as inevitable. I deprecate, however, your suggestion that we have regarded as our first duty to facilitate such growth. What we have regarded as our first duty is to facilitate such dispersal of the growth as will make it healthier than it will be if it is left to go on as at present . . . I remember when I was the first executive of the Garden City Company in England, I thought it possible – as you appear to do – that the building of garden cities would tend towards stopping the growth of London. What it has done is to make the growth of London better and to spread rather than contract the big city. We all wish it had been otherwise, but that has been the experience.
>
> I agree with you that there is no reason for hoping that the increased growth and vast expenditure will be compatible with a sufficient provision of open spaces and housing facilities, *if* you judge solely from past experience. But we are of the opinion that past experience has little bearing on what will happen under the conditions of the next fifty years. I am surprised that you should say that we have the growth and maintenance of land values as an end in view because one of our chief ends has been to destroy the fallacy that land values matter at all when human values are at stake. I prefer to put it this way, however, that high land prices mean low value because it is the price situation with regard to land that presents the difficulty of getting ample spaces . . .
>
> I cannot possibly see any benefit from submitting a regional plan that will set up an impossible ideal or fails to accept facts as they are. A city must always possess the weaknesses of the human beings who inhabit it and of the governments that control it. We cannot assume perfection in the city any more than in human nature. I am inclined to defend the City Plan Commissioners of 1811 against those who criticize them because all the defects that have occurred in Manhattan are the result of not following the Plan and limiting the density of building to the street widths that were provided.
>
> You will have plenty of opportunity of seeing a continuance of muddle and shortsightedness. There will always be a sufficient disregard of planning and sound principle, however much improvement may be made. It is right and proper that you should criticize the plan in respect to what you conceive to be its defects. I hope, however, that in founding this criticism on the assumption that the city will cease to grow, you will show that you have a reasonable basis for this expectation. I confess that it seems to be a case in which you are prepared to let the wish become father to the thought. How happy I would be if I could do the same![22]

Mumford responded by suggesting that Adams should have examined the reports of the Regional Planning Association of America in the *Survey Graphic* of May 1925 and Henry Wright's report to the New York State Housing and Regional Planning Commission of May 7, 1926. Now, four years later, it was too late for the decentrists' idea to have much impact on the Regional Plan. Intellectual and political commitments had been made and now could not be undone. A few days later Adams wrote back that he had reviewed the RPAA reports but noted that they had dealt with the subject of 'state regional planning and not of regional planning in relation to any community of the character of New York'.[23]

Mumford's close friend and associate, Benton MacKaye, the originator of the Appalachian Trial, took an even stronger stand against the Regional Plan in a review of R.L. Duffus's popularized version of the Plan, entitled *Mastering a Metropolis*.[24] MacKaye refused to accept the underlying premise of the plan – that ten million people would be added by 1965 to the ten million already in the region in 1930. Even if this growth were inevitable, it would be better, thought MacKaye, *not* to provide for it in advance. 'Why deliberately plan to achieve something that looks nothing like an asset and something like a liability? One way *not* to get [ten million more people] is *not* to make "swifter and less painful" subways', MacKaye opined. Build some new cities he suggested, down South, out West, anywhere but in the New York Region. 'The American city', MacKaye concluded, 'is no longer a city problem, it is a national problem'.[25]

MacKaye was wrong, of course, to assume that not building transportation would keep people out of New York. Only a few new subway lines were in fact built, and yet nearly nine million additional people settled in the Region by 1965, the horizon year of the plan. MacKaye's notion of a national policy was more firmly premised, but too advanced a concept for its time. How could a nation as a whole agree on a desirable population distribution when individual large metropolitan areas were too fragmented to carry out plans on a regional basis? And if the ten million new people were therefore inevitable, why not provide in advance for their transportation and other needs?

The most memorable and detailed critique of the Regional Plan came two years later when in June of 1932 Mumford's long-awaited analysis was published in the *New Republic*.[26] It was a devastating treatment revealing the very different premises upon which the two groups were operating. Mumford labelled the plan a 'monumental' failure both as a specific enterprise for the benefit of New York and as a model for other cities. If its example were widely followed, the results, Mumford warned, would be disastrous.

The plan, according to Mumford, contained many internal contradictions. Proponents of garden cities as well as of concentration could find support for their positions at different points in the text. What the plan lacked was a fertile theoretical base upon which concrete proposals might be made. The plan, Mumford thought, was characterized by its drift into the future and its unquestioning assumption of continued growth. There were other shortcomings: the geographic and historical studies which should have been basic to the plan were perfunctory and arranged in no logical order; the choice of the planning region as an area of metropolitan influence based on an hour's commutation time to the centre was, he suggested, arbitrary and too confining; the population projections, modelled on the process of fruit fly multiplication in a closed container, was inappropriately applied to a metropolitan area.

Mumford noted that New York's peak of centralization had occurred about 1910 and was declining thereafter as the effects of automobile and electricity transmission decreased the advantages of metropolitan concentration. The plan and survey, he asserted, ignored this trend and had been erroneously based on growth statistics from the period 1900–1912.

Mumford further criticized the plan for offering solutions capable only of immediate implementation when what was needed was a plan flexible enough to be operative over thirty or forty years. He criticized the plan's failure to serve as a forum where citizens could learn about the critical problems facing the region – an educational process that Mumford viewed as a prerequisite to change. He also saw class bias and interest underlying the values on which the plan had been devised:

> It may be more effective, as well as more clearsighted and honest, to say that no comprehensive planning for the improvement of living conditions can be done as long as property values and private enterprise are looked upon as sacred, than it is to draw pictures of parks that may never be built . . . and garden cities that will never be financed . . .
>
> The Russell Sage planners did not take advantage of their theoretical freedom; they were so eager to fasten to a viable solution, a solution acceptable to their committee full of illustrious names in financial and civic affairs, to the business community generally, to the public officials of the region, that they deliberately restricted the area of their questions.[27]

Mumford attacked the plan for its willingness to compromise on a number of issues. While it called for more light and air, it endorsed the skyscraper and proposed dense residential and institutional development along the riverfront. It called for garden cities and yet proposed a denser concentration in the centre; precisely the opposite,

Mumford thought, of the prime objective of building garden cities. It called for better housing for low-income people but offered no new governmental or economic techniques for achieving it. In essence, he contended, the plan falsely substituted heavy investment in transportation for a community development programme.[28]

Mumford's sharpest criticism was directed at Adams's failure to look at alternative strategies which might require far less capital investment. Mumford proposed an alternative solution: lessen the pressure of congestion in lower Manhattan by recentralizing the metropolitan business districts; lay down new cities and direct the exodus of industries to these new cities outside the Region's congested areas; rebuild the blighted areas and take care of part of the increase in population by a process of 'intensive internal colonization', by which Mumford meant establishing denser neighbourhoods with more open space. By diverting new growth to redevelopment inside the city boundaries, Mumford hoped that the suburban drain of urban resources could be deterred. This alternative conception, an extrapolation of the ideas of Ebenezer Howard, Patrick Geddes, and Henry Wright, was not a denial of the metropolis but of what Mumford deemed to be its unnecessary expansion at the expense of amenity, community, and the vitality of civic institutions.

Mumford summed up his criticism by comparing the regional plan to the efforts of the previous generation of 'City Beautiful' planners. If the latter were superficial, they at least left parkways and civic centres on the American scene and a greater feeling of spaciousness and elegance. The regional plan, because it lacked aesthetic sensibilities, was even more shallow and unredeemed. For Mumford, the regional plan was a badly-conceived pudding, into which many ingredients had been poured, some appealing but many distasteful, by a cook who tried to satisfy every appetite.

> The mixture is indigestible and tasteless: but here and there is a raisin or a large piece of citron that can be extracted and eaten with relish. In the long run, let us hope, this is how the pudding will be remembered.[29]

Other writers also sharply criticized the plan for its failure to come to grips with the housing problem, but it was Mumford's general attack which aroused Adams to a written rebuttal.[30] Labelling Mumford an 'esthete-sociologist', whose ideas were 'pathetically immature', Adams denied that he or his staff had tried to find a solution 'acceptable to the committee consisting of a caste of bankers', or that they had deliberately restricted the area of their inquiry.[31]

Adams invoked his past association with Patrick Geddes and Ebenezer Howard, asserting that both would have approved the plan's basic ideas. Mumford's ideals, Adams acknowledged, were high, but unwork-able. What was essential to progress in reform, Adams asserted, was 'movement'. And for movement, 'one must keep to the road and as nearly the middle of it as possible, if any improvement is to be made'. It was this 'movement' toward progress which Geddes would have applauded, he suggested, and not Mumford's unrealizable Garden City idea. As for Howard, Adams contended, he would have approved the notion of garden suburbs close to the city, for had he not sited his second Garden City, Welwyn, seventeen miles closer to London than the first, Letchworth?[32]

Adams denied categorically that skyscrapers were incompatible with garden cities, that the proposed highways and rail systems were substitutes for housing, and that the boundaries chosen for the region were too close in to allow for new town proposals in the countryside. And, disputing Mumford, he vehemently contended that the plan would reduce congestion, not add to it. Because the criticism was based on a 'wrong diagnosis', Adams asked that Mumford's conclusions be dismissed.[33]

Adams and Mumford, both committed reformers, had sailed past each other like ships in the night. Their differing perceptions and values precluded any communication on fundamentals. Mumford's words still stand tall after fifty years, his vision of human community untarnished by the passage of time. By contrast, Adams's detailed plans and his arguments in defence of them seem more dated, embedded in an era and a place. For Adams the object of the plan was to formulate a usable public agenda acceptable within the bounds of public opinion. To go beyond this was to risk failure and impotence. But for Mumford, the object of a plan was to stretch the limits of opinion itself, and to provide new images of a humane community. Adams sought solid but incremental improvements in the city and region as it existed in reality. Mumford sought to change that political and social reality. Mumford's words seem more durable because the realities are still in need of change. Adams's plans seem dated because they were fitted to the perceived need of the time. If Adams had indeed concocted a raisin pudding by assembling in one place the ideas of a myriad of actors and agencies, he had fashioned it out of the fragmented regional political economy which was itself a pudding even more indigestible.

Mumford and Adams epitomized two consistent strains of American reform. One radically grounded and visionary, the other conservative and pragmatic, they have often clashed bitterly. But just as often the first has prepared the way for the achievements of the second, though only after enough time has passed for the visionary to come to seem the possible. Thus after a half century Mumford's ideas strike a responsive chord, while Adams's seem timid by comparison.

But the contrast is due not only to the passage of time and the difference in reform styles. Mumford's criticism of Adams proved accurate in many particulars. The plan was indeed timid in the crucial matter of housing, a direct consequence of the pressure placed on Adams by the conservative members of the Committee he served. And certainly the imageries of Manhattan redevelopment conjured up by the plan's architectural teams called for more densely populated environments than the abstracted rhetoric of Adam's written version of the plan. But these were matters largely beyond the control of Adams who was by personality and position more synthesizer than commander. These failings of the regional plan were regarded as sufficiently serious as to cause George B. Ford, Adams's successor in 1930, to contemplate abandoning the plan and starting over. Yet Adams's achievement ought to be properly recognized. Lewis Mumford's vision of the future New York Region was more attractive than that of the regional plan. But the region became a better place having had Adams's plan than it would have been without it.

THE IMPACT OF THE REGIONAL PLAN OF NEW YORK AND ITS ENVIRONS

Whatever its flaws, the 1929 Regional Plan of New York and Its Environs left a considerable imprint on metropolitan New York. The infrastructure in place today was created in large measure through the successful completion of many of the proposals contained in the plan. Important new agencies and institutions, such as the New York City Planning Commission and the National Resources Planning Board, were established or assisted by the existence of the plan and the work of the Regional Plan staff. Franklin Roosevelt, as President, knew of the value of planning as a result, in part, of his acquaintance with the regional plan. When Frederic Delano accepted his nephew Franklin's invitation to lead the new National Resources Planning Board, the experience of the regional plan of New York was there to guide him.

Planning education was also greatly influenced by the regional plan project. The first graduate degree programme in city and regional planning was established – at Harvard University – directly in response to the need for skilled professional planners which had become apparent in the course of developing the plan.[34]

The plan's physical planning concepts provided the framework for much of the subsequent development of the region. The great bridges and tunnels that knitted together the pieces of the region were located according to the recentralizing principles laid out by Thomas Adams and were accelerated in their construction by the existence of the plan.

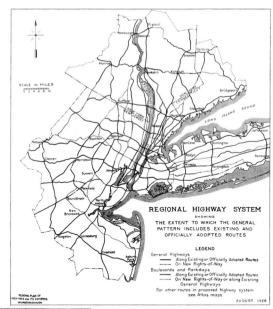

Figure 6. Plan: Proposed Highway System, Regional Plan of New York and Its Environs, 1928 (*Source*: Regional Plan of New York and Its Environs, *The Graphic Regional Plan*)

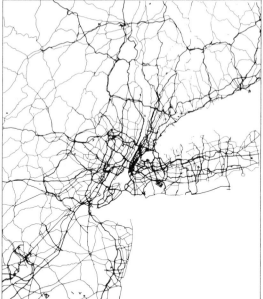

Figure 7. Reality: Major Expressways, Parkways, and State Highways, 1965. (*Source*: Regional Plan Association)

The circumferential highways in the plan were adopted by engineers and state highway departments. New grade–separated freeways were originated or accelerated by the plan (figures 6 and 7). The acquisition of parklands was also spurred by the proposals contained in the regional plan (figures 8 and 9). City waterfronts were rebuilt along the principles of the plan, though their use for highways took more

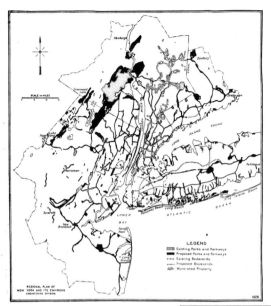

Figure 8. Plan: Existing and Proposed Park and Parkways, Regional Plan of New York and Its Environs, 1928. (*Source*: Regional Plan of New York and Its Environs, *The Graphic Regional Plan*)

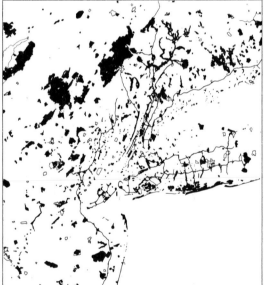

Figure 9. Reality: Open Space and Watersheds, 1965. (*Source*: Regional Plan Association)

priority over the amenity and recreational values recognized in the plan. In the growing centres of the cities, especially Manhattan, new structures were spread further apart to allow for better circulation and more light and air, in accordance with the images and ideas of the plan. If many of these projects and concepts did not originate with the regional plan, it nevertheless brought them together in a unified presentation, making them far more widely known and accepted.

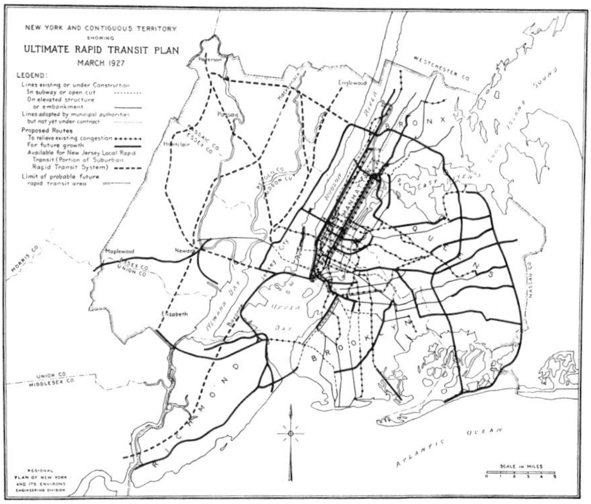

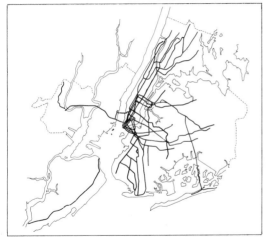

Figure 10. Proposed
Ultimate Rapid Transit
Plan. Engineering
Division, Regional Plan of
New York and Its
Environs, 1927. (*Source*:
Regional Plan of New
York and Its Environs,
Transit and Transportation)

Figure 11. Reality: Operating
Rapid Transit Routes, 1963.
(*Source*: Regional Plan
Association)

    The plan resulted in many positive successes, but it also failed in serious ways, both in its fundamental conception and in its implementation. The plan failed to address the long-term implications of vastly increased automobile ownership, despite accurate predictions of the increase. It failed to address the problem of providing housing for low- and lower-middle income families. And it was ambiguous in its support of new communities, affirming the concept, on one hand, and reluctant to indicate where or how new communities might be built, on the other.

    The plan also failed to realize its bold rail proposals, thanks largely to the fragmented, private ownership of the railroads, and it failed to realize its too modest proposals for rail transit, because of the difficulty of coordination across state boundaries, the reluctance of the Port Authority to assume a leadership role in a financially unattractive venture, and the reluctance of New York City transit officials to permit suburban trains on city subway system tracks (figures 10 and 11). The result was progress in public highway construction without parallel development of transit facilities, leaving a decentralized region by 1965 rather than the 'recentralized' region envisioned by Thomas Adams. The plan also failed to make adequate provision for new or expanded business centres, even though it was quite apparent that a considerably increased and recentralized population would require such centres.

Despite its failures, the regional plan unquestionably had a significant effect on the physical development of the region. And it also brought important changes in the institutional and public bodies concerned with regional development. Numerous planning and zoning agencies were established at the county and municipal level as a direct result of field work by the staff of the regional plan. State policies toward regional development also were augmented. The Port of New York Authority was greatly aided in its uncertain early years by the support of the Regional Plan Committee. Differences occurred, of course, but the influence of the regional plan on the Port Authority was usually salutary and broadening, as in the convincing case made in the plan for providing rapid transit capacity in the design of the George Washington Bridge. The ultimate location of the bridge at 178th Street was also influenced by the regional plan's conception of a 'Metropolitan Loop' of which the bridge was a key element. The loop was intended to move traffic around the centre rather than into it, as would have been the case with the earliest versions of a trans-Hudson bridge proposed for 22nd and, later, 57th Streets (figures 12, 13 and 14).

Robert Moses, in his positions of New York City Park Commissioner and chairman of both the Long Island State Park Commission and the Triborough Bridge Authority, carried many of the plan's highway and park proposals for New York City and Long Island to completion. The regional plan undoubtedly provided Moses with an agenda of public works. But more important, it created for Moses a climate of opinion among the business and political leadership in New York favourable to his programme. Though he would never credit the plan as being of much value, Moses's ascendancy to power was considerably aided by this climate.

Much of the progress made toward the partial though considerable realization of the plan during the Depression years from 1929 to 1941 was due to the vigorous efforts of the Regional Plan Association which pressed local governments to undertake park and transportation projects. In a number of instances, the Association provided detailed

Figure 12. Proposed North River (Twenty-Second Street) Bridge, Gustav Lindenthal, Engineer, 1896. (*Source*: Harrison, *History of the City of New York: Externals of Modern New York*)

Figure 13. Proposed North River (Fifty-Seventh Street) Bridge, Gustav Lindenthal, Engineer, 1921. (*Source*: *The Hudson River Bridge*, Regional Plan papers, Cornell University Library)

Figure 14. Proposed Hudson River Bridge at 178th Street, Cass Gilbert, Architect; O.H. Ammann, Engineer, 1927. (*Source*: Regional Plan papers, Cornell University Library)

design proposals based on the plan which directly resulted in acquisition and development.

The Regional Plan Association, created to carry out the proposals of the regional plan, is perhaps the most enduring and significant institutional heritage of the efforts of the Russell Sage Committee. The Association continues to play a unique watchdog and research role in the New York Metropolitan Region.[35]

The plan's impacts on the theory and techniques of urban and regional planning were also important. Population forecasting, economic base theory, and Clarence Perry's neighbourhood theory, were all fostered or spawned by the plan. Edward Bassett, in his work on the regional plan, refined the zoning tool he had helped to create in 1916. As a consequence of the plan, local zoning was adopted earlier and more widely in the New York Region than elsewhere. Bassett also significantly developed the law of public open space and shorefront rights in connection with his work on the plan.

The plan gave early warning of several urban problems which continue to be serious: the pollution of air and water, the inequitable social effects of large-lot zoning, and the destruction of public investment in highways by marginal commercial development. But perhaps its most important contribution was to articulate the connections between the physical framework of the city region and its social and economic conditions. No longer could engineering or architectural works be promoted solely on narrow grounds of individual project efficiency. Relationships between public investments in infrastructure and the distribution of jobs and people would have to be taken into account. The plan and the regional survey persuasively demonstrated the need to consider complex connections among basic regional systems.

The new ideas and principles promoted by the plan spread rapidly through the region and the nation in the decade following its publication in 1929. Former members and consultants of the regional plan staff took up important positions and tasks, not only in the New York area, but in other American cities and universities, carrying with them ideas and concepts evolved in their work for the Regional Plan Committee.[36]

Long after the plan became only of historic interest, the values and images, and the premises and goals, of American planners continued to be influenced by those embodied in the Regional Plan of New York and Its Environs. When the New York World's Fair opened in Flushing Meadows in 1939 an enormous three-dimensional model of the regional plan was placed on display in the New York Building (figure 15). In the midst of economic depression the Fair provided millions of visitors a glimpse of the future possibilities of new tech-

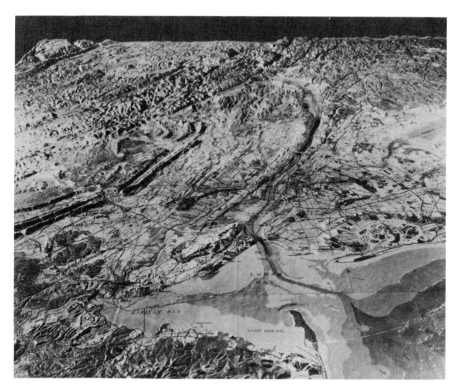

Figure 15. Model of the Regional Plan of New York and Its Environs on display at the New York World's Fair, 1939–1940. (*Source*: Regional Plan papers, Cornell University Library)

nologies. The regional plan had anticipated some of those technologies, though by 1939 it must have seemed somewhat backward-looking to fairgoers dazzled by television and robots.

When the Fair closed in 1940 with the outbreak of hostilities in Europe, the plaster model of the New York regional plan was given to the U.S. War Department to aid civil defence planning around the harbour. The gesture was somehow fitting. The plan was born in part out of the demands and pressures of World War I. Now it was to be put aside in response to the exigencies of World War II. After the war was over, low-density suburban development would spread rapidly in the fringe areas made accessible by the parkways and highways promoted in the regional plan. But the region that evolved, with its sprawling suburbs and decaying central cities, resembled neither the humane vision of Lewis Mumford nor the recentralized plan of Thomas Adams.

NOTES

1. Regional Plan of New York and Its Environs (1929) *Physical Conditions and Public Services*. Vol. VIII. New York: Committee on Regional Plan of New York, pp. 164–65.

2. Mandelbaum, Seymour J. (1965) *Boss Tweed's New York*. New York: John Wiley, pp. 116–17.

3. Fein, Albert (ed.) (1968) *Landscape Into Cityscape: Frederick Law Olmsted's Plan for a Greater New York City*. Ithaca: Cornell University Press, pp. 158–59.

4. Olmsted, Jr., Frederick Law (1914) The town planning movement in America. *Annals of the American Academy of Political and Social Sciences*, **51** (January), pp. 172–81.

5. New York City Improvement Commission (1907) *Report to the Honorable George B. McClellan, Mayor of the City of New York*. New York, p. 9.

6. City Plan Number, *Brooklyn Daily Eagle*, January 18, 1914.

7. *Ibid.*

8. See Caro, Robert A. (1974) *The Power Broker: Robert Moses and the Fall of New York*. New York: Alfred A. Knopf, pp. 341–44, for a description of Moses's 1930 version of the plan. Moses, of course, characteristically refused to acknowledge any debt to the reform planners.

9. For a description of the tremendous impact of the completion of the Panama Canal on the American business community, Rush, Thomas E. (1920) *The Port of New York*. Garden City: Doubleday, Page, and Co.

10. Bard, Erwin Wilkie (1942) *The Port of New York Authority*. New York: Columbia University Press, chapters 1 and 2.

11. New York, New Jersey Port and Harbor Development Commission (1920) *Joint Report with Comprehensive Plan and Recommendations*. Albany.

12. Kantor, Harvey A. (1973) Charles Dyer Norton and the origins of the Regional Plan of New York. *Journal of the American Institute of Planners*, **39**(3), pp. 35–41.

13. Committee on the Regional Plan (1923) *Draft Report of the Advisory Planning Group, November 12, 1923*. New York: The Committee.

14. Committee on the Regional Plan (1929) Vol. 1: *The Graphic Regional Plan*. New York: Regional Plan of New York and Its Environs, p. 401.

15. Mumford, Lewis (1925) Realities or Dreams. *Journal of the American Institute of Architects*, **13**(June), pp. 191–99. For another account of the 1925 International Town, City and Regional Planning and Garden Cities Congress, see Mumford, Lewis (1925) Bigger and better cities? *The Survey*, May, p. 216.

16. New York State Commission of Housing and Regional Planning (1926) *Report*, (May 7). Albany.

17. Mumford (1926) *op. cit.*; see also Mumford, Lewis (1926), The intolerable city: must it keep growing? *Harper's*, February, pp. 283–93.

18. Mumford, Lewis (1930) The booby prizes for 1929. *New Republic.* January 8, pp. 190–91.

19. Thomas Adams to Lewis Mumford, January 9, 1930. Regional Plan papers, Cornell University Library.

20. Lewis Mumford to Thomas Adams, January 18, 1930. Regional Plan papers, Cornell University Library.

21. Shelby Harrison to Thomas Adams, January 24, 1930. Regional Plan Papers, Cornell University Library.

22. Thomas Adams to Lewis Mumford. January 27, 1930. Regional Plan Papers, Cornell University Library.

23. Lewis Mumford to Thomas Adams, January 31, 1930; Thomas Adams to Lewis Mumford, February 3, 1930. Regional Plan papers, Cornell University Library. See also Lubove, Roy (1963) *Community Planning in the 1920's: the Contribution of the Regional Planning Association of America.* Pittsburgh: University of Pittsburgh Press, pp. 107–27, and Simpson, Michael (1985) *Thomas Adams and the Modern Planning Movement.* London: Mansell, pp. 38, 53–58.

24. Duffus, R.L. (1930) *Mastering a Metropolis: Planning the Future of the New York Region.* New York: Harper and Row.

25. MacKaye, Benton (1930) New York: a national peril. *Saturday Review of Literature*, August 23, p. 68.

26. Mumford, Lewis (1923) The Plan of New York, *New Republic*, June 15, pp. 121–26; Mumford, Lewis (1932) The Plan of New York: II. *New Republic*, June 22, pp. 146–54.

27. Mumford (1932) *op. cit.*, pp. 124–25.

28. *Ibid.*, p. 125.

29. Mumford (1932) The Plan of New York: II, *op. cit.*, p. 154.

30. Other prominent critics of the plan were Norman Thomas and Edith Elmer Wood. Thomas, Norman and Blanshard, Paul (1932) *What's the Matter with New York: A National Problem.* New York: Macmillan, pp. 314–16; also Wood, Edith Elmer (1931) *Recent Trends in American Housing.* New York: Macmillan, pp. 279–86.

31. Adams, Thomas (1932) A communication in defence of the Regional Plan, *The New Republic*, July 6, p. 207.

32. *Ibid.*, p. 208 Patrick Geddes was acquainted with both the Regional Plan Committee and its staff, and with Mumford's group, the Regional Planning Association of America. Geddes visited both groups on his final trip to America in the Spring of 1923.

33. *Ibid.*, p. 210.

34. For a detailed analysis of the impact of the plan see, Johnson, David A. (1974) *The Emergence of Metropolitan Regionalism: An Analysis of the Regional Plan of New York and Its Environs*, Ithaca: Cornell Dissertations in Planning, pp. 365–85.

35. Hays, Forbes B. (1965) *Community Leadership: The Regional Plan Association of New York*, New York: Columbia University Press.

36. Simpson, Michael (1982) Meliorist versus insurgent planners and the problems of New York, 1921–1941. *American Studies*, **16**(2), pp. 207–28.

Chapter Eight

The New Deal and American Planning: the 1930s

JOHN HANCOCK

On first impression, the soaring 1920s and depression 1930s in the United States seem Janus-faced. Beginning with elated public relief that the 'world' war was over and prosperity 'just around the corner', the era ended with ten years of the most severe economic depression in the nation's history followed by a second and greater world holocaust. Yet in American urban and regional planning, as in the rest of American life, the two decades were closely related. The Crash and deepening depression proved that the private market and local government could not sufficiently lead the nation's economic, physical, and social development. The New Deal strategy of federal intervention was a blend of old and new ideas that amended but did not fundamentally alter the American system of development.[1]

The idea of 'planning' – which Frederick Law Olmsted, Jr. described in 1910 as 'the new social ideal of unified and comprehensive city planning' and which the first generation of modern American planners had extended in the 1920s to region and state[2] – became a central element in the New Deal approach to recovery and future national well-being. The New Deal made planning not only fashionable but imperative in the Depression – and in federal–local relations ever since.

The focus of this chapter is the New Deal's impact on American planning policies and practices. After 1932, virtually all planning activity in the United States – in rural areas, towns and cities, states, regions, and the nation – was a direct result of New Deal policies. A look at the interaction between federal policy and planning activity in the 1930s helps to explain why certain concepts took hold and survived while others slipped into the archives of American intellectual history with little effect on landscape or society.

CONTINUITY WITH THE PAST

New Deal planning policies came from the ideas and experience of several previous presidential administrations; from professional planners, academics, businessmen, and local officials flocking to Washington; and from urgent Depression conditions. Federal interest in natural resource and rural planning went back to at least Theodore Roosevelt's presidency (1901–1908); and in city and state planning to William Taft (1909–1912) and Woodrow Wilson (1913–1920).[3] As Secretary of Commerce (1920–1928) and then as President (1929–1932), Herbert Hoover kept alive federal interest in planning by encouraging state adoption of model zoning and city planning enabling legislation and by commissioning data-gathering and policy studies on land use, conservation, public works, home ownership, airports, highways, social trends, slums, and unemploy-ment.[4]

Hoover saw the federal government's role as a passive one of promoting and facilitating voluntary compliance and cooperation in planning and resource management at state and local levels. His approach was 'to centralize ideas and decentralize execution'.[5]

As the Depression deepened after the Crash, Hoover continued to encourage state and local governments to undertake public works, expanded federal public works, and reluctantly asked Congress to create the Reconstruction Finance Corporation (RFC) to lend public funds to private banks, corporations, and municipalities for 'self-liquidating' projects, and to states which had exhausted their direct unemployment and work relief funds. Hoover's administration spent more federal money on public works than all administrations of the previous thirty-six years combined, but nothing in the approach was new.[6]

City planning was one of the first local public functions to cease in the general paralysis of the early Depression years. By 1931 the majority of city planning commissions were completely inactive, including those in thirty of the fifty largest cities and in more than half the next 168 cities (25,000 to 100,000 population range). By mid-1932, desperate city mayors formed the U.S. Conference of Mayors to advocate direct federal aid for redevelopment.[7]

Widely publicized ideas for a more active federal role in recovery all emphasized 'planning' by industry, business, and government.[8] In 1931 Charles Beard of Columbia University, probably the best-known historian and political scientist of the day, made a ringing call for a

Federal Council to make a 'Five Year Plan for America' with the federal government buying up marginal lands, building highways and electrical transmission lines, authorizing 'corporate farming' and massive low-cost rehousing, and employing

> an army of two or three million men to tear down and build cities decent to live in and delightful to the eye, summoning to its aid the best architectural talent in the country ... In the end there would be millions of acres of model farms and thousands of houses fit to live in. If the scheme fails, the properties can be sold ... But the plan is not utopian: it involves the extension of practices already in effect, and brains and materials are available.[9]

PLANNING AND THE NEW DEAL

Franklin Roosevelt, who took office on March 4, 1933, was more familiar with modern American urban and regional planning than any of his predecessors and – more importantly – was determined to use planning as a major weapon to fight the Depression and achieve prosperity. Whereas President Hoover had pursued *relief* and *recovery*, using the government's 'reserve powers' to protect citizens temporarily against 'forces beyond their control', President Roosevelt (1933–1945) also pursued *reform*, using federal powers to achieve more efficient and equitable use of human and natural resources. To guide us, he explained in 1934, 'the time called for and still calls for planning'.[10] Indeed, he said in his Message to Congress that year,

> I look forward to the time in the not too distant future when annual appropriations, wholly covered by current revenue, will enable the work to proceed with a national *plan*. Such a plan will, in a generation or two, return many times the money spent on it; more important, it will eliminate the use of inefficient tools, conserve and increase national resources, prevent waste, and enable millions of our people to take better advantage of the opportunities which God has given our country.[11]

Attacking the nation's ills on several fronts, Roosevelt tried eight major planning programmes between 1933 and 1940 – temporary work relief, major public works, and agricultural, industrial, housing, resettlement, regional, and national planning. All were efforts at economic and social as well as spatial planning; all utilized the services of professional planners. All originated from omnibus 'emergency' legislation in the famous 'First Hundred Days' of the New Deal (March 9 to June 16, 1933), amplified by over a dozen subsequent bills.

These programmes affected every American and covered every kind of habitat in the nation (table 1). The scale was new, but as Walker

Table 1. Major New Deal Acts Affecting Planning in the United States.

	Passage date	Affects mainly:
Federal Emergency Relief Administration Act (FERA)	5/12/33	all areas, unemployed
Tennessee Valley Authority Act	5/18/33	parts of 7 states
Home Owners Refinancing Act Extended & liberalized 4/27/35, phased to FHA 7/1/36	6/13/33	non-farm mortgages, lenders, homeowners, builders
National Industrial Recovery Act Title II: Public Works Admin. Housing Division Subsistence Homesteads Division National Planning Board (6/20)	6/16/33	all areas, declared unconstitutional 1935
Civil Works Administration Terminated 3/34, functions go to FERA	11/8/33	all areas, unemployed
National Housing Act Created Federal Housing Admin.	6/28/34	all areas, lenders, builders, homeowners
Soil Conservation and Domestic Allotment Act★	4/27/35	rural areas, farmers
Emergency Relief Appropriation Act	4/18/35	all areas, unemployed
Resettlement Administration Executive Order, under FERA powers, absorbed by Farm Security Admin. 1937	5/1/35	rural, suburban, urban
Rural Electrification Administration By Executive Order, under FERA powers★	5/11/35	rural areas
U.S. Housing Act (Wagner-Steagall Act) Created U.S. Housing Authority	9/1/37	rural–urban, especially cities
Administrative Reorganization Act Consolidates 24 agencies into Federal Loan Agency, Federal Security Agency, and Federal Works Agency; Transfers Bureau of Budget and National Resources Planning Board (7/1) to Executive Office	4/3/39	all areas

★Not discussed in this Chapter

Lippmann suggested in 1935, both Hoover's and Roosevelt's policies were 'the continuation of a [reform] movement in American politics which goes back at least fifty years'.[12]

Roosevelt got most of his planning ideas from the profession. On entering office he formed a National Land Use Planning Committee under Dr. L.C. Grey, Chief of the Bureau of Land Economics, U.S. Department of Agriculture (USDA), which included American City Planning Institute (ACPI) members Alfred Bettman, Jacob Crane, Frederic Delano (Roosevelt's uncle), Charles Eliot II, and John Nolen. Canvassed 'to get the views of a representative group of planners . . .

with reference to the technique of making planning effective', they recommended a coordinated national planning policy with a new federal agency to direct its research.[13] The ACPI members called this task 'social planning'. Much more than just land use planning,

> The general objectives of all social planning are to conserve human resources and maintain the nation and the race; to enhance the plans of living; to promote a balanced social economy with a better distribution of wealth; and to conserve natural resources.

Their recommendations led directly to creation of the *ex officio* National Planning Board and a short-lived Civil Works Administration.[14]

NATIONAL PLANNING

For planning writ large, the most important early bill was the June 16, 1933 National Industrial Recovery Act, whose purpose was to revive the economy and to reduce unemployment. Title I, which established the National Recovery Administration to supervise industrial self-planning, was ruled an unconstitutional violation of antitrust laws in 1935, but the activities under Title II survived and were of great importance to American planning. Title II set up the Public Works Administration (PWA) under Secretary of Interior Harold Ickes, who established three other programmes within it: a Housing Division under Robert Kohn to undertake slum clearance and public housing; a Subsistence Homesteads Division under M.L. Wilson to build resettlement communities; and a National Planning Board.

National planning was a matter of highest New Deal priority when Ickes created the National Planning Board within PWA in August 1933. However, since Congress never officially empowered it, the Board remained an *ex officio* organization under various titles. (National Resources Board (July 1, 1934 to June 7, 1935), National Resources Committee (June 8, 1935 to June 30, 1939), National Resources Planning Board (NRPB, July 1, 1939 to August 31, 1943). Hereinafter I call all the above 'NRPB', since that was its function throughout.

The NRPB reported directly to the President after 1933, and finally was relocated in the White House Executive Office from 1939 until its demise in 1943. In its decade of life, it reviewed all public policy for natural and human resources; stimulated the creation of city, state, and regional planning bodies; unofficially served as 'permanent long-range commission' for research, policy planning and coordination of all publicly funded programmes; and publicized ways to 'conserve and extend the benefits of American resources' to all citizens. In effect

NRPB became the administration's chief researcher, integrator, and advocate of national development policies – functions served by no single federal counterpart since.[15]

A diverse and bright group closely tied to the planning and academic communities, NRPB had a Washington staff of eight people, 200 more in regional offices, and 250 consultants. It also directed thousands of workers on public relief to do planning, engineering, and socio-economic surveys for states and local municipalities. NRPB was headed by a governing board of three 'citizen' advisers – Delano, political scientist Charles Merriam, and economist Wesley Mitchell – plus Ickes (1933–39), four other Cabinet secretaries, Emergency Relief administrator Harry Hopkins, and Roosevelt (1934 on). Chairman of the Board Delano, Roosevelt's 'favourite uncle' and 'crony', had headed the National Capital Park and Planning Commission. Executive Director Charles Eliot, 2nd, who had come from a similar job at NCPPC, claims that he and Delano first suggested the idea of a national planning committee. This body met several times a month, and less frequently with the President. The younger staff and consultants included future Nobel Prize winners Milton Friedman, Paul Samuelson, and Wassily Leontief; Milton Eisenhower and Gilbert White; Robert Weaver who in 1965 became the first Secretary of the Department of Housing and Urban Development; John Galbraith and others including every nationally known planner in the nation in the 1930s.[16]

NRPB produced no national plan, but had some minor success in carrying out two of its basic roles: (1) to promote planning and construction of public works, and (2) to coordinate federal planning activities; and had exceptional success in efforts (3) to stimulate city, state, and regional planning, and (4) to gather data and conduct research. By 1938, NRPB had helped create planning authorities in forty-one states, 500 regions and counties, and 400 additional towns and cities; and had provided consultation and information to whomever wanted it. By Marion Clawson's careful count, NRPB produced at least 370 major reports (among some 1600 published items) covering the American spectrum: natural resources, transportation, socio-economic conditions, urban government, housing, welfare, income, public works, industrial and agricultural capacity, to name a few – an enormously rich, relatively available, and unused shelf of studies. Its Urbanism Committee, as we shall see, produced the first major study of American cities in metropolitan, regional, and national context. But with no structural authority, few funds or political supporters, NRPB became essentially a research body and finally died in 1943 when Congress simply refused to re-fund it.[17]

REGIONAL PLANNING

The organization and implementation of regional planning – in the 1920s largely unofficial, voluntary responses to interstate and other cross-jurisdictional issues – got a big boost from the New Deal. In July 1933 NRPB set up eleven regional planning commissions, each run by a distinguished regional leader and the heads of all state planning boards in the region, plus a small technical and clerical staff and consultants. Their purpose was to collect data on regional resources and conditions, to make planning studies of needed interstate public works (e.g. dams), to focus attention on the region as an entity, and to promote regional and state planning. A 'region's' boundaries were flexibly defined, by economic networks or natural features. While these bodies had official status, they had no authority or control over action programmes.[18] The Tennessee Valley Authority (TVA), on the other hand, was a federal administrative or action agency, not principally a planning authority – although it was, and still is, the most notable example of regional planning *implementation* by the federal government.

The TVA Act of May 18, 1933 initiated an American regional planning programme of world wide significance. The most comprehensive New Deal planning effort of any kind, TVA was the largest public works project in the modern world to that time. It covered the 41,000-square-mile basin of the Tennessee River which spilled into parts of seven states – Alabama, Mississippi, Georgia, North Carolina, Virginia, Kentucky, and Tennessee. The Valley's 2.27 million residents were overwhelmingly rural, white, Protestant, native born, and poor, with per capita income lower than in forty-seven of the forty-eight states. The region's economy was chiefly extractive (e.g. timber), and the soil was too poor to provide adequate farm incomes.[19]

TVA is a classic American example of the federal government's difficulty in making and carrying out comprehensive planning policy. The planners' purposes were to build a hydroelectric power and river system fostering a strong economy, a prosperous society, and natural resource conservation. Roosevelt envisaged TVA as the prototype for a network of regional power authorities in all the major river valleys of the nation, to be established and coordinated by a National Power Authority.

The planning component apparently was a last-minute addition to the TVA legislation. According to Eliot, 'there was no mention of planning whatsoever' in the original TVA bill.

Jack [Nolen, Jr., his assistant at NCPPC] and I were agitated and got an appointment to see [Senator George] Norris [Republican, Nebraska] with Delano's help. We had drawn up a planning section for the bill and told Norris, rather sold Norris, that it ought to go in. Norris said, 'Is that all, gentlemen?' and put the recommendation in. Thus Sections 22 and 23 went in verbatim in the TVA bill, and those planning sections, of course, were responsible for the enormous planner influence in TVA.[20]

Section 22 gave the President undefined social, economic, and physical planning power. According to Earle Draper, who became head of TVA's Division of Land Planning and Housing, these sections

> were inserted in the Act with practically no discussion and were probably considered by Congress (if examined at all) as well-meaning generalities that were of little moment. Yet they contained planning powers that were later delegated by the Executive Order of the President to the TVA.[21]

Dams were TVA's most visible result, and helped to achieve some of its priority goals. Seven major dams were constructed along the River and its tributaries between 1933 and 1941, bringing electrification to the area, improving navigation and flood control, reviving the region's agricultural and industrial potential, and creating several new towns and vast public recreation grounds, which became second only to manufacturing in the region's economic growth.[22]

However, TVA failed as an experiment in town planning. Norris, Tennessee (planned for an ultimate population of 5,000 permanent TVA employees and families) was conceived as a federal demonstration town by planners Draper and Tracy Augur, who hoped to make it the prototype for a string of similar small communities built by government or private enterprise throughout the Valley. Encouraged 'to make a complete reappraisal of essential and non-essential points in housing and town planning', the planners emphasized simplicity, harmony with regional architecture, greenbelt protection from other towns, preservation of natural advantages, full local employment, an industrial/agricultural economic base, subsistence farms for homesteaders, fully electrified homes, a large common and community centre, and a freeway connection to state roads – all ideas familiar to American planners.[23] Congressional and business opposition, and disagreement among the directors, so modified the plan that only a third of Norris was built by 1940.[24]

If town planning proved difficult, TVA's social planning record was dismal. The agency intended to relocate more than 3,000 families (some 15,000 persons) displaced from 153,000 acres needed for Norris Dam. They were to receive better land, modern homes and new schools, health and other public services, and to share in the general economic benefits expected from the creation of new industries. As a recent study shows, no organized system of resettlement was planned or implemented, no relocation monies were provided, no displaced

Figure 1. (above) Houses demolished to make way for Norris Dam.
Figure 2. (below) TVA Model Homes built in Norris.
(*Source*: TVA Information Office, Knoxville, Tennessee)

families were resettled in Norris, and the displaced generally received below market price for their land with no allowance for inflated land value – forcing most families to settle on poorer, less productive land than before in the five-county river basin. There is also evidence that TVA failed in the long run to redistribute economic benefits more equitably: residents of the Norris Dam region outside of Norris continue to have one of the lowest living standards in Tennessee today.[25]

Thus TVA, probably the best-known New Deal programme, became essentially a public power utility. Comprehensive planning was virtually dead by 1936, when Congress drastically reduced funding for town and social planning. Finally in 1938 the U.S. Army Corps of Engineers led a successful fight to prevent Congress from passing Roosevelt's proposal for a national power agency and seven other TVA-like regional authorities across the land.[26]

URBAN PLANNING

In contrast, New Deal policies for urban America were unambitious and piecemeal. Although cities and towns received funds or services from over seventy federal programmes, none were exclusively 'urban'-directed. Five of these programmes – plus the work of NRPB's Urbanism Committee – constitute what can be called New Deal urban planning and development policy. They are: (1) temporary public works for unemployment relief (2) permanent federal/state and local public works; (3) rental public housing and slum clearance; (4) home ownership protection; and (5) new town resettlement.

Emergency Work Relief

Following some banking, budget-cutting, and other fiscal measures, the first New Deal approach to recovery was to fund temporary public works providing immediate jobs for the unemployed. On May 12, 1933, the Federal Emergency Relief Administration (FERA) was created under Harry Hopkins to coordinate all emergency relief. State and local authorities identified projects to be undertaken, and the RFC (Hoover's creation) provided funds to the states to distribute locally. FERA made direct grants (in contrast to Hoover's loans) to the states for unemployment relief, and an equal sum in matching loans ($1 federal for $3 state and local) for public works. Big city mayors objected to the matching provisions and to funnelling grants through the states, but the hundred largest cities got about half the funds, which helped some of them to avoid bankruptcy.

To help offset a rise in unemployment as winter neared, Congress passed another bill on November 8 creating the short-lived Civil Works Administration (November 1933 to April 1934), a separate relief organization also under Hopkins's direction. While its primary purpose was to provide temporary employment and raise income and purchasing power, CWA gave a much-needed boost to local planning capacity: it employed 4.2 million people during the winter of 1933–34 on some 200,000 projects including construction and repair of 500,000 miles of roads, 40,000 schools, playgrounds, and public buildings; provided planning services to all levels of government; and was the first federal agency to collect reliable nationwide data on twentieth century urban housing, income, and land use. Nearly 10,000 people made urban data studies and plan surveys, including the first urban Real Property inventory in U.S. history. Covering sixty-four cities of varied size, the study revealed a widespread pattern of slums, substandard housing, and poverty in urban America. This information became the basis for New Deal housing policies, and for local government revision of zoning ordinances and general plans based on hard information, not guesswork or abstract national standards.[27]

Both relief programmes were replaced by the more extensive and direct approach of the Works Progress Administration (WPA), created by the Emergency Relief Appropriations Act of 1935. Also under Hopkins, WPA awarded grants or loans directly to local governments, and left a permanent imprint on the American landscape. The largest federal employment programme, WPA during its lifetime (1935–1943) employed 8.5 million people on 1,140 projects and spent 85 per cent of its funding for wages. When WPA provided over half of its funds to the fifty largest cities, it was a great victory for mayors and city planners who had been pressuring Washington for unencumbered money since the summer of 1932. WPA labour built and repaired over 651,000 miles of highways and streets (10 per cent urban), 853 airports, 125,110 libraries, schools, museums, and other local public buildings, and over 25,000 parks, playfields, swimming pools, community centres; made many planning surveys; and paid the salaries of over 50,000 bureaucrats and local professionals, including planners. Few communities in the United States today are without evidence of WPA's impact. However, with growing opposition from business, Congress cut relief funds 50 per cent in 1936 and 1937, 60 per cent in 1938, and in 1939 began to require a minimum local contribution of 25 per cent.[28]

Basic Public Works

A second and equally well-known programme had nearly as much impact on cities and a greater one on city planning: the Public Works Administration (PWA), created as part of NIRA. PWA was a 'pump-priming' programme to stimulate the construction industry and related businesses, consumer spending, and employment though a combination of loans and grants to build large-scale public works. Costs were divided 45/55 (originally 30/70) between the federal and state/local governments. Applications were carefully reviewed by a central professional staff working closely with colleagues in local government and in newly-created local public development authorities which could condemn land, borrow, and plan independently of the municipality. Ickes used NRPB to coordinate, advise, and assist federal, state, and local governments in getting projects under way. More than half of PWA's $4.8 billion went to urban areas.

PWA funded expressways, water and sewage systems, gas and electric power plants, hydroelectric dams, civic centres, federal buildings, public housing/slum clearance projects, schools, hospitals, bridges, tunnels, aircraft carriers, a rapid transit system, and so on. Like WPA, PWA spent over a third of its funds on highways and roads. Yet PWA was not a notably successful 'pump primer' because it worked too slowly, centrally, and sometimes in conflict with local politicians. (Over half of its 34,500 projects between 1933 and 1939 were federal.) Ickes, notorious for his desire to avoid waste and any appearance of political partisanship, put much stress on planning, expertise, central review, and coordination with independent local public development authorities. Nevertheless, *unlike* WPA, PWA projects generally had the support of local businessmen, developers, and contractors.[29]

Slum Clearance and Rental Public Housing

Housing has major socio-economic significance. In 1930 it covered about 60 per cent of developed urban land in the United States. Thirty-eight per cent (11 million units, 55 per cent non-farm) of *all* U.S. housing was 'substandard'. Construction (all kinds) was the nation's second largest industry (after automobiles), and nearly 30 per cent of the jobless in 1933 were in the building trades.

In slum clearance and housing policies, New Dealers essentially fashioned two distinct federal programmes: rental public housing in slum areas for low- to moderate-income groups; and home ownership (especially suburban) for white, middle- to upper-middle income groups. Together these policies reinforced rather than loosened the segmented socio-economic character of American habitat and attendant problems of racism, poverty, and central city decay.

Slum clearance and public housing, conceived as one programme,

Figure 3. New Civic Centre, Oklahoma City, 1939. City Building, Court House, Municipal Auditorium and Public Safety Building constructed with PWA/ WPA funds on four blocks of centre city land acquired in 1935 from the railroads, which were rerouted to the city edge's in accord with the city plan made in the 1920s.

Figure 4. Key West Highway, 1938. Built with PWA/WPA funds in 1936–1938, this portion (34 miles, 20 foot wide road surface) replaced 11 washed-out railroad bridges connecting Key West and the other Keys to Miami (145 miles total route). (*Source*: PWA, *American Builds*)

was an early New Deal goal, based on proposals by housing reformers and planners since *c*.1911. In 1932 Hoover's RFC loaned money to private corporations to construct two low-cost housing projects. These were absorbed by PWA's Housing Division, whose first decision was to let private enterprise do the job, making loans up to 85 per cent of project cost to developers who would agree to certain profit limitations. But the results were poor in the seven projects funded: rents were beyond low-income means, and all projects were erected on vacant land, thus undermining PWA's objectives to demolish slums and to build on the cleared sites rental housing which slum-dwellers could afford.

In December 1933, the Housing Division created the Federal Emergency Housing Corporation (FEHC) to make grants and loans to states and local authorities to build 'demonstration' projects showing private enterprise what could be done by clearing slums and building low-rent housing in 'planned neighbourhoods'. Preference in FEHC projects went to localities with proposals that conformed to a city's general plan (if one existed). Plans for Neptune Gardens, East Boston, were the first approved, but the City of Boston and the State of Massachusetts failed to provide condemnation laws and matching funds – an early indication that public housing and slum clearance might be more popular with social reformers than with politicians, business, and perhaps the general public. Fifty-one projects (21,769 rental units) in thirty-eight cities were completed before the programme was terminated in 1937. Not too costly ($136 million total, $6,200/unit), they were superior in design, materials, and space to anything private enterprise built for comparable income groups. Residents had to be employed to qualify and had to leave if monthly family income surpassed six times their rent. Ickes insisted that these homes were for people of all ethnic and racial groups, but the projects were segregated.[30]

In a landmark case midway through this programme, the U.S. Circuit Court of Appeals (U.S. v. Certain Lands in the City of Louisville, July 12, 1935) blocked FEHC's efforts to condemn a slum site for a public housing project, on grounds that housing was not a federal purpose and that FEHC could thus not exercise eminent domain. The handwriting was clear: it convinced government policy-makers that the federal government's roles should be those of major financier, standard-setter, and technical consultant – leaving legal control, planning, design, and construction to local authorities empowered by state governments. By December 1936, thirty states had passed enabling legislation for local public housing authorities, and forty-seven city housing authorities had been established, with support from organized labour, housing officials, planners, and social workers.

On September 1, 1937, Congress finally passed the U.S. Housing Act (Wagner-Steagall Act). To get the bill passed over opposition from the housing industry, Senator Robert Wagner (Democratic,

Figure 5. (above) Chicago slums demolished in 1934 to make way for the Jane Addams PWA Housing Project.

Figure 6. (below) Courtyard of the Jane Addams Houses with WPA play statues. Completed in 1938, this project was located on Grenshaw Street, two blocks from the Loop and one-half mile west of Hull House. It was the largest (1,027 unites) of three PWA housing projects completed in Chicago in the 1930s.
(*Source*: The Chicago Historical Society)

New York) restricted beneficiaries to low-income groups, reduced quality standards and construction costs, and required the demolition of one substandard housing unit for each unit of public housing built – which changed the purpose of the legislation from that of producing rental public housing for a wide income range to clearing slums and rehousing the poor in the cleared areas.

The U.S. Housing Authority (USHA) created by this legislation absorbed all other public housing programmes, and under Nathan Strauss attempted to provide 'decent, safe, and sanitary dwellings' for families with incomes under $1,500 (median U.S. income was $1,800) who could not afford comparable housing in their community. For the first time, a federal agency could lend up to 30 per cent of total development cost at low interest to a local authority over a sixty-year period. As with the U.S. Housing Corporation in World War I, local communities qualified by assuming certain operational responsibilities such as exempting the projects from taxes, drawing up precise zoning and condemnation laws, and providing a master plan of community work priorities – a provision which unfortunately was not enforced, though it helped to revive local planning in some cities. Thanks to social, functional, and architectural standards established by Edith Wood, Catherine Bauer, and other seminal figures in public housing, USHA and PWA projects in the 1930s were generally suited to family needs, available to black families (but segregated), low-rise, sited on well-landscaped grounds with limited road access, and of good quality. Although Congress cut off funding in 1939, USHC built 130,000 units by 1941 (almost a third of the units for black families), and demolished 79,000 units of slum housing in the same areas – which extended the concentration and segmentation of low-income neighbourhoods in big cities.[31]

Home Ownership Protection

When war in Europe broke out again in September 1939, the United States still had an estimated 10 million units of substandard housing, but residential construction passed the billion dollar mark for the first year during the Depression. This achievement can be credited largely to the New Deal's ready assistance to middle- and upper-middle-income homeowners, loan institutions, and the housing industry in general – in sharp contrast to its reluctant support of rental public housing. In addition to outright social prejudice, this double standard reflects traditional American values of home ownership and the lobbying power of business and civic leaders concerned with overcoming economic problems more than social blight.

The purpose of the Home Owners Refinancing Act of June 13, 1933 was to prevent foreclosure on non-farm homes and to stimulate housing construction. Going beyond Hoover's Home Loan Bank Board, set up in 1932 to create discount banks for home mortgages, the Home Owners Loan Corporation (HOLC) created long-term, self-amortizing, uniform-payment home loans, by insuring against loss investment banks which would make low-interest twenty-year loans up to 90 per cent of costs for new and second mortgages, and up to 50 per cent for repair, renovation, and expansion. (Prior to 1933, a typical bank mortgage was for 58 per cent of costs after 30 per cent or more down payment, financed at high interest rates for five to ten years, with quick repossession for nonpayment.) One million homeowners – a sixth of all owner-occupied, non-farm home mortgages – were saved by this means from 1933 to June 1936, when HOLC's functions were absorbed by the new Federal Housing Administration (FHA). FHA secured loans up to 93 per cent of cost and extended payment to thirty years, which further reduced monthly payments and foreclosure rates, though not for everyone. While some homes in declining city neighbourhoods were insured, 80 per cent were those mortgaged to upper-middle-income families (above $2,000 annual income).

HOLC/FHA also systematized appraisal methods nationwide by dividing communities into neighbourhoods classified and rated according to the head of household's occupation, income, and ethnicity; the unit's type, condition, age, price range, and demand; and the neighbourhood's location and comparative socio–economic condition in the community. This rating system explicitly prevented racial mixing and undervalued older, dense, functionally and socially mixed neighbourhoods – especially poor, non-white, non-Protestant, inner-city ones – applying 'notions of ethnic and racial worth to real estate appraising on an unprecedented scale', as historian Kenneth T. Jackson says.[32]

Measured by their own goals, HOLC/FHA policies were very successful. Written in close cooperation with Secretary of Treasury Henry Morgenthau, other bankers, and Herbert Nelson, chief lobbyist for the National Association of Real Estate Boards (NAREB), the bills reflected the administration's faith in private enterprise, and Roosevelt's and the electorate's belief that home ownership signified an investment in community and citizenship as well as good personal economic sense. Under these policies, the New Deal accelerated home ownership and suburbanization in the 1930s: residence in metropolitan areas grew twice as fast as in central cities. The administration was far more committed to urban decentralization than to city renewal and to privately built or owned than to public or rental housing.[33]

However, the New Deal also sped up the process of inner-city decay by making it far easier to build in new areas than to get loans for home repair and modernization in old ones, and by accelerating racial and income segregation in home financing, thus preventing the use of

FHA funds to develop heterogeneous neighbourhoods and city growth. Measured by New Deal values of more opportunity and equality of condition, then, the net result of these programmes was to extend the *status quo*.

New Town Resettlement

Urban decentralization got another boost from a fifth New Deal approach to cities and planning: building new communities to resettle families under more favourable living and working conditions than available in crowded cities or on submarginal farmlands. This small programme – only ninety-nine communities were built – generated much public interest, strong opposition, and some practical lessons for professional planners, who were heavily involved. Another viable American tradition, resettlement had long appealed to Roosevelt as a way to merge agricultural and industrial development in regional planning.[34] Although New Deal resettlement communities took several forms, all are additional cases of comprehensive planning experiments undercut before they were fairly tested.

These experiments got under way in the Summer of 1933 when FERA and the USDA's Rural Rehabilitation Division planned thirty-five agricultural and industrial communities to be built in ten states over the next two years by state corporations using FERA funds. Simultaneously, PWA's Subsistence Homesteads Division (SH), under agricultural economist Milburn Wilson, planned sixty-three 'demonstration' towns in every region of the country, ranging from resettlement of stranded mine workers (Arthurdale, WVa), full-time farmers (Penderlea, NC), part-time farmers and industrial workers near cities (Dayton Homesteads, OH) or decentralized industry (Longview Homesteads, WA), industrial workers wanting to live in cooperatives (Jersey Homesteads, NJ), and black industrial workers and farmers (Aberdeen Gardens, VA). These projects were too small, narrow, or slow getting under way to make much difference in national economic recovery or in urban decentralization: transferred to the newly created Resettlement Administration (RA) in May 1935, only twenty-eight of FERA's and thirty of SH's sixty-three contemplated projects (5,730 units) were actually completed by 1940. Between 1935 and 1940 RA planned and built another thirty-seven communities (5,208 units), all but four of them rural.[35]

In its brief lifetime, RA was the most powerful and revolutionary planning authority created in the United States to that time, or since. As Paul Conkin notes, RA had the 'clearest mandate yet for the initiation of new communities'. It directly supervised all federal community and land rehabilitation programmes (two-thirds of them rural), with unlimited emergency authority to select and purchase land and to plan new communities.[36] Its purpose, said director Rexford Tugwell, was 'to put houses and people together in such a way that the props under our economic and social structure will be permanently strengthened'.[37] Aside from Roosevelt, the New Deal's best known 'planner' and most controversial figure, Tugwell – a former economics professor – believed with Roosevelt that neither rural resettlement nor slum clearance would solve the problems of poverty or congestion, and urged building 'satellite cities as an alternative'. 'My idea', he said, 'is to go just outside centres of population, pick up cheap land, build a whole community and entice people into it, then go back into the cities and tear down whole slums and make parks of them'.[38]

The 'greenbelt' towns were his major demonstration of this idea. NRPB made a preliminary study of the 100 largest cities, looking at housing, industrial employment, wages, real estate fluctuation, population profile and growth, municipal indebtedness, and prior local planning record. RA's Suburban Resettlement Division selected and acquired the local tract; made a master plan integrated into the local landscape, society, and economy; designed and constructed all buildings; and – unlike SH – *rented* the dwellings. The planners (a separate team planned and developed each town) emphasized high quality site planning, infrastructure, and housing mix; open–space separation from other suburbs; minimal commuting; nearby or in-town employment; resident-owned cooperative businesses; community centre facilities; and plenty of room for recreation – not a suburb but a whole community, planned as a physical, social, and political entity. Again, none of the planning, design, or administrative ideas were new. As Tugwell explained in defence of the programme,

[We] accepted a trend instead of trying to reserve it. Greenbelt refers to land, to the fixing of plan, to the fundamental uses of area, to the better living to be had by protection from crowding from within and encroachment from without.[39]

Intending to build twenty-five towns in the next several years, Tugwell received funding from Roosevelt to develop four towns near existing large cities: Greenbelt, Maryland (Washington, D.C.); Greenhills, Ohio (Cincinnati); Greendale, Wisconsin (Milwaukee); and Greenbrook, New Jersey (New Brunswick).

The greenbelt town planners began with great hopes, but within twenty months RA was dismantled because of continuing opposition from the courts, Congress, and the private sector, which claimed the towns were 'socialistic', added nothing to local taxes, and adversely affected land values by bringing poor people into the area. In May 1936, the D.C. U.S. Circuit Court of Appeals ruled Greenbrook (then

Figure 7. (above) Showing each tenement with its outhouse, this photo was part of the Resettlement Administration's documentation of poverty – in this case, perhaps to justify nearby projects like PWA's Laurel Homes and RA's Greenhills. (Photo by Carl Mydans)

Figure 8. (below) Residential street ready for occupancy, Greenhills, Ohio, October 1938. (Photo by John Vachon)

Figure 9. (above, right) Workers going home from work, Greenhills, Ohio, February 1937. Paid by WPA funds, these workers were therefore ineligible to live in the model community they were building. (Photo by Russell Lee)

(*Source*: Historical Section, RA, Farm Security Administration Collection, Prints and Photographs Division)

in plan) 'an unlawful delegation of legislative power to the President', who had no authority 'to regulate housing or to "resettle" population', and an unconstitutional use of federal funds for activities that 'have no connection with the general welfare'. Tugwell resigned, and Congress dismantled RA on December 31, putting all its programmes, including the three greenbelt towns, under the Farm Security Administration in the USDA until funds ran out in June 1938.[40]

While demonstrating some site design and community benefits of centralized comprehensive planning,[41] the greenbelt towns had some serious shortcomings. Dormitory suburbs more than functionally mixed communities, they neither provided for light industry nor attracted any to their borders as hoped. The number of people who would have benefited was small, even had all twenty-five towns been fully built (about 200,000 people). Because of underfunding, only 2,267 housing units (about 60 per cent of the total planned) were built (another 1,000 were added to Greenbelt in 1941 by the war emergency). Building costs were high, though not to the resident or for comparable quality in the private market.

Above all, the towns reinforced traditional social biases. They were in fact middle-income white family towns. Applicants had to have an income of $1,200–$2,000 per year, be married (preference to families with children) with one but not both spouses working (generally the male) in a permanent (not relief) job, and exhibit (to the Family Selection Section in each town) acceptable family and social behaviour. There were over 12,000 applicants – roughly six times the numer of units available. Black families were totally excluded, along with white families below middle income. In 1938 the average annual industrial wage was $1,100, and 45 per cent of all employed industrial workers earned less than $1,000 – which excluded from the greenbelt towns most factory workers, all relief workers constructing the towns, and over 8 million unemployed people.[42]

NRPB and the Cities

For all its attention to planning and cities, the New Deal never developed a policy for cities or urban regions. The closest it came was in the work of NRPB's Urbanism Committee, formed in 1935 to study the city's role in national life. In three major and twenty-two other studies made through 1939, the Urbanism Committee advocated replanning and building up central cities in metropolitan context, departing slightly from enthusiastic federal intervention in urban decentralization. Original members of this Committee, headed by former Cincinnati city manager Clarence Dykstra, included public administrator Louis Brownlow, sociologist Louis Wirth, Milburn Wilson (who represented rural interests), and planners Eliot, Arthur Comey, and Ladislas Segoe, director of the studies. The Committee's major work was a three-part study, *Our Cities: Their Role in the National Economy*, and two supplements, *Urban Government* and *Urban Planning and Land Policies.*[43]

Our Cities is a brief but impressive work, deserving NRPB's claim that it was 'the first major national study of cities in the United States'. The Committee drew policy-makers' attention to the fact the United States was an urban nation, noted trends and forces in urbanization, identified fourteen major emerging urban problems and recommended 'general policy' to help solve these problems.

Noting that economic security, higher and more equitable incomes, and 'quality of life' were the greatest needs, the authors made eleven major policy recommendations for federal help, including partial funding of social welfare, crime prevention, public utilities, and slum and blight eradication; and a national policy 'for [public and private means of] re-housing the low income groups at acceptable minimum standards' with federal funding to cities 'conditioned on the existence of a comprehensive city plan and a housing programme meeting satisfactory standards – all of which have since become part of the federal-local agenda. They made many other suggestions which have not, including (congressional) creation of a 'permanent national planning board' to encourage and coordinate planning by federal, state, and local authorities; congressional enablement of interstate metropolitan compacts with 'greatly improved', broad authority to plan and manage 'government functions of regional scope'; a permanent urban data division in the Census Bureau; dividing the metropolis into coherent, politically enfranchised neighbourhoods or communities; and 'far more fundamental and much more effective planning at all levels of government.[44] It was a familiar wish list to planners, most of it ignored by politicians.

A NEW DEAL FOR AMERICAN PLANNING?

The federal government became an indispensable force in the well-being of American society in the 1930s, and remains so. Did this New Deal benefit American planning and planners? Did its policies change how planning was done, or the results? Public policy-making is a reciprocal process, an interaction of framers' goals and values with those in the larger, more pluralistic political system: policies, programmes, and results don't match precisely. New Deal planning was tempered by legislatures, courts, local governments, organized business opposition, and citizens far more receptive to reform in Roosevelt's first term than thereafter. Still, the 1930s was a time of unprecedented *experimentation* with and *implementation* of planning in the United States: planning moved from the conceptual, technical, and limited practical achievements of a small band of pioneering professionals to centre stage in federal policy and its impact on American habitat. Unquestionably, American planning benefited unevenly from the ensuing successes, and failures.

The sheer amount and variety of planned development makes the 1930s arguably the most significant era in American planning history. There were small but unprecedented breakthroughs in public housing/slum clearance, national planning, rural and suburban community planning, natural resource planning, and federal 'demonstration' projects. There were significant gains in public works (including roads), home financing, land reclamation, regional modernization, planning data, and intergovernmental planning coordination.

Clearly the New Deal vastly enlarged planning capacity in the United States. Local, state, and regional planning, dormant by 1932, did not resume in the decade without federal help. Even caretaking chores like zoning were paid for with relief funds.[45] By 1940 a planning apparatus was in place in every state and major urban region, over 1,500 counties, metropolitan regions and cities, and 200 federally funded local public authorities therein. While mostly underused and underfunded, the nation's public planning structure was dramatically enlarged and beginning to change from peripheral citizen advisory bodies to operational departments near centres of executive power.[46]

Reflecting planning's growing importance in the public arena, government (all levels) replaced the private sector as the chief employer of professional planners and stimulated demand for more planners. NRPB's staff alone was larger than the entire ACPI membership in the 1930s. Similarly, planning education expanded geographically beyond its largely northeastern concentration to every region of the country, and substantively beyond design and engineering to public administration and the social sciences, although there was little agreement on what constituted planning education.[47]

The profession underwent significant intellectual change in the 1930s. Realizing the inadequacy of their narrow focus on physical order and their ignorance of American social, economic, and political realities, planners opened their eyes and minds to new sources of ideas – particularly to the plight of low-income people and the need for more equitable distribution of resources. The growing number of social scientists and public administrators holding important planning positions also increased the influence of their ideas on planning thought and practice. Still, the profession remained divided over many critical issues. Thus between 1935 and 1938 ACPI officially revised its goals statement to include metropolitan and regional planning, but could not agree on the proper role of social and economic planning therein.[48]

This diverse expansion of practice, education, and ideas produced more fragmentation than integration of fields in planning. As new questions were posed about planning's role in the nation's development, planners also began differentiating planning administration from plan implementation, spatial from social or economic planning, short-range from long-range goals – without putting it all back together, which renewed without clarifying debate over the proper boundaries of planning and how to make it work. Christine Boyer concludes that the physical planning idea was destroyed as it merged with economic and political policy in the 1930s:

> The more the disciplinary control of planning intervened in the economy and the political order, the more it met with resistance from private and local municipal spheres. The more it was beaten back, the more it turned inward toward abstract policy formulation, research, and information collection . . . Badly fragmented, planning would reach out to join hands with the administrative process of policy-

making and abandon finally its physical intention: to order the American city.[49]

Political gains in the emerging era of close federal–local relations brought notable new alliances for urban planning. New Deal programmes tended to reinforce more than to change the physical, social and economic character of cities, but 'each successive relief and recovery measure opened up new lines of communication between the two levels of government',[50] as Mark Gelfand observes.

Businessmen were key participants in the new planning alliances. Very selective – and successful – lobbyists, they considered public housing and slum clearance, and most comprehensive federal projects, to be costly, unfair competition and un-American when their participation, and the profit motive, were eliminated. Asking planners to join 'us' (2,400 land developers and home builders) in lobbying Congress to terminate NIRA, Kansas realty king J.C. Nichols wrote: 'If the Government would just stop interfering in business, the unemployment in this country would soon be solved . . . It certainly is destroying all initiative in private property'.[51] While distressed by non-profit public programmes, Nichols and associates lobbied successfully for federal mortgage protection and were impressed by federal studies and demonstrations showing that the economic costs of 'blighted' areas – decaying commercial and industrial zones – were between two and ten times greater than revenues cities received from them; that publicly funded neighbourhood improvement districts could arrest decline; and that cities with general comprehensive plans linked to capital budgets appeared least hurt by the Depression, best able to plan for new public works, and most successful in attracting federal money. (Examples most often cited were New York City, Richmond, Cincinnati, Milwaukee, and San Diego). These findings argued for planning's closer alignment with public policy-making and administration.[52] They also encouraged businessmen to join planners and local politicians in urging federal redevelopment grants to cities to purchase and sell large tracts of blighted land at below-market rates to private companies to develop within specific local planning guidelines – precisely as was done after World War II in the housing and urban renewal acts of 1949 and 1954.[53]

Comprehensive planning – tested more thoroughly by the New Deal than ever before or since – was the most notable failure of the decade. The failure was due partly to the controversial pronouncements of some of its leading administrators like Tugwell, to negative media coverage (e.g. the New York *American* [October 29, 1936] called Greendale 'the first Communist town in America'), and to the belief of some Americans that any public 'planning' was a radical, fascist, or elitist ideology imposed on unwitting citizens by narrow-minded or impractical experts and bureaucrats. Ickes removed the word 'planning' from the National Planning Board in 1934, renaming it the National Resources Board for this reason; the term was put back in 1939 when NRPB was lodged in the White House. To counter opposition to national planning, Roosevelt emphasized its local character: 'national planning should start from the bottom, or, in other words, the problems of townships, counties, and states should be coordinated through larger geographical regions and come to the capital of the nation for final coordination'.[54] Draper differentiated American 'grass-roots' regional and urban planning from 'totalitarian' planning.[55]

A more important reason for the failure of comprehensive planning was the New Dealer's political myopia – the belief that traditional politics could be transcended. Not surprisingly, New Deal attempts to eliminate localism and privatism from planned visions of American 'community' aroused widespread business and political opposition. Organized business opposition, for instance NAREB, the American Banking Association, and the U.S. Chamber of Commerce, argued that the New Deal method of slum clearance *cum* public housing served only a small portion of low-income families but was paid for by all taxpayers, went mostly to cities (which was incorrect) but returned no city taxes, raised businessmen's taxes but reduced their potential sources of profit, and stigmatized the poor by removing them from the housing market. Politicians from Congress to city council's disliked large, comprehensive projects like TVA and RA because they threatened the patronage system. As Barry Karl suggests, 'The distribution of resources and federal funds was the lifeblood of a congressman's career. To turn that distribution over to the President, let alone to scientific planners, was a direct threat to congressional power'.[56] Politicians also were 'accustomed to thinking in terms of houses and highways rather than communities'.[57]

From their national perspective, most New Dealers and many planners had quite a different view, of course. To old Progressive Republicans like Ickes, the times cried out for a 'new social vision of the future . . . to the testing of new social values . . . if it is our purpose to make industrial gains to serve humanity then national planning will become a major governmental activity'.[58] Looking backward five years later, FDR's cabinet and agency heads pronounced their efforts 'the most impressive collection of progressive policies and public achievement since the days of Washington and Hamilton and Jefferson and Gallatin'.[59] Nolen, a pioneer modern planner and a special consultant to every major New Deal planning programme until his death in 1937, felt NRPB *et al.* had 'done the most distinguished and important piece of planning work yet conceived in this country, breaking ground in an original way and in a new field'.[60] Looking backward forty years, Andrew Lepawsky, a student of Merriam's who wrote several major NRPB studies, felt that '[d]espite a lack of sophistication, especially in the economic realm, the New Deal remains the high water mark of American planning thought and practice'.[61]

Underlying these opposing views are two planning styles (and values) which reflect countervailing tensions in historic American culture. One is a localist or Jeffersonian style – self-governing, small-scale, piece-meal, permissive, and 'merit'-based. The other is a centralist or Hamiltonian style – managerial, large-scale, comprehensive, mandatory, and 'equity'-based. Both styles exalt (in name if not in practice) civil rights, private property, individual enterprise, and limited government.

New Dealers intertwined these styles unsuccessfully, with negligible attention to the former. In general they took a comprehensive approach in the first term but settled for piecemeal programmes as resistance to basic reform stiffened. To Otis Graham this federal intervention was 'a divided and confusing counsel', and so national planning 'failed during the most favourable circumstances history has yet provided in the United States'.[62] However, from the beginning New Dealers espoused no single philosophy of comprehensiveness but took a 'let's-try-what-works' approach: their planning policies served varied, sometimes conflicting, political interests – which is to be expected in a pluralistic society. Unfortunately, they were inattentive to programme coordination and local differences, and they were biased along class and racial lines. Significantly, there was no specific New Deal policy for cities, and categorical programmes were administratively weak and uncoordinated at the national as well as the local level. Typical of later legislation, the USHA did not even require that public housing programmes be coordinated with city plans, though planners and NRPB repeatedly urged it in the 1930s. What emerged from the political infighting instead was what planner George Galloway called in 1941 a 'broker state' New Deal: 'sectional, restrictive, and uncoordinated . . . It consisted of a series of stopgaps designed, as Mrs. Roosevelt said, 'to give us time to think'.[63]

In my judgement, the New Deal's planning problems were as much internal as external. The broker state followed from both the New Dealers' failure to appreciate the need for and their inability to achieve the *integration* of consolidated and decentralized systems to accomplish democratic planning and equitable results at every scale in the United States. Democracy and comprehensive planning are *not* inherently incompatible, but they have to be applied from the ground up as well as from the top down. In this regard the New Deal planning vision was strong but one-sided. The formula continues elusive.[64]

During the Depression the political environment seemed most receptive to comprehensive planning, yet ultimately rejected it. The New Deal never achieved a clearly formulated, consistently followed, or widely supported 'unified and comprehensive' policy for national, regional, or urban development. Yet the federal *endeavour* to undertake social, economic, environmental, and spatial planning from neighbourhood to national scale is a benchmark legacy in our planning history – along with the failure to place it in the American grain.

NOTES

1. There is a vast literature on the New Deal and surrounding decades. See, for example, Hicks, John (1960), *Republican Ascendancy, 1921–1933*. New York: Harper & Brothers; Karl, Barry (1983) *The Uneasy State: The United States from 1915 to 1945*. Chicago: University of Chicago Press, pp. 80–181; Leuchtenburg, William (1963) *Franklin Roosevelt and the New Deal, 1932–1940*. New York: Harper & Row; Louchheim, Kate (ed.) (1983) *The Making of the New Deal: The Insiders Speak*. Cambridge: Harvard University Press; Mollenkopf, John (1983) *The Congested City*. Princeton: Princeton University Press, pp. 3–96; Mowrey, George and Brownell, Blaine (1981) *The Urban Nation, 1920–1980*. New York: Hill & Wang, pp. 3–110; Rozwenc, Edwin (1959) *The New Deal: Evolution or Revolution?* Boston: D.C. Heath; Wilson, William (1974) *Coming of Age: Urban America, 1915–1945*. New York: John Wiley & Sons.

2. (1910) Basic Principles of City Planning. *Proceedings of the Second National Conference on City Planning*. Boston: NCCP, pp. 3–4, quoting; Hancock, John (1967) Planners in the changing American city, 1900–1940. *Journal of the American Institute of Planners (JAIP)*, **33** (September), pp. 290–304; Scott, Mel (1969) *American City Planning Since 1890*. Berkeley: University of California Press, pp. 110–269.

3. Hays, Samuel (1959) *Conservation and the Gospel of Efficiency: The Progressive Movement and Conservation 1890–1920*. Cambridge: Harvard University Press; West, Myron (1919) The great opportunity for city planning. *American City*, **20**, February, pp. 129–30; Wilson *Messages and Papers*. Shaw, Albert (ed.) (1924) New York: Macmillan, Volume II, pp. 673–74.

4. Clements, Kendrick (1984) Herbert Hoover and conservation, 1921–1933. *American Historical Review*, **89**, pp. 67–88; For some of Hoover's planning-related views see his (1951–52) *Memoirs of Herbert Hoover*. New York: Macmillan, 3 volumes. Volume II, pp. 61–78, 132–38, 183–85, 226–309.

5. Clements *op. cit.*, pp. 67–88, quoting Hoover, p. 69.

6. Hoover *op. cit.*, Volume II, pp. 61–78.

7. Shurtleff, Flavel (1932) What are plan commissions doing? *American Civic Annual*. Washington: ACA, p. 178; editorials (August 1932, January 1933) What are 'self-liquidating' public works?, and Self-liquidating projects flow in sluggish streams. *American City*, **47**, p. 5 and **48**, p. 5. The latter also notes only 1 per cent of the RFC funds were used for municipal projects.

8. Beard, Charles (ed.) (1930) *Whither Mankind? A Panorama of Modern Civilization*. New York: Longmans Green, pp. 406–7; Coyle, David (1931) Public Works and Prosperity. *American City*, **45**, p. 83; editorial (January, 1933) Economists urge decreased federal aid to states and cities. *Ibid*. **48**, p. 54.

9. Beard, Charles (1931) A five-year plan for America. *American City*, **45** p. 108.

10. Hoover (1951–52) *Memoirs*, *op. cit.*, Volume II, quoted p. 78; Roosevelt (1934) *On Our Way*. New York: John Day, quoted xii.

11. Roosevelt (March 4, 1934) *Public Papers and Messages*. Rosenman, Samuel (ed.) (1938–45) New York: Random House, 13 volumes, III, p. 11.

12. Lippmann (1935) The permanent New Deal. *Yale Review*, **24** (June), pp. 650–51.

13. Crane, Jacob *et al.* (April 27, 1932) Report of the National Land Use Planning Committee. Mimeographed, quoted ACPI file, Nolen Papers (NP) Cornell University; the conference was held on February 15–18, 1933.

14. Bettman, Alfred *et al.* (June 13–14, 1933) Memorandum, ACPI Committee on Rural Zoning in collaboration with National Land Use Planning Committee, USDA, quoting; Crane, Jacob to Committee members (April 27, 1933) Memorandum on the Relation of Emergency Relief Work to Planning. Mimeographed, both in ACPI file (NP).

15. (December 1, 1934) A Plan for Planning. *Report*. Washington: U.S. National Resources Boards, PWA, p. 3.

16. Roosevelt, James and Shalett, Sidney (1959) *Affectionately F.D.R.: A Son's Story of a Lonely Man*. New York: Harcourt Brace, quoting Roosevelt p. 290 and p. 316; Eliot, 2nd, Charles (1933) Planning by the Federal Government. *Planning and National Recovery*. Washington, NCCP, 38; Clawson, Marion (1981) *New Deal Planning: The National Resources Planning Board*. Baltimore: Johns Hopkins University Press, pp. 52–85 and *passim*; Krueckeberg, Donald (1983) From the backyard garden to the whole USA: A conversation with Charles W. Eliot, 2nd, in Krueckeberg (ed.) *The American Planner: Biographies and Reflections*. New York: Methuen, pp. 355–57; Karl, Barry (1974) *Charles E. Merriam and the Study of Politics*. Chicago: University of Chicago Press, pp. 244–82.

17. Clawson *op. cit.*, pp. 86–186, 322–47, *passim*; Ickes, Harold and Fletcher, Robert in Perkins, Francis *et al.* (1938) *The Federal Government Today: A Survey of Recent Innovations and Renovations*. New York: American Council on Public Affairs, pp. 25–27, 55–61, 92–93. The key source for NRPB archives is Eliot, Charles 2nd and Merrill, Howard (1943) *Guide to the Files of the National Resources Planning Board and Predecessor Agencies: Ten Years of National Planning, 1933–1943*. Washington: NRPB, mimeographed, 188pp, in Records Group 187, National Archives.

18. Technical Committee on Regional Planning of the National Resources Committee (December 1937) *Regional Factors in National Planning*. Washington: GPO, pp. iii–xii and *passim*; Draper, Earle (1941) Regional Planning, in Galloway & Associates (ed.) *Planning for America*. New York: Henry Holt and Company, pp. 507–22; Clawson, *op. cit.*, pp. 80–81, 125–31, 166–70, 189–98, 248–49. The regions were: I New England, II Middle Atlantic, III South-eastern, IV Ohio-Great Lakes, V South Central, VI Missouri Valley, VII Intermountain & Great Plains, VIII Southwest, IX Pacific Northwest, X Alaska, XI Caribbean.

19. Schaffer, Daniel (1984) Environment and TVA: Toward a Regional Plan for the Tennessee Valley, 1930s. Paper presented to the American Collegiate Schools of Planning, annual meeting, Minneapolis, pp. 1–15; McDonald, Michael and Muldowny, John (1982) *TVA and the Dispossessed: The Resettlement of Population in the Norris Dam Area*. Knoxville: University of Tennessee Press, pp. 69–123.

20. Eliot interview with author (March 4, 1965), Cambridge, MA.

21. Draper, *op. cit.*, pp 518–519 (Roosevelt's Executive Order, Conservation and Development of the National Resources of the Tennessee River Drainage Basin, was June 18, 1933.); Sections 22 and 23 reprinted in Draper, 518. Section 22 authorizes the President:

> by such means or methods as he may deem proper within the limits of appropriations made therefore by Congress, to make such surveys of and general plans for [the region] as may be useful to the Congress and the several states in guiding and controlling . . . development . . . all for the purposes of fostering an orderly and proper physical, economic, and social development of said areas, and to do so in cooperation with the states or subdivisions thereof, cooperative and other organizations, and to make such studies, experiments, or demonstrations as may be necessary or suitable to that end.

22. Schaffer, *op. cit.*, pp. 6–25; Gough, Herbert, Seavey, Clyde, and Caromicli, John in Perkins *et al. op. cit.*, pp. 72–84; Droze (1965) *High Dams and Slack Waters: TVA Rebuilds a River*. Baton Rouge: Louisiana Press; Holley, Donald (1975) *Uncle Sam's Farmers: The New Deal Communities in the Lower Mississippi Valley*. Urbana: University of Illinois Press includes several Mississippi towns like Tupelo that emerged from TVA's impact.

23. U.S. Tennessee Valley Authority (1947) *The Norris Project*. Washington: GPO, pp. 174–75 (quoting), pp. 15–68, 161–220; Augur, Tracy (1936) The planning of the town of Norris. *American Architect*, **148** (April), pp. 18–26.

24. *Ibid.*, pp. 161–200; Draper (1933) The new town of Norris, Tennessee. *American City*, **48** (December), pp. 18–26; Augur, Tracy to Nolen (September 19, 1935), TVA file (NP); Johnson, David (1984) Norris, Tennessee on the occasion of its fiftieth anniversary. *Planning History Bulletin (PHB)*, **6**(1), pp. 32–40. Norris was sold to a private purchaser in 1946, and remained a small dormitory community whose population has slowly declined over the years from 2500 to 1374 residents, mostly TVA employees and retirees. Scott *op. cit.*, says Norris was 'the only town built in the 1930s by the federal government that brought a price greater than its total cost, p. 315.

25. Unsigned (1936) TVA Replaces a Town. *American City*, **51** (January), pp. 58–60; McDonald and Muldowny (1982), pp. 215–72.

26. See McGraw, Thomas (1970) *Morgan vs. Lilienthal: The Feud Within the TVA*. Chicago: Loyola University Press; and (1971) *TVA and the Power Fight, 1933–1939*. Philadelphia: Lippincott.

27. Gelfand, Mark (1975) *A Nation of Cities: the Federal Government and Urban America, 1933–1965*. New York: Oxford University Press, pp. 27–43, 82–83; U.S. Bureau of Public Records (1955) *Highway Statistics: Summary to 1955*. Washington: GPO, p. 59; Crane, Jacob (April 27, 1933) Memorandum on Relation of Emergency Relief Work to Planning, enclosed in letters to Nolen and L. C. Grey, FERA file (NP); FERA (March 2, 1934) *Bulletin D–3*; Schwartz, Bonnie (1984) *The Civil Works Administration 1933–1934*. Princeton: Princeton University Press.

28. WPA (1939. Renamed Works Projects Administration in 1939) *Report on Progress of the Works Program*. Washington: GPO; Federal Works Administration (1942) *Final Report of the WPA, 1933–1939*. Washington: GPO; Gelfand, *op. cit.*, pp. 44–46; Mollenkopf *op. cit.*, pp. 66–67.

29. Ickes (1933) Federal Emergency Administration of Public Works. *Planning and National Recovery*. Baltimore: National Conference on City Planning (NCCP), pp. 19–26; PWA (1939) *America Builds: The Record of PWA*. Washington: GPO, pp. 1–23 and *passim*; Gelfand, *op. cit.*, pp. 46–49; Mollenkopf, *op. cit.*, pp. 65–66; Wilson (1974) pp. 184–87. While eighty-six cities proposed rapid rail transit plans, PWA funded only one, Chicago, see Foster, Mark (1981) *From Street-car to Superhighway: American City Planners and Urban Transportation, 1900–1940*. Philadelphia: Temple University Press, pp. 132–76.

30. Ickes and Strauss, Nathan in Perkins *et al.*, *op. cit.*, pp. 25–27; Ickes (1935) Government and Housing, in *Planning for the Future of American Cities*. Cincinnati: American Society of Planning Officials (ASPO), pp. 172–76; unsigned (1933) Organization Complete of the Federal Emergency Housing Corporation. *American City*, 48 (December) p. 72; Wood, Edith (1935) *Slums and Blighted Areas in the United States*. Washington: GPO, pp. 7–15; Blumenthal, Yvonne (March 1935) Summary of the Activities of the Federal Agencies Affecting Housing. *Housing Study Bulletin* 6 (PWA), pp. 3–6; Scott, *op. cit.*, pp. 127–33; Nolen to Robert Kohn (September 20, 1932), to John Milton (June 19, 1933), Nolen and William Parker (July 25, 1933) Planning Neptune Gardens, Low-Cost Housing Project, Summary of Report Submitted by the City Planning Board; Boston, Mass., on Civil Works Project No. 3512, 193035; Boston *Herald*, August 18, 1934; all in Neptune Gardens file (NP); PWA (1939) *America Builds*, pp. 206–17, 291; Bowly, Devereaux Jr. (1978) *The Poorhouse: Socialized Housing in Chicago, 1895–1976*. Carbondale: Southern Illinois University Press, pp. 17–33; Trout, Charles (1977) *Boston: The Great Depression and the New Deal*. Chicago: University of Chicago Press. PWA claimed Techwood Homes in Atlanta was the first 'public' slum clearance and low-rent housing project in American history.

31. Mollenkopf, *op. cit.*, pp. 67–69; Scott, *op. cit.*, pp. 316–22; Gelfand, *op. cit.*, pp. 59–65; Kohn, Robert in Perkins *et al.*, *op. cit.*, pp. 25–27, 92–94; Crane, Jacob in Galloway (ed.), *op. cit.*, pp. 394–410; Birch, Eugenie (1983) Woman-made America: the case of early public housing policy, in Krueckeberg (ed.), *op. cit.*, pp. 149–75.

32. Strauss, Nathan and Fahey, John in Perkins *et al.*, *op. cit.*, pp. 95–103; Jackson, Kenneth (1980) Race, Ethnicity, and Real Estate Appraisal: The Home Owners Loan Corporation and the Federal Housing Administration. *Journal of Urban History*, 6, pp. 419–42, quoted p. 424; Wecter, Dixon (1948) *The Age of the Great Depression, 1929–41*. New York: Macmillan, pp. 123–53.

33. Keyserling, Leon in Louchheim, (ed.), *op. cit.*, pp. 196–204.

34. See for example Roosevelt, Franklin in Beard, Charles (ed.) (1932) Actualities of agricultural planning. *America Faces the Future*. Cambridge: Harvard University Press, pp. 326–47.

35. Press Release #98609 (April 1935) Subsistence Homes and Housing. USDI, Div. SH; Wilson in Perkins *et al.*, *op. cit.*, pp. 11–16; Wilson (1934) The misuse of the nation's land leads to a new policy. *New York Times Magazine*, July 11; Conkin, Paul (1959) *Tomorrow a New World: The New Deal Community Program*. Ithaca: Cornell University Press, pp. 1–145, 237–304, 332–37; Holley, Donald (1975) pp. 65–283 (covers Arkansas, Louisiana, Mississippi); Dreier, John in Louchheim *op. cit.*, pp. 244–46.

36. Conkin, *op. cit.*, pp 131–145, quoted p. 145.

37. Tugwell (1936) Housing Activities and Plans of the Resettlement Administration. *Housing Officials Year Book*. Chicago: National Association of Housing Officials, 28.

38. Tugwell (1937) The Meaning of the Greenbelt Towns. *New Republic* 80 (February 17), pp. 42–43, quoted; it appeared first in his Diary, March 3, 1935, see Myhra, David (May 1974) Rexford Guy Tugwell: initiator of America's Greenbelt New Towns, 1935 to 1936. *JAIP*, 40, p. 181.

39. Tugwell (1937), *op. cit.*, p. 43 quoted; RA (September 1936) *Greenbelt Towns: A Demonstration in Suburban Planning*. Washington: GPO, p. 1–15; Mayer, Albert (1939) Housing for All the People. *Thirty-first Proceedings of the National Conference on Planning*. Boston: ASPO, pp. 16–20; Augur (1940) City Planning and Housing – May They Meet Again. *Thirty-second Proceedings of the National Conference on Planning*. San Francisco: ASPO, pp. 157–65; Conkin, *op. cit.*, pp. 305–25; Arnold, Joseph (1971) *The New Deal in the Suburbs: A History of the Greenbelt Town Programs, 1935–1954*. Columbus: Ohio State University Press, pp. 24–109, 148–90.

40. Franklin Township in Somerset County, N.J. *et. al.* v. Tugwell *et. al.* (May 18, 1936) *Federal Reporter: Second Series* 85, #6619 (October–December 1936), pp. 209, 219–220 quoted; Schaffer, Daniel (1983) Resettling industrial America: the controversy over FDR's greenbelt town program. *Urbanism Past and Present*, 8 (Winter/Spring), pp 18–32; Myhra (May 1974) pp. 184–88; Arnold, *op. cit.*, pp. 36–53; 124–35, 191–217; Eden, Joseph and Alanen, Arnold (1983) Looking backward at a New Deal town: Greendale, Wisconsin, 1935–1980. *JAPA*, 49 (Winter), pp. 40–58.

41. Augur, Tracy and Blucher, Walter (1938) The Significance of the Greenbelt Towns. *Housing Yearbook, 1938*. Chicago: National Association of Housing Officials, 218–225. From my own childhood recollections of the physical amenities in PWA's Neighbourhood Gardens, St. Louis 1937, Greenhills 1939–40, and Public Housing Authority's Elmwood, Connecticut

project 1943–1947, Greenhills was by far the best place to live.

42. Farm Security Administration (1939) *Annual Report*. Washington: GPO, pp. 1–18; Arnold (1971), *op. cit.*, pp. 22, 112–15, 136–47. Conkin, *op. cit.*, pp. 320–31; Bone, Hugh (February 1939) Greenbelt Faces 1939. *American City* **54**, pp. 59–61; U.S. Census Bureau (1975) *Historical Statistics of the United States: Colonial Times to 1970*. Washington: GPO, Series F pp. 297–348 and G pp. 306–18, 243–45, 284–305; Mayer, Albert (1967) Greenbelt towns revisited. *Journal of Housing*, **24** (January, February, March), pp. 12–26, 80–85, 151–60.

43. Urbanism Committee of the National Resources Committee (June 1937) *Our Cities: Their Role in the National Economy*. Washington: GPO; (1939) *Supplementary Report of the Urbanism Committee, I: Urban Government*; and (1939) *Supplementary Report . . . II: Urban Planning and Land Policies*. Washington: GPO. Clawson, *op. cit.*, pp. 162–64; Gelfand, *op. cit.*, pp. 71–104, who (pp. 58–59) notes the only bill passed by Congress with any urban reference in the title was the Municipal Debt Adjustment Act, 1935. No city over 30,000 population ever used it, and in 1936 it was declared an unconstitutional infringement of state responsibilities.

44. Urbanism Committee (June 1937) *Our Cities*, quote pp. v–xii, 80 and 85, see also v–xii, 55–85.

45. Buttenheim, Harold (1931, 1932, 1933) Trends in Present-day city and regional planning in the United States. *City Planning*, **8**, pp. 110–15; **9**, pp. 73–86; **10**, pp. 63–77; ASPO *News-letter* (1936–1939) pp. 2–5 (# 1), pp. 1–2 all issues; *cf.* Abbott, Carl (1983) *Portland: Planning, Politics and Growth in a Twentieth-Century City*. Lincoln: University of Nebraska Press, pp. 103–24.

46. Segoe, Ladislas in Galloway & Associates (ed.) (1941) City and County Planning, pp. 536–43, and Kizer, Benjamin, State Planning, *Ibid.*, 523–528. National Resources Committee (May 15, 1937) Status of City and County Planning in the United States. *Circular Letter X*; Lowitt, Richard (1984) *The New Deal and the West*. Bloomington: Indiana University Press, pp. 218–28.

47. Feiss, Carl (1938) Education for Planning in the United States. *National Conference on Planning: Proceedings*. Minneapolis: ASPO, pp. 143–57.

48. Unsigned (1935) Revised Constitution. *Planners' Journal*, **1**, pp. 13–18; ACPI Committee on Urban Land Policies (1937) Report: Increased Public Ownership of Urban and Suburban Land. *Planners' Journal*, **3**, pp. 98–99; Black, R. Van N. (1938) President's Report. *Planners' Journal*, **4**, pp. 19–22.

49. Boyer (1983) *Dreaming the Rational City: The Myth of American City Planning*. Cambridge: MIT Press, pp. 203–23, quoting p. 205.

50. Gelfand, *op. cit.*, p. 65 quoting, see also pp. 66–69, 198–237, 381–89. Mollenkopf, *op. cit.*, pp. 47–96; *cf.* Romasco, Albert (1983) *The Politics of Recovery: Roosevelt's New Deal*. New York: Oxford University Press.

51. Nichols to Nolen (April 26, 1935), Nichols file NP; Thorpe Merrill (January 1938) Fever Chart of a Tugwell-Town: Electric Dryers for Greenbelt Housewives; Morris, George (November 1938) Another Social Experiment Goes Sour; and Thornhill, Edward and De Armand, F. (October 1940) $16,000 Homes for $2000 Incomes, all in *Nation's Business*, **26**, p. 13, **26**, pp. 21–23, and **28**, pp. 23–25.

52. McNeal, Donald (May 1941) Waverly – A Study in Neighbourhood Conservation. *National Conference on Planning*. Philadelphia: ASPO, 216–22; Gillette, Howard, Jr. (August 1983) The evolution of neighborhood planning from the progressive era to the 1949 Housing Act. *Journal of Urban History*, 9 pp. 427–34; NRPB (1941) *Long-Range Programming of Municipal Public Works*. Washington: GPO, pp. 1–72; Walker, Robert (1941) *The Planning Function in Urban Government*. Chicago: University of Chicago, pp. 106–220.

53. Nelson, Herbert (1935) The Share of the Realtor. *Planning for the Future of American Cities*. Cincinnati: ASPO, pp. 90–94; U.S. Chamber of Commerce (1937) *Balanced Rebuilding of Cities: A Statement Issued by the Construction & Development Committee*. Washington: USCC, pamphlet; Bartholomew, Harland (February 1938) Neighborhood rehabilitation and the tax-payer. *American City*, **53** pp. 56–57; unsigned (August 1938) For large-scale city rebuilding. *American City*, **53**, p. 5 quoting Nelson; Gelfand (1975) pp. 111–15, 139–40; Scott (1969) pp. 377–86, 404–29, 462–67, 486–531.

54. Roosevelt (1937) quoted in Karl, *op. cit.*, p. 165; see also pp. 111–13, 161–81.

55. See for example Draper, *op. cit.*, pp. 508–12.

56. Karl, *op. cit.*, p. 161.

57. Gelfand *op. cit.*, pp. 236.

58. Unsigned (1933) City Planning Merges into National Planning. *American City*, **48** (November), p. 5 quoting Ickes.

59. Perkins, *et al.*, *op. cit.*, pp. 2. See also Louchheim, *op. cit.*, *passim* for enthusiasm of younger New Deal staff.

60. Nolen to Delano (July 6, 1935) NRPB file (NP).

61. Lepaswky (January 1976) The planning apparatus: a vignette of the New Deal. *JAIP*, **42**, p. 19; Clawson (1981) p. 258, and Beckman, Norman (May 1960) Federal long-range planning – the heritage of the National Resources Planning Board. *JAIP* **26**, pp. 89–97, see the New Deal a more effective stimulator of ideas than a coordinator of public actions.

62. Graham (1976) *Toward a Planned Society: From Roosevelt to Nixon*. New York: Oxford University Press, quoting pp. 8, p. xiii, 45, 68, see also pp. 1–68. Wilson, David (1979) *The National Planning Idea in U.S. Public Policy: Five Alternative Approaches*. Boulder: Westview Press, looks at national planning c. 1900–1972 to assess 1973–75 issues.

63. Galloway in Galloway & Associates (ed.) (1941) The Climate of Opinion, p. 48 quoting, see also pp. 46–49.

64. See for example Needlemans, Martin and Carolyn (1974) *Guerillas in the Bureaucracy: The Community Planning Experiment in the United States*. New York: John Wiley; Burchell, Robert and Sternlieb, George (eds.) (1979) *Planning Theory in the 1980s*. New Brunswick: Center for Urban Policy Research, Rutgers University; Meltzer, Jack (1984) *Metropolis to Metroplex: The Social and Spatial Planning of Cities*. Baltimore: Johns Hopkins University Press.

Chapter Nine

The Paradox of Post-War Urban Planning: Downtown Revitalization versus Decent Housing for All

JOHN F. BAUMAN

On August 28th, 1964 the attempt by two police officers to remove Mrs. Odessa Bradford and her husband from their car at the intersection of 22nd and Diamond in the heart of North Philadelphia's black ghetto triggered three days and nights of rioting, burning and looting. Two people were killed, 399 were wounded, and 308 were arrested. Investigations following the riot cited three principal causes of the conflagration. Slum housing headed the list of grievances together with poor public schools and high unemployment.[1]

Just two months later Philadelphia's acclaimed urban planner and renaissance architect, Edmund Bacon, appeared on the cover of *Time* magazine. 'Of all the cities under the planner's knife', remarked *Time's* cover story, 'none has been so deeply or continuously committed to renewing itself as the city where the Declaration of Independence was signed'. *Time* praised Philadelphia's redevelopment programme as 'the most thoughtfully planned, thoroughly rounded and skillfully coordinated of all the big-city programs in the U.S.'.[2]

A city glorified for its quintessential revitalization and yet just months earlier wracked and ablaze with ghetto violence offers a perfect urban stage for analysing post-war housing and planning. Not only was the city's housing and redevelopment policy acclaimed as 'shelter-oriented', but critics also awarded Philadelphia's revitalization effort high marks for its socially sensitive architecture and design. In addition, such Philadelphia post-war housing and planning personalities as Edmund Bacon, Louis I. Kahn, Oscar Stonorov, Henry Churchill, Robert Mitchell, William Wheaton, Martin Meyerson, and William Rafsky, to mention a few, achieved considerable distinction in the realm of planning, and exerted recognizable influence in shaping the milieu for post-war housing and redevelopment nationally. Therefore, the 'Philadelphia story' provides a particularly good vantage point from which to observe and understand the success or failure of housing and planning during the critical years of urban redevelopment and renewal, 1945–1964.[3]

WEAVING A THEORY OF SLUMS AND URBAN BLIGHT, 1945–1949

The Great Depression had a devestating effect upon the economy and environmental quality of American cities. Plant closings and massive unemployment eviscerated the urban economy, undermined the urban tax base and compelled the delay or abandonment of much needed public works. By 1943, despite federal aid from the Public Works Administration (PWA), the Works Progress Administration (WPA), the HOLC, FHA, CWA, and other New Deal alphabet agencies, and despite the passage in 1937 of the Wagner-Steagall (public) Housing Act, basic urban services such as water delivery, sewer, lighting, and education had deteriorated, leaving an ever expanding area of urban slums and blight.[4]

While World War raged in Europe and the Pacific, housers and planners, dreading the spectre of a post-war housing crisis and post-war unemployment, began planning for a revitalized post-war city.[5] Organizations such as the National Resources Planning Board, the Division of Urban Studies of the National Housing Agency, the National Association of Housing Officials and the National Association of Real Estate Boards, debated the nature of the urban crisis and spawned visions of a better-planned and better-housed urban America. Victory in Europe and Japan and the return of thousands of veterans anxious to form families and enjoy the fruits of warborn prosperity not only precipitated a housing shortage, but also intensified national concern for jobs and the rebuilding of slum-scarred cities.

Between 1945 and 1949 this discussion of the future of cities continued, with most of the debate centering on housing and redevelopment legislation first introduced in Congress in 1945 by Senators Robert Wagner (Democrat, New York) Robert Taft (Republican, Ohio), and Allen J. Ellender (Democrat, Louisiana). Among other things the Wagner-Ellender-Taft bill called for federal aid for 'land assembly, for participation by private enterprise in development or redevelopment programs', and for the continuation of public housing and the rehabilitation of older buildings for the use of low–income families.[6]

By 1949, the year the Wagner-Ellender-Taft housing bill was passed, planners had defined urban blight and concocted a remedy for its cure. William Ludlow, a planner with the Philadelphia Redevelopment Authority, in 1953 defined blight tersely as land overcrowding, inadequate light, poor ventilation, insufficient play space, dirt, and social ills. Others stressed 'physical deterioration', and 'obsolete structures', but instead of land overcrowding, emphasized 'the loss of population in residential districts'.[7]

Regardless of the definition, most housers and planners deplored the high population density associated with American central cities.[8] Nurtured as planners on a steady diet of anti-congestion invectiva, planners in the 1940s still equated slums and blight with land over-crowding and they recited a litany of correlative evils such as poverty, high typhoid and tuberculosis rates, crime, delinquency and low levels of literacy.[9]

Architects, planners and housers often traced the roots of urban social and physical decay to the haphazard urban growth pattern inherited from the nineteenth century.[10] To invert the phrase used by the scholar of land-use patterns, Constance Perrin, everything was not in its place.[11] Manufacturing competed for downtown space with commercial warehouses and retail establishments. And amid the airless, dank spaces and dark shadows created by these buildings sat hundreds of two and three-storey tenement buildings, artifacts of the nineteenth century, and which, perforce, still performed the vital function of housing the urban poor.[12]

Following the terminology of urban sociology and the urban design principles of Eliel Saarinen, post-war planners leaned heavily on a biological model of the city (especially the etiology of disease) to understand the process of blight and slum formation. Cities had hearts capable of pulsating with health, but were instead congested with population. City streets were arteries clogged with traffic. However, the most dreaded killer was the cancer of blight which vitiated the urban core, then spread its deadly tentacles outward to devour one vital neighbourhood after another. Planners such as Coleman Woodbury and Edmund Bacon espied blight, which they claimed destroyed not only the physical, but also the social-psychological city. In this phase blight invaded the neighbourhood morale, robbed pride, and produced general slovenliness. Woodbury equated blight with social-psychologist Emile Durkheim's idea of 'anomie', a condition caused by the loss of a sense of belongingness and the disintegration of social norms. Although some planners considered Woodbury's social interpretation of blight to be specious, it nevertheless tinctured much of post-war urban redevelopment theory, especially in Philadelphia. Like the biological model of the city and the etiology of disease, it helped undergird the rationale for development and neighbourhood planning.[13]

PLANNING PRACTICE: CURING URBAN BLIGHT

Defining urban blight as a cancer suggested that cities required radical and costly surgery. Conservative businessmen, civic leaders, planners and liberal housers for various and sometimes conflicting reasons concurred that urban revitalization necessitated federal intervention.[14] As a result, by 1945 schemes for federal participation in urban redevelopment increased in number and popularity. During the war, economically motivated redevelopers and planners including Harlan Bartholomew fashioned a convincing economic argument to justify a federal-urban partnership in city-rebuilding. Blight, they argued, threatened the existence of the downtown and thereby endangered the bastion of urban wealth and urban culture. However, petty, rackrenting landlords impeded redevlopment by refusing to surrender their tottering slum property at a 'reasonable price'. Therefore, the need arose for the creation of local redevelopment authorities armed with the power of eminent domain and flaunting a tantalizing package of federally underwritten tax incentives and low-interest, tax-free bonds. Indeed, between 1940 and 1948 twenty-seven states, including New York and Pennsylvania, passed redevelopment authority legislation.[15]

These early redevelopment authority laws codified the aspirations of businessmen and civic leaders fearful about the future of the central city. In its first *Annual Report* (for 1947), the Philadelphia Redevelopment Authority praised Pennsylvania's new redevelopment law as 'a socially important interpretation of the use of condemnation, . . . [and as the] missing link between planning . . . [and] redevelopment'.[16] Under the 'power broker', Robert Moses, the New York City Redevelopment Authority previously had provided eminent domain and tax incentives to lure New York's Metropolitan Life Insurance Company to build the massive and much ballyhooed Stuyvesant Town housing development, a project opening in 1943 that would serve as a model for post-war development.[17]

Planners and housers meeting at the Chicago Conference on Redevelopment in 1948 emphasized the economic as much as the social benefits to be gained from urban rebuilding. Modern, well-planned neighbourhoods, argued the conferees, would turn back the tide of suburbanization by enhancing the appeal of the city. Their emphasis rested on a belief in progress and modernization. Therefore Philadelphia architects in 1950 contrasted the city's 'dull and deadening row housing' with the 'fine [luxury] housing projects . . . correspond[ing] to 20th century need', that will rise in the next five years. Referring to the modern high-rise, middle-income housing proposed for Philadelphia's city centre Triangle Redevelopment Area, Samuel Zisman, a former Executive Director of the Citizens Council on City Planning(CCCP), talked excitedly about the 'fresh and unashamed architecture that symbolizes Philadelphia's awakening in the second half of the century'.[18]

Yet amidst many testimonials exalting the economic and aesthetic benefits of redevelopment, other voices were heard imploring planners and redevelopers to fashion social as well as physical development goals for city-rebuilding. Guy Greer, Catherine Bauer, Coleman Woodbury, G. Holmes Perkins, and architect Walter Gropius, to mention a few, believed that urban redevelopment was doomed unless coupled with a broadscale, federally-subsidized housing programme. Moreover, they insisted that the gravity of the post-war housing shortage dictated regional not narrowly conceived local solutions to the rehousing-redevelopment task. Catherine Bauer, the renowned houser and author in 1934 of *Modern Housing*, implored post-war planners not to resist, but to control, the global force of suburbanization by planning and building decentralized, socially diverse communities. Impressed by Great Britain's Town and Country Planning Act of 1947, American housers and planners such as Bauer and Woodbury lobbied vigorously for federal legislation expediting the orderly resettlement of congested urban populations into planned suburban communities. This 'natural decongestion', argued Bauer, would deflate exaggerated inner-city land values, and provide a reasonable basis for reconstructing the central city.[19]

Still, as early as 1953, Bauer and Woodbury confessed that America's route to better housing and urban redevelopment had diverged from the desired British solution. Woodbury bemoaned that post-war city planners had not designed modern, decentralized communities and had opted instead for the negative approach of slum clearance and blight removal.[20] An enduring and stolid champion of the European 'communitarian' approach to city planning, Catherine Bauer remained the most committed to wedding modern housing and urban revitalization. As she had during the 1930s, Bauer ascribed the real cause of slums to the so-called 'filter system' – which rather than trickling down safe and sanitary housing to the urban poor, spawned abominable slums instead. In 1946 Bauer also debunked talk among housing policy-makers that America could solve its housing shortage 'by the back door of employment', that is by making work for the building trades rather than building good housing 'for its own sake'. She particularly deplored the inevitable consequence of poor post-war planning, 'the profusion . . . of ragged, formless [urban] fringes graying the last remaining open country in our metropolitan areas'. Bauer observed in her biting rhetorical style that 'far from getting rid of blight, most planning and housing officials were 'busy as bird dogs [in 1946] relaxing standards and throwing up Quonset huts on playgrounds and squeezing two families in where only one was before'.[21]

Bauer's communitarian passion for planned regional community development wonted a popular base of support. But her argument about the critical importance of public housing in the redevelopment process attracted numerous adherents. In 1945 Alfred Bettmen, the Cincinnati lawyer-city planner, underlined the crucial distinction between redevelopment goals and the aims of public housing. Redevelopment, observed Bettman, mainly sought the elimination of blight and the reuse of valuable land for commercial and industrial purposes. On the other hand, public housing specifically addressed the housing needs of low-income families. However, in its terseness, Bettmen's distinction ignored the functional role played by public housing in sheltering families displaced by redevelopment activity.[22]

More characteristically, post-war defenders of public housing stressed the housing shortage. Guy Greer, senior economist of the Board of Governors of the Federal Reserve System, and author with Harvard economist Alvin Hansen of the post-war housing and planning pamphlet entitled *After Defense-What?*, estimated in 1944 that the United States would need 1,600,000 new dwellings annually for ten years. In light of the low-incomes of many Americans, Greer concluded that public housing would be a necessary supplement to any post-war housing and planning effort.[23]

But, where to build all the new public housing? Naturally, considering her decentralist bias, Bauer favoured building it on inexpensive, vacant land outside the city. Pointing to the achievement of Scandinavia, Bauer advocated incorporating public housing into planned community development 'which ideally', she wrote, 'involved the federal government aiding non-speculative private enterprise carrying through the whole program and operating through metropolitan public or semi-public agencies'.[24]

Woodbury, too, imagined a comprehensive programme of urban renewal operating in tandem with public housing construction. In Woodbury's mind the atomic bomb and the spectre of nuclear war made the decentralized approach to urban redevelopment and housing imperative. 'If space is our only defense', he argued, 'then

Figure 1. Catherine Bauer Wurster and the Philadelphia reformer and housing authority member Walter I. Phillips examining a map showing projected sites for public housing c. 1952.

industry as well as low-income housing must be decentralized'. But as fervently as Bauer and Woodbury pressed for public housing on the urban periphery, the majority of post-war planners and redevelopers urged that public housing should be located in the central city. In his summary of the 1948 Chicago Conference on redevelopment, planner Frederick Gutheim observed that redevelopment officials pictured public housing as 'short term', low-income shelter, constructed on 'cleared land in or near the redevelopment site and close to [the] . . . friends, institutions and places of employment of those displaced'. According to Gutheim, these redevelopment planners surmised that most displaced families would 'return to the old area after redevelopment, provided, of course, re-use were for housing that they could afford'.[25]

Between 1948 and 1953, therefore, redevelopers and planners outlined a functional relationship connecting public housing and urban redevelopment; it was, however, a marriage predicated upon building housing projects on central city sites. As early as 1947 Dorothy S. Montgomery, the managing director of the Philadelphia Housing Association, a progressive housing organization founded in 1911 to oversee the betterment of city housing conditions and promote the enactment and enforcement of city housing ordinances, fretted over the narrow economic focus of post-war central city planning. Writing in 1947 to Catherine Bauer Wurster (Bauer had married the architect William Wurster in 1947), Montgomery commiserated with her housing ally about the lack of political support for housing; it seems 'a waste of time to run a housing program', sighed the PHA chief. Montgomery praised Pennsylvania's two year old model redevelopment law, but simultaneously registered dismay at the five gentlemen appointed by the governor to the Philadelphia authority. Four of them, she complained, 'are clearly out of the real estate business'. They 'may only be interested in central city commercial areas with high potential tax yield', she sneered. 'We will be pleasantly surprised if we do not have to disagree with their recommendations which should be out pretty soon'.[26]

THE PHILADELPHIA CASE: REFORM-BASED REDEVELOPMENT

Philadelphia's experience illustrates exquisitely the untoward consequences of shackling public housing to urban redevelopment. Yet no other American city struggled more valiantly to unify the goals of good housing with the vision of urban renaissance. Tragically, the dubious outcome of Philadelphia's effort to mesh housing and redevelopment obscured the nobility of the city's intentions.

Philadelphia's unique 'shelter-oriented' approach to redevelopment originated in the late 1930s among a band of young, liberal-minded lawyers, housers, and architects who believed that planning in the words of one eager patrician reformer, Walter Phillips, offered a 'non-political, non-controversial way' to accomplish political reform. In addition to Phillips, Philadelphia's band of 'young Turks' included houser Dorothy Schoell Montgomery, lawyers Abraham Freedman, Joseph Sill Clark and Richardson Dilworth, G. Holmes Perkins of the University of Pennsylvania School of Fine Arts, and architects Oscar Stonorov and Edmund Bacon. Phillips, Montgomery, Stonorov, Perkins, Freedman, and Bacon were all associated with the Philadelphia Housing Association. Indeed, from 1940 until he joined the Navy in 1942, Edmund Bacon served as the Managing Director of the PHA.[27]

By 1942 these Young Turks had teamed with the Junior Board of Commerce and the Lawyers Council on Civic Affairs to form the Joint Committee on City Planning, later the Citizens Committee on City Planning (CCCP).[28] From this early wartime planning and housing activity sprang a newly constituted, activist planning commission headed by Edward Hopkinson, an illustrious civic leader and the great grandson of the signer of the Declaration of Independence. For the commission's new executive director the CCCP selected Robert Mitchell, the planner who had just recently headed the Urban Section of the now defunct National Resources Planning Board. Triumph in 1942 only intensified the reformers' ardour. Accordingly, by 1945 Abraham Freedman helped draft Pennsylvania's urban redevelopment law, and in January 1947, having defeated a taxpayer's challenge to its legality, Philadelphia reformers celebrated the birth of the city's urban redevelopment authority.[29]

These early years of planning and redevelopment produced more bluster than solid accomplishment. In the city's defence, before any neighbourhood could be certified for redevelopment, the state's redevelopment law required Philadelphia to conduct time-consuming, house-by-house surveys. Meanwhile, in concert with the PHA and the CCCP the Planning Commission and Redevelopment Authority drummed up popular support for urban revitalization by staging a gala 'Better Philadelphia Exhibit'. Designed by Oscar Stonorov and Louis I. Kahn, the exhibit featured a magnificient scale model of the city that dramatically contrasted the city of the present with the city to be reborn through planning. Stonorov and Kahn used lights, bells, and other visual special effects to spotlight the exciting physical changes taking shape on the planner's drafting tables. Displayed at Gimble's large downtown department store, the Better Philadelphia Exhibit attracted over 700,000 visitors in 1947.[30]

As Phillips and the Young Turks had hoped, the reality of urban decay, crime and political graft clashed disconcertingly with Stonorov's and Kahn's vision of a renewed Philadelphia. Soon, the dream of physical rebirth helped ignite political reform. In 1949 liberal Democrat Joseph Clark won election as City Controller clinching a significant victory over the city's creaking Republican machine. As one of his first acts Clark revamped and streamlined the city's somnambulent housing authority. Two years later, while the city reverberated with talk of reform, Philadelphians elected Clark mayor and approved a new city charter. It was a 'sunlit hour', an era of surging hope for an aging industrial city wracked by the sizeable loss of industry, commerce, and middle class tax payers.[31] Not only had Philadelphia elected a progressive mayor committed to achieving efficient government, professional city planning, and housing betterment, but the city affirmed its dedication to urban modernization by arming Clark with a new city charter. Philadelphia's new charter vested considerable authority in a strong mayor-council form of government, and created within the mayor's office a powerful bureaucracy, including a managing director and a cabinet status Commission on Human Relations. Furthermore, the charter preserved the city planning commission, and charged it to produce an annually updated six-year comprehensive plan.[32]

Congressional passage of housing and redevelopment legislation in July 1949 greatly strengthened Joseph Clark's ability to promote the goal of a Better Philadelphia. Lauded by planner William L.C. Wheaton as 'the most significant event in the development of city planning in recent history', the Housing Act of 1949 established the national goal of 'a decent home in a decent environment for every American'. Title I authorized a first year outlay of one billion dollars in federal loans, and $500 million in grants to local redevelopment authorities to help purchase and clear slum land. But, despite the boon to redevelopment, this was primarily housing legislation. Ohio Senator Robert Taft insisted that areas redeveloped under the law should be for 'primarily residential' reuse. Toward that end the law linked new public housing to rehousing families displaced by slum clearance. Consequently, the legislation resuscitated the long dormant public housing programme by scheduling the construction of 810,000 units of new public housing, 135,000 yearly for six years.[33]

Housing and redevelopment ranked equally high on Joseph Clark's agenda for Philadelphia. A Harvard and University of Pennsylvania-educated Philadelphia aristocrat whose mother, Kate Avery, had inherited Louisiana oil wealth, Clark in the vein of his idol, Franklin Delano Roosevelt, believed that the survival of the republic necessitated government intervention on behalf of the common man. Fighting in 1953 to rescue public housing from the death grip of Republican critics who branded it 'socialistic', Clark charged that 'if the housing program is not carried through there is danger that there will not be sufficient houses for our residents and that will mean democracy cannot work'. In the mid-1950s Clark's faith in the positive behavioural effects of public housing was widely shared. Even Philadelphia's conservative congressman, Hugh Scott, saw public housing rescuing slum-scarred juveniles from a life of crime.[34] As the *Housing Yearbook* explained in 1955, 'public housing projects made life better for people. They sleep better, they join organizations. [Their] . . . incomes rise and [they are] finally able to afford a private house again'.[35]

But behind a concern for the plight of the city's ill-housed and a belief in the benefits of public housing, scintillated the iridescent vision of the 'Better Philadelphia'. Like his colleagues in the National Conference of Mayors, Clark believed that to compete with suburbia, the aging, begrimed central city had to be transformed into a hub of commerce, higher education, medical services and modern finance capitalism.[36] Furthermore, the success of the Better Philadelphia Exhibit underscored urban design as the path to a glorious urban future. Under Edmund Bacon, Philadelphia's planning commission made design its hallmark. A graduate of Cornell University in architecture, and later a student of city planning under Eliel Saarinen at Cranbrook Academy, Bacon taught that the planner's principal task was to arrange space into a functional, three-dimensional expression of the internal urban structure.[37]

Architect-planners such as Bacon, Oscar Stonrov, and Louis Kahn advocated good design and good architecture as an antidote to the planlessness of the modern city. Good design would connect the fragmented parts of the city and restore what planners called 'coherence'. For example, in their 1948 report on the Triangle Redevelopment Area, a wedge shaped tract bounded by the Benjamin Franklin Parkway, Market Street, and the Schuylkill River, planners Kahn and Stonorov castigated the area's muddle of warehouses and shabby housing. 'Our redevelopment can give assurances of economically sound growth to the Triangle, making it', they wrote, 'a component part of the Central City District. Whereas the 1947 tax levy [from the Triangle] to the city amounted to $956,287.59, they [sic] should be increased to $3,932,717, and probably more upon ultimate development . . . '. Kahn and Stonorov hailed the Triangle as 'the biggest single promotion job for the Better Philadelphia of tomorrow that begins today'.[38]

The theme remained unchanged four years later. Calling 1952 'a turning point in the city's planning history', the *Philadelphia Inquirer* applauded the demolition of the city's gargantuan Chinese Wall – a mammoth stone pile ushering the tracks of the Pennsylvania Railroad down Market Street right to the doorsteps of City Hall. Replacing the brooding Chinese Wall with the modern Penn Centre office complex, stated the *Inquirer*, 'offers Philadelphia the opportunity to revitalize the heart of the city'.[39]

However, Bacon believed that building the new efficient city entailed more than erecting skyscraper canyons. Philadelphia planners in fact scorned the Corbusian scale visible in Robert Moses' New York City. Bacon contended that good design demanded the balance of work and residence, of large as well as small scale. Still, the planners' basic motive for balance was largely economic. Efficient planning, wrote Bacon in 1960, 'bolstered the central city economy by providing good housing for office workers and executives and assuring the preservation of the historic section of the city by restoring living values to the city'. Lofty ideals notwithstanding, the planners' ambition to recreate the central city as a socially and physically revitalized habitat of glass offices, apartment towers, and restored eighteenth-century townhouses, involved serious social consequences, particularly the displacement of low-income families.[40]

SHELTER ORIENTED REDEVELOPMENT, 1950–1953

Planners in the early 1950s concurred with their houser brethren that for urban revitalization to succeed redevelopment and housing must proceed together. Philadelphia's American Public Health Association *Housing Quality Surveys* (completed in 1951) described central city housing conditions that were predominately substandard, 'and to a serious degree'. Furthermore, early redevelopment planning in the Temple Redevelopment Area revealed that over 7,500 families would be displaced. No wonder, then, that David Walker, the Executive Director of the Philadelphia Redevelopment Authority, announced in 1950 that Philadelphia 'redevelopment stresses housing'. Although the Triangle Area project offered 'dramatic possibilities equal to that anywhere, . . . the Redevelopment Authority', conceded Walker, 'must take first things first, must meet the most urgent needs, those pertaining to housing'.[41]

Philadelphia proudly trumpeted its redevelopment as 'shelter-oriented'. The city was 'clearing slums with penicillin, not surgery', extolled the *Architectural Forum* in 1952. Rather than Robert Moses's 'monstrous single project solution', explained the *Forum*, 'Philadelphia, cut redevelopment areas into small, distinctive projects that local capital can underwrite, and involves a minimum of dislocation of present inhabitants'. Deeply imbued with Eliel Saarinen's feeling for the 'continuity of life', Philadelphia's redevelopment strategy (under Bacon's guidance) aimed to preserve the existing neighbourhood fabric including the churches, schools, and clubs; in this respect, it reflected particular sensitivity to the past. Applying Saarinen's design principles, then, Philadelphia planners strove to restore spatial harmony, that is 'over-all coherence', to fragmented urban neighbourhoods. In turn, the planners expected rehabilitated areas to act as 'spores', spreading outward and invigorating the surrounding blighted region.[42]

The city's first area redevelopment exuded this 'shelter-orientation'. Plans for 'East Poplar', as the area was called, originated with Francis Bosworth, the director of the Society of Friend's Neighbourhood Guild, a settlement house at Eighth and Brown Streets. Shortly after assuming directorship of the Guild in 1943, Bosworth embraced the idea of using self-help labour and mutual ownership to transform a group of aged, but structurally sound, Civil War vintage row houses into decent, low- to moderate-income housing units. Bosworth's project, which was aided by the Title I provisions of the Housing Act of 1949, became the centrepiece of East Poplar redevelopment. In a second East Poplar Area project, the RA assisted the construction of the 173-unit Penn Town apartments, a privately managed, garden type housing complex for middle-income families. Elsewhere in East Poplar, the Philadelphia Housing Authority built the 203-unit Spring Garden low-income housing project. When the redeveloped East Poplar tapestry finally and fully unfolded, it revealed an interweave of

Figure 2. Cambridge Plaza (c. 1962). Like nearby Harrison Plaza, Cambridge Plaza's two 14-storey high rises and its 124 townhouses fronted a wide concrete esplanade. However, despite the luxury of its open space, the island-like project seemed stranded and austere amidst North Philadelphia's sea of small streets and brick row houses.

housing authority and privately undertaken projects (including a landscaped Reading Railroad right-of-way, and the historic preservation of the residence where poet Edgar Allen Poe wrote 'The Raven').[43]

Despite Bacon's and Stonorov's orchestration of the various elements of East Poplar redevelopment, the Housing and Home Finance Administration charged the city with 'piecemeal or spotty development'. Washington's accusation forced the city planning commission to seak greater integration in its plans for the Temple University and Mill Creek Area redevelopment. The Temple Area plan owed its main inspiration to the firm of Louis I. Kahn, Louis A. McAllister, Douglas Brandt and Kenneth Day. Christopher Tunnard of Yale University coordinated the area's landscaping. With an emphasis on housing similar to East Poplar, Kahn's design featured 1,428 rental units in addition to several blocks of purchase housing and a community shopping complex. Attractive, lawn fronted row housing set back from the main street, greenways and off-street cul-de-sac parking embossed Kahn's signature on the area.[44]

The 10-acre Harrison Plaza housing project supplied 300 of the 1,428 units of rental housing in the Temple Area. Harrison Plaza featured a fifteen-storey tower and 188 units of row housing. Sprawling over parts of four city blocks, Harrison boasted a community building, 'tot lots', and sitting areas that bordered a long open concrete mall. Theoretically, at least, projects such as Harrison Plaza, and its North Philadelphian neighbour, the 372-unit Cambridge Plaza, with their large play areas and other community facilities helped anchor the Southwest Temple neighbourhood both socially and physically; presumably, then, Harrison and Cambridge Plaza functioned as spores for Central North Philadelphia revitalization.[45]

However, it was West Philadelphia's 'shelter-oriented' Mill Creek – not Southwest Temple – which represented Kahn's *piece de resistance*. At Mill Creek Kahn attempted to incorporate low-income public housing as an integral part of the overall neighbourhood design. A Philadelphian by birth, Kahn had spent his childhood in a poor section of the city, an experience that persuaded him that slums could be a 'most closely knit social neighborhood . . . full of more kindness and more natural behavior than anywhere else'. Therefore, at Mill Creek Kahn attempted to identify and preserve the community elements that 'gave a neighborhood its patriotic unity'. He situated the 218-unit Mill Creek public housing project at the centre of his plan. City streets were vacated and the recovered open space transformed into a verdent pedestrian walkway. This mall acted as a 'linear community green' with churches and community services bordering it and a redeveloped shopping centre stationed at each end. The spore theory radiated from Kahn's plan. According to *Architectural Forum*, the redesigned neighbourhood with its greenways, parklets, shopping malls, and modern and rehabilitated housing would 'rally the ambitions of people . . . to save their homes from blight'. In Bacon's words, 'it was the purpose of Mill Creek to prevent the spread of blight from the eastern and southwestern portions of West Philadelphia into the predominately sound western portions . . .' and act, explained Bacon, 'as a major step in the conservation of West Philadelphia'.[46]

Cooperation between the Housing Authority and the Redevelopment Authority marked the shelter-oriented phase of Philadelphia's urban renaissance. The relationship, of course, had a symbiotic quality. While the Housing Authority helped rehouse some families displaced by slum clearance, Title I underwrote the excessive cost of purchasing and clearing central city housing project sites. But if inter-agency harmony promoted the housing and redevelopment authorities' goal of achieving a variety of housing types and designs in the Temple, Mill Creek and Poplar areas, it proved useless in helping the Housing Authority solve the greater problem of finding more and better project sites. By 1953 the Philadelphia Housing Authority located most sites in heavily populated, often black occupied, slum sites.

Moreover, to the consternation of the Philadelphia Housing Association and the CCCP, and in the face of University of Pennsylvania anthropologist Anthony F.C. Wallace's verdict against building high-rise buildings for family occupancy, most of the HA's eleven new developments announced in its annual report for 1953 exhibited high-rise architecture.[47]

CURA AND THE DEVOLUTION OF PUBLIC HOUSING

In both theory and practice Philadelphia planners in the mid-1950s abandoned the shelter-oriented approach to redevelopment visible at Mill Creek, East Poplar and Southwest Temple. Several factors explain their disenchantment. First America's white middle class no longer experienced a housing crisis. Homebuilders built a record 1,396,000 new homes in 1950 and another 2,218,300 between 1951 and 1953. Half the new homes occupied suburban sites. By 1953 the 'cool, green, rim' of American cities such as Philadelphia blossomed with Levittowns, Drexel Hills, Ridley Parks, and Radnors. Of equal importance for the demise of shelter-oriented redevelopment, a sea of black migrants from North Carolina, Georgia and Virginia flowed in behind the tide of out-migrating whites. Increasingly, therefore, white Philadelphians poisoned by racial predjudice viewed the black inner city as 'the jungle', an unredeemable and enlarging blotch of deepening poverty, crime and immorality.[48]

Thirdly, faced with the prospect of this amorphous and irreversible spread of inner-city black poverty and economic disintegration, planners and redevelopers rejected the spore theory that 'islands of good favorably affected the surrounding swamp of bad'. Research by the Redevelopment Authority disclosed that families displaced from the East Poplar and Southwest Temple redevelopment areas 'moved to the streets immediately adjacent, further overcrowding the houses there and turning what were sometimes only bad into totally bad'.[49] Contemplating the trash and grafitti-scrawled walls of the once 'spic and span' Richard Allen Homes, the despondent public relations director of the Philadelphia Housing Authority, Drayton Bryant, bemoaned in 1953 that contrary to the spore theory 'neighborhoods . . . have a strong effect upon the public housing development'.[50]

Finally, housers, planners and redevelopers bristled at the lax pace of urban redevelopment. Blighted or not, financiers and bankers balked at investing in central city neighbourhoods. The urban crisis worsened while isolated 'spots' of redevelopment languished as beleagured outposts in a wasteland of blight.[51] William Wheaton, G. Holmes Perkins, and Martin Meyerson of the Citizens Committee on

City Planning pressed the city to fashion an overall housing and urban renewal policy, and urged a massive assault on the slum together with an enlarged public housing programme.[52]

Criticized for 'projectitus' and being lacklustre, redevelopment in Philadelphia and the nation underwent an early season of reassessment between 1953 and 1955. Impressed by the neighbourhood revitalization work in Baltimore's Waverly neighbourhood, Chicago's Woodlawn, and Philadelphia's East Poplar, the planner William Slayton summoned his colleagues to shift their emphasis from rebuilding to rehabilitating old urban areas. However, rather than Slayton, it was Miles Colean, author in 1953 of *Renewing Our Cities*, who exerted the greatest influence on reshaping urban policy in the mid-1950s. Colean attacked redevelopment officials for their 'narrow, intermittent surgery' approach, and in chorus with Slayton beseeched a coordinated, full-scale attack on blight and stressed conservation, code enforcement and rehabilitation.[53]

Taking Colean's lead, President Dwight David Eisenhower in 1953 created the Advisory Commission on Government Housing Policies and Programs which in addition to Colean included businessmen James Rouse and the distinguished Cincinnati planner Ernest J. Bohn. The 1954 law, which emerged from the deliberations of Eisenhower's commission, made renewal the centrepiece of urban revitalization, and established the federal Urban Renewal Administration to orchestrate a new comprehensive approach to solving the urban crisis. The 1954 law embraced neighbourhood conservation and housing rehabilitation while discouraging 'intermittent surgery' by requiring all communities seeking federal renewal aid to submit a detailed 'workable plan'.[54]

Eisenhower's Advisory Commission aimed to enlist businessmen and the investment community in the renewal effort. But while the new Housing Act of 1954 greatly enhanced the advantages of Title I to the development community by softening the rule requiring 'primarily residential' land reuse, it did not ignore public housing. On the contrary, by limiting the allocation of new public housing units to the number of families displaced by urban renewal activities, the Housing Act of 1954 gradually dubbed public housing a handmaiden of renewal rather than a blushing bride of redevelopment, as it had been under the law of 1949. Yet, while the law still recognized the important role of public housing in renewal, Eisenhower and a politically conservative Congress did not. Between 1954 and 1960 Washington reduced its annual scheduling of public housing units from the 135,000 units promised in 1949 to fewer than 35,000.[55]

Philadelphia's renewal programme underscored the decreasing importance of housing in the hierarchy of goals set for urban revitali-

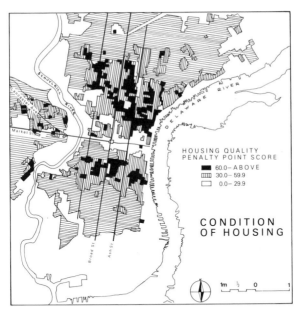

HOUSING QUALITY
PENALTY POINT SCORE

■ 60.0 – ABOVE
▥ 30.0 – 59.9
☐ 0.0 – 29.9

CONDITION
OF HOUSING

Figure 3.

zation. While deeply concerned about Washington's diminution of the public housing programme, Joseph Clark, William Rafsky, and Philadelphia housers such as Dorothy Montgomery could at least rejoice that the 1954 Housing Act installed the 'Philadelphia approach' to renewal. Led by city housing and redevelopment coordinator, William Rafsky, the city undertook a comprehensive study of the central urban renewal area. Rafsky's Central Urban Renewal Area plan (CURA) announced in February 1956 treated the entire central-city area bounded by Erie Avenue on the North, the Navy Yard on the South, Sixty-third Street on the West, and the Delaware River to the East. CURA assigned an 'A', 'B', and 'C' rating to every residential section of the central city and prescribed a renewal strategy appropriate to each classification.[56]

The CURA approach amounted to urban *triage*. CURA branded the blighted, largely black occupied, inner rings of the central city as either 'A' (most blighted), or 'B' (moderately blighted). These 'A' and 'B' areas corresponded closely to sections of the central city earning an APHA housing quality penalty – scores above 30 (figure 3). Discouraged by past failures to arrest urban decay, city planners recommended a policy of benign neglect for 'A' and 'B' areas. While the city continued such projects as East Poplar and Southwest Temple in the grey areas, other than this, CURA advised 'limited action' for these areas, including demolishing tax-delinquent properties and utilizing cleared land for parking lots and playgrounds.

At the same time that CURA sounded retreat from the 'Gray Areas', it signalled bold initiatives for the 'C' or 'conservation' areas bordering the slums. Here the city proposed a concentrated $15.2 million programme of slum clearance, code enforcement, housing rehabilitation, social programmes, and the construction of small, low-rise, tastefully designed public housing projects.[57]

If Philadelphia in the mid-1950s pursued a fresh strategy for establishing bridgeheads in the conservation neighbourhoods, the city moved just as unswervingly to restore its sagging economy by attracting commerce and industry and by luring the prodigal middle class back to the city. 'If we don't make an effort to keep industry from abandoning Philadelphia', pleaded William H. Ludlow, Director of Programs for the Redevelopment Authority, 'how are we ever going to pay for any kind of renewal? Industry and commerce supply the tax money to keep us going. If they leave', warned Ludlow, 'the city perishes . . . Certainly we want to get houses built for the low-income families, but that doesn't mean we should not also try to get back into the city the kind of families that pay more taxes, spend more liberally at our stores, contribute to our cultural institutions and require somewhat less in the way of health, welfare and public services'.[58]

Benign neglect of the slums, code enforcement in the conservation areas, and downtown renewal all involved residential displacement. Therefore, notwithstanding Washington's starvation of the federal housing programme, public housing activity in Philadelphia in the mid-1950s proceeded, although at an inadequate level in the houser's estimate. Despite these efforts, by 1956 the city confronted the need to find sites for 2,500 new public housing units. Seeing the opportunity to combine social with physical planning, some housers and planners urged the Philadelphia Housing Authority to locate its new housing developments outside the black, central city ghetto in the all-white 'C' areas and beyond.[59]

Aided by the Housing Authority's Joint Committee on Site Selection (a body comprised of representatives from both the Philadelphia Housing Association and the Citizens Committee on City Planning), and by William Rafsky's own Interagency Committee on Sites, the Housing Authority designated locations for twenty-one proposed housing projects. With few exceptions the sites were scattered throughout the urban periphery in such white strongholds as Roxborough, Manyunk, Oak Lane, and Olney. And just as in Chicago where outraged white neighbourhoods had mobilized in 1951 to defeat the Chicago Housing Authority's effort (under Elizabeth Wood) to decentralize and integrate public housing, so in 1956 neighbourhood fury in Philadelphia blocked Rafsky's and the Housing Authority's plan to decentralize public housing. Forced to retreat ignominiously from its original twenty-one sites, Philadelphia's chastened housing officialdom selected alternative sites located in uncontested areas – either already racially mixed, too isolated, or too environmentally undesirable to threaten the territorial equilibrium of the city.[60]

This debacle aggravated the gnawing feeling of despair over public housing shared by housers and planners alike. Not only did the withering political assault from the real estate and homebuilding industry render the size of the government programme inadequate, but substantial criticism arose from within the housing movement itself. As early as 1955 Lee Johnson and Ira Robbins of the National Housing Conference plaintively assured the membership of the NHC that housers were 'not a group of tired liberals', that the problem of the slum and the housing shortage . . . persist[s]'. Yet, 'we have failed', cried Johnson. 'We have wearied of the long fight. We are jealous of the bureaucracy we have built; we fear innovation; we have failed to make housing a challenging profession and we have failed to enlist public support'.[61]

Two years later the pall enshrouding the housing movement darkened. In her 'The Dreary Deadlock of Public Housing' the once stalwart ideologue of public housing, Catherine Bauer Wurster, harangued the movement for delivering unimaginative, regimented housing. 'Overcautious, rigid, uncreative public housing administrator[s]', recounted Wurster, 'had produced repulsive, institutionalized fortresses', islands which turn their backs on the surrounding neighbourhoods. 'Public housing', confessed Wurster, 'is not the way most American families want to live'.[62]

A year later the *New York Times* carried Harrison Salisbury's series of ghastly descriptions of the social and environmental squalor prevailing in New York's Fort Green housing project. In fact, Daniel Seligman, a disenchanted houser, later quoted Salisbury, and in doing so plumbed the depths of liberal despair with public housing. 'Once upon a time', mused Seligman, but using Salisbury's words, 'we thought that if we could only get our problem families out of those dreadful slums, then papa would stop taking dope, mama would stop chasing around, and junior would stop carrying a knife. Well, we got them into a nice new apartment with a modern kitchen and a recreation center. And they're still the same bunch of bastards they always were'.[63]

In 1958 Elizabeth Wood, then with the New York Citizens Housing and Planning Council, blamed the shattered vision of public housing partly on the housers' and planners' desire to erect giant neighbourhood projects not on sites that met the test of long-range planning, but on the 'best piece of land we could get approved by city council'. Therefore, complained the insightful Wood, 'year by year most of us have been building in minority occupied slums, regardless of the housing shortage, regardless of the mounting housing needs of in-migrant minority families . . . regardless of the relocation problem, regardless of the ultimate effect on enlarging and hardening ghetto patterns . . . '. Rejected by 'normal families', housing projects, lamented Wood, 'have become increasingly segregated – economically, socially and racially – diminishing their value to the city . . . '.[64]

Neither Seligman, Wood, Nathaniel Keith, Lee Johnson, nor Warren Vinton, who in 1958 retired from the National Public Housing Administration, abandoned their support for public housing. Hoping to reintegrate public housing more fully into national housing and renewal policy, the National Housing Conference pressed in 1958 for the creation of a Department of Housing and Urban Development.[65] Nevertheless, the concept of public housing as modern, safe and sanitary waystations for the mobile working-class faded in the late 1950s. In its 'Basic Policies for Public Housing', the Housing Associ-ation and CCCP joint Public Housing Committee chaired by Dean Jefferson Fordham of the University of Pennsylvania Law School, explained government-built housing as 'only one tool for combatting blight'. The Fordham Committee scorned monolithic projects and called instead for small units, architecturally and socially integrated into their neighbourhoods. Furthermore, the committee urged that over-income tenants be permitted to purchase their units; and to facilitate owner-occupancy, the Fordham Committee recommended that the housing authority buy and rehabilitate used housing. Finally, the committee protested the Housing Authority's exclusion of so-called 'problem families'. Public housing, insisted the committee, should perform a social service as well as a real estate function.[66] And, indeed, a few years later, under Marie McGuire, the Commissioner of Public Housing under President John F. Kennedy, social service became the priority of public housing policy-makers.[67]

THE GOLDCOAST AND THE SLUM

Observers of the city from Benjamin Disraeli and writers Charles Dickens, Charles Booth, and Stephen Crane, to sociologists Harvey Zorbaugh, and the President's Commission on Civil Disorders have observed and rued the widening social chasm dividing the city of affluence from the city of poverty. It is a social and economic dichotomy as visible and troubling in the modern metropolis as in the Gotham of Dickens and Booth. Indeed, today's gentrifying cities with their gleaming office towers and scrubbed historic districts contrast starkly with scabrous slum zones. Only instead of the cacophony of teeming Ludgates and bulging Five Points, modern slums are more often characterized by rubble, housing abandonment and gloom. To the degree that post-war redevelopment and renewal restored scintillating vitality to the modern city, they also bequeathed the conundrum of ghetto neighbourhoods scarred with fire-gutted buildings, blotched with vacant lots, and redolent with crime, vice, violence and despair.[68]

The bitter contrast between the city of blitheness and vitality and the city of poverty and decay sharpened in the early 1960s as the pace of downtown renewal quickened. To cope with the sagging economy, President Kennedy in 1961 pumped two billion dollars into the federal urban renewal programme. Philadelphia alone received $120,000,000 in renewal funds. By 1963 the Urban Renewal Administration was underwriting 1,400 projects in 682 cities. And as in the case of Philadelphia, the target for most of this renewal activity was the central city.[69] Philadelphia's Comprehensive Plan, which finally appeared in 1960 after nine years in the making, stated emphatically and unabashedly that the first objective of planning was the 'develop[ment] of the Centre City ["the heart of a metropolitan region"] to its full potential including an emphasis on new office space, [and] on revitalized retail space . . . '. The plan also stressed, but less effusively so, the goal of the city 'to be a people city', which required improving housing quality. In theory at least, economic growth produced by a revitalized central city would enhance the quality of urban life throughout the city.[70]

In the early 1960s the literature on Philadelphia redevelopment exuded great expectations about the future of a downtown renaissance. For example, the Redevelopment Authority predicted that the new 971-unit Penn Town apartment complex rising at the edge of the Triangle Renewal Area 'would increase the [city's] annual [tax] yield from $18,000 to $250,000'.[71] Downtown Philadelphia pulsated with renewal activity. In Society Hill, part of the Washington Square Redevelopment Area, the Old Philadelphia Development Corporation cross-fertilized historic preservation with strains of modern, but tastefully designed, low- and high-rise architecture. The result was a magnificent, and posh, inner-city residential neighbourhood. Through Title I, in Society Hill the Redevelopment Authority cleared acres of tottering slum dwellings, ancient warehouses, and grimy commercial fronts. Historic structures left standing were restored according to the rigorous design standards of the OPDC and the city's historical commission. The interstices were then transformed into charming open space or infilled with modern but architecturally harmonious townhouses.[72]

Bacon and the OPDC allowed one exception to the gracious

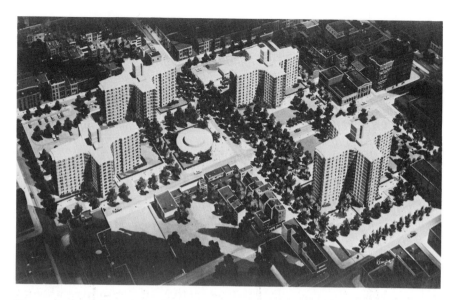

Figure 4. An architect's model of the 1122-unit Raymond Rosen project (c. 1954). Contrary to the vision embodied in the artist's portrayal, the Rosen project was quickly engulfed by the surrounding North Philadelphia slum.

eighteenth-century human scale that they sought for their Society Hill tapestry. To anchor the historic area to the city and affirm its axial relationship to the reborn downtown, the city commissioned noted architect I.M. Pei to design three apartment towers overlooking Penn's Landing on the Delaware River to the east, and City Hall and the new Penn Center towers on the west.

Elsewhere, city bulldozers cleared acres of blighted residential property for the redevelopment of the West Philadelphia University City expansion, demolished old downtown commercial and residential structures for the Jefferson Medical Center complex, and in North Philadelphia continued to assist the growth of Temple University.[73]

Notwithstanding the Redevelopment Authority's fervent and frequent declaration that the agency was as concerned about people as about bricks and mortar, between 1950 and 1962 in North Philadelphia alone urban renewal projects displaced over 6,250 families. In time the grey 'A' and 'B' slum zones absorbed the bulk of these refugees. An earlier 1957 Philadelphia Housing Association study of the relocation issue indicated the grim human dimension of the displacement problem. The mean income of those relocated in Philadelphia from 1955 to 1957 was $2,500. Sixty-five per cent of displaced families earned under $3,000 and 95 per cent were black.

Figure 5. One of two high rise towers comprising Oscar Stonorov's highly acclaimed Schuylkill Falls housing project (c. 1960). Paradoxically, the project failed as an environment for living. Plagued by notoriously high maintenance costs, the high rises were closed in the late 1970s.

Even more ominous, the Housing Association's *Relocation Study* estimated that between a third and a quarter of those relocated could be designated 'problem families', having members with 'police records involving dope, prostitution . . . armed robbery or assault, accute addiction to alcohol, extremely poor housekeeping, . . . or comprised of an unmarried mother of two or more children'. Shunned by most landlords – even by the Philadelphia Housing Authority – such problem families drifted from one substandard dwelling to another. Frequently, despite the determination of the Housing Authority to bar their admittance, the problem family ended its odyssey in a central-city housing project.[74]

The sordid consequences of urban renewal did not escape notice. Until blacks were free to move more freely within the metropolitan housing market, observed William Grigsby in 1962 and Scott Greer in 1963, displaced poor blacks would be concentrated in the grey area, 'aggravating and intensifying the problem of blight'.[75] Wurster also dreaded that unless America pursued the goal of a 'vast and varied democracy offering housing choices to everyone . . . ', urban renewal would accelerate the 'long trend toward economic class division between the central city and suburbia'.[76]

Tragically – in light of the vision of urban community which originally inspired it – public housing helped congeal this ignominious pattern of urban segregation and even added another invidious dimension to its form. In Philadelphia, by 1964, 81 per cent of the population living in mammouth public housing complexes such as the Richard Allen Homes, Harrison Plaza, Raymond Rosen, and the Cambridge Plaza homes were black.[77] Moreover, distraught public housing officials labelled more and more of these tenant families as 'problems'. Concerned about the rising number of female-headed families living in his project, in 1961 the manager of the 1,112 Raymond Rosen Homes expostulated on why one woman in the project desired to leave. 'She is the only one on the floor with a husband', explained the manager.[78]

By 1964 large central-city housing projects such as New York's Fort Green Homes, Saint Louis' Pruitt-Igoe housing, Chicago's Grace Abbott, Cabrini and Robert Taylor Homes, and Philadelphia's Allen, Norris, Rosen and Schuylkill Falls projects were 'home' for a black underclass. In contrast to the revitalizing centre city, public housing neighbourhoods unfolded as a deprived, perilous world of social malaise and instability. The milieu bespoke not only scarred walls and unkempt, urine-fouled hallways, but also less visibly the growing population of non-modal families, the deepening pool of jobless and dependent families, and the sullen atmosphere of anger and hopelessness. Not surprisingly, the Philadelphia black riot of 1964 raged through streets and alleys darkened by the shadows of the Raymond Rosen Homes.[79]

CONCLUSION

The 1964 riot made frighteningly clear that the other side of the redevelopment coin bore the physiognomy of the slum. For a while after World War II, impressed by the magnitude of the urban housing shortage, and mindful of the political clout of big labour and housing-starved veterans, Philadelphia housers and planners fashioned a shelter-oriented redevelopment programme. Their 'penicillin cure' for blight produced such celebrated area designs as East Poplar, Mill Creek, and Southwest Temple where low- and moderate-income housing was woven into the neighbourhood fabric.

But as critics noted, although tastefully designed, these projects lacked coherence as part of an overall plan for urban renewal. Fearful about the galloping advance of blight – especially the physical and financial erosion of the downtown – and alarmed by middle-class flight to suburbia and the imminent loss of vital urban civic and educational institutions, in the mid-1950s, Philadelphia planners shifted their redevelopment goal from supplying shelter to saving the downtown. In concert with the authors of the Housing Act of 1954, the designers of Philadelphia's CURA plan as well as the architects of its 1960 comprehensive plan, enlisted public housing in the cause of resuscitating the heart of the city, the downtown.

However, without the urban-suburban regional framework for housing reform urged by Wurster, Woodbury, and Grigsby, and without the enforcement of open housing laws beseeched by Charles Abrams, planners reluctantly tucked public housing into the crevices of the cityscape, wherever, that is, the political repercussions from site decisions promised to be least violent.

Clearly, by 1964 public housing had been shorn of its waystation mission. Instead of safe and sanitary havens for the mobile working class, projects increasingly functioned as warehouses for the poor, and in particular the severely disadvantaged black poor. Looming sternly from the wilderness of the urban ghetto, these brooding human receptacles stood in 1964 as grim testimonials to the egregious failure of America to grapple imaginatively and humanely with the housing needs of low-income families.

NOTES

1. On the North Philadelphia riot of 1964, see Berson, Lenora E. (1966) *Case Study of a Riot: The Philadelphia Story*. New York: Institute of Human Relations Press, pp. 25–35; also Citizens Emergency Committee of North Philadelphia, Minutes of Meeting, August 29, 1964, in Box 47, Folder 38, Wharton Center Papers, Temple Urban Archives, Philadelphia, Pa. [Hereinafter TUA].

2. See 'The city: under the knife or all for their own good', *Time* Magazine, **84**, November 6, 1964, p. 58.

3. For a discussion of the paradoxical history of urban planning, see Marcuse, Peter (1980) Housing policy and city planning: the puzzling split in the U.S., 1893–1931, in Cherry, Gordon E. (ed.) *Shaping an Urban World*. London: Mansell, pp. 25–51; and Friedman, Lawrence (1978) *Government and Slum Housing: A Century of Frustration*. Chicago: Rand McNally and Company.

4. On the impact of the Great Depression, see Bauman, John F. (1969) The City, The Depression and Relief: The Philadelphia Experience, 1929–1941, unpublished Ph. D. diss., Rutgers University; on water, see *Philadelphia Record*, October 19, 1943, p. 1.

5. Note that in 1943 Charles Ascher, a staff member of the federal National Resources Planning Board, charged that the 'urban community of the future must be a nobler embodiment of the democratic responsibility for the worth of the individual, if our war effort is to be justified. Urban Planning could redeem dying city districts . . . create better home conditions in both cities and suburbs, banish apple selling and leafraking in the days to come, [and] underwrite a sounder prosperity than America has ever known', see Gelfand, Mark I. (1975) *A Nation of Cities: The Federal Government and Urban America, 1933–1965*. New York: Oxford University Press, p. 125.

6. See Bauman, John F. (1980–1981) Visions of a post-war city: a perspective on urban planning in Philadelphia and the nation, 1942–1945. *Urbanism Past and Present*, 6 (11), pp. 8–10; on veterans and the housing shortage, see Davies, Richard O. (1966) *Housing Reform During the Truman Administration*. Columbia, Missouri: University of Missouri Press, pp. 41–43.

7. Ludlow, William (1953) Urban densities and their costs, in Woodbury, Coleman (ed.) *Urban Redevelopment: Problems and Practices*. Chicago: University of Chicago Press, p. 202.

8. See Woodbury, Coleman (1953) Essays on redevelopment, in Woodbury, Coleman (ed.) *The Future of Cities and Redevelopment*. Chicago: University of Chicago Press, pp. 58–63.

9. Lubove, Roy (1962) *The Progressives and the Slums: Tenement House Reform in New York City 1890–1917*. Pittsburgh: University of Pittsburgh Press; also, Philadelphia Redevelopment Authority (1947) *Our City Today and Tomorrow*. Philadelphia: Philadelphia Redevelopment Authority, in Housing Association of Delaware Valley (HADV) pamphlets, TUA; and Better Housing League of Cincinnati (1948) *Going Home: Thirty-Second Annual Report of the Better Housing League of Cincinnati*. Cincinnati: Better Housing League, in HADV pamphlets, TUA.

10. Ludlow, *op. cit.*, p. 203, bemoaned that during the first half of the twentieth century cities merely 'patched onto the nineteenth century pattern many bulky multi-storied structures, rapid transit, and some costly but inadequate highway and parking.

11. Perrin, Constance (1977) *Everything in its Place: Social Order and Land Use in America*. Princeton: Princeton University Press.

12. Ludlow, *op. cit.*, p. 199; and Jackson, Kenneth (1980) Race, ethnicity, and real estate appraisal: the Home Owners Loan Corporation and the Federal Housing Administration. *Journal of Urban History*, 6 (4), pp. 419–52.

13. See Gruen, Victor (1964) *The Heart of Our Cities: The Urban Crisis, Diagnosis and Cure*. New York: Simon and Schuster; on the cancer model, see Philadelphia Redevelopment Authority (1947) Report on the Redevelopment Authority: City of Philadelphia, mimeographed, in HADV pamphlets, TUA; and on socio-psychological definition of blight, see Woodbury, Coleman and Gutheim, Frederick A. (1949) *Rethinking Urban Redevelopment*, Urban Redevelopment Series Number 1. Chicago: Public Administration Service, p. 3.

14. Post-war planners at the Chicago Conference in 1947 wished to make

over blighted areas 'so that they become parts of the new and better urban community envisioned in the comprehensive plan for the locality', see Woodbury, and Gutheim, *op. cit.*, p. 3; a few years later Edmund Bacon imagined redevelopment remaking older decaying neighbourhoods into pleasant, desirable communities, transforming 'ugliness', he incanted, 'into beauty', see Philadelphia Chapter American Institute of Architects (1950) *Challenge 1950: Yearbook of the Philadelphia Chapter of the American Institute of Architects.* Philadelphia, p. 7; also Bauman, (1980–1981), *op. cit.*, p. 7.

15. On Seward Mott, see Scott, Mel (1969) *American City Planning Since 1890.* Berkeley: University of California Press, p. 418; on Harlan Bartholomew, see Gillette, Howard Jr. (1983) The evolution of neighborhood planning: from the progressive era to the 1949 Housing Act. *Journal of Urban History*, 9 (4), pp. 437–39.

16. See Philadelphia Redevelopment Authority (1947) Report of the Redevelopment Authority; City of Philadelphia, mimeographed, in HADV pamphlets, TUA.

17. Built just prior to World War II, the New York City Metropolitan Life Insurance Company's Stuyvesant Town represented the 'spot' or 'spore' theory of redevelopment. The project, aided by a tax-incentives and eminent domain programme pushed through the New York legislature by Robert Moses, earned notoriety by refusing to admit blacks, see Caro, Robert (1974) *The Power Broker: Robert Moses and the Fall of New York.* New York: Alfred Knopf; and Gillette, *op. cit.*, pp. 437–39.

18. On the Chicago Conference, see Woodbury and Gutheim, *op. cit.*, p. 307; on dull and deadening row housing, see American Institute of Architects (1950) *Challenge 1950: Yearbook of the Philadelphia Chapter of the American Institute of Architects.* Philadelphia, p. 12.

19. See Bauer, Catherine (1946) Is urban redevelopment possible under existing legislation? in American Society of Planning Officials, *Planning 1946.* Chicago, pp. 62–70; see also Woodbury and Gutheim, *op. cit.*, p. 307; and Gropius, Walter (1952) Faith in planning, in American Society of Planning Officials, *Planning 1952.* Chicago, pp. 4–15.

20. Perkins unfolded a glittering vision of 'the better city . . . [set amidst a "balanced" urban region] and [reflecting] the full-fledged redevelopment of the old city with congestion eliminated and light and life let into the old stagnate areas', see Perkins, G. Holmes (1953) The regional city, Woodbury, Coleman (ed.) *The Future of Cities and Urban Redevelopment.* Chicago: University of Chicago Press, pp. 26, 29.

21. Bauer, *op. cit.*, pp. 65–70; Bauer in 1946 also recognized the vicious nexus between redevelopment and family displacement, 'an obstacle', she wrote, which would 'stand in the way of most redevelopment projects for many years to come . . . unless means are available to rehouse low-income families elsewhere, beforehand', *ibid.*

22. For Bettman quote, see Scott, *op. cit.*, p. 418.

23. Greer, Guy (1944) The why of planning: the economy needs an immense building programme and the people need a better environment. *Fortune*, November, 1944, reprint. In TUA.

24. See Memorandum from Catherine Bauer to Dorothy Montgomery, April 18, 1949, in Box 330, folder 6427, in HADVP, TUA.

25. Woodbury, Coleman (1953) Industrial locations and urban renewal, in Woodbury, Coleman (ed.) *The Future of Cities and Urban Redevelopment.* Chicago: University of Chicago Press, p. 169.

26. Dorothy Montgomery to Catherine Bauer Wurster, October 30, 1947, in Box 330, folder 6427, in HADVP, TUA.

27. On city reform, see Wallace, David A. (1960) Renaissanceship. *Journal of American Institute of Planners*, **XXVI** (August), pp. 157–76; Bacon, Edmund (*ca.* 1943) How city planning came to Philadelphia. n.d., in Series III, folder 60, in HADVP, TUA; and Lowe, Jean (1967) *Cities in a Race With Time: Progress and Poverty in America's Renewing Cities.* New York: Random House.

28. *Ibid.*, see also on the CCCP and its role in reform, Levine, Aaron (1960) Citizen participation. *Journal of the American Institute of Planners*, **XXVI** (August), pp. 195–200.

29. See Lowe, *op. cit.*, p. 322; on redevelopment laws, see Wallace, *op. cit.*, p. 159; and *Martha Belovsky v. Redevelopment Authority of City of Philadelphia.* Brief for the Redevelopment Authority, by Abraham Freedman. Number 68, June Term 1946, in PHAP.

30. On early years of Philadelphia Redevelopment Authority, see Philadelphia Redevelopment Authority (1947) Report of the Redevelopment Authority: City of Philadelphia, mimeographed, in HADV pamphlets, TUA; on 'Better Philadelphia Exhibit', see Bacon, Edmund (1960) A case study in urban design. *Journal of the American Institute of Planners*, **XXVI** (August), pp. 224–35. Churchill, Henry S. (1950) City redevelopment. *Architectural Forum*, December, p. 72; and Dorothy Montgomery to Bryn Hovde, May 21, 1951, Box 170, folder 1657, HADVP, TUA.

31. For assault on Republican Party machine, see Fink, Joseph R. (1971) Reform in Philadelphia, 1946–1951. Ph.D. dissertation, Rutgers University; and Lowe, *op. cit.*, p. 328; and Petshek, Kirk (1973) *The Challenge of Urban Reform: Politics and Progress in Philadelphia.* Philadelphia: Temple University Press; an ecstatic Dorothy Montgomery wrote to Bryn Hovde, a prominent houser-planner friend, then on the faculty of the University of Wisconsin, begging him to join Philadelphia's crusade. Hovde had to refuse, but nevertheless, he congratulated Montgomery that 'after all those years wandering in the wilderness, so to speak, you see the promised land. Now clearly you are set to really get things done', see Montgomery to Hovde, November 14, 1951, Box 170, folder 1657, HADVP, TUA; and Hovde to Montgomery, November 18, 1951, *ibid.*

32. On the new Philadelphia City Charter see, Philadelphia Housing Association and City Charter Commission (April 1950) Housing and the City Charter: Recommendations of the Philadelphia Housing Association and the City Charter Commission, mimeographed, in HADV pamphlets, TUA; also Philadelphia Charter Commission (February 14, 1951) Proposed Philadelphia Home Rule Charter, mimeographed, in HADV Pamphlets, TUA.

33. On the Wagner-Ellender-Taft legislative battle, see Friedman, Lawrence (1968) *Government and Slum Housing: A Century of Frustration*. Chicago: Rand McNally, p. 149; also Davies, *op. cit.*, pp. 11–12, 29, 70; Freedman, Leonard (1969) *Public Housing and the Politics of Poverty*. New York: Holt, Rinehart and Winston, p. 76; and Keith, Nathaniel (1973) *Politics and the Housing Crisis Since 1930*. New York: University Books, pp. 76, 85–91.

34. On Joseph Clark, see Reichley, James (1959) *The Art of Government*. New York: Fund for the Republic; Neal, Steve (1975) Joseph Clark: our last angry man. *Today Magazine*, August 3, 1975, p. 1; for Clark's social philosophy, see Clark, Joseph (1955) The Future of Urban Shelter. Speech Given at Luncheon Meeting of Metropolitan Housing and Planning Council, Chicago, May 6, 1955, in Box 9, folder 196, Philadelphia Chapter National Association for the Advancement of the Colored People Papers (NAACPP), TUA; Clark quoted on river wards and democracy in 'Clark suggests public plea for housing' *Philadelphia Inquirer*, April 18, 1953; for Scott's view of public housing, see 'A decent place to live: Philadelphia Housing Authority will be biggest landlord in the state'. *Philadelphia Inquirer Magazine*, June 24, 1954, p. 4.

35. Mrs. D.G.D. (1955) New houses, new people, in National Housing Conference, *The Housing Yearbook 1955*. Washington, D.C., pp. 29–31.

36. On Joseph Clark's philosophy, see Clark, Dennis (n.d.) The Urban Ordeal: Reform and Policy in Philadelphia, 1947–1967. Integrative Paper Series, Paper Number 1, in TUA.

37. On Bacon, see 'The city: under the knife or all for their own good.' *Time Magazine*, **84**, November 6, 1964, pp. 69–70; also Bacon, Edmund (n.d.) Personal history, in Series III, folder 44, HADVP, TUA; also consult, Saarinen, Eliel (1943) *The City: Its Growth, Its Decay, Its Future*. Cambridge: Cambridge University Press.

38. See Associated City Planners (March 22, 1948) Excerpts from Report on the Triangle Development, mimeographed, p. 12, in HADV Pamphlets, TUA; and Bacon, Edmund N. (1961) Downtown Philadelphia: a lesson in design for urban growth. *Architectural Record*, May, pp. 131–43.

39. See 'Turning Point 1952', in *Philadelphia Inquirer Special* Section, May 10, 1952, p. 1; see too, Philadelphia City Planning Commission and Redevelopment Authority of Philadelphia (1950) *Progress in Rebuilding Philadelphia, 1947–1950: What Has Been Accomplished or Started Since the Better Philadelphia Exhibit*. Philadelphia, in HADV Pamphlets, TUA.

40. Bacon, *op. cit.*

41. Walker, David (1950) Philadelphia Stresses Housing in Philadelphia Chapter American Institute of Architecture. Philadelphia, p. 10; see also, Philadelphia City Planning Commission, Redevelopment Authority of Philadelphia, and Philadelphia Housing Authority (1949) *Philadelphia Housing Quality Survey: Mill Creek Area Report*. Philadelphia, in HADV Pamphlets, TUA [a *Philadelphia Housing Quality Survey* appeared for each of the redevelopment areas]; on displacement, see $20,000,000 Housing Projects Gets Nod, *Philadelphia Inquirer*, August 16, 1951, p. 19.

42. See The Philadelphia cure: clearing slums with penicillin, not surgery. *Architectural Forum*, April, 1952, pp. 113–15, in HADV Pamphlets, TUA; on spore theory see, Keith, C. Allen (1954) Mill Creek area housing gets under way. *Philadelphia Inquirer*, October 10, p. 3.

43. On East Poplar, see ACTION Research Memorandum (ca. 1956) Case Study: Quaker 'Self Help' Rehabilitation Programme in Philadelphia, mimeographed, in HADV Pamphlets, TUA; also Memorandum from George Bedell, Race Relations, Public Housing Administration Field Office, Philadelphia, 'East Poplar Redevelopment Area Plan, Philadelphia, Pa., With Special Reference to Project Area I, and Project Area II', December 29, 1950, in Program Files, Race Relations, Department of Housing and Urban Development Records (HUDR), Record Group (RG) 207, National Archives, Washington, D.C; on Penn Town, see Philadelphia City Planning Comission, Press Release, 'East Poplar Redevelopment Policy', July 1, 1949, in PHAP; and Slayton, William L. (1953) Urban redevelopment short of clearance, in Woodbury, Coleman (ed.) *Urban Redevelopment: Problems and Practices*. Chicago: University of Chicago, pp. 383–5.

44. On Southwest Temple, see Redevelopment Authority of the City of Philadelphia (December 31, 1951) *Annual Report*, pp. 15–16; see also Redevelopment Authority of the City of Philadelphia (December 31, 1958) *Annual Report*, pp. 4–13; and 'The Philadelphia cure: clearing slums with Penicillin, not surgery'. *Architectural Forum* (April 1952), pp. 113–15.

45. See the brochure, Philadelphia Housing Authority (May 29, 1956) *Dedication of Harrison Plaza* in PHAP; and Philadelphia Housing Authority (August 1956) *Project Analysis: Harrison Plaza, PA–2–15*. Philadelphia, pp. 1–13, in PHAP.

46. On Kahn's ideas, see Kahn, Louis I. (1953) Toward a plan got midtown Philadelphia. *Perspecta: The Yale Architectural Journal*, 2, pp. 10–23.

47. On cooperation between the PHA and RA, see Redevelopment Authority of Philadelphia (December 31, 1950 *Annual Report*, p. 7; on displacement and site difficulties, see Redevelopment Authority of Philadelphia December 31, 1951) *Annual Report*; and Philadelphia Housing Authority (1953) *New Thresholds: Report of the Philadelphia Housing Authority for 1953*. Philadelphia, pp. 9–19; on high rise issue, see Wallace, Anthony F.C. (1952) Housing and Social Structure: A Preliminary Survey with Particular Reference to Multi-Storey, Low-Rent Housing Projects, mimeographed, in TUA; also see Dorothy Montgomery to Catherine Bauer Wurster, June 12, 1951, Box 330, folder 6428, HADVP, TUA.

48. On FHA see Jackson, Kenneth (1980) Race, ethnicity, and real estate appraisal: the HOLC and the FHA. *Journal of Urban History*, 6 (August), pp. 419–53; on North Philadelphia as 'jungle' see memorandum from John Azar, 'Poplar Community Holds Protest on "Jungle" Issue', February 15, 1957, in Box 85, folder 131, HADVP TUA; see also Cybriwsky, Roman (1976) *Philadelphia: A Study of Conflicts and Social Cleavages*. Cambridge: MIT Press.

49. Wallace, (1960) *op. cit.*, pp. 157–76; see also 'Special Report to the Advisory Commission of the Philadelphia Housing Authority on the

Relocation of 342 Families from the Site of the East Poplar Project', October 8, 1952, mimeographed, in Box 230, folder 3355, HADVP, TUA.

50. See Memorandum from Drayton Bryant to Walter Allesandroni, June 3, 1953, in Box 230, folder 3353, HADVP, TUA.

51. On lax pace of renewal, see Scott, *op. cit.*, pp. 498–520; Gelfand, *op. cit.*, p. 172; and on reluctance of financiers to invest in slum areas, see Rafsky, William L. (1956) 'Summary of Activities [a detailed log of meetings and activities with reflective annotations. Both Mayor's Clark and Richardson Dilworth requested their department heads to keep such a log], June 18, in Box 1, William L. Rafsky Papers, TUA.

52. Wheaton, William L.C. *et al.* (1955) A Statement on Housing and Urban Renewal Policy for Philadelphia, mimeographed, in Box 321, folder 6163, HADVP, TUA.

53. Slayton, William L. (1953) Rehabilitation and conservation – studies and a little experience, in Woodbury, Coleman (ed.) *Urban Renewal: Problems and Practices*. Chicago: University of Chicago Press, pp. 371–75; Colean, Miles (1953) *Renewing Our Cities*. New York: the Twentieth Century Fund.

54. On Eisenhower's Advisory Committee, see Scott, *op. cit.*, p. 496; see Presidents Advisory Commission on Government Housing Policies and Programmes (December 4, 1953) A Report to the President of the United States, mimeographed, in Box 658. Program Files, HUDR, Record Group 207, NA; see also Foard, Ashley A. and Fefferman, Hilbert (1966) Federal urban renewal legislation, in Wilson, James Q. (ed.) *Urban Renewal: The Record and the Controversy*. Cambridge: Harvard University Press, pp. 71–125.

55. Abrams, Charles (1965) *The City is the Frontier*. New York: Harper and Row, p. 84; Keith, *op. cit.*, p. 117.

56. See Philadelphia public housing programme heading for quick death. Philadelphia *Daily News*, October 14, 1954; on CURA, see Redevelopment Authority of City of Philadelphia (*ca* February 1956) Summary of Urban Renewal Policy and Program, mimeographed, in Box 249, folder 3988, HADVP, TUA; also Office of Development Coordinator (December 1956) A New Approach to Urban Renewal for Philadelphia, mimeographed, in HADVP, TUA.

57. *Ibid*; Dennis Clark, a staff member of the Philadelphia Housing Authority, used the expression 'roundhouse renewal' to characterize the CURA approach in a letter to William Rafsky, December 16, 1955, Box 272, folder 4624, HADVP, TUA; George Schermer, Chairman of the Philadelphia Commission on Human Relations, interview with author at his home in Washington D.C., February 18, 1983.

58. For Ludlow quote, see William H. Ludlow's response to a series of articles by Edward S. Kessler critical of urban renewal in Philadelphia, No pause in attack on slums, *Germantown Courier*, January 19, 1961, p. 1.

59. See Snarl on sites threatens plans for low-rent housing', Philadelphia *Evening Bulletin*, February 26, 1956; and 'Philadelphia Procedure for Selecting Public Housing Sites', mimeographed, n.d., *ca.* 1956, in PHAP.

60. 'Philadelphia Procedure for Selecting Public Housing Sites', mimeographed, n.d., *ca* 1956, in PHAP; on Joint Committee on Site Selection, and Interagency committee, see Dorothy Montgomery to Frank C. Walther, August 11, 1955, Box 234, folder 3465, HADVP, TUA; on publishing sites, see Walter Allesandroni to Edmund Bacon, April 2, 1956, stating that 'we are submitting to you at this time for approval by the Philadelphia City Planning Commission a list of 21 sites . . . These sites will make possible the construction of the 2,500 homes', found in PHAP; see also, Philadelphia *Evening Bulletin*, June 4, 1956; also, 'Civic groups urge city to OK twenty-one sites'. Philadelphia *Daily News*, May 15, 1956; on neighbourhood opposition, see Residents petition demands housing projects be dropped. *Mayfair Times*, May 3, 1956; on retreat from sites, see 'Notes of Telephone Conversation from Allesandroni, October 30, 1958', in which Allesandroni referred to sites as a 'collection of junk', in Box 279, folder 4823, HADVP, TUA; on Chicago case, see Hirsch, Arnold R. (1983) *Making The Second Ghetto: Race and Housing in Chicago, 1940–1960*. New York: Cambridge University Press, pp. 213–58.

61. Johnson, Lee (1955) What's the matter with housing, in National Housing Conference, *Housing Yearbook 1955*. Washington, D.C., p. 12; and Robbins, Ira (1955) Forward. National Housing Conference, *Housing Yearbook 1955*. Washington, D.C., pp. 3–4.

62. Wurster, Catherine Bauer (1957) The dreary deadlock of public housing. *Architectural Forum*, **106** (May), pp. 141, 221.

63. Salisbury, Harrison (1958) Problem youngsters spring from the housing jungle. *New York Times*, March 29, 1958; Seligman, Daniel (1957) The enduring slum, in the Editors of Fortune, *The Exploding Metropolis*. Garden City: Doubleday and Company, p. 106.

64. Wood, Elizabeth (1958) New York Citizens Housing and Planning Council (1958) *Planning 1958*. Chicago: American Society of Planning Officials, pp. 198–99.

65. Vinton, Warren J. (1958) Public Housing. American Society of Planning Officials, *Planning 1958*. Chicago, pp. 195–7; also Johnson, Lee F. (1958) The long fight: 1937 to 1958, a prescription for achieving a well-housed America, in the National Housing Conference, *The Housing Yearbook 1958*; Washington D.C., pp. 5–8.

66. On Fordham Committee report, see Committee on Public Housing Policy, Jefferson Fordham Chairman, December 12, 1956, in Box 282, Folder 4934, HADVP, TUA; and Fordham, Jefferson *et al.*, 'Basic Policies for Public Housing of Low-Income Families in Philadelphia: A Report on Public Housing Policy', mimeo, November 1957, in Box 282, folder 4905, *ibid.*

67. On Kennedy Administration approach to housing and renewal, see 'Legislative history of public housing traced through twenty-five years' in *Journal of Housing*, 8, 1962, pp. 442–45; also Housing and Home Finance Administration Department Study Draft (*ca* 1963) A Demonstration Programme to Deal With Human Problems Related to Urban Renewal and Housing Program, n.d., mimeographed, in Box 119, Correspondence Files,

Weaver, HUDR, Record Group 207, NA; on 'People Oriented' programmes, see Robert Weaver to Marie McGuire, October 23, 1963, in Box 116, Subject Correspondence Files, Weaver, 1961–1968, HUDR, Record Group 207, NA.

68. See *Report of the National Advisory Commission on Civil Disorders*. New York: The New York Times Company, 1968, p. 1; Bremner, Robert (1967) *From the Depths: The Discovery of Poverty in the United States*. New York: New York University Press, pp. 3–15.

69. City of Philadelphia Redevelopment Authority (1961) *Annual Report*, pp. 5–8; Slayton, William L. (1966) The operation and achievement of the urban renewal programme, in Wilson, James Q. (ed.) *Urban Renewal: The Record and the Controversy*. Cambridge: Harvard University Press, pp. 189–231.

70. Redevelopment Authority City of Philadelphia (1963) *Annual Report*, p. 5; Redevelopment Authority City of Philadelphia (1962) *Annual Report*, p. 4; Row, Arthur (1960) The Physical Development Plan. *Journal of the American Institute of Planning*, **XXVI**, August, pp. 177–81.

71. Redevelopment Authority City of Philadelphia (1961) *Annual Report*, pp. 9–21; Redevelopment Authority City of Philadelphia (1962) *Annual Report*, pp. 12–26; and 'Philadelphia . . . city reborn!' in Redevelopment Authority City of Philadelphia (1960) *Annual Report*, pp. 4–19.

72. *Ibid*; on OPDC, see Lowe, *op. cit.*, pp. 344–47.

73. Bacon (1961) *op. cit.*, pp. 134–35; see also 'Philadelphia . . . city reborn'. In Redevelopment Authority City of Philadelphia (1963) *Annual Report*, pp. 5–7.

74. For date on displacement in North Philadelphia, see Bauman, John F. Muller, Edward K. and Hummon, Norman (1985) Public Housing, Family and Economic Opportunity in North Philadelphia, 1945–1965. Paper delivered at the Temple University Conference on North Philadelphia. unpublished, University of Pittsburgh; also Philadelphia Housing Association (1958) *Relocation of Philadelphia*. Philadelphia: Philadelphia Housing Association, pp. 10–23; and Memorandum from George Dunn, Director of Management of Philadelphia Housing Authority, regarding 'Problem Families', May 27, 1957, in box 285, folder 5006, HADVP, TUA.

75. See Grigsby, William (1962) *Housing Markets and Public Policy*. Philadelphia: Institute for Urban Studies, University of Pennsylvania Reprint Series; and Greer, Scott (1963) Key issues for the central city, in American Society of Planning Officials, *Planning 1963*, p. 123.

76. Catherine Bauer Wurster quoted in 'Meeting of Six Minds: The Record of the Great Housing Debate at the Annual Meeting of the Conference', in National Housing Conference, *Housing Yearbook 1962*. Washington, D.C., p. 10.

77. Data on percentage of black occupancy from Public Housing Administration, Stastistical Branch, 'Reports on Occupancy', Box 32, Microfilm Reel 39, HUDR, Record Group 207, NA.

78. On husbandlessness in the Rosen homes, see Memorandum for the File,

Subject: 'Interview with George Dunn', October 29, 1961, Box 281, folder 4890, HADVP, TUA.

79. On black underclass, see Glasgow, Douglas G. (1980) *The Black Underclass: Poverty, Unemployment and Entrapment of Ghetto Youth*. San Francisco: Jersey-Bass Inc and Sowell, Thomas (1975) *Race and Economics*. New York: Donald McKay and Company.

Chapter Ten

The Post-War American Suburb: A New Form, A New City

ROBERT FISHMAN

FRANK LLOYD WRIGHT, PROPHET OF THE NEW CITY

Over fifty years ago Frank Lloyd Wright exhibited at Rockefeller Center a three-dimensional scale model of his American utopia, Broadacre City. This meticulously-detailed 'cross section of a complete Civilization' showed an automobile-age America from which all large cities had disappeared; their people and industry dispersed along the great superhighways that Wright envisioned. The city had 'gone to the countryside': all citizens enjoyed as much land as they could use on large homesteads which were both family homes and working farms; factories and offices had decentralized and now nestled among the homesteads and fields; shopping and cultural centres sprang up wherever the superhighways crossed. This new city had no centre and no periphery. As Wright put it, 'the true centre (the only allowable centralization)' in Broadacre City was the individual homestead. Yet the superhighway system brought each homestead into convenient contact with as many jobs and services as the average family could conveniently reach in the largest city.[1]

The Broadacre City plan has interested historians largely for what it reveals about Wright's own mind and the anti-urban Jeffersonian tradition which inspired him. (That certainly was my own emphasis when I discussed Broadacre City in my *Urban Utopias in the Twentieth Century* [1977]). But I now fear that such an approach does not do justice to the truly 'prophetic' character of Wright's ideas. To be sure, the city has not – as he devoutly wished – disappeared; nor have most of us adopted part-time farming. Wright, however, did see very early and very clearly that 'the big city is no longer modern'.[2] As he remarked as early as 1922, 'In the days of electrical transmission, the automobile and the telephone', urban concentration 'becomes needless congestion – it is a curse'.[3]

He also saw clearly that the automobile would not merely promote further suburbanization, that is further growth at the periphery of large cities while the fundamental law of urban concentration within a region remained unaltered. The destiny of the automobile was for a far more radical decentralization, one that dissolved all traditional boundaries of town and country and created vast new regional cities which were neither urban nor rural nor suburban in the usual meaning of these words.

This new kind of city Wright called Broadacres, the city that was 'everywhere or nowhere', that would 'absorb all needless cities and towns where they stood'.[4] A half-century after his model we can now begin to recognize its essential features in the world around us. The decentralization of formerly highly-concentrated urban functions into vast 'non-place urban fields' (John Friedmann's phrase) has now been largely accomplished, and for exactly the reasons that Wright foresaw in the 1920s and 1930s. The dispersal of manufacturing to the outer rings of large cities and to rural areas beyond them has proceeded with government encouragement and without it, but perhaps even more significant has been the movement of service jobs as well. The 1980 Census clearly indicates that the areas of outstanding growth both of jobs and housing have been precisely these outer rings and the (relatively) rural areas beyond them.[5]

Central cities, of course, have survived and, in their skyscraper and gentrifying districts, prospered. Nevertheless, for the vast majority of Americans, these central cities have in fact disappeared – from their daily lives and experiences. The 'outer city' has become a self-sufficient world of its own, with varied housing, extensive employment opportunities, a full range of educational and cultural institutions, and, of course, the ubiquitous malls which Wright foresaw in his model. If the residents of the outer city look beyond their world, it is usually not to the dim and threatening inner city – it is to the rural counties even further out, the expected sites for new homes, factories, malls, and office complexes.

In short, Broadacre City already exists, and most Americans are already living in it. If this new city is not recognized as such, it is because American culture is still preoccupied with the suburb and the idea that 'the growth of the suburbs' is the pre-eminent fact of post-World War II America. As I hope to show, the new American city of the 1980s may be hard to define, but it is definitely not a suburb.

BROADACRE CITY VERSUS THE SUBURB

Even when the Broadacre City model was first exhibited, Wright was accused by many cities of advocating universal suburbanization. This he hotly denied, in part because he despised suburbia but also because he realized that confusing Broadacre City with the suburbanization of his time represented a crucial misunderstanding of his ideas. For Wright, the suburbanization of American cities in the late nineteenth and early twentieth centuries was in fact pseudo-decentralization, the appearance of decentralization that masked a growing concentration of population and production in central cities.

This was perhaps most obvious in the case of the classic middle-class residential suburb of the turn of the century, such as Oak Park, Illinois where Wright himself lived from 1889 to 1911. Supposedly a 'flight from the city', the residential suburb actually extended the central city into the countryside. Its residents were wholly dependent on jobs and services in the central business district; without rapid rail transportation into the centre, the residential suburb could not exist. Every new suburban house thus marked a corresponding increase in the demand for office space, department stores, theatres, restaurants, etc. in centre city. The middle-class suburbanites might live in a setting that resembled a small country town, and they might (at least at weekends) maintain a lifestyle borrowed from an older generation of independent small-town gentry. But these suburbanities were in fact integral parts of a corporate economy based on increasingly large organizations found in the great cities. This corporate economy was rapidly centralizing production and distribution in the industral metropolis, thus draining population from the small towns and undermining that very class of independent proprietors which suburbia strove to imitate. While preserving the style of the small town, the turn-of-the-century residential suburb represented the triumph of the metropolis.

If the middle-class suburb supported the dominance of the central city, so too did the working-class industrial suburb. These factory towns at the edge of a great city were another important innovation of the period 1890–1930, but here again an apparent agent of decentralization in fact promoted the centralizing tendencies of the industrial metropolis. To be sure, workers in these peripheral 'satellite cities' lived close to their factories, and they and their families seldom ventured into the central business district. Nevertheless, these suburban factories were as dependent upon the central city as were the suburban homes of the middle class. Almost all such plants were established by businesses which had been founded in the central city and whose management remained there. The plants looked to the central business district and the older factory zones around it for specialized services, skilled workers, and even transportation facilities. (The rail link that connected a factory in a satellite city with an inner-city railyard was as important for suburban production as the commuter link to the central business district was for suburban residence.) The new industrial suburbs drained population and production from older, smaller centres and thus contributed in their own way to the centralizing tendencies of the industrial metropolis.

Yet, as Wright prophesied, centralization as the dominant force in the American environment had run its course by 1930, though the Great Depression and World War II prevented the emergence of a counter trend until after 1945. This post-war decentralization, although it appeared to be the culmination of the suburbanization of 1890–1930, had the exact opposite significance. At issue here is not the number of new factories, housing units, offices or stores built since 1945 on the outskirts of the older industrial metropolis, impressive though these numbers may be. It is that these peripheral regions came to constitute a *new city* functionally independent of the old.

The Emergence of Broadacre City

As in Wright's Broadacre plan, the true centre of this new city is not in some downtown central business district but in each residential unit. From that central starting point, the members of the household create their own city from the multitude of destinations that are within suitable driving distance. One spouse might work at an industrial park two exits down the interstate; the other at an office complex five exits in the other direction; the children travel by bus to comprehensive schools in their district or drive themselves to the local branch of the state university; and the family shops at several different malls along several different highways. All they need and consume, from the most complex medical services to fresh fruits and vegetables, can be found along the highways. Once a year, perhaps at Christmas, they go 'downtown' but never stay long.

If families and individuals have detached themselves from the central cities, so too have the manufacturing and service industries which form the economic heart of the new city. In this era of national and international corporations, headquarters for a manufacturing plant in an industrial park or an insurance office in a shopping mall is as likely to be across the continent as it is to be in the nearest central business district. Nor do plants look to the central city for raw materials or special services: these are almost always conveniently available somewhere along the highway.[6]

Personnel officers have discovered that they no longer need dense 'urban' concentrations of workers to ensure a sufficient pool of workers, nor do they need urban school systems or technical institutes to provide them with vital skills. A good location where, say, an interstate ring road crosses another interstate, can make their plant or office accessible to as many workers as a location along an urban subway system. Indeed, one of the great attractions of the new city is that it taps a labour pool of middle-class and working-class women – single, newly-married without children, or returning to work after child-raising – whose family situation and housing preferences have placed them squarely in the outer city and who are unwilling or unable to commute into the centre. To this group one can add the large numbers of college students who live at home and work part-time. Such workers are usually more attractive to employers than inner-city minorities.

On these twin foundations of massive growth in housing and jobs, the outer city has overcome its former status as a suburb or satellite of the central city. It has generated urban *complexity* without traditional urban *concentration*. Housing is no longer confined to the single-family tract house; it includes cluster housing, garden apartments, even high-rise towers: a range of housing types for a full range of incomes and needs. The shopping mall has shown an astonishing capacity to reproduce the range of choice available even in a large downtown shopping district.

Even in the higher regions of culture, the new city can frequently point to advanced research universities (many of which were quiet teachers' colleges only a generation ago); an impressive choice of regional theatres, music festivals and first-run movie houses; and elaborate new school systems and hospitals, often superior to their urban equivalents.

Perhaps most importantly, the new city has become the locus of the country's most advanced technological innovations. At the turn of the century, new industries tended to locate at the edge of an older commercial city; the belt of automobile plants that surrounded Detroit in the 1910s and 1920s was perhaps the best example. But the equivalent of Detroit for the 1980s is not an urban area at all. It is Silicon Valley, the highly decentralized region between San Francisco and San José which has proven the most congenial setting for high technology. And Silicon Valley has its equivalent in other outer cities throughout the country: the high-tech research and production centre has become almost as familiar in the new city as the shopping mall.

The industrial metropolis had achieved its privileged status because it brought together technical innovators, entrepreneurs with access to risk capital, and an ample supply of both skilled and unskilled labour. As the location of high-tech industries demonstrates, these pre-conditions for growth now exist most fully *outside* the metropolis. The fundamental relationship between 'city' and 'suburb' has thus been reversed. The new city that Frank Lloyd Wright predicted a half-century ago has emerged as the central American environment, while the old metropolis has been pushed to the margins of our economy and society.

A NEW URBAN FORM: NEW PROBLEMS AND NEW OPPORTUNITIES

Any attempt to write the history of the new American city must confront this paradox: the new city required massive government aid to be created, but the creation of a new kind of city was never the conscious aim of this aid. The subsidies that built the new environment were either proposed to facilitate old-style suburbanization or had no apparent connection to urbanization. Indeed, the programmes that did the most to destroy the hegemony of the industrial metropolis were precisely those designed to save it.

This can be seen most clearly in the crucial area of transportation policy. Wright had grasped the basic point in his Broadacre City plan: a fully-developed highway grid eliminates the primacy of a central business district. It creates a whole series of highway crossings which can serve as business centres, while promoting multi-directional travel which prevents any single point from attaining undue importance. Not surprisingly, the politicians and bureaucrats who actually planned the American highway system lacked Wright's prophetic insights and systematically misunderstood the meaning of their plans.

From Robert Moses to the present, highway planners have imagined that the new roads, like the older rail transportation, would enhance the importance of the old centres by funnelling cars and trucks into the downtown and the surrounding industrial belt. At most, the highways were to serve traditional suburbanization; that is movement from the periphery into the core during morning rush hours and the reverse movement in the afternoon.

When, for example, Los Angeles highway planners of the 1930s laid out their ambitious design for a regional network of freeways, these freeways generally followed the path of the older trolley lines: a radial pattern converging at the downtown.[7] Ironically, the Los Angeles downtown was already in decline in the 1930s; by the time the freeways were actually built in the 1950s and 1960s, the decline of the downtown was virtually complete and few motorists made it their destination. For most residents of the region, the downtown was simply a point of meaningless convergence and congestion. Retail trade and offices had already moved *out* along the freeways and other highways, distributing itself throughout the whole Los Angeles basin.[8]

As Mark Rose has shown, the planners of the federal interstate highway system brought a similar misunderstanding to the whole nation.[9] The superhighways were intended to move people and goods from one central city to another. In fact they made cheap land outside the centres more convenient for auto and especially truck transportation than the relatively congested factory zones of the core. In conjunction with the unplanned but devastating collapse of the railroad system, the interstates virtually negated the transportation advantage which had been a crucial advantage of the industrial metropolis.

Especially striking has been the unanticipated importance of the ring roads of 'beltways' around major cities. These were built into the interstate system simply to allow through traffic to avoid going directly through an urban core. In fact, they became the 'Main Street' of the new city, a high-speed traffic artery that put every part of the urban periphery in close contact with every other part, without passing through the central city at all. In short, the federal government created a Broadacre City system of highways without comprehending the consequences.

The impact of new highway construction was vastly increased by a corresponding post-war surge in housing construction. Here again, government failed to understand the meaning of its actions, especially those of the Federal Housing Administration. The FHA-insured mortgage, the centrepiece of a vast re-housing of the American people, was never intended to achieve such sweeping ends. The National Housing Act of 1934 which created the FHA was passed as emergency aid to a housing industry which had been in a deep recession for almost a decade. After massive foreclosures on the short-term 'balloon mortgages' of the 1920s, the long-term, low-interest mortgages insured by the FHA were intended to save the industry from total collapse and to provide for a slow but steady pace of new housing.

If the original aims of the FHA were essentially limited and defensive, the post-war boom made the FHA a vital link in a massive wave of land speculation and housebuilding at the urban fringe. Its guarantees created a virtually risk-free environment in which large corporations could undertake the complete transformation of rural land into sprawling subdivisions. The speed and scale of this process – augmented at every stage by government subsidies and guarantees – had an especially devastating effect on the older cities by the (again unforeseen) consequenes of FHA policies that directed its aid almost exclusively toward new building on the urban periphery.

These policies also derived from the 1930s and the FHA's obsessive fear of losing money through mortgage investment in 'blighted' areas. At a time when all housing investment seemed risky, FHA assessors applied the most conservative standards that led them to favour homogeneous suburban zones over ethnically-mixed city neighbourhoods. The impact of this policy during the 1930s was minimal, but when it was carried over into the post-war period it ensured the rapid deterioration of many urban areas at the same time that capital for building and home improvement was freely available at the outskirts.[10]

In housing as well as highways, the government pursued a policy of radical decentralization – without even knowing it. A comparable unconsciousness affected the private sector, where economic concentration led, paradoxically, to physical decentralization. As corporations grew larger, they developed elaborate management and communications structures which made it possible for them to operate efficiently with plants and offices scattered widely in a region, in a nation, and ultimately throughout the world. Factories were thus free to gravitate anywhere that goods could be produced and shipped most cheaply. In the post-war era, this meant moving to the outskirts where cheap land for sprawling, single-storey factories – the design best adapted to the needs of mass production – was most easily obtained, and where convenient highway links were also available. In the Boston region, for example, 80 per cent of the new industrial building undertaken between 1954 and 1967 took place on the suburban fringes.[11] By the end of the 1960s, Route 128 – the Boston beltway – had become an international symbol of the new industrial environment: modern research centres and assembly plans on landscaped sites overlooking the superhighway.

At the same time, inner-city factories were left to run down. The historic link between the growth of the corporation and the growth of the inner city was thus broken. In the heyday of that linkage – 1890 to 1930 – efficient corporate operation seemed to require the concentration of production in some single location near 'headquarters' where constant supervision by top management was possible. As corporations expanded in this period, rural areas and towns lost their small factories to massive plants in the factory belt of the metropolis. By the 1950s, however, further corporate expansion was having the opposite effect, draining jobs from the inner city and transferring them to the peripheries. By the 1960s, three-quarters of all new manufacturing jobs were being created in areas that the Census classified as 'suburban'.[12]

If manufacturing could move to the outskirts, so too could management and its support services. "Headquarters" might move to a prestigious suburb, but even if it remained in a downtown high-rise the backoffice could leave the city and remain tied to headquarters electronically. The decentralization of office work is perhaps the most important element in job location in the 1970s and 1980s, just as the decentralization of the factory had been the key element of the 1950s and 1960s.

One might see the growth of the shopping mall as simply one more aspect of the ability of the large corporation to function effectively in a decentralized environment. The great metropolitan department store of the turn-of-the-century can be viewed as an example of the concentration of corporate capital and management in a single 'plant' located at the core. As early as the 1920s, downtown department stores began to establish suburban branches to serve customers with automobiles, but only in the 1950s and 1960s did department stores reorganize themselves to create a decentralized network of large stores serving the entire region. Each store in the network reproduces the extensive selection of goods which was once possible only in a central location. Even the small shops in a mall are not usually small businesses but branches or franchises of a corporation that operates regionally or nationally.

This capacity of the large corporation to 'cover ground' – to establish decentralized branches on widely scattered sites – has been integral to the larger decentralization of the American city. Frank Lloyd Wright had assumed that physical decentralization would inevitably result in economic change: the break-up of large concentrations of capital and power, and the emergence of an economy based on small-scale units. If anything, the opposite has been the case. The large corporation has adapted so well to the new city that genuine small business is nowhere more at risk than in the outer city. Where Wright had hoped to see a culture and a society based on individuality and independence, there has emerged the heartland of the mass media and the mass produced.

THE FUTURE OF BROADACRE CITY

Unplanned, unsought, and unanticipated, the new city is now a fact. As I tried to show, it arose out of government policies whose real effects were misunderstood as well as out of deeper economic trends whose meaning was ignored. It also reflects, I should add, innumerable individual choices of 'where I want to live' as well as innumerable attempts to profit from those choices. Local government, as always, followed rather than led, seeking to provide a reasonably-workable crazy-quilt of services for the new city. In any case, the American people have voted with their feet for Broadacre City.

We might now ask whether Wright's ultimate prophecy will be fulfilled: the disappearance of the big city. Is the present-day boom in downtown office construction and inner-city gentrification simply a last hurrah for the old city before deeper trends in decentralization lead to its ultimate decay?

To me, the final triumph of Broadacre City such as Wright envisaged it seems unlikely, if only because Wright underestimated the force of economic and political centralization that continues to exist in this country. If physical decentralization had indeed meant economic decentralization, then the urban cores would indeed be ghost towns. But large and powerful organizations still seek out a central location that validates their importance, and the historic core of great cities meets that need better than any other location. And the corporate and government headquarters attract a wide variety of specialized support services – law firms, publishing, media, restaurants, culture, etc. – that continue to make the centre cities viable.

The old factory zones around the core have also survived, but only in the painfully ironic sense of housing those too poor to earn admission to the new city of prosperity at the periphery. Here, Wright was all too accurate in predicting the decay of centralized production areas. What he did not see was that these areas would serve as the last resort for a seemingly permanent underclass.

The big city, therefore, will not disappear in the foreseeable future, and outer-city residents will therefore continue to confront uneasily both the economic power and elite culture of the urban core and the poverty of the inner city. Nevertheless, both the elite and the under-class will surely remain distant from the everyday experience of most Americans. The question must be: how will Broadacre City continue to evolve?

Perhaps the most striking finding of the 1980 Census is that even the energy crisis of the 1970s has not slowed the trend toward further decentralization. For the first time since 1820, Census figures show rural population growing faster than urban; but these figures simply reflect a decentralization of formerly urban functions into areas so remote from cities that demographers cannot call them 'urban'.[13] A recent *New York Times* article describes a large, high-tech factory located at the intersection of two interstate highways in a rural district of Illinois. Its workers live scattered in six counties that cover over 2,000 square miles of farmland.[14] This is truly Broadacre City; it is also representative of the fastest-growing areas in the nation.

The question is not, I think, whether some new and more severe energy crisis will force a return to the cities. So much decentralization has occurred that such a return would be like forcing toothpaste back into the tube. The question is whether decentralization will reach the extremes that Wright predicted in the 1930s – and now seem to be occurring in the 1980s – or if energy costs, government policy or some other constraints will keep the new city relatively confined to its present dimensions. The Atlanta metropolitan area, for example, was defined by the 1970 Census to include five counties with a population of 1,390,000. By the 1980 census Atlanta covered *fifteen* counties, and, though population in the central city shrank by 15 per cent, total metropolitan population increased by 44 per cent to 2,000,000.[15] Will the 1990 Census show growth mostly 'filling-in' within the fifteen counties, or will even this vast area be subsumed in a still-larger regional pattern? The trend of the 1980 Census points clearly to the latter outcome of more radical decentralization; that is Broadacre City.

Whatever the quantitative measures of the new city, there remains the final qualitative question: what kind of city are we building for ourselves? Wright believed that decentralization provided the opportunity for the creation of a classic American landscape in which the demands of the machine age and the natural beauties of the countryside would finally be reconciled. 'Broadacres', he wrote, 'would be so built in sympathy with Nature that a deep feeling for the beauty of the terrain would be a fundamental qualification in the new city-builders'.[16] Openness and diversity would be built into the plan, as they could not be in the 'petty diverse partitions of property' in the suburbs or the inhuman congestion of the city.

Compared to these ideals, the reality of the new city is best summed up in the inevitable word 'sprawl'. Ada Louise Huxtable called the new settlements 'slurbs' and wrote that life there is 'no voyage of discovery or private exploration of the world's wonders, natural and man-made; it is cliché conformity as far as the eye can see, with no stimulation of the spirit through quality of the environment'.[17]

The case against the new American city can be easily summarized. Compared even to the traditional suburb, it is impossible to comprehend. It has no clear boundaries; it includes discordant rural, urban and suburban elements; and it can best be measured in counties rather than city blocks. Consequently, the new city lacks any recognizable centre to give meaning to the whole. Major civic institutions – schools, shopping malls, hospitals, etc. – seem scattered at random over an undifferentiated landscape.

Even planned developments – however harmonious they might appear from the inside – can be no more than fragments in a fragmented environment. A single house, a single street, even a cluster of streets and houses – these can be and frequently are well-designed. But true public space is lacking, impoverished, or (in the malls) totally commercialized. Only the remaining pockets of undeveloped farm land maintain real openness and these are inevitably developed, precipitating further flight and further sprawl.

The case for the new city can only be made hesitantly and conditionally. First, all new urban types appear in their early stages to be chaotic. 'There were a hundred thousand shapes and substances of incompleteness, wildly mingled out of their places, upside down, burrowing in the earth, aspiring in the earth, mouldering in the water, and unintelligible as any dream'.[18] This is Dickens describing London in 1848. As I have tried to indicate, 'sprawl' has a functional logic which is perhaps not apparent to those accustomed to more traditional cities. If that logic is understood imaginatively, as Wright tried to do in his Broadacre City plans, then perhaps a matching aesthetic can be devised.

We must remember that even the most 'organic' cityscapes of the past evolved slowly after much chaos and trial-and-error. The classic late-nineteenth-century railroad suburb – the standard against which critics judge today's sprawl – evolved out of the disorder of nineteenth-century metropolitan growth. First, planners of genius like John Nash and Frederick Law Olmsted comprehended the process and devised aesthetic formulas to guide it. These formulas were then communicated – slowly and incompletely – to speculative builders who nevertheless managed to capture the basic idea. Finally, individual property owners constantly upgraded their holdings to eliminate discordant elements and bring their community closer to the ideal.

We might hope that a similar process is now at work in post-suburban America. As a starting-point, there are Wright's Broadacre City plans and drawings which still repay study by anyone seeking a vision of a modern yet 'organic' American landscape. More useful still is the American New Town tradition, starting from Radburn, with its careful designs intended to reconcile decentralization with older ideas of community. New Town designs have been adopted by speculative builder, not only in a highly-publicized project like the Rouse's Columbia, Maryland, but in hundreds of smaller 'planned communities' which are beginning to leave their mark on the landscape.

At the level of civic architecture there is Wright's Marin County Civic Center to serve as a model for public monuments in a decentralized environment. The most recent multi-level enclosed shopping malls have attained a spaciousness not unworthy of the great urban shopping districts of the past, while newly-built college campuses and campus-like office complexes and research centres add significantly to the environment. Some commercial highway strips have been rescued from ugly cacaphony and have managed to achieve a liveliness that is not tawdry. (This evolution parallels the evolution of the nineteenth-century downtown, a remarkably ugly clutter of small buildings and large signs around 1850 which was transformed into a reasonably dignified centre for commerce by the turn of the century.)

Most importantly, there is a growing sense that open land must be preserved as an integral part of the landscape, through regional land-use plans, purchases for parklands, and tax abatements for working farms. These governmental measures, combined with thousands of thousands of small-scale efforts by individuals, could create a fitting new environment for the new city. These efforts, moreover, could provide the starting-point for a more profound diversification of the outer city. An increased understanding and respect for the landscape of each region could lead to a growing rejection of a mass culture that erases all such distinctions.

Wright himself, despite his professed love of democracy, had little respect for the capacity of ordinary people to create the great new city he envisaged. In his utopian society all matters affecting the environment, i.e., *all* political and economic questions, would be judged by an all-powerful 'County Architect', an obvious projection of Wright himself. But Wright believed that the new city must be a totally integrated whole, organized around his organic architecture; and, as Jane Jacobs reminds us, 'A city cannot be a work of art'.[19] Precisely because the outer city includes all the urban functions, it will necessarily have its ugly, discordant, and chaotic elements. Nevertheless, we need not yield to the critics' vision of sprawl and slurbs. Between this horrific image and Wright's utopian vision of a total organic environment there lies an immense field for individual and governmental initiative. The new city will never be a utopia, but it might evolve into something worthy of Wright's ideal: the plastic form of a genuine democracy.

NOTES

1. Wright, Frank Lloyd (1958) *The Living City*. New York: Horizon Press.

2. Wright, Frank Lloyd (1932) *The Disappearing City*. New York: W.F. Payson, p. 20.

3. Wright, Frank Lloyd (1923) *Experimenting With Human Lives*. Hollywood, California: Fine Arts Society, p. 9.

4. Wright, Frank Lloyd (1958) *The Living City*. New York: Horizon Press, p. 157.

5. *New York Times*, 23 March 1980, p. 1.

6. The suburbanization of the corporation, in Masotti, Louis H. and Hadden, Jeffrey K. (eds.) (1974) *Suburbia in Transition*. New York: New Viewpoints, pp. 82–100.

7. Brodsly, David (1981) *L.A. Freeway: An Appreciative Essay*. Los Angeles: University of California Press, p. 78.

8. *Ibid.*, p. 120.

9. Rose, Mark H. (1979) *Interstate: Express Highway Politics 1941–1956*. Lawrence, Kansas: Regents Press of Kansas.

10. Jackson, Kenneth T. (August 1980) Race ethnicity, and real estate appraisal, *Journal of Urban History*, 6, pp. 419–52.

11. Berry, Brian J.L. and Cohen, Yehoshua S. (1973) Decentralization of commerce and industry in Masotti, Louis H. and Hadden, Jeffrey K. (eds.) *Urbanization of the Suburbs*. Beverly Hills, California: Sage Publications, p. 442.

12. The rapid growth of suburban employment, in Masotti, Louis H. and Hadden, Jeffrey K. (eds.) (1974) *Suburbia in Transition*. New York: New Viewpoints, p. 99.

13. *New York Times*, 12 December 1981, p. 8.

14. *New York Times*, 23 March 1980, p. 50.

15. *New York Times*, 1 February 1981, p. 1.

16. Wright, Frank Lloyd (1945) *When Democracy Builds*. Chicago: University of Chicago Press, p. 58.

17. Huxtable, Ada Louise (1974) An alternative to 'slurbs', in Masotti, Louis H. and Hadden, Jeffrey K. (eds.) (1974) *Suburbia in Transition*. New York: New Viewpoints, p. 187.

18. Dickens, Charles (1848) *Dombey and Son* (1848), quoted in Sheppard, Francis (1971) *London 1808–1870: The Infernal Wen*. Berkeley, California: The University of California Press, p. 133.

19. Jacobs, Jane (1961) *The Death and Life of Great American Cities*. New York: Random House, p. 372.

Chapter Eleven

Problems of Governance and the Professions of Planners: The Planning Profession in the 1980s

HOWELL S. BAUM

For most people other than planners, Peter Marris has observed, planning is an episodic response to the disintegration of purpose in action.[1] The power of planners, he suggests, lies in their ability to use their professional method to solve a conceptual crisis. This chapter is an account of a current crisis regarding the purposes of public action. Planners' methods, developed in response to past crises, have become, in turn, a source of new crisis as the demands of the polity have changed. The first section of this chapter reviews the historical evolution of planners' proclaimed expertise and the resultant contemporary crisis. The second section examines planners' perceptions of the situation and their role in it. The concluding section presents alternative scenarios for planners' future.

THE EVOLUTION OF PLANNING AND THE CONTEMPORARY CRISIS

Progressive urban reformers became active at the end of the nineteenth century in response to the physical and social disorder of American cities under growing industrialization. New factories attracted millions of immigrants to rapidly swelling cities. Crowded tenements not only posed risks to the health of those who occupied them but also endangered their wealthier neighbours. The invasion of impoverished, often discontented, workers from foreign cultures threatened dominant American values and the established economic order. The reformers offered a variety of physical and social interventions to improve urban living conditions. Those who subsequently became known as planners emphasized architectural and other skills of physical intervention.

First housing congestion in New York, then the encroachment of garment factories against Fifth Avenue salons, presented challenges to these practitioners. As defined by local government and business interests, these were physical problems calling for expertise in architecture and landscape design. However, the challenge to the commissions charged to resolve these issues reflected not simply substantive problems in urban development, but also a conceptual crisis. The tangible problem was that more and larger buildings were being constructed throughout the city; the conceptual crisis was that private enterprise, presumed to have a hidden but benevolent and effective hand, had failed to regulate itself in such a way as demonstrably to serve the public welfare. Thus the charge to a growing body of self-identified planners – such as Edward Bassett, Benjamin Marsh, and Lawrence Veiller – was to devise a regulatory procedure which justified public intervention without significantly challenging private initiative.

The resultant proposal for zoning was a procedural innovation which legitimated public regulation of urban physical development. Planners' proffered expertise in landscape and building design justified private trust in public zoning actions. At the same time, any disruption from public regulatory power over private development was moderated by the ways in which zoning regulations tended to endorse dominant business interests.[2]

The proliferation of the automobile in the 1920s presented a new challenge to planners. The automobile raised new requirements for street construction and posed threats to safety. Still more significantly, by increasing mobility, it threatened the stability of urban businesses and property values. Local commercial and civic groups turned to planners for advice. Although imbedded in these problems was the major political question of balancing urban and suburban development, planners responded to downtown anxieties by formulating the problems as primarily technical. They emphasized their expertise in surveying traffic, identifying 'laws' of traffic movement, and developing standards for street design.

Planners proposed that traffic plans be linked to local government zoning ordinances. Because planners' biases led them to design road systems that favoured the dominance of central-city development, local businesses endorsed their proposal. In this way, city planning moved more securely into local government.[3] Planners solidified their claims of expertise in physical design which could solve problems of urban development, and they reinforced their position that marginal problems of development should be regulated by technical advisors who served a relatively restrained local government. This important procedural position was reinforced by the national movement of technocratic urban administrative reform.[4] As earlier, public intervention received much of its legitimacy from its fundamental support for private urban development. This intervention could be justified as representing the public interest, insofar as the public interest was identified with business interests.

The spread of planning was uneven but unceasing. Even though local interests were sometimes uncertain whether city planning was important or useful, the number of city planning commissions, master plans, zoning regulations, and transportation elements grew through the early 1930s. The Depression depleted local governments' budgets, and concerns about economic survival often supplanted interests in public regulation.[5] Still, planners had established themselves in local government.

Both the economy and the physical stock of cities declined during the Depression and the Second World War. During the war both the federal government and local governments began to plan for the post-war renewal of cities. Again the balance of urban and suburban development was at issue. Again most planners tended to side with downtown business interests.[6] The culmination of these efforts was the national urban renewal programme, enacted in the Housing Acts of 1949 and 1954. The programme represented an effort by the federal government to provide massive infusions of money to local governments for physical planning by and in support of private business interests.

However, at the same time that the extent of urban decay made such far-reaching public-private intervention into urban development tenable, the city had changed in a number of ways which made these traditional programmes less broadly acceptable. The combined post-war migration of blacks to the cities and movement of whites to the suburbs created a metropolis increasingly characterized by racial segregation and social and economic inequality. At the same time, the Civil Rights Movement spearheaded the organization of blacks and other ethnic minorities to insist that decisions about urban economic and social development take them into account.

The urban renewal programme, as earlier planning activities, tended to benefit organized business interests to the neglect of the poor and racial minorities.[7] However, in the 1960s this programme was challenged by the poor and racial minorities with growing questions about the principles on which planners had established their claims for professional status. First, substantively, the poor criticized the physicalist bias of urban renewal: planners conceptualized urban problems superficially in terms of the city's physical stock and did not recognize the intangible social structures which support communities. Massive displacement of the poor from expert-defined 'slums' epitomized this insensitivity to community social structures.

Insofar as displaced persons were publicly relocated, they were moved to new dwellings which did not respond well to the workings of extended families, the ties of neighbourhood helping networks, or the importance of local social and recreational activities. Far from solving the problems of poverty, urban renewal projects increased them. Consequently, it became increasingly difficult to see the benefits of public planning.

In addition, the poor and racial minorities took the position that they were entitled to a fair, if not a compensatory, share of benefits from public programmes. Hence they raised a second, procedural, objection to the planning model which underlay urban renewal. Not only was the programme ineffective because it was based on faulty substantive expertise, but it lacked authority because decisions – and the procedures by which they were achieved – did not represent broadly affected interests. Massive dislocation was not only harmful; it was illegitimate.

As the War on Poverty gave support to the claims of the urban poor and racial minorities, the Model Cities Programme was formed in response to these criticisms of the traditional planning model. Substantively, physical interpretations of urban problems were supplemented with social interpretations. Thus some planners became concerned with not simply the physical quality of housing, but also the occupants' employment opportunities. High-rise public housing was supplemented by scattered-site public housing. Model Cities plans included social programmes. At least as important, Model Cities incorporated a procedural innovation. Citizens affected by the plans were invited to participate in the planning process – directly through public meetings and indirectly through the representations of advocate planners. Planners' traditional emphasis on giving technical advice to governing officials was moderated by encouraging public participation in the deliberations and decisions.

These concerns presented a new public image of city planning.[8] The traditional image emphasized technocratic advice (on limited public intervention) in support of private physical and economic development. The new image portrayed public planning as social welfare planning, guiding deliberately redistributive efforts by government. Social welfare planning was concerned with social problems created by or left after private capital accumulation and investment. Whereas planners traditionally had been concerned simply with expanding the urban economy, now some planners advocated a more equitable distribution of urban wealth and income.

This second image of city planning affected responses to the Model Cities Programme and planning.[9] On the one hand, Model Cities offered a new model of planning and increased public demand for participation in planning. On the other hand, its demise encouraged cynicism, particularly among the poor, about the likely results of participation. The most recent decade, characterized by troubled economic times, has complicated the planning process. Working-class and middle-income citizens have become concerned about their economic security and, prodded by Presidents Nixon and Reagan, have identified programmes like Model Cities as unfair – illegitimate – interventions by government into the distribution of life-chances, somehow favouring the poor over others. Although President Carter identified himself as a planner – in the first model, not the second – his administration demonstrated the inefficacy of government as an institution for solving problems. President Reagan's excoriation of planners and bureaucrats articulates a growing belief that self-interest should guide public and private action, that planners are obstacles to progress, and that, simply, 'government does not work'.

In the face of such developments, planners' traditional professional claims are unpersuasive. The limitations of a purely physicalist view of urban problems have in some measure been recognized and supplemented with a small but growing interest in cities as social systems. Still, it is not merely the restricted substantive expertise which planners offer, but also their implicit procedural claims, which are challenged. Planners' traditional claims that they have approached urban problems with rationality have not persuaded the poor and racial minorities who have been consistent losers. Planners' subsequent advocacy of participation and redistribution frighten insecure middle-income citizens. In short, planners' claims that their recommendations serve a public interest are not convincing.

Thus government today, and public planning with it, confront a conceptual crisis. Public action is difficult to justify because so many interests regard government as serving and representing someone else. Both the future of government and the future of planners depend on planners' ability to devise new decision-making procedures which satisfy broad, diverse expectations of participation and representation. Development of these procedures depends on a sensitivity to social issues as well as to the physical environment. Although seeds of such procedures may be found in the participatory experiments of the Model Cities Programme, the new model must incorporate more interests and somehow reconcile their conflicts.

PLANNERS' PERCEPTIONS OF THE SITUATION

There are no simple ways for planners to respond to public expectations that government be more accountable to citizens. In general, these expectations require more explicit attention to how decisions tacitly represent or exclude specific interests. In particular, these expectations call for planners to make deliberate procedural interventions – to act in ways which broaden public participation and representation in planning decisions.

Many planners share public perceptions that public decision-making has become stalemated. Planners commonly complain that they have little influence on public (let alone private) problem-solving.[10] How do planners interpret this situation? Do they perceive a conceptual crisis restraining public action? Do they believe that their accustomed role is inconsistent with public expectations? Do they consider developing new relationships with public constituents as a means of changing the situation?

Studies of planners produce contradictory answers to these questions. When planners are asked about the situation of planning in general, they are likely to acknowledge some aspects of the crisis identified by contemporary interest groups. However, when planners are asked about the implications of such observations and the need to transform their roles, most are likely to insist on strengthening – rather than altering – their traditional roles as substantive experts working independently of public pressures. When planners are asked about including procedural interventions in their repertoire of professional skills, a minority respond favourably.

Because different questions have been asked of different samples, it is impossible to reconcile divergent findings with any certainty. The studies below suggest two complementary interpretations. The first is that there are two groups of planners, a relatively small group who recognize a procedural crisis and a relatively large group who resist that possibility. The second interpretation is that there is also a third group of indeterminate size who somehow hold both beliefs but ultimately remain ambivalent about procedural interventions.

Analysis of the Situation

Michael Vasu, a political scientist concerned with planners' political views, surveyed a national sample of planners in 1974 and found signs of recognition of a conceptual crisis for planning.[11] Traditionally, planners have claimed that their expertise enables them to discern a public interest which transcends competing private interests. This public interest serves as the legitimating basis of planners' recommendations. Thus planners are able to remain neutral with respect to any particular interest and to put forth positions which favour all. In Vasu's study, however, a majority of planners believe that the complexity of competing interests inevitably makes planning an interested activity itself. Fewer than half (43 per cent) believe that it is possible to identify a solitary public interest (40 per cent disagree, with 17 per cent uncertain). A majority of planners (50 per cent) accept the implication that a planner is not simply a neutral judge of the public interest (only 27 per cent disagree). A strong majority (78 per cent) agree that the planning process is value oriented. An overwhelming majority (88 per cent) believe that no plan can be neutral, that a plan must benefit some interests and discriminate against others.[12]

Implications for Planners' Roles

Such an analysis would suggest that planners should become more sensitive political analysts, that they should consider whether advocative roles are not inescapable, and, at the least, that they should embrace more deliberately procedural roles intended to re-shape participation in planning decision-making. However, when planners are asked about modifying their roles, most tend to resist.

Vasu's planners fail to draw consistent conclusions from their own analysis. A majority (53 per cent) assert that it is still possible for government to plan comprehensively in a pluralistic society (30 per cent disagree). When asked about their own role preferences, the largest group (48 per cent) still prefer a 'technician' role, in which the planner neutrally judges the public interest, makes recommendations on professional rather than political bases, and avoids lobbying or other political activity. Only 20 per cent prefer a contrasting 'advocate' role, and 32 per cent choose an intermediate or combined role, which Vasu designates 'moderate'. Apparently, despite recognition of political changes which challenge the traditional planning role, many planners still insist on the correctness of that role.

Power to the Planners

Planners in my own 1977–78 study of a sample of Maryland practitioners offer compatible responses.[13] These planners frequently express frustration at their limited influence. However, in recommending changes which would improve planners' opportunities to practise effectively, most assume that the traditional technocratic planning role is appropriate.

When advocating reforms in their working conditions, most of these planners emphasize moves which would 'let planners be (traditional) planners'. Ten per cent argue that they are held back by administrators who are overly cautious and who must be replaced. Bolder administrators would aggressively negotiate with other departments on behalf of the planners. However, planners do not mean that their recommendations are negotiable – rather, that their authority to impose them should be.

Another 20 per cent of the planners argue that the planning process should be 'depoliticized', that planners' expertise should have more weight than politicians' interests. A number of planners regard citizen boards or advisory councils not as means for incorporating public concerns into planning analyses, but as means whereby politicans and private interests collude to stifle the influence of rational planning in decisions. Some planners advocate increasing the statutory authority of planning departments, so that planners' recommendations can have the force of law.[14] The following report from a county planning director is representative of these interests in removing politics from planning:

> We're trying to work now to change the planning process and the planners – changing the level of responsibility which planners take within the local government. We're trying to stick it to them [the planners]! Out here the Council are the planners. I'd like to see them not see themselves as the planners. What I see ultimately as helping us to do a better job is changing the roles and responsibilities and organi-zational structure of the county.[15]

Underlying these sentiments is a deep faith in the reasonableness of planners' substantive expertise. There is little recognition that political constraints on planners' influence may reflect public concerns about limiting the role of experts in democratic decision-making. At the least, there is little acknowledgement of such procedural concerns in proposing 'depoliticized' procedures.

Forty-two per cent of the planners reinforce this position by arguing that planners should have more power, should receive more support for their efforts, and should have larger budgets for their efforts. Interestingly, planners repeat public complaints about restrictive bureaucratic standards, but planners want the standards removed so as to increase discretion. In addition to stifling creativity, some planners believe, regulations and review processes generate side-games which focus on controlling aspects of the review process, rather than devising sensible outcomes. A number of planners argue that planning agencies and programmes should have larger budgets, both as a signal of planners' importance and as a means of ensuring their influence. Several planners complain that legislative bodies and citizens generally have little appreciation for the imagination and rationality which planners can contribute to public decision-making; they contend that the public must be educated about planning. One local planner expresses many of these concerns:

> We need the ability to influence the decision-making process. This is

how it is in this country. It is thought the planners cannot be trusted to make decisions. This is really a big problem for the planning profession. Every one has a board (which decides on planners' recommendations). In a country where private sector interests are considered to be godly, planners will always have this problem.

In these sentiments, as elsewhere, there is considerable confidence in the rightness of planners' substantive expertise. Relegation of planners to a subsidiary role is regarded mainly as short-sightedness. Again, there is little recognition that the public may have given some thought to the procedural relationship between planners and elected decision-makers and that, consequently, planners might do likewise.

Limited Citizen Participation

This emphasis on substance over procedure is evident when planners are asked directly about citizen participation. Citizen participation has been justified on both substantive and procedural grounds. Substantively, lay citizens may have information which planners lack and which should be incorporated into decisions. Procedurally, citizen participation may give legitimacy and support to subsequent decisions. Some planners do recall with satisfaction various projects where citizen participation both informed proposals and generated political support for the proposals. And most planners acknowledge that laypersons have useful information. However, many planners discount citizens' knowledge by maintaining that their primary contribution to problem-solving is parochial information. Residents have intimate knowledge of neighbourhood conditions, as a long-time local planner argues:

> A well-informed citizenry can be very helpful in helping the professional understand a neighborhood . . . There is something which is qualitative which is not apparent in the numbers. There is a need for interpretation of quantitative data. Neighborhood groups can provide guidance on customs of the neighborhood.[16]

Accordingly, 78 per cent of planners regard citizen participation as important in the beginning of planning, when problems are identified.

At the same time, most planners contend that planning should be guided by broad cognitive considerations. Spatially, planning decisions should incorporate some notion of a public interest or, failing that, at least the interests of a whole metropolis or region. Temporally, planning decisions should consider the long-term future. Many planners feel that most citizens lack the training or ability to contribute in these important ways. Hence, once community members have finished describing local conditions, many planners want to exclude them from further participation. Initial statements of problems must be interpreted in order to formulate meaningful action goals; only 48 per cent of the sampled planners believe that citizens have the requisite reflective ability to contribute helpfully. They observe that citizens 'can best describe what they envision', or that citizens are most capable of 'evaluating their communities, evaluating their needs, gaps between needs and present level of services, setting goals, development of aspirations'. Once goals have been established, alternative strategies must be developed and evaluated for their feasibility; at this point only 38 per cent of the sample believe that citizens have sufficient abstractive ability to understand the choices involved. Only a minority would accept a county planner's view that citizens

> can provide a sense of what is acceptable and what is not acceptable to the community. They can make the planner more knowledgeable about opportunities. They are useful in reviewing the alternatives which are developed. Depending on the project, they can evaluate cost-effectiveness.[17]

Thus most of these planners think of the planning process as an intellectual activity in which substantive expertise, the planners' forte, is the primary requirement. Even though these assumptions tend to exclude citizens from participating in planning activities, few planners mention associated questions of planners' procedural accountability or legitimacy. There is little recognition that public apprehensions about planners' isolation and independence may be expressed in the resistance which planners accurately identify as a constraint on their effectiveness. A majority of these planners, as of Vasu's, insist on reasserting a traditional planning role without, or in spite of, acknowledgement that public expectations of planning have changed.

Planners' Repertoire of Skills

Still, such statements about the political environment and even about planning roles are relatively abstract and may express professional ideology rather than describing actual practice. Even though these abstract formulations of their actions emphasize technical analysis rather than conceptual crises and procedural interventions, it is possible that some planners do act in ways which deliberately modify public decision-making procedures.

The Ethics of Procedural Intervention

A study by Elizabeth Howe and Jerome Kaufman sheds some light on this question. Interviewing in 1977 a national sample similar to Vasu's, Howe and Kaufman asked planners whether they regarded certain hypothetical actions as ethical.[18] The actions in question involved procedural intervention responding to political interests and affecting the structure of participation in the planning process. Scenarios included three types of actions: modifying the emphasis in analysis and presentation of information in order to favour particular interests; distributing information to interests not formally involved in the planning process; and actively working with interested parties to affect the outcome of the planning process.

Modifications in the emphasis in analysis and presentation of information included distortions or extreme emphases which favourably portray positions which planners prefer, as well as changes in technical judgments in response to administrative pressure. Distribution of information to interests not formally involved in the planning process included releasing draft recommendations in response to requests and leaking information either without or against authorization to do so. Active involvement with or on behalf of interested parties included putting expendables into plans as goods for a tradeoff; dramatizing problems to get support for action; organizing a coalition to support planners' positions; using legal authority as a bargaining threat to get support for a plan; and working independently as advocate for a citizen group.

Planners' approval of actions in these categories varies consistently. Although analysing and presenting information is most congruent with the traditional role of the planner as provider of substantive in-formation, the act of modifying the interpretation is perceived as a clear violation of the rational imperative which accompanies that role. Planners as a group regard such actions as 'probably unethical', with a mean score of 3.66 on a scale of 1 (clearly ethical), 2 (probably ethical), 3 (not sure), 4 (probably unethical), to 5 (clearly unethical).[19]

Planners are less unfavourable toward the interventions which entail distributing what may be considered valid information to interests not formally participating in the planning process. As a group, planners still regard such actions as not ethical but are close to being 'not sure' about them (average of 3.16). In conflict with one of Vasu's findings, planners view favourably the variety of lobbying, advocacy, and negotiating activities which are most overtly procedural interventions. In these cases the planners are not content to let valid information 'speak for itself' but favour active work in its support. Although close to 'not sure' about these actions, the group is inclined to regard them as ethical (average of 2.72).[20]

Howe and Kaufman go on to identify distinct groups of planners who differ in the approval which they accord to procedural interventions. Asking planners about their preferred roles, Howe and Kaufman identify three groups similar to Vasu's, although the proportion favouring a traditional planning role is smaller: 27 per cent are 'technicians'; 18 per cent are 'politicians'; and 51 per cent are 'hybrids'.[21] Howe and Kaufman find that approval for procedural interventions is consistently related to role preferences, with politicians most favourable and technicians least favourable. In particular, politicians as a group view both distribution of information and active involvement as ethical and are least disapproving of modifications of emphasis.

The political developments which have stimulated public concern about procedural issues have led to perceptions by a growing variety of groups that they are poorly represented in decisions. Thus planners' actions which increase the access of only some interests are hardly likely to satisfy this diversity of constituents. Hence it is important to inquire on behalf of whose interests planners may approve procedural interventions. Specifically, if planners favour increased participation primarily for those who have already dominated planning decisions, then the traditionally excluded will not be satisfied.

Howe and Kaufman's research permits observations about this question as well. Their scenarios may be classified according to the interests served: whether they would benefit the poor or racial minorities; business, developers, or a white citizens' group; or the physical environment, which may serve many interests.[22] Planners as a group most strongly approve procedural intervention related to environmental issues and regard only those as definitely ethical (average of 2.53). Actions benefiting either the poor or business are adjudged somewhat more unethical than not (averages of 3.27 and 3.29, respectively). Although role differences are probably not statistically significant, the politicians are more likely to approve interventions for the poor than for business, and the opposite is true for technicians.

These findings indicate that, although many planners are sceptical about the possibility of discovering a unitary public interest, planners are most likely to approve of procedural interventions when they appear to benefit everyone. They apparently would be inclined against interventions which would support one interest against another, perhaps because such actions would be likely to involve planners themselves in conflict. This seeming even-handedness toward business and the poor may express a belief, contrary to Vasu's finding, that neutrality is both desirable and possible.

The Ability to Intervene

Do planners act as they say they should? Because planners' actions have not been systematically studied, it is impossible to answer this crucial question definitively. Howe and Kaufman report that for each of their hypothetical scenarios at least 75 per cent of their respondents say that they would act consistently with what they prescribe.[23] My study of planners offers another indication of planners' likely actions.

Planners were asked what they regard as their personal strengths as practitioners. Responses were categorized according to whether planners emphasized intellectual or interpersonal expertise. Although there is not exact correspondence of those terms to the terms of this essay, intellectual expertise is generally substantive expertise, and interpersonal expertise is normally procedural expertise. Asked to describe their practical strengths, 42 per cent mentioned intellectual expertise exclusively; another 26 per cent mentioned intellectual expertise primarily with a secondary mention of interpersonal expertise; 8 per cent mentioned interpersonal expertise first with a secondary mention of intellectual expertise; and 22 per cent mentioned interpersonal expertise exclusively. [24] Although these responses are not unambiguous, one can group them into a majority of approximately two-thirds who emphasize intellectual expertise exclusively or primarily and approximately one-third who emphasize interpersonal expertise exclusively or primarily.

These two groups emphasize distinct abilities. The two-thirds who refer to intellectual expertise speak of competence in physical planning, social planning, or both. They emphasize expertise in such matters as waterfront ecology, road layout, housing programmes, hospital design, and social service policies. In contrast, many of those who refer to interpersonal expertise focus on procedures in the organizational realm where planning takes place. For example, one administrator emphasized his skills 'as a manager, synergist, where I can bring together different disciplines, where I can orchestrate things, and out of it comes something physical'.[25] Another observed that he had

> been able to break through barriers and get people to talk with each other. We have to resolve differences which will occur unless we do communicate. Coordination, communication is so vital to these things.[26]

Some of these planners represent themselves as tacit mediators of conflicting world-views and interests; others portray themselves as overtly political negotiators.

Along with claimed competence, the cognitive maps of these two groups also differ. The minority who believe they have interpersonal competence perceive a world of people and politics: actors have interests, their interests come into conflict, and planning entails some mediation of these conflicts. In such a world, political experiences challenge the possibility of discovering a unitary public interest or of establishing a neutral position on a planning issue. Procedural difficulties are paramount. Typically, a regional planner calls attention to

> coordination and synthesis and understanding what different people mean – finding some language which both can understand and agree on. In an organization like this, it is like a United Nations. You have all sorts of disciplines inside. On the council you have all sorts of disciplines on the outside. Some of them don't use the same words. Some of them use the same words to mean different things. A lot of the air needs clearing [in order to understand] what is being said, what is meant.[27]

In contrast, the majority who believe they have intellectual competence perceive a world of impersonal ideas and information: data about the world are available, and planning entails some logical organization of those data. The available data are not political, but more or less technical. These data do not tangibly affect a belief in a unitary public interest or political neutrality. Procedural problems do not arise. Indeed, a fantasy world, free from political conflict, is clearly portrayed by a veteran architect-planner:

> The best and worst things that have happened in the physical environment have happened under despots and patrons. It means that important things that have happened in the design aspect of the physical world when people were in the position to make physical acts of will – the redevelopment of Paris under von Haussman, Baroque Rome, Pope Sixtus, Imperial Rome, Greece, all those city planning design achievements, Italian Renaissance, Medicis, Louis of France Versailles . . . There has to be control. If people like myself are going to create good environments, we have to have an opportunity to do it.[28]

Thus planners' beliefs about their competence are congruent with specialized world-views. How such a correspondence comes about is unclear. Other comments by planners suggest that those claiming interpersonal competence are more comfortable working with people and their feelings than are planners claiming intellectual competence. As a result, the interpersonal planners are able to see a world in which personal and political interests exist and matter. In contrast, many of the intellectual planners tend to be anxious in personal contacts and may retreat to intellectual activities because these provide greater security. Consistently, they do not see political actors in their worlds, but only impersonal technical data.[29] Such an explanation would help to interpret the contrast between the high proportion of planners, mentioned earlier, who want more power and the considerably lower proportion, described here, who speak without any specificity about the political relations which such a change would involve. Only the interpersonally competent may be sufficiently secure to see and think about political strategies required to empower planners.

These findings help to explain apparent paradoxes in responses to Vasu's survey. Questions about a public interest and value neutrality do not necessarily engage planners' personal practice. In responding, they may refer to their own conflicts over planning as an indication of a breakdown in social consensus. However, for planners with intellectual, impersonal, cognitive maps, these questions are abstract: the data to which they refer are not those which these planners normally encounter and, as a result, do not necessarily affect personal role formulation. Further, the implication that breakdown in political consensus requires planners to work directly with interested actors arouses anxiety for many planners. Thus specific questions about planners' roles may continue to evoke strongly felt commitments to politically neutral roles. These are roles in which a majority of planners feel both most comfortable and most confident.

Interpretations

Because of differences in frameworks and methodologies, as well as the aggregate character of published data, it is difficult to draw firm conclusions from comparing these studies. Howe and Kaufman suggest that conflicting data be interpreted as the expressions of relatively discrete groups of planners. Thus a small group (approximately one-fifth) of planners, labelled 'politicians', may both perceive a conceptual crisis in public action and favour experimental procedural interventions by planners. A relatively larger group, perhaps one-half of planners, labelled 'technicians', probably do not perceive a conceptual crisis and insist instead on planners' traditional technical role of substantive expert. A third group, of uncertain size, possibly around one-third of planners, who may be called 'hybrids', hold less clearly interpretable beliefs about the political environment and about appropriate planning roles; perhaps they combine political and technical roles.[30]

My own study helps to interpret conflicting data in terms of planners' feelings about their actions. Howe and Kaufman's portrayals of 'politicians' and 'technicians' are consistent with these study findings. However, this study offers an alternative interpretation of the 'hybrids'. What may characterize many 'hybrids', more than intellectual compromise between political and technical terms, is psychological ambivalence between them. The 'hybrids' may include many planners who, on the one hand, accurately perceive a breakdown in consensus on traditional planning roles but, on the other hand, anxiously resist more active efforts to influence planning procedures.

Thus they may vacillate between the political and technical positions, ultimately settling on the more traditional technical role because it is the one in which they feel most comfortable.[31]

These two interpretations are complementary. They converge in identifying two basic responses to the crisis of public action. Only a minority regard planning as part of a political field. Some even explicitly formulate planning challenges in the terms of this essay, but most generally conceptualize their work as finding reasonable courses of action which draw support from a wide range of active political interest. Still, only some of these 'political' planners are especially interested in including the traditionally excluded, while others tend toward the traditionally powerful.

In contrast, a majority of planners regard planning as an essentially intellectual activity. Some acknowledge a crisis in public action – or, at least, in support for planning – but believe that the crisis is the responsibility of professional politicians. In some way or another, most believe that their recommendations serve a public interest, but few consider specifically what the public interest might mean, and few give special attention to groups which have not been represented in past planning decisions. Drawing on the profession's past, these 'technical' planners see themselves as disinterested experts serving the public at large.

The problem with which this position leaves planners is that, insofar as the poor and racial minorities believe that they have been poorly represented in planning decisions, such efforts at neutrality may not satisfy them or persuade them that public planning 'works' for them. By retreating from the ethnic, racial, and economic conflicts which explicit advocacy would evoke, planners do not avoid these conflicts or contain the conceptual crisis but only intensify them.

THE FUTURE OF PLANNERS

Public action in America is constrained by a conceptual crisis, in which there is little consensus among diverse groups about purposes for governmental action. As designers of governmental programmes and projects, planners suffer from this withdrawal of legitimacy. Planners suffer additionally from their identification with a social planning model which emphasizes participation of the traditionally excluded and which portends increased public conflict. If planners are to influence the future design of the physical and social environments, they must persuade members of the public that their services are useful. Above all, they must persuade citizens that they can solve the important problem of providing new rationales for public interventions which affect private interests and promote a public good.

There are no easy prescriptions for planners who hold such interests for both themselves and the public. To regain legitimacy, planners must develop an understanding of the social, as well as the physical, environment. In terms of substantive expertise, planners will need to learn more about the problems of poverty, racial discrimination, unemployment, and the growing anxiety over decreased opportunities. More importantly, planners must develop new procedural expertise. Planners must recognize their role as procedural actors and must understand how their actions affect the structure of participation in government.[32] In particular, planners must recognize that their traditional technocratic role has lost public legitimacy, and they must work to broaden their constituencies by developing new models of participation and planning. This does not mean that planners should drop intellectual rigour to become purely political actors. Rather, they should learn to recognize political interests when they formulate problems and recommend solutions for them.

Planners' future depends on which of the two basic groups dominates the profession's thinking and actions. Each group suggests a different scenario. One rests on the possibility that most planners will continue to do what most planners do now. In this future, planners tender advice on specific substantive issues, and they refrain from involvement in procedural problems, for several reasons. Some believe that procedural intervention, because apparently political, would be unprofessional. Some believe they lack the competence to intervene effectively. Some find confrontation anxiety-inducing and choose to withdraw. In the end, most continue to work as technical advisors in public bureaucracies while the legitimacy of those bureaucracies and government continues to decline.

Although it is unrealistic to imagine that planners alone can resolve a growing national crisis, their action, nevertheless, leaves initiatives to other actors, such as lawyers and politicans. Their attempts to instill public action with new purpose, however, mainly amplifies the tendencies which contributed to the crisis. A growing number of conflicts become embroiled in litigation. Although lawyers are concerned with conflict resolution, their procedures are adversarial. The lawyer's job is to help one private client defeat another, rather than to foster a compromise between the two. Although lawyers are concerned with procedural problems, their concern is conservative: they adhere to past procedures, rather than searching for new ones. Thus growing litigation to resolve conflicts only increases the procedural crisis.

As this scenario progresses, the procedural crisis becomes overtly politicized. Legislative initiatives typify the orientation of all branches of government: they are concerned primarily with defending narrow well-organized private interests, rather than creating shared, public, interest. Growing stalemates over government budgets register the breakdown of confidence in a collective public interest justifying collective action. No interest in devising new principles for conflict resolution may be found in legislative bills, executive initiatives, or court decisions. Because dominant public principles favour private market actions, the scope of government activity diminishes. The wealthy and powerful are most often the beneficiaries of government decisions, and the poor, powerless, and racial minorities are most often the victims. Further, as trust in public action wanes, partisans bypass legislative processes and seek to establish their interests in ballooning federal, state and local constitutions and charters. Although this course of events appears to protect the middle and working classes from challenges by the poor, particularly by racial minorities, the losers increasingly despair of getting any redress from public action. Polarization increases. Public action loses still more accepted purpose.

As the public domain contracts, planning agencies have fewer legal mandates. Public agencies which continue to operate generally find their recommendations ignored. When private developers are forced to present proposals to planning departments, the developers inevitably get their way, because their staffs of planners, economists, and attorneys persuasively defend their proposals against weak notions of public interests forwarded by the planning agencies. Planners gradually become a moderately respected, small, and rarely consulted profession.[33]

This scenario is likely if planners resist grappling with the crisis of legitimacy for public action. An alternative scenario arises from the possibility that planners recognize the loss of public purpose as a planning problem and seek to fashion new purposes which have the assent of members of a heterogeneous society. Crucial in this scenario is planners' efforts to articulate the meaning of the crisis, both in their encounters with clients and constituents and in statements issued by planning agencies. Here, planners begin to make explicit – and thus discussable – matters which have concerned numerous citizen groups for a considerable time: bias in governmental actions, exclusion from public decisions, and fear of continual defeat or elimination by other interests. Planners' articulation of these issues in itself gives them greater credibility with groups who feel increasingly disenfranchised and ignored.

Planners are guided in this effort by several traditional planning principles. Perhaps most important is a belief that planning recommendations should be informed by some notion of public interest which transcends private interests. Planners do not deceive themselves about the simplicity of such a pub'ic interest or the ease of discovering one. However, this concern leads them to think about collective interests and conflict resolution, rather than win-lose situations and zero-sum proposals. Faith in the possibilities of devising collective actions is bolstered by planners' traditional interest in design. Planners are concerned with creating both physical environments and social institutions which respond to diverse, often conflicting, requirements. A new group of planners approach the design of new decision-making procedures as a challenge like that of designing complex living environments. One other traditional planning principle makes planners sensitive to the complexity of design and yet pushes them further when procedural design seem difficult: concern with the future consequences of present actions. Planners appreciate that failure to work on procedural problems will only lead to disintegration of support for government, including planning agencies.

As this scenario unfolds, a growing number of planners resume experiments in social planning and they attempt to increase public participation in problem-solving. In doing so, they search for models which would include traditional losers in planning and reconcile some of their interests with those of middle-income earners and businesses. Planning departments strengthen or re-establish community planning divisions; they send planners to work with local communities, particularly those of the poor and racial minorities. These community planners offer technical assistance to neighbourhood associations and submit proposals to the associations for review and comment. Planning departments develop the policy of inviting all interested parties not only to public hearings, but also to informal staff consultations, in order to explicate and attempt to resolve differences.

Participation in these forums is not always easy, nor is it without conflict. Further, it is often difficult for planners to avoid taking sides – or, at least, to be perceived as taking sides. However, planners' insistence on including more parties, as well as efforts to articulate their interests, adds to public confidence in public institutions. Meetings often bog down in confused debate, but frequently participants leave with growing faith that these meetings express a sincere interest in incorporating ideas of the public into the decision-making process. Although citizens initially resist the conclusion, many gradually come to believe that these meetings force them to take responsibility for decisions. Thus motivated, they sometimes put forth new ideas which contribute to new ways of making decisions. Other times, even though overt conflicts do not seem to be intellectually resolved, participants feel as if they were listened to, and even traditional types of decisions seem acceptable.

At the same time, the national professional association of planners initiates two projects which move planners beyond their traditional domains to work with others who influence social decision-making procedures. The association establishes a work group to identify the range of governmental units whose actions affect procedural design and to define new roles for planners in these units. For example, in the executive branch, planners begin to work in departments of justice and a variety of regulatory agencies. Planners join the staffs of legislative committees in preparing middle-range agendas. In addition, some planners begin work with federal and lower courts in analysing strategies for hearing cases on appeal.

The association's second project is to assemble multidisciplinary study groups which will examine the sources of the crisis in public purpose and identify directions for formulating new public consensus. Dropping earlier concerns about protecting professional boundaries, the planners' association convenes meetings with lawyers, designers, sociologists, community psychiatrists, mediators, political scientists, administrators, analysts, anthropologists, judges, organizers, legislators, historians, and others. In initiating these task groups, the association is doing what planners traditionally have done: when they encounter problems, they call on whoever has relevant expertise. Normally, these problems have been substantive problems, and planners have called on substantive experts. When the problems are procedural, now planners assemble new networks of experts. These work groups slowly begin to formulate policy recommendations for public and private action and initiate meetings with policy-makers to discuss implementation.

It can hardly be said that planners' efforts alone will resolve the conceptual crisis in government. However, the initiatives of their professional association send forth ripples which create a new public dialogue on matters of public purpose. New programmes recognize the problems of poverty and racial exclusion and organize a public attack on them. Simultaneously, the re-opened channels of participation in local planning persuade diverse citizen groups that new language of public purpose is matched by intentions to incorporate a broad range of interests in public programmes. In small but growing ways, the public comes to regard 'planners' as experts who can be of assistance to them in helping to confront and solve some urgent public problems. The identity of 'planners' changes. Not only are many substantive experts, but many are acquiring expertise in procedural matters as well.[34]

The Professions of Planners

Planning is built on the premise that action guided by intelligence is preferable to action without intelligence. And yet at present there is disagreement about where action should be taken and which intelligence may be a useful guide. Planners' future depends on the ways in which their own internal conflicts about these issues are resolved. Indeed, it may be accurate to say that planners comprise two professions, each with a different image of society and a different norm for practice. Although most planners express concern for the public interest, design, and the future, the two professions of planners interpret these concerns quite differently.

The 'technocratic' profession concentrates on gathering intelligence on traditionally-defined problems. It recognizes crisis neither in public purpose nor in planners' relations with clients, and it adheres to a faith that intelligence of any kind will eventually find its constituency. The other planning profession is difficult to name; the labels 'social', 'political', and 'participative' each contribute helpful connotations, although none is sufficient. This profession recognizes a crisis in public purpose and haltingly attempts to respond. Uncertainly, members of this profession acknowledge that planners' conventional role must be considered a problem to be resolved. Although the technocrats' faith in the power of intelligence is an affirmation of the role of reason in public affairs, this second planning profession is concerned that the technocrats may be providing thoughtful solutions for simply the wrong problems. This second planning profession is concerned not only about using reason in public affairs, but also about finding reasons for public affairs.

In the end, the future of the planning profession, while important to planners, is a small stake compared to the future of government in society. Although planning is carried out in many realms, the activities of the planners described here have long been tied to the public sector, and the uncertainties in their future reflect conflict over the extent and direction of public activities in society. As planners deliberate about their own future, they need to recognize these larger, contextual issues. Thus planners may identify their own private interests with a public purpose as well.

NOTES

1. Marris, Peter (1982) *Community Planning and Conceptions of Change.* London: Routledge and Kegan Paul, p. 62.

2. See Lubove, Roy (1962) *Progressives and the Slums: Tenement House Reform in New York City, 1890–1917.* Pittsburgh: University of Pittsburgh Press, chapter 8; Marcuse, Peter (1980) Housing policy and city planning: the

puzzling split in the United States, in Cherry, Gordon (ed.) *Shaping an Urban World*. London: Mansell, 23–58; and Scott, Mel (1969) *American City Planning Since 1890*. Berkeley: University of California Press, chapter 3.

3. See Brownell, Blaine A. (1980) Urban planning, the planning profession, and the motor vehicle in early twentieth-century America, in Cherry, Gordon (ed.) *Shaping an Urban World*. London: Mansell, pp. 59–77.

4. See Callow, Alexander B. (1982) The crusade against the tweed ring, in Callow, Alexander B. Jr. (ed.) *American Urban History*, 3rd ed. New York: Oxford University Press, pp. 191–209; Chudacoff, Howard P. (1981) *The Evolution of American Urban Society*, 2nd ed. Englewood Cliffs: Prentice-Hall, chapter 6; Glaab, Charles N. and Brown, A. Theodore (1983) *A History of Urban America*, 3rd ed. New York: Macmillan, chapters 9 and 10; and Hays, Samuel P. (1982) The changing political structure of the city in urban America, in Callow, Alexander B. Jr. (ed.) *American Urban History*, pp. 240–61.

5. See Kent, T.J. Jr. (1964) *The Urban General Plan*. San Francisco: Chandler Publishing Company, chapter 2; Scott, Mel (1969) *American City Planning Since 1890*. Berkeley: University of California Press, chapters 3 and 4; and Wilson, William H. (1983) Moles and skylarks, in Krueckeberg, Donald A. (ed.) *Introduction to Planning History in the United States*. New Brunswick: Centre for Urban Policy Research, Rutgers University, pp. 89–121.

6. For discussion of the alignments of different groups of planners with different sides in the post-war redevelopment debate, see Bauman, John F. (1983) Visions of a post-war city: A perspective on urban planning in Philadelphia and the nation, 1942–1945, in Krueckeberg, Donald A. (ed.) *Introduction to Planning History in the United States*, pp. 170–89. For analysis of a prototypical privately funded urban redevelopment programme, see Lubove, Roy (1969) *Twentieth-Century Pittsburgh: Government, Business and Environmental Change*. New York: John Wiley and Sons, chapters 6 and 7. For evaluation of the class interests served by public urban renewal programmes, see Weiss, Marc (1980) The origins and legacy of urban renewal, in Clavel, Pierre, Forester, John F. and Goldsmith, William W. (eds.) *Urban and Regional Planning in an Age of Austerity*. New York: Pergamon Press, pp. 53–80.

7. See also Fainstein, Susan S., Fainstein, Norman I., Hill, Richard Child, Judd, Dennis and Smith, Michael Peter (1983) *Restructuring the City: The Political Economy of Urban Redevelopment*. New York: Longman.

8. In an important sense, the Model Cities Programme resurrected concerns of some of the early urban reformers. In particular, housing reformers continued to advocate social interventions and redistributive programmes. However, their interests were submerged in the formal organization and expression of the planning profession. For a reminder of the connections between interests of contemporary housers and early urban reformers, see Bauman (1983) *op. cit.*, pp. 170–89. For an analysis of reasons for the limited influence of the housers, see Marcuse, *op. cit.*, pp. 23–58.

9. For an interesting analysis of changes in planners' claimed expertise, see Bailey, Joe (1980) *Ideas and Intervention: Social Theory for Practice*. London: Routledge and Kegan Paul, chapter 5.

10. See Baum, Howell S. (1983) *Planners and Public Expectations*. Cambridge: Schenkman Publishing Company.

11. Vasu, Michael Lee (1979) *Politics and Planning: A National Study of American Planners*. Chapel Hill: University of North Carolina Press. Vasu mailed a questionnaire on planning roles and political values to a random sample drawn from the 1974 roster of members of the American Institute of Planners, the national professional association of planners. There were 775 respondents.

12. Howe, Elizabeth (1983) Planners' Views of the Public Interest, Paper presented at the Annual Meeting of the Association of Collegiate Schools of Planning, San Francisco, presents preliminary study findings which indicates that most planners still favour the concept of a public interest as a justification for their recommendations. However, planners have adjusted the meaning of the concept in various ways to deal with the reality of conflict in which there are disgruntled losers as well as satisfied winners. Some planners make ungrounded assumptions about the legitimacy of the planning process as justification for a recommendation serving a putative public interest. Others elevate the concept of public interest to sufficient abstraction as to overlook the realities of defeat and dissatisafaction.

13. Baum *op. cit.* The author conducted 1½ hour semi-structured interviews on planning roles and values with a random sample of members of the Maryland Chapter of the American Institute of Planners. The fifty interviewees resembled American planners generally in age, sex, race, income, and place of employment.

14. The following discussion of these study findings refers to 'a number of planners', 'some planners', 'several planners', and so forth. Sometimes the qualitative character of the data prevents greater precision. In addition, where small parts of a relatively small sample are involved, greater precision would be misleading. These references to groups of planners in this section may be understood to identify subgroups of the larger groups of 10 per cent, 20 per cent, and 42 per cent of the sample as a whole. Similar references in subsequent sections may be interpreted in the same way. For more extensive statistical summaries of findings, see Baum *op. cit.*

15. Baum *op. cit.*, p. 98.

16. *Ibid.*, p. 123.

17. *Ibid.*, p. 124.

18. Howe, Elizabeth, and Kaufman, Jerome (1979) The ethics of contemporary American planners. *Journal of the American Planning Association*, **45**, pp. 243–55. Howe and Kaufman developed a series of planning vignettes and asked respondents to assess the ethics in the stories; in addition, the researchers asked respondents about their planning and political values. Their randomly selected sample of members of the American Institute of Planners included 616 respondents.

19. For purposes of this analysis, I have categorized Howe and Kaufman's scenarios in the following way: modifications in emphasis include scenario numbers 2, 3, 10, and 11; distribution of information includes 1, 4, 7, 9, 12, and 14; and active involvement includes 5, 6, 8, 13, and 15. It should be kept in mind that a *lower* mean score on Howe and Kaufman's rating system

corresponds to a *higher* percentage stating that an action is ethical.

20. This surprising finding may be related to specific elements in the five scenarios which I have included in this category. Two of the five focus on actions by planning directors, who may be expected to act more politically than subordinate staff. One other refers to advocacy by a planner on private time, a matter which may not concern others in their professional roles. More speculation than this is difficult, since average scores do not reveal anything about the distribution of responses.

21. Approximately 5 per cent were not classified into any role. These percentages exceed 100 as a result of rounding off.

22. For this analysis, I have categorized Howe and Kaufman's scenarios as follows: those benefiting the poor and racial minorities include 2, 4, 6, 7, and 10; those benefiting business or a white citizen's group include 3, 7, 11, 12, and 14; and those benefiting the environment include 1, 9, 13, and 15. One scenario benefits the planning department in general but no other interests in particular.

23. Howe and Kaufman, *op. cit.*, p. 248.

24. One person did not respond to the question. See Baum, *op. cit.*, chapter 2.

25. *Ibid.*, p. 59.

26. *Ibid.*, p. 59.

27. *Ibid.*, p. 191.

28. *Ibid.*, pp. 194–95.

29. *Ibid.*, chapter 6.

30. It should be clear that, while the labels for the groupings are Howe and Kaufman's, the estimates of their distribution are drawn from all three studies.

31. For an elaboration of this analysis, see Baum, Howell S. (1983) Politics and ambivalence in planners' practice. *Journal of Planning Education and Research*, 3, pp. 13–22.

32. For an excellent examination of the ways in which planners are inescapably procedural intervenors, see Forester, John (1982) Know your organizations: planning and the reproduction of social and political relations. *Plan Canada*, 22, pp. 3–13.

33. For a description of a number of these developments as recent history, see Fainstein, Susan S. *et. al.* (1983) *Restructuring the City*. New York: Longman.

34. Some of the forecasted modifications in planners' practice are resurrections of practices from the Model Cities and community planning experiments of the 1960s. For critical analyses of these practices, see Marris, Peter, and Rein, Martin (1982) *Dilemmas of Social Reform*, 2nd ed. Chicago: University of Chicago Press; and Needleman, Martin and Needleman, Carolyn Emerson (1974) *Guerrillas in the Bureaucracy*. New York: John Wiley. An example of the development of work groups on societal problems is the American Academy of Arts and Sciences' 1965–1966 meetings of the Commission on the Year 2000, reported in Bell, Daniel (ed.) (1969) *Toward the Year 2000: Work in Progress*. Boston: Beacon Press.

Chapter Twelve

The Future of the Metropolitan Region

DAVID R. GOLDFIELD

For the metropolitan region in the United States, the future is the past. The current configuration of our evolving regions represents the acting out in spatial terms of an American culture extending back to the white man's early settlements, when the sheer abundance and expanse of the land astounded the European to whom land spelt wealth and power. The availability and temptation of the land even dissected and dissipated the tight New England communities, the new zions in the wilderness that eventually fell from the mountaintop to serve as commercial depots for an expanding farm hinterland. True enough men settled in cities, but urban land, too, occupied a major role as a sought-after commodity, a planning base, and an accessible status symbol. And some men, as fast as they could sell it, left, for the centrifugal forces that have pushed urban settlement and settlers outward for more than a century came as natural as the land itself.

THE URBAN REGION

In 1821, not long after the commissioners fixed a relentless grid on New York City, Phillip Hone noted that long-time city residents were moving out to the periphery 'in flocks', where 'orchards, cornfields, or morasses' vied for space with the new suburbanites. There they pitched their characteristic dwelling – the single-family home accompanied by a plot of land – a land-use pattern that had already assumed the characteristic of a cultural moré. 'A man is not a whole and complete man', Brooklyn poet Walt Whitman intoned, 'unless he owns a house and the ground it stands on'. And the outward trend provoked the same concern that such movement generates today; the *New York Tribune* expressed this concern in 1847:

> Property is continually tending from our city to escape the oppressiveness of our taxation; many who have made fortunes here carrying them away to be expended and enjoyed . . Thus, while every suburb of New York is rapidly growing, and villages twenty and thirty miles distant are sustained by incomes earned here and expended there, our City has no equivalent rapidity of growth, and unimproved property here is often unsalable at a nominal price.[1]

The proclivity documented by the *Tribune* was a new phenomenon in the western world; elsewhere, the city centre had assumed a thick layer of cultural meaning that riveted affluent residents. The wanderlust of Americans may be explained, as Hector de Crevecoeur noted two centuries ago, by their love of newness and nature. When H.G. Wells predicted the future shape of the American metropolis in 1902, he explained that 'The passion for nature . . . and that craving for a little private imperium are the chief centrifugal inducements . . . The city will diffuse itself until it has taken upon considerable areas and many of the characteristics of what is now country . . . We may call . . . these coming town provinces "urban regions".[2] Of course, the peripatetic American would not be able to satiate these passions were it not for the abundance of land and the growth of an affluent, consumer-oriented society – attributes present in considerably lesser quantities in most of the industrialized world.

The spatial diffusion represented by these 'urban regions' reflects the general diffusion of our lives. Delos F. Wilcox noted as early as 1907 that 'a man's most intimate associates may be scattered over the whole city, while he scarcely knows his next door neighbor's name'.[3] In the post-World-War-II era, it is even possible to speak of national rather than regional communities. As geographer, Brian J.L. Berry observed, 'the experiences of national community may be more frequent and real than experiences of local community'.[4] Little wonder, as Frank Lloyd Wright foresaw, that the home would become the centre of the local universe while we live out our lives in regional and national contexts. As Kevin Lynch averred: 'Our senses are local, while our experiences are regional'.[5]

Indeed in some metropolitan areas, we have arrived at the cityless or centreless metropolis. Our sports teams are no longer named for cities, but for states or regions: the Minnesota Twins, California Angels, Golden State Warriors, and the New England Patriots, for example. Even more traditional designations reflect anachronism rather than reality. The New York Jets and the New York Giants now play in suburban New Jersey; the Los Angeles Rams have abandoned the city for suburban Anaheim; and the Detroit Lions play their home games in the indoor comfort of the Silverdome in Pontiac. But the decreasing identification between our beloved teams and their cities merely reflects our general propensity for drift within an amorphous metropolitan region. As one Orange County, California resident put it: 'I live in Garden Grove, work in Irvine, shop in Santa Ana, go to the dentist in Anaheim, my husband works in Long Beach, and I used to be the president of the League of Women Voters in Fullerton'.[6]

A SLOWING OF SUBURBAN SPRAWL

This does not imply that we are forever condemned as some Thomas Wolfe character to a lifetime of wandering in and about the regional periphery; indeed, there are some indications that America's chronic mobility may be slackening, and that there is a settling down and a growing up in erstwhile suburbia. There is evidence that subtle but nonetheless perceptible changes have occurred over the past decade within the nation's metropolitan areas to indicate the emergence of new spatial trends. The central city is becoming less and less, both in perception and reality, the victim of chronic outward expansion. From the perspective of the 1960s and 1970s, the existence of an urban crisis was a given. The graphic portrayals of civil disturbance, the political pilgrimages to the South Bronx, and the news stories about dying, bankrupt, and decaying industrial cities stoked the perception. It was not merely media hyperbole, of course; statistics reflected staggering demographic and economic losses. If concentration and density were the pathologies of the early twentieth-century city, then the evisceration of the city a half century later became the new anxiety.

But by the 1980s, a new type of city, or more properly, three types of cities, emerged from the expanding urban region. The first type, representing an old model is the city that has failed to adjust to the post-industrial economy, a city that is doggedly clutching its weakened industrial infrastructure hoping like Mr. Micawber that something better will turn up – cities such as Gary, Detroit, and Youngstown – cities with a history of domination by one major industry that are unable to shake the deadly dependence accumulated over decades. These cities usually preside over declining urban regions as well. Then, there are the transitional cities: those urban places, formerly dependent upon an industrial base that are in the process of shifting to a diversified post-industrial economy through an expanded government sector, educational activities, and corporate services (legal, accounting, and computing services, for examples). A range of cities including Philadelphia, Chicago, Baltimore, and Birmingham comprise this growing category.

Pittsburgh is perhaps the most notable and remarkable entry in this category because of its historic ties to a domestic steel industry that collapsed in the 1970s. Today, the University of Pittsburgh is the city's leading employer. Since 1980, the steelmaking workforce has declined from 90,000 to 45,000, but the city has gained 40,000 new jobs in high-tech industries. The 'Golden Triangle' area – the point where the Allegheny and Monongahela Rivers converge to form the Ohio River – has become an international showcase of architecture and activities. An airline magazine asked recently, 'What city offers waterfront dining, international cuisine, trolley cars, and one spectacular view after another?' Perhaps visitors are not yet leaving their hearts in Pittsburgh, but a stocked city treasury indicates they are leaving other momentos behind.[7]

The transitional city, however, has not come about without some significant adjustment pains involving a public sector adaptation of private industry techniques such as personnel cutbacks, the institution of labour-saving devices, service retrenchment, and a triage concept applied to neighbourhoods and people designed to salvage what is most salvageable in human and physical terms. The transitional city is leaner, having experienced significant population and job losses. But even here, as Pittsburgh officials note, there can be advantages as the exodus of blue collar workers there and in Memphis, for example, has moderated politics and reduced service demands as well as eliminated crowding and opened the way for more propitious land use. In addition, the influx, however modest, of single and adult-oriented professionals to work in the new economy has countered population loss to some degree and has helped to maintain property values.

THE NEW CITY

The third type of city is what might be termed the new city. These are the urban areas in the South and South-west, the so-called 'Sun Belt', where 89 per cent of the nation's urban growth has occurred since 1970. These are the cities that grew up in the automobile era, located in states with liberal annexation laws, equipped with the latest infra-structure, devoid of bitter ethnic and racial legacies, and sporting a service and administrative economic base: Austin, Phoenix, and San Diego are among the more prominent of a group that also stresses lifestyle amenities. These new cities are the heirs to the regional dominance once enjoyed by the old industrial cities, although, in truth, the newer urban entities are often so vast as to be indistinguish-able from the surrounding countryside.[8]

In general terms, successful central cities, whether transitional or new, must become specialized functionally rather than attempting to generate an all-purpose environment as offered by their late-nineteenth-century predecessors. Corporate heads will continue to prefer central locations because, as sociologist John Kasarda maintains, face-to-face encounters remain essential for establishing mutual trust. Also, a Fifth Avenue or Union Square address still reflects significant prestige. And visiting executives much prefer the culture and entertainment of central cities once the business day is concluded rather than the look-alike lounges and clubs attached to freeway-oriented hotels far from the city centre. In the future, it is likely that major corporate decisions will require increased interaction, and hence proximity to the support services that have traditionally occupied the city centre, such as law firms, large banks, and insurance companies.[9]

Gone are the industries and much of the general retail trade. The changing national economy, industrial technology, and cheaper land and labour on the metropolitan periphery closed out the city's industrial function while readily accessible, comprehensive shopping centres reduced the downtown's retail potential. Although central city pedestrian malls have revived retail trade in a handful of cities, and some places such as Minneapolis and Houston have successfully duplicated the enclosed, temperate suburban malls, the retail future of the city is directed more to specialty shops that cater for an affluent office clientele and for transient customers such as convention-goers and travelling businessman. The boutique has become a retail commonplace in the central city.

The upscale retail function reflects the changing downtown workforce, a workforce becoming as specialized as the urban economy. Between 1953 and 1980, New York City lost more than 525,000 jobs in manufacturing and construction while gaining 650,000 in information-processing industries. Similar transformations occurred in the economies of Chicago, Philadelphia, and Boston. By 1980, the information-processing portion of the private-sector economy in New York had jumped, in just one decade, from 22 to 45 per cent; from 12 to 43 per cent in Philadelphia; and from 22 to 53 per cent in Boston.[10]

While many of the nation's cities were overcoming or outrunning the urban crisis of the late 1960s and early 1970s, the suburban segment of the metropolitan area was undergoing transformation as well. We may be entering what Robert Fishman referred to as the 'post-suburban' era, a period when the small residential suburban community, that venerable post-war prototype of the good life, recedes in importance or becomes part of larger relatively self-contained nodes or regional units that sociologist Jack Meltzer refers to as 'subcities'. These entities are frequently multi-purpose centres containing the ubiquitous shopping mall, hotel, office and industrial activities, and adjacent residential areas that possess not only the traditional single-family home, but condominiums and apartment houses as well.[11]

The configuration and concentration of these places has resulted from a number of factors which are likely to persist, if not accelerate, in the near future. First, the character of suburban development (some would say sprawl) depended in part on a combination of cheap energy, constantly-improving standards of living, the economic ability to sustain mass production of single-family homes in leap-frog development patterns, and massive federal subsidies. These conditions have modified to some degree or at least governments and citizenry are challenging their viability. While energy resources are not the dire problem of a decade ago, their cost remains a factor in development, both in terms of density and in distance from the workplace. In addition, the general costs of single-family homes combined with double-digit interest rates and a stabilized wage structure for the younger generation of workers have rendered the traditional dwelling and the generous land on which it rested more difficult to attain for young families in the 1980s than for their predecessors in the 1960s.

Then, of course, there are fewer young families. Single and adult-oriented households or single-parent families now comprise nearly one-half of the metropolitan housing market. For these households, the traditional dwelling may not only be beyond reach financially, but may be inappropriate to lifestyle needs. These new demographics fed the inner-city housing revival of the late 1970s and are currently providing a market for higher-density units in the suburbs, especially as the post-industrial economy finds attractive quarters on the urban periphery.

Economic and demographic conditions immediately following World War II were crucial elements in detonating the exploding metropolis. But federal policy provided the flint upon which these volatile elements could act and react. The Federal Housing Administration, established in 1934, lowered the cost of home-buying significantly, guaranteeing loans which reduced interest rates and stretching out the amortization period to twenty-five or thirty years which lowered the average monthly payment. In some cases, it became cheaper to buy than to rent. Federal income tax provisions further enhanced home ownership. By 1984, the subsidy in the form of interest payment and property tax deductions amounted to $53 billion per year. Finally, the interstate highway system, whatever its initial purpose, became from the late 1950s onward, a facilitator of suburban land development for residential and especially for commercial and industrial uses. Since 1945, in fact, 75 per cent of federal expenditures for transportation have gone to highway construction. Federal subsidies shifted, however, after the passage of the Housing and Community Development Act in 1974 which funnelled money into conservation, rehabilitation, and even to mass transit. While tax breaks remain in place, new tax provisions, especially the investment tax credit, favour urban areas. The interstate highway system is complete or, at least, built to the limits of financial and political endurance. And the FHA presence as a silent developer has diminished, especially for new residential construction.[12]

The new combination of factors – economic, demographic, and governmental – have led historian Kenneth T. Jackson to predict a 'new kind of spatial equilibrium' emerging by the early twenty-first century, a greater spatial balance between city and suburb, even the densification of the metropolitan periphery.

The outlines of the new peripheral subcities are already becoming evident, particularly as the elements of the post-industrial economy sort themselves out spatially within the metropolitan context. For the teenager or part-time worker, entry level positions abound in fast food establishments and retail outlets. For professional, highly-educated men and women, the periphery has become the new focus of technology and innovation in the metropolitan area. Out there, the sleek new research facilities, of which the Research Triangle Park in the Raleigh-Durham-Chapel Hill area of North Carolina is a proto-type, typify the attractions of peripheral locations – inexpensive land, bucolic surroundings, highway accessibility, and the proximity of a high-skilled labour pool. These concentrations are likely to mushroom in the future. Already outside Princeton, New Jersey, corporate giants such as Exxon, Xerox, Merrill Lynch, and Siemens A.G. have congregated on former potato fields taking advantage of a classy address and the educational and labour benefits of the New York-New Jersey conurbation. By 1992 office space in the Princeton area will equal downtown Milwaukee's office space and by the year 2000, the growing collection of research, office, and industrial parks will be the largest city in the state. Though Princeton Mayor Barbara Boggs Sigmund has referred to this agglomeration outside her corporate borders as 'a soulless, congested, harassing anti-city', corporations and their employees increasingly prefer such multi-purpose locations.[13]

While both the scale and diversity of these concentrations may be new phenomena of the 1980s, the beltway industries of the 1960s and 1970s were precursors and predictors of this trend. Boston's famed Route 128 led the way as far back as the 1950s. In Philadelphia it has been Route 202 and in Washington D.C. it has been the Capital Beltway. Much as the major downtown streets of yesterday functioned as magnets for the city's economic activities, these newer roads have attracted shopping centres and industries, drawn now not by efficacious rail and river connections, but by highway and airport proximity.

Both the new central city and the sometimes competing, sometimes complementary subcities have combined to present a new metropolitan prospect, a prospect more amorphous and boundaryless than census definitions would have it. The British-spawned word 'conurbation' comes to mind – a formless urban mass oozing out into the countryside with little differentiation and seemingly little order. Political scientist John J. Harrigan calls the new form a 'multicentered metropolis' which depicts well the diversity of functions once exclusively the province of the central city, now coming together in nodes some of which are far from and independent of the central city.[14] But the image of multiple centres may be too neat to describe what is in reality a more chaotic pattern of development. Jack Meltzer prefers the term 'Metroplex', which Dallas leaders first used to describe their agglomerating metropolis and which Meltzer employs to describe the collection of subcities. The Metroplex, according to Meltzer, is a 'multinucleated central place'. The inclusion of the geographer's phrase, central place, confuses the issue, as it is not clear whether the subcities include the central city and the remaining autonomous, primarily residential, suburbs that still are very much in existence in the modern metropolis.[15]

Robert Fishman's imaginative resurrection of Frank Lloyd Wright's much-maligned Broadacre City concept adds a fresh perspective in defining and describing the new metropolitan entity. But in discounting the role of the central city and in emphasizing the single-family home, Wright missed the growing diversity and specialization of the late-twentieth-century urban region. Nevertheless, the focus on the superhighway and the insight of diminishing suburb-city interdependence serve the new model well.

The evolving metropolitan configuration for the last decade of the twentieth century more closely resembles an abstract painting – a concentration of colour here, an amorphous shape over there, without any seeming connection between the various parts though artists claim there is indeed an order and a discipline to abstraction. But, identifying the future region, its components, and the factors that conspired to generate the new form are only some of the issues that lie ahead for citizens and decision-makers during the remainder of the century. Obviously, it is important to know the dynamics of the contemporary metropolitan process in order to establish policies to ensure a more equitable and efficient working of these regions. At the same time, it is also vital to discern a policy agenda and its limits in order to direct efforts toward appropriate objectives. Specifically, there are two interrelated policy concerns – governance and equity – that will determine the quality of life within the metropolitan container of the present and future.

GOVERNING THE NEW METROPOLIS

The multiplicity of governments and the complications and dupli-cations arising therefrom are well known. During the 1960s the ardour for some form of metropolitan government was especially strong, but beyond the Twin Cities Metropolitan Council and the consolidations in Nashville, Miami, and some smaller cities and counties, the interest in administrative reform at the metropolitan level subsided.

While formal government arrangements were rare in the 1960s and after, metropolitan commissions performing occasional planning review functions, gathering data, and issuing reports proliferated. In 1960 there existed only sixty-three metropolitan planning commissions, but by 1970 that figure had jumped to two-hundred. The increase was due less to keen interest in metropolitan planning than to federal government requirements of a metropolitan-wide review authority passing on federal grant applications. Purportedly the review process was to ensure that local government projects utilizing federal funds were in harmony with regional plans. Councils of Governments (COGs) dutifully followed review procedures and prepared attractive plans but their actual impact on regional planning was minimal (although smaller suburban governments found the data-gathering function of such organizations helpful in devising their own short-range plans). Planning, being a political process, did not fare well in COGs since the councils lacked a firm political base, answered to no constituency, and were supported on a strictly voluntary basis. As Edward Banfield has noted: 'No competent politician will sacrifice votes that may be needed in the next election for gains, however large, that may accrue to the public ten, twenty, or thirty years hence'.[16] Even assuming metropolitan planning could gather a consensus from the diverse constituency inhabiting contem-porary urban regions, it is doubtful that they could move politicians interested in immediate results and short-term policies.

The waning sentiment for metropolitan governance and planning has led John J. Harrigan to refer to the 1980s as 'a post-reform period'.[17] This should not imply that the various entities within today's urban regions are like so many planets spinning wildly off their axes and eventually out of the solar system altogether. Local governments are becoming more resoureful in areas of service provision and management, often looking to 'extra-terrestrial' bodies to perform certain functions. Elected officials, in fact, are increasingly circumscribed in their powers. Federal programmes in the post-war era generated local bureaucracies – housing authorities, social service agencies, transportation commissions, and semi-public development corporations – that siphoned policy-making roles away from the direct political process. In addition, in the service realm, some financially-strapped suburban governments have privatized functions, contracting with private firms for garbage collection, for example. Or, they have cooperated with neighbouring governments to contract out certain services. Special districts have become a particularly favourite service provision tool since, unlike localities, the districts need not adhere to state debt and revenue-raising restrictions. The special district rose to prominence to administer federal programmes in public housing, community development, and natural resources. There are also metropolitan districts to handle transit, sewage, water supply, and airport services, and in some urban regions multi-purpose metropolitan districts have formed in order to improve coordination of these functions. So while formal metropolitan-wide government remains the unusual case in regional governance, there is a back-door movement to capitalize on the economies of scale. A major problem looming in the future, however, is reduced accountability – both fiscally and politically – as these bodies multiply. In fact, the average suburban resident today probably has little conception of who provides certain services and who pays for them.[18]

While there has been some centripetal movement with respect to service provision, the legacies of the late 1960s and 1970s in terms of decentralization of authority remain to provide a participatory, grass roots counter to the bureaucratic-technocratic government arising almost surreptitiously in the urban region. Neighbourhood-based governance received a significant boost from a variety of converging trends two decades ago. First, there was widespread revulsion against the depredations of the federal urban renewal programme: the destruction of neighbourhoods, the failure to provide sufficient numbers of housing units in return, and the deleterious impact of freeway systems on the social and structural fabric. Second, and related to the first, there was increasing interest in historic preservation, not only as a result of supportive federal legislation in 1966 and the bicentennial celebration a decade later, but also from the growing consciousness of the finitude of resources and the importance of maintaining links with the past in America's highly-mobile society. The civil rights movement also provided a motivation for neighbourhood organizations with its emphasis on minority political power and its successful challenges to at-large electoral systems. Finally, orgies of annexation in some cities and skewed allocation of services and resources in others prompted citizens from a broad socioeconomic range to challenge local government.[19]

One result of the neighbourhood movement was to decentralize the planning function and alter the traditional thrust of planning work. City officials found it politically expeditious and, after the passage of the 1974 Housing and Community Development Act, legally necessary, to consult with citizens at some point in the planning process. Thus, at a time when local governments were erecting bureaucratic mechanisms that reduced electoral account- ability, they began to create procedures designed to enhance citizen- government relations. The planner became a key actor, frequently serving as a liaison between neighbourhood and government. As an individual who perceived the city from an interdisciplinary perspective and who possessed the ability to communicate relatively free of jargon, the planner assumed more the role of a social service worker than a neutral technocrat engaging in comprehensive planning. The danger for the planner and his profession, however, was that identification with neighbourhood groups, especially those comprised of minority residents, could reduce both his credibility and effectiveness. The change in emphasis to process as opposed to plan expands the planner's purview at the same time as it might narrow his influence. The result could be that neighbourhood groups that believe they have a conduit to city hall may be frustrated when they discover that avenue leads nowhere. Already, the ardour over neigh- bourhood self-governance is waning among local officials and some cities, notably Atlanta, have reduced the formal linkages between planners and neighbourhood organizations. As it is, these officials are increasingly beseiged by what Ken Auletta has termed 'a plethora of special interest groups', of which the neighbourhoods comprise a vocal and potent portion. The danger is policy paralysis, a disease which gripped New York City during the late 1970s, and which circumscribes even further the boundaries within which local government can act.[20]

Increasingly, therefore, as local government delegates service re- sponsibilities and as its leaders feel constricted by the realities of interest group politics, the metropolitan area has become a beehive of economic development activity. Politicians can argue that economic development is a neutral activity that ultimately benefits the entire community. Further, they point to the necessity of keeping pace with the changing national economy. The examples of Cleveland and Newark are frequently injected as reminders of the fate that awaits laggards – and also the fact that the federal well, so deep and swiftly flowing for nearly a half century, is running dry.

Of course, the emphasis on economic development is not a new metropolitan phenomenon. City officials learned quickly after World War II, as John Bauman notes, to utilize federal housing legislation for developmental purposes having little relationship to shelter provision. Suburban governments, relying heavily on the property tax as a revenue base, and confronted with primarily residential land use and mounting service costs, actively sought industry and shopping centres to reduce individual tax burdens. The federal government subsidized these urban and suburban recruitment efforts, unwittingly or otherwise. The federal system itself implied relatively wide local discretion with federal funds. The urban renewal programme was the first major indication of loose local interpretation of federal intent. More recently, the Community Development Block Grant (CDBG), in effect since 1974, though designed to upgrade poorer neighbourhoods and their residents, has been employed increasingly for economic development projects such as industrial parks and downtown revitalization programmes.[21]

Since the Carter Administration, federal urban policy has been decidedly entrepreneurial, reinforcing local tendencies in that direction. President Carter evolved an elaborate framework of tax credits, interest rate subsidies, and other incentives to lure private investors to troubled areas of cities. The only remnant of his programme to attain reality was the Urban Development Action Grant (UDAG), an outright grant to local government for economic development programmes that local officials employed to clear blighted areas and offer an incentives package to prospective firms for constructing offices or factories on the cleared sites. President Reagan cut UDAG funds because 'they encouraged companies to invest in high cost and economically inefficient areas'. Instead, he proposed urban enterprise zones, areas designated by the Department of Housing and Urban Development (HUD) where new businesses would be eligible for tax, minimum wage, and environmental concessions. In addition, the Reagan Administration widened local discretion with respect to the utilization of CDBG and UDAG funds, though it reduced the amount of funding.[22]

In fact, the entrepreneurial thrust of federal urban policy over the past fifteen years has been the only coherent element of national urban endeavours. Though President Carter attempted to form a comprehensive national urban policy, divergent views within his administration – those who advocated aid to distressed cities and their poorer residents and those who discounted the fiscal and political efficacy of such assistance and who opted for more general policies – undermined his objectives, not to mention foreign policy and management distractions. The Reagan Administration has sorted out the debate by eschewing most previous policies in favour of a comprehensive economic development agenda that would benefit cities, among other entities, in the national economy. This is not to say that, given another administration, an alternative is possible, or even preferable. The federal government, especially Congress, is buffeted by a similar array of special interest groups that constrain policy formulation on the local level. Moreover, the enormity of the federal deficit precludes the maintenance of urban-related pro- grammes at 1970s levels, not to mention the addition of new programmes. The entrepreneurial bent of federal policy has the dual virtue of limiting federal responsibility and satisfying numerous interest groups. It is not surprising the local jurisdictions emphasize economic development priorities.[23]

Local policy-makers feel even more motivation to secure economic development, especially as the competition for such development sharpens and especially as the federal government reduces its social service obligations which must be picked up by state and local authorities. Mayors today are more akin to development officers than they are to their politician-predecessors. Globetrotting Atlanta Mayor Andrew Young, for example, perceives the development function as the highest priority of his administration, especially as his social service bill mounts and suburbs continue to siphon off the city's population and economic base. Local administrators will also confront an increasing need in the future to develop an infrastructure suitable for the new technology, i.e., as John D. Kasarda has suggested, a computer network to enable businesses 'quickly and efficiently [to] receive, process, store, and transmit immense amounts of data and information'. Kasarda recommends municipally-owned computer facilities and other information processing infrastructure to facilitate the administrative activities of the computer age.[24]

As government direction at all levels narrows and becomes primarily entrepreneurial, the serviceable dichotomy which has existed between public and private sectors will be less functional, if not largely irrelevant in the coming years. Of course, the dividing line has never been sharp, as David Hammack notes in his essay, but increasingly as cities assume a larger entrepreneurial role and adopt administrative techniques from private firms, the line will grow dimmer. Local officials in recent years, of necessity, have learned to slash workforces, as Tampa's Mayor (and now Governor of Florida) Bob Martinez and Baltimore Mayor Don Schaefer have done, contract out some services, install computers, devise 'work management systems', hunt for municipal profit-making endeavours such as Harrisburg, Pennsylvania Mayor Stephen Reed did when he began to burn trash and sludge and sold the resulting steam to industrial customers, or institute user fees for new development and services as many California communities did after Proposition 13. As James Peterson of the Council for Urban Economic Development has observed, 'The old mayor [spent his time] dividing up the pie for special-interest groups and going to the state and federal governments for help. The new mayor is the manager'.[25]

In keeping with the theme, major projects in the metropolitan area frequently offer a mixed-enterprise approach. Again, this is not a new development, but it represents an acceleration of public–private cooperation. In Charlotte, North Carolina, for example, the NCNB Development Corporation, the development arm of a local bank, worked closely with the city and with some federal assistance, revitalized an abandoned central city neighbourhood, the Fourth Ward, that has become a national showcase of the benefits of such cooperation. With cities renovating homes and with private firms collecting garbage, the future metropolis will be a boundless economic development engine with all cylinders working toward fiscal solvency, even profitability.

A QUESTION OF EQUITY

Just as the civil disturbances and social upheavals of the late 1960s exercised a chastening effect on government at all levels, so the financial distress of the 1970s and the realigned federal relations of the 1980s have reordered metropolitan priorities. This situation does not imply that the conditions which precipitated the social movements of the 1960s have dissipated or even moderated; indeed, there is evidence that those conditions have worsened in the ensuing two decades. Rather, local governments today find it difficult, regardless of the colour of the policy-makers, to devise strategies for *both* economic development *and* social equity. The feeling is either that the former will eventually generate the latter, or that race-specific or place-specific policies have proven unsuccessful in the past and have merely served to drain resources from the rest of the city.

As a result, three social realities have emerged in our metropolitan areas over the past two decades and will likely continue. First, blacks (and to a lesser extent, Hispanics) are overwhelmingly central-city dwellers while the types of employment most suitable to their skill levels are typically located in the suburbs. Second, within the cities a two-tier society is being formed and the gap between them is widening: between those whose skill levels fit the informational and technological requirements of the post-industrial economy and those whose skills suit a bygone industrial era or who possess no marketable skills at all. Finally, a regional imbalance has emerged with employment and affluent population shifting to favour the South and West, while poor minorities become locked into the decaying central cities of the North and Mid-West.

In 1940, less than 50 per cent of the nation's blacks resided in cities; by 1985 that figure had risen to over 80 per cent. Blacks are especially concentrated in the largest cities of the so-called Snow Belt. More than three out of four blacks reside in the central cities of the Snow Belt metropolitan areas while only one in four whites remains. The metropolitan area not only reflects a racial segmentation, but an economic division as well. In the five largest metropolitan areas of the North – New York, Chicago, Detroit, Philadelphia, and Boston – the average median family income of blacks in 1980 was $13,000, compared with $24,000 for white families; one out of three blacks lived below the poverty line, only one in thirteen whites did so. Some might argue that these doleful statistics represent a historic pattern of racial divergence, but, in fact, the gap has widened particularly over the past two decades, ironically in the aftermath of path-breaking civil rights legislation and the unprecedented entrance of blacks into the middle class.[26]

When Daniel Patrick Moynihan published his controversial book, *The Negro Family: The Case for National Action* in 1965, nearly one-quarter of all black births were out-of-wedlock; by 1980, the figure was one-half of all black births. In 1965, 25 per cent of all black families were female-headed; fifteen years later that number had increased to 41 per cent. Although blacks comprised only one out of every nine Americans, they accounted for 50 per cent of the murder arrests in 1980, with nearly half of their victims being black. In the more than three decades since the historic Supreme Court ruling in *Brown v. Board of Education of Topeka, Kansas*, the black-white unemployment ratio has remained two to one.[27]

Black sociologist William Julius Wilson argues that these statistics, coupled with the rapid expansion of the black middle class, invalidate claims that racial discrimination is responsible for the current miserable condition of the inner-city blacks and the corresponding bipolar metropolitan economic and social structure. To be sure, historic discrimination has handicapped blacks, but Wilson cites several other factors such as the concentration of the black population, a concentration maintained especially by the welfare system that limits or discourages the mobility necessary to break the cycle of dependence.[28] As John D. Kasarda has noted, 'By relying . . . on place-oriented public housing, nutritional, health care, income maintenance, and other assistance programmes, a large minority underclass has become anchored . . .'. Imagine, Kasarda asks, if black Southerners who migrated to Northern cities earlier in this century 'had been sustained in their distressed localities by public assistance'.[29]

Wilson also attributes the contemporary black metropolitan condition to the consistent nature of black migration which unlike European immigration never slowed substantially enough to allow for consolidation and absorption, though this may be happening in the 1980s. Most of all, Wilson argues, the basic shift in the American economy, its impact upon cities where blacks are most heavily concentrated, and upon the low-skilled and blue collar workforces plunged an already-depressed black urban population deeper and more permanently into poverty. By the 1980s, another complication had set in – the rapid increase in a diverse Hispanic population, less racially-identifiable, more dispersed residentially, and equally willing to compete for the finite number of menial positions available in the post-industrial economy.[30]

In 1980, President Carter's National Commission for an Agenda for the Eighties recommended that 'The nation should reconcile itself to current redistribution patterns and seek to discover in them opportunities to do new things well and old things better'. Two years later, President Reagan's *National Urban Policy Report* similarly rejected federal interference in the current intrametropolitan and interregional distributions of population and economic base: 'Urban growth in a free society is the result of decisions by many individuals, households, and firms acting independently, to cluster together in particular places'.[31] Rather than upset private decision-making, the Reagan Administration, as noted earlier, favours macroeconomic solutions to urban fiscal and social dilemmas.

Indeed, it may be that the Snow Belt-Sun Belt dichotomy is overstated – there are signs of revival even in the former rust belt and between 1980 and 1985 venerable cities such as Boston and New York added population for the first time in decades. In addition, the portrait of decaying central cities and thriving suburbs is similarly exaggerated, even inaccurate. Inner suburbs in particular are experiencing problems familiar to central-city policy-makers and the economic revivals underway in Pittsburgh and Baltimore bely the dire forecasts of the early 1970s. The Reagan Administration would point to these examples as vindication of its macroeconomic perspective, but it is not yet evident that the two-tiered employment structure and the plight of the poor have been much affected by prosperity.

What we have today and likely into the 1990s is the anomalous metropolis in terms of social equity. Gleaming downtowns will vie with peripheral office parks, while decaying neighbourhoods and hope-lost people crouch in the shadows. It is a Dickensian setting for the future – the best of times and the worst of times – what geographer Brian J.L. Berry has called a *'mosaic culture* – a society with a number of parallel and distinctively different lifestyles'. As for the incendiary potential of this 'mosaic culture', Berry is rather sanguine: 'While one result is divisive tendencies for the society as a whole, at another level, mutual harmony is produced by mutual withdrawal into homogeneous communities, exclusion and isolation from groups with different life styles and values'.[32] Jane Jacobs and others would cringe at this privatized metropolis of the future, but the devolution of government as well as the seeming prosperity of all entities within the metropolitan configuration encourage this perspective. If so, are there any policies on the horizon to respond specifically to equity questions increasingly subsumed under economic development strategies?

Planning theorist, Harvey S. Perloff, suggested two policy scenarios for the future metropolis, both emanating from past practice. First, there are what he terms the 'hard' solutions – those policies that emphasize fixed, physical structures and technology. Government agencies and private-sector corporations have historically wielded such metropolitan remedies with the current emphasis on economic development representing a melding of public and private 'hard' policies. A second policy approach, according to Perloff, involves 'soft' solutions that stress individual initiative, institutional flexibility, and social innovation. The neighbourhood movement represented a prominent example of the 'soft' approach.[33]

It may be that 'soft' policies, especially with a diminished presence of formal government institutions which are frequently too rigid and too closely identified with corporate power, could provide some amelioration to the administrative and particularly, the equity issues raised by the new metropolis. Specifically, self-help movements and voluntarism are emerging to fill some of the vacuum created by the reorientation of public policy. There is deep historical precedent for this approach: the parish churches and local businesses of the early twentieth-century immigrant neighbourhoods were schools and supporters of upward mobility. In addition, there is growing awareness that the tendency among black leaders of the 1970s to celebrate the strengths of the black community, even to the point of romanticizing the ghetto and its institutions is waning and with it a new consciousness that the best 'ghetto enrichment' policy would be its dismantling. As Orlando Patterson noted in 1977, black ethnicity had become by that date, 'a form of mystification, diverting attention from the correct kinds of solutions to the terrible economic condition of the group'.[34]

By now, the veil has lifted somewhat and black-owned and run development corporations have appeared to upgrade transitional neighbourhoods; black leaders are encouraging tough attitudes toward education; and black residents are managing public housing properties. In addition, the predominantly-white voluntary action organizations scorned in the 1970s are re-surfacing with innovative programmes in central-city neighbourhoods.[35] Moreover, the sharp decline in black central city in-migration should ease housing, employment, and discriminatory problems, according to William Julius Wilson. In this increasingly private age, when the hearth is often the limit of our social responsibility, and the automobile and personal computer its technological manifestations, solutions are apt to be private as well. If this strikes some as a resurgence of a frontier mentality it is well to note that the modern metropolis in the United States is a unique phenomenon in the world. For nowhere has the attainment of the personal dream of land and a home been so wide-spread. The challenge for the future is to increase the accessibility to that dream by providing a variety of residential and employment options for all citizens of the modern metropolis and to keep in mind Lewis Mumford's challenge: 'Does a city exist to promote the life of its citizens? Or do the citizens exist in order to increase the size, importance, and the commercial turnover of the city?'.[36] Whether through governmental or voluntary devices, the future metropolis must respond to these questions.

NOTES

1. Hone, Whitman and the *Tribune* quoted in Jackson, Kenneth T. (1985) *Crabgrass Frontier: the Suburbanization of the United States*. New York: Oxford University Press, pp. 21–22, 50, 29–30.

2. Crevecoeur and Wells quoted in Berry, Brian J.L. (1976) The counter-urbanization process: urban America since 1970, in Berry J.L. (ed.) *Urbanization and Counterurbanization*, vol. 11, Urban Affairs Review Annual. Beverly Hills: Sage, pp. 25, 26.

3. Wilcox quoted in Berry, Brian J.L. (1973) *The Human Consequences of Urbanization*. New York: St. Martin's Press, p. 11.

4. *Ibid.*, p. 49.

5. Quoted in Ebner, Michael essay, this volume.

6. Quoted in Jackson, *op. cit.*, p. 265.

7. *Los Angeles Times*, 1984, September 8; *Washington Post*, 1984, December 27.

8. Kasarda, John D. *et. al.*, (1985) Demographic and Economic Shifts in the Sunbelt. Presented at Sunbelt Research Conference, Miami, FL, November 3.

9. Berry, Brian J.L. (1985) Islands of renewal in seas of decay, in Peterson, Paul E. (ed.) *The New Urban Reality*. Washington, D.C.: The Brookings Institution, pp. 69–96; see also, Meltzer, Jack (1984) *Metropolis to Metroplex: the*

Social and Spatial Planning of Cities. Baltimore: Johns Hopkins University Press, pp. 18–20.

10. Kasarda, John D. (1984) Urban change and minority opportunities, in Peterson (ed.), *The New Urban Reality.* Washington, D.C.: The Brookings Institution, pp. 45–49.

11. Meltzer, *op. cit.*, p. 18.

12. See Jackson, *op. cit.*, pp. 204–6, 250, 294.

13. Peirce, Neal (1985) As jobs move to suburbs, opportunity goes along. *Washington Post*, August 31.

14. Harrigan, John J. (1985) *Political Change in the Metropolis*, 3rd ed. Boston: Little, Brown and Co., p. 280.

15. Meltzer, *op. cit.*, p. 8.

16. Quoted in Harrigan, *op. cit.*, p. 351.

17. *Ibid.*, p. 341.

18. *Ibid.*, pp. 265–71, 280.

19. See Fisher, Robert (1984) *Let the People Decide: Neighbourhood Organizing in America.* Boston: Twayne; Silver, Christopher (1985) Neighbourhood planning in historical perspective. *Journal of the American Planning Association*, **51** (Spring), pp. 161–74.

20. Auletta, Ken (1980) *The Streets were paved with Gold: the Decline of New York. An American Tragedy.* New York: Random House, p. 224; on the changing and limiting role of planners, see Brooks, Michael P. (1970) *Social Planning and City Planning.* Chicago: ASPO; (1977) Process vs. task in social planning. *Social Work*, **22** (May), pp. 178–83; Krumholz, Norman (1982) A retrospective view of equity planning: Cleveland, 1969–1979. *Journal of the American Planning Association*, **48** (Spring), pp. 163–74.

21. Glickman, Norman (ed.) (1980) *The Urban Impacts of Federal Policies.* Baltimore: Johns Hopkins University Press; Peirce, Neal (1984) Community development: an anniversary review. *Washington Post*, December 29.

22. Levine, Myron A. (1983) The Reagan urban policy: efficient national economic growth and public sector minimization. *Journal of Urban Affairs*, **5** (Winter), pp. 17–28.

23. Eisinger, Peter K. (1985) The search for a national urban policy, 1968–1980. *Journal of Urban History*, **12** (November), pp. 3–23.

24. Kasarda, *op. cit.*, p. 64.

25. Quoted by Peirce, Neal (1985) 'New' mayors slash staff, act like corporate boss. *Washington Post*, May 4.

26. Peterson, Paul E. (1985) Introduction: technology, race, and urban policy, in Peterson. (ed.) *The New Urban Reality.* Washington, D.C.: The Brookings Institution, pp. 13–21.

27. Moynihan, Daniel Patrick (1985) *The Negro Family: the Case for National Action.* Washington, D.C.: U.S. Department of Labor; Wilson, William Julius (1985) The urban underclass in advanced industrial society, in Peterson (ed.)

The New Urban Reality. Washington D.C.: The Brookings Institution, pp. 133–42.

28. Wilson presents a full explication of his ideas in (1978) *The Declining Significance of Race: Blacks and Changing American Institutions* . Chicago: University of Chicago Press.

29. Kasarda, *op. cit.*, pp. 61–62.

30. Wilson, *op. cit.*, pp. 147–60.

31. President's Commission for a National Agenda for the Eighties (1980) *Urban America in the Eighties: Perspectives and Prospects*. Washington, D.C.: Government Printing Office, p. 4; U.S. Department of Housing and Urban Development (1982) *The President's National Urban Policy Report*. Washington, D.C.: Government Printing Office, p. 23.

32. Berry, (1973) *op. cit.*, p. 66.

33. Perloff, Harvey S. (1980) *Planning the Post-Industrial City*. Washington, D.C.: American Planning Association.

34. Patterson, Orlando (1977) *Ethnic Chauvinism: the Reactionary Impulse*. New York: Stein and Day, p. 155.

35. Peirce, Neal (1985) Religious groups ministering to the homeless. *Washington Post*, January 19; *Washington Post*, May 3.

36. Quoted in Schaffer, Daniel (1982) *Garden Cities for America: the Radburn Experience*. Philadelphia: Temple University Press, p. 62.

Index